International Arbitration Discourse and Practices in Asia

'Globalisation means that corporations are increasingly turning to arbitration to settle disputes. This book offers important insights into current arbitral practices across a range of major Asian contexts. Its fascinating account of convergent trends in a swiftly changing landscape is essential reading for everyone involved in Asian business law.'

Ruth Breeze, University of Navarra, Spain

International business exchanges between and with Asian countries have increased enormously over the last few years. As a natural consequence, this has brought about an increasing number of trade disputes that are being resolved through arbitration as an effective alternative to more expensive litigation. This volume offers a variety of perspectives on this important international dispute resolution practice in Asia. Essentially interdisciplinary in approach, it brings together specialists in law, international commercial arbitration and discourse analysis. The contributing authors include practitioners as well as academics. Together, they explore the interrelations between discourses and practices in the field of arbitration in Asia. The work also investigates the extent to which the 'integrity' of arbitration principles, typical of international commercial arbitration practice, is maintained in various Asian contexts. The authors focus particularly on arbitration norms and practices as they are influenced by local juridical, cultural and linguistic factors.

The book will be a valuable resource for academics and practitioners working in the areas of arbitration and dispute resolution, as well as researchers with an interest in language, communication and discourse analysis.

Vijay K. Bhatia, formerly Professor of English, City University of Hong Kong, is now Adjunct Professor at Chinese University of Hong Kong, and Visiting Professor at the Hellenic American University, Athens (Greece). He is also the founding President of the Languages for Specific Purposes and Professional Communication Association for Asia-Pacific. His research interests include Critical Genre Analysis; academic and professional discourses in legal, business, newspaper and promotional contexts; ESP and Professional Communication; simplification of legal and other public documents; intercultural and cross-disciplinary variations in professional genres.

Maurizio Gotti is Professor of English Language and Translation and Head of the Department of Foreign Languages, Literatures and Cultures at the University of Bergamo, Italy. He is also the founder and director of CERLIS, the research centre on specialised languages based at the University of Bergamo. His main research areas are the features and origins of specialised discourse, both in a synchronic and diachronic perspective. He is also interested in English syntax and English lexicology and lexicography, with particular regard to specialised terminology and canting. He is a member of the Editorial Board of a number of national and international journals.

Azirah Hashim is a Professor in the English Language Department, Faculty of Languages and Linguistics and currently, Director of the Centre for ASEAN Regionalism (CARUM) and Executive Director at the Asia-Europe Institute (AEI), University of Malaya. Her research interests include Language Contact in the Region, English as a Lingua Franca in ASEAN, Language and Law and Academic and Professional Discourse.

Philip Koh has over 30 years of expertise in three arenas: the academic, professional and industry. His specialisations include contract and investment laws, financial services and securities, corporate law and governance, commercial and civil litigation and public law. He is a member of the Financial Stability Executive Committee of Bank Negara Malaysia, Private Sector Group Global Corporate Governance Forum, Board member of Minority Shareholder Watchdog Group, and he has previously held the posts of Adjunct Professor at Deakin University and visiting Fulbright Scholar attached to the Harvard University Economics Department. He is senior counsel at High Court, Court of Appeal and Federal Court cases involving commercial and civil disputes and a panel arbitrator of the Kuala Lumpur Regional Center for Arbitration and has sat and written awards as Arbitrator.

Datuk Professor Sundra Rajoo is the Director of the Kuala Lumpur Regional Centre for Arbitration (KLRCA) and current President of the Chartered Institute of Arbitrators (CIArb) Global. He was Founding President of the Society of Construction Law, Malaysia and the Past President of the Asia Pacific Regional Arbitration Grouping (APRAG), which is a federation of nearly 40 arbitral institutions in the Asia-Pacific region. He serves on the panel of numerous international arbitral institutions and organisations. He is a visiting professor at the University of Technology Malaysia and the National University of Malaysia. He is the author of a number of books on arbitration and contract law.

Law, Language and Communication

Series Editors

Anne Wagner, Université du Littoral Côte d'Opale, France and Vijay Kumar Bhatia, formerly of City University of Hong Kong

This series encourages innovative and integrated perspectives within and across the boundaries of law, language and communication, with particular emphasis on issues of communication in specialised sociolegal and professional contexts. It seeks to bring together a range of diverse, yet cumulative research traditions in order to identify and encourage interdisciplinary research.

The series welcomes proposals – both edited collections as well as single-authored monographs – emphasising critical approaches to law, language and communication; identifying and discussing issues; proposing solutions to problems; offering analyses in areas such as legal construction, interpretation, translation and de-codification.

Other titles in the series

Shari'a in the Secular State
Evolving Meanings of Islamic Jurisprudence in Turkey
Russell Powell
ISBN 978-1-4724-7954-9

Language and Culture in EU Law
Multidisciplinary Perspectives
Edited by Susan Šarčević
ISBN 978-1-4724-2897-4

Towards Recognition of Minority Groups
Legal and Communication Strategies
Edited by Marek Zirk-Sadowski, Bartosz Wojciechowski and Karolina M. Cern
ISBN 978-1-4724-4490-5

The Ashgate Handbook of Legal Translation
Edited by Le Cheng, King Kui Sin and Anne Wagner
ISBN 978-1-4094-6966-7

Legal Lexicography
A Comparative Perspective
Edited by Máirtín Mac Aodha
ISBN 978-1-4094-5441-0

https://www.routledge.com/Law-Language-and-Communication/book-series/LAWLANGCOMM

International Arbitration Discourse and Practices in Asia

Edited by
Vijay K. Bhatia, Maurizio Gotti,
Azirah Hashim, Philip Koh
and Sundra Rajoo

Routledge
Taylor & Francis Group
LONDON AND NEW YORK

First published 2018 by Routledge

2 Park Square, Milton Park, Abingdon, Oxfordshire OX14 4RN
52 Vanderbilt Avenue, New York, NY 10017

Routledge is an imprint of the Taylor & Francis Group, an informa business

First issued in paperback 2020

British Library Cataloguing-in-Publication Data
A catalogue record for this book is available from the British Library

Library of Congress Cataloging-in-Publication Data
Names: Bhatia, V. K. (Vijay Kumar), 1942–, editor. | Gotti, Maurizio, editor. | Azirah Hashim, editor.
Title: International arbitration discourse and practices in Asia / edited by Vijay K. Bhatia, Maurizio Gotti, Azirah Hashim.
Description: New York, NY: Routledge, 2017. | Series: Law, language and communication | Includes bibliographical references and index.
Identifiers: LCCN 2017010650 | ISBN 9781138282216 (hardback)
Subjects: LCSH: Dispute resolution (Law)—Asia. | International commercial arbitration—Asia. | Arbitration (International law)
Classification: LCC KM500 .I58 2017 | DDC 347.5/09—dc23
LC record available at https://lccn.loc.gov/2017010650

ISBN: 978-1-138-28221-6 (hbk)
ISBN: 978-0-367-59482-4 (pbk)

Typeset in Galliard
by codeMantra

IN MEMORIAM

Rizul Jai

It is with profound sadness that we relate the loss of a beautiful life, full of infinite potential that had just started to blossom. In Rizul Jai, the legal profession has lost one of its youngest members.

Contents

Contributors

Patrizia Anesa holds a PhD in English Studies from the University of Verona and is a Research Fellow at the University of Bergamo (Italy), where she teaches courses in the field of English Language and Translation. Her research interests lie mostly in the area of specialised discourse, with particular reference to the investigation of knowledge asymmetries in spoken interaction. She is a member of AIA (Associazione Italiana di Anglistica); ESSE (The European Society for the Study of English); CERLIS (Centro di Ricerca sui Linguaggi Specialistici); AIDEL (Associazione Italiana di Diritto e Letteratura) and ILLA (International Language and Law Association).

Janet Ainsworth is the John D. Eshelman Professor of Law at Seattle University. She is a licensed attorney in the United States, has litigated well over 100 jury trials and is admitted to practice in the United States Supreme Court appellate bar. Her research interests lie at intersection of law, language and culture. Her most recent publications include *Speaking of Language and the Law*, coedited with Lawrence Solan and Roger Shuy; and *Consent and Coercion in the Law: A Discursive Analysis*, coedited with Susan Ehrlich and Diana Eades, both published in 2016. She currently serves as coeditor of the Oxford University Press series, Studies on Language and the Law.

John K Arthur is a barrister at the Victorian Bar of over 27 years standing. An experienced advocate, his principal area of practice is general commercial litigation, including contract, sale of land, property, equity, professional negligence, corporations, insolvency and succession. He is a Fellow of the Chartered Institute of Arbitrators (CIArb) and ACICA, and has been empanelled with KLRCA as Arbitrator, Adjudicator and Mediator. He is a National Councillor of CIArb (Australia). John has published and presented many papers in Australia and internationally on topics in varied areas of law and practice, including equity, contract, practice and procedure, alternative dispute resolution (ADR) and international arbitration. He is a coauthor of Lexis publications, *Civil Procedure Victoria*, Lexis Nexis and *Australian Uniform Evidence*. He also contributes to other publications. He is a member of the IBA, Law Institute of Victoria, Asialink Chairman's Club and the Asian Australian Lawyers Association.

Ulisse Belotti teaches English for Business and Law studies at both undergraduate and postgraduate level at the University of Bergamo (Italy). His research interests concern word formation in IT language, genre analysis, business and legal discourse. His recent work centres on the genre characteristics of business and law-related documents through the analysis of specialised corpora. His publications are mostly in the areas of specialised discourse, particularly legal (arbitration) and business communication, and he is currently researching genre and conversation analysis in the domain of arbitration and business-related subjects.

Vijay K Bhatia is Adjunct Professor at the Chinese University of Hong Kong, and Visiting Professor at the Hellenic American University in Athens (Greece). His research interests include (Critical) Genre Analysis of academic and professional discourses in legal, business, promotional and in new media contexts; ESP and Professional Communication. Three of his books, *Analysing Genre: Language Use in Professional Settings, Worlds of Written Discourse: A Genre-based View* and *Critical Genre Analysis*, are widely used in genre theory and practice.

Mariacarla Giorgetti, born in Milan on 19 October 1969, graduated in law in 1992 with 110/110 *magna cum laude*. She presented a thesis on civil trial law and obtained a PhD in 1997. She holds the chair of Civil Trial Law, of Arbitration Law and of Bankruptcy at the Law Faculty of Bergamo University. She is the author of numerous publications on questions concerning civil trial law, arbitration law and bankruptcy law. She is a member of the editorial committee of the "*Rivista di diritto processuale*", a member of the Scientific Committee of the Chamber of Arbitration and Conciliation at the Foundation of Chartered Accountants of Milan. She acts as solicitor in Milan, Bergamo and Ancona. She has acquired many years' experience in arbitration, bankruptcy and composition litigation, nationally and internationally.

Maurizio Gotti is Professor of English Language and Translation, Head of the Department of Foreign Languages, Literatures and Cultures and Director of the Research Centre for LSP Research (CERLIS) at the University of Bergamo. His main research areas are the features and origins of specialised discourse (*Robert Boyle and the Language of Science,* 1996; *Specialized Discourse: Linguistic Features and Changing Conventions*, 2003; *Investigating Specialized Discourse,*[3] 2011). He is also interested in English syntax and English lexicology and lexicography, with particular regard to specialised terminology and canting. He is a member of the Editorial Board of national and international journals, and he edits the *Linguistic Insights* series for Peter Lang.

Azirah Hashim is the Executive Director of the Asia-Europe Institute, Director of the Centre for ASEAN Regionalism and a Professor in the English Language Department, Faculty of Languages and Linguistics, University of Malaya. Her areas of research interests include Language Contact in Southeast Asia, Language and Law and Higher Education in ASEAN. She sits on the executive committee of the Asia Pacific Languages for Specific Purposes and Professional Communication Association, is a former executive committee member of the International Association of Forensic Linguists and is currently President of the Malaysian Association of Applied Linguistics, an affiliate of the International Association of Applied Linguistics. She is on the editorial board of *English Today, Journal of Sociolinguistic Studies, Journal of Intercultural Communication (Nordic Network), Asian Journal of English Language Studies* and is Chief Editor of the *Asia-Europe Institute Insights Journal.*

Rizul Jai, a law graduate from Symbiosis International University, Noida, India, was considering furthering his legal education in the United Kingdom, when fate cruelly snatched him away in November 2016. Being born and brought up in a distinguished family of lawyers and blessed with an analytical and incisive mind, he was a dynamic and vibrant personality with unlimited potential and promise for a bright career in legal profession.

Lam Wai Loon is a founding partner of Messrs. Harold & Lam Partnership, a law firm based in Malaysia. Mr Lam is a Chartered Arbitrator and Fellow of the Chartered

Institute of Arbitrators (UK), a member of the Kuala Lumpur Regional Centre for Arbitration's Panel of Arbitrators and Adjudicators. He has sat in numerous arbitrations and adjudications involving construction disputes. He is the current chariman CIArb, Malaysia Branch (2016/2017); the Deputy President of the Society of Construction Law, Malaysia (2016/2017) and the Vice President and a founding member of the Malaysian Society of Adjudicators (2016/2017). His other publications include a coauthored comprehensive text titled 'Construction Adjudication in Malaysia' (CCH-Kluwer, 2013); a coauthored Chapter on 'Arbitration in Malaysia' published in 'International Commercial Arbitration in Asia (JurisNet LLC, 3rd Edition, 2013) and the author of Chapter 17: Construction ADR in Malaysia in "Arbitration in Malaysia: A Practical Guide" (Sweet & Maxwell, 2016).

Philip Koh Tong Ngee, LLB (Hons) (Malaya), LLM (University of London), M.A.(Theology) Australian Catholic University, is an Advocate and Solicitor at the High Court of Malaya. He is also a member of the Panel of Arbitrators of the Kuala Lumpur Regional Centre for Arbitration and Senior Partner of Mah Kamariyah & Philip Koh. Koh maintains an interest in law and language. He has participated in and chaired forums on the relationship between law, discourse analysis and literature.

Net Le (PhD in Law from London School of Economics, UK) is a partner in charge of LNT & Partners' Infrastructure and Financial Services practice group. In 2012, Dr Le was awarded the title of "Lawyer of the Year" by Vietnam's Ministry of Justice. He is a lecturer of civil law at the Ho Chi Minh City University of Law and has authored textbooks that have been published in Vietnam and internationally. He is an arbitrator at the Vietnam International Arbitration Centre (VIAC), in which he has chaired or co-arbitrated more than 30 cases. He is also a member of the Chartered Institute of Arbitrators (CIArb) and International Council for Commercial Arbitration (ICCA).

Piera Pellegrinelli received her doctorate in Civil Procedural Law at the University of Milan. Currently, she has a fellowship to undertake research activities at the Department of Law, University of Bergamo, where she is also adjunct professor of Law of Arbitration. She is the author of several publications on arbitration, such as 'The Management of a Mediation Organization According to the Italian Law' (*Beijing Law Review*, 2012), 'Il termine per la pronuncia del lodo' and 'Profili critici in tema di responsabilità degli arbitri' (both in*La giustizia sostenibile. Scritti vari*, Roma 2014), 'Commento all'art. 817 c.p.c. (in A. Briguglio/B. Capponi (eds) *Commentario alle riforme del processo civile*, Padova 2009). She is a lawyer.

Richard Powell is professor of English at Nihon University in Tokyo, with responsibility for the International Course at the College of Economics. Before getting involved in linguistics, he studied history, politics and law, and his research interests include forensic linguistics, language planning, professional communication and cross-cultural pragmatics. He has published books and articles in all four areas. His main research sites are in Southeast Asia, but he has also conducted studies in East Asia; South Asia; the Pacific Islands and southern, eastern and western Africa. Richard sits on the board of directors of the Japan Association of Law and Language and on the editorial board of several academic publications, including the International Journal for the Semiotics of Law.

Datuk Professor Sundra Rajoo is the Director of the Kuala Lumpur Regional Centre for Arbitration (KLRCA) and President of the Chartered Institute of Arbitrators (2016).

His roll of honour includes being Founding President of the Society of Construction Law, Malaysia and the Malaysian Society of Adjudicators. He is also the Past President of the Asia Pacific Regional Arbitration Grouping (APRAG), which is a federation of nearly 40 arbitral institutions in the Asia Pacific region. Datuk Professor Sundra Rajoo is a Chartered Arbitrator and an Advocate and Solicitor of the High Court of Malaya (non-practising). Sundra is a Professional Architect, Registered Town Planner and a Fellow of the Royal Institution of Chartered Surveyors. He has had numerous appointments as chairman, co-arbitrator of three-man panels and sole arbitrator in international and domestic arbitrations. He is visiting professor at the Faculty of Built Environment, University of Technology Malaysia and past visiting professor at the Law Faculty, National University of Malaysia. He is also a member in the Monetary Penalty Review Committee set up under the Malaysian Financial Services Act 2013.

Charu Sharma is an Associate Professor, Associate Dean (Student Initiatives) and Executive Director, Center for Environment and Climate Change at School of Law, O P Jindal Global University, Sonepat, Haryana, India. Her research interests lie in environmental law, natural resources law, tort and contracts. Dr Sharma holds an LLM from university of Delhi, India and a Phd from Macquarie, Sydney, Australia. Her most recent publications include Tort Liability for Environmental claims in India: A Comparative View, LexisNexis, (March 2017), "Sale of Goods" in *CHITTY ON CONTRACTS: Hong Kong Specific Contracts*, fifth edition, Sweet & Maxwell, December 2016, "Sexual Harassment Law and Policy: Hong Kong and China", Springer Global Encyclopedia of Public Administration, Public Policy, and Governance Chapter No: 2541–1 (2016). Before joining OP Jindal Global University, she lived and taught in Hong Kong for over 15 years.

Rajesh Sharma is currently teaching at RMIT University, Melbourne, Australia. Dr Sharma has taught and researched on WTO Law, international trade, foreign investment arbitration and ADR. Dr Sharma is the Associate Director of the Hong Kong WTO Research Institute; a member of Asian WTO Research Network; a panel arbitrator of Korean Commercial Arbitration Board; a panel arbitrator at Indian Institutes of Arbitrators; a member of the Centre for Global Studies; a Researcher at China-Latin America Legal Research Centre, Shanghai; Fellow of International Academy of Belt and Road and elected Associate Member of Academy of Comparative Law. Dr Sharma is the first Indian to hold PhD in Law from China. He holds PhD from the Chinese University of Political Science and Law, Beijing, a Master of Business Law from Monash University, Australia. Dr Sharma's recent book is "Dispute Settlement Mechanism in the FTAs of Asia".

Elena Signorini is a Research Fellow and Adjunct Professor of Labour Law and of Welfare Law at the University of Bergamo. She has written on unquestionable rights of the worker, health protection in the workplace, employment promotion and fair work, informal economy and undeclared work, youth employment, labour market discrimination and labour law. She is the author of several publications, such as 'Diritto al lavoro. Crisi. Lavoro dei Giovani' 2013; 'Le politiche di contrasto al lavoro sommerso nei Paesi dell'Unione Europea' (co-autor with M. Sala Chiri) 2014; 'Invecchiamento attivo: il senso delle stagioni della vita. Evoluzione o sfida ai sistemi?' 2014; 'La salute mentale, ritmi, assenze e presenze: nuovi rischi sul fronte del lavoro?' 2014; 'Apprendistato: modulabilità della formazione' 2012; 'Il lavoro decente' 2012. She is a lawyer, and arbitrator and mediator at the Chambers of Commerce of Bergamo and Modena.

Ashok Kumar Singh is a Senior Advocate with 38 years of practice at the Supreme Court of India and High Courts of Delhi, Uttrakhand, Meghalaya. A good volume of the cases conducted by him has been referred to Reporters by the Courts. He has a vast experience of conducting International and Domestic Arbitrations. He is also on the Panel of Arbitrators of the Kuala Lumpur Regional Centre for Arbitration, BANI Arbitration Centre, Indian Council of Arbitration, National Internet Exchange of India, The International Center for Alternative Dispute Resolution, Indian Institute of Arbitration & Mediation, Chandigarh Arbitration Centre and Delhi International Arbitration Centre, India. He is a member of various International and National associations. He is the author of various articles and has attended numerous National and International conferences as a speaker or delegate.

Dr Shahrizal M Zin FCIArb is an Advocate and Solicitor of the High Court of Malaya. He was called to the Malaysian Bar in 2003 and commenced legal practice in a leading law firm in Kuala Lumpur soon after. He graduated with LLB (Hons) and LLM from University of Malaya, Malaysia. He holds a PhD from Monash University, Australia, with a thesis investigating the WTO dispute settlement mechanism. He is currently acting as a senior lecturer at the Faculty of Law, University Technology MARA. His teaching expertise includes public international law and international commercial arbitration. He has been awarded a diploma in international commercial arbitration from the Chartered Institute of Arbitrators (CIArb), UK and was admitted as a fellow.

Introduction

In the current environment of globalisation of trade and commerce, International Arbitration is being increasingly regarded as an economical and effective alternative to litigation for settling commercial disputes, and it is being widely adopted for the settlement of domestic and international disputes in Asia. Indeed, international business exchanges between and with Asian countries have increased enormously over the last few years, and even the recent economic recession has not slowed down this growth. As a natural consequence, this increase in business deals and contracts has brought about an increasing number of trade disputes that are being resolved through arbitration.

This volume brings together a selection of chapters from, though not limited to, the international conference on 'Arbitration Discourse and Practices in Asia' organised by the Centre for ASEAN Regionalism University of Malaya (CARUM), and Kuala Lumpur Regional Centre for Arbitration (KLRCA), in collaboration with a research project on Asian Arbitration Law and Discourse, University of Bergamo (Italy) and Hong Kong, focusing on the analysis of arbitration in action by undertaking a legal, contextual, and discourse-based analysis of data drawn from discursive and professional practices in arbitration.

In order to explore the interrelations between discourses and practices in the field of arbitration in Asia, the present volume also investigates the extent to which the 'integrity' of arbitration principles typical of international commercial arbitration practice is maintained in various Asian contexts, focusing in particular on arbitration norms and practices as they are influenced by local juridical, cultural, and linguistic factors from a number of different perspectives, such as legal, discourse analytical, and arbitration practice.

This book offers a number of unique, interdisciplinary perspectives on Arbitration in Asia as international dispute resolution procedure, focusing both on discursive as well as professional practices. It is essentially interdisciplinary in nature, bringing together specialists in law, international commercial arbitration, and discourse analysis. The authors contributing to the volume are interdisciplinary scholars, as well as practitioners from the field, and their differing backgrounds and concerns highlight some of the key aspects of the multidimensional nature of this important alternative dispute resolution practice. Moreover, these perspectives are, in some sense, unique to Asia, though increasingly international in scope, as commercial arbitration is essentially an international practice.

The volume is organised into four sections

Section I on *Asian Perspectives on Arbitration* opens with an overview of arbitration in Asia by Vijay K. Bhatia, highlighting developments in arbitration in six of the major Asian countries, i.e., China, India, Hong Kong, Singapore, Malaysia, and Japan, focusing in particular on the perceptions and attitudes of the legal community in Asia. He further identifies and discusses the concept of public policy exception in these countries, especially the way it is interpreted in the formulation of national policies and guidelines in Asian jurisdictions.

John K. Arthur focuses specifically on how the concept of public policy exception is interpreted and used in the courts in cases seeking to set aside or enforce international arbitral awards.

Another issue investigated in this section by Janet Ainsworth is the relevance for Asian arbitration parties of the structural advantages of repeat players in litigation dispute resolution practices.

Section II on *Discursive Practices in Arbitration* offers discursive perspectives on arbitration focusing on different Asian countries. Maurizio Gotti, Piera Pellegrinelli, and Elena Signorini investigate the texts of both the PRC Arbitration Law and the Law on Mediation and Arbitration of Labour Disputes in order to examine, in particular, the norms concerning the combination of conciliation/mediation and arbitration in Chinese legislation. This combination clearly shows how typical traits of the Chinese legal tradition and social culture have greatly influenced the characteristics of the arbitration process in this country.

Patrizia Anesa's chapter analyses arbitration in India, making use of the results obtained from a questionnaire and structured interviews conducted with experts in the field operating in the Indian subcontinent. It also offers a comparative analysis with similar studies carried out by experts in other Asian countries, such as Singapore, as well as in some Western countries, such as Italy.

A similarly comparative study is carried out by Ulisse Belotti, who investigates how arbitration practitioners from two very different cultural and professional backgrounds – Italy and Singapore – see arbitration practice. Using two corpora of interviews of Italian and Singaporean arbitration practitioners, he analyses the state of the art of arbitration in the two countries and investigates the linguistic realisations that these experts, mainly counsels and arbitrators, have employed, using English as either a lingua franca for the Italian respondents or as a mother tongue for the Singaporean interviewees.

The next chapter, by Patrizia Anesa and Net Le, focuses on the developments that international arbitration has undergone in Vietnam, combining a legal perspective with a cultural one. At first, the chapter delineates the main legal aspects that typify arbitration in Vietnam, illustrating the general legal framework, within which arbitration develops. In its second part, it investigates the opinions and perceptions of professionals operating in the arbitration field in order to identify the main prospects and challenges in that context.

In the final chapter in this section, Richard Powell outlines the historical development of arbitration in Japan, particularly focusing on how professional practitioners and academic scholars comment on and explain the gap between the country's modern arbitral infrastructure and its low profile in Asian and global contexts.

Section III on *Professional Practices in Arbitration* then takes up various issues concerning arbitration in action, in particular, offering professional perspectives on laws from various Asian countries from the point of view of arbitration scholars and practitioners. Sundra Rajoo focuses on the recent innovations introduced in institutional arbitration in Malaysia, pointing out its successful developments. The study particularly centres on the KLRCA, highlighting its innovative practices, such as the 'Fast Track Rules' (aiming to speed up the arbitration process) as well as a specific set of rules designed for its regional users. As Malaysia is a hub for Islamic finance, KLRCA has recently developed a Shariah-compliant scheme for disputes that relate to Islamic transactions.

Lam Wai Loon, instead, analyses a few critical aspects of arbitration in Malaysia, attributing the decline in the number of arbitration cases to both the improved efficiency in the speed of case disposal by the judicial court system and the higher costs of arbitration than court proceedings. The decrease in arbitration cases could also be due to the introduction of the Construction Industry Payment and Adjudication Act (CIPAA), which provides for an interim summary procedure for the resolution of construction payment disputes. Further factors are then investigated to account for the weaker confidence in arbitration there.

Rizul Jai's chapter provides a detailed presentation of the evolution of arbitration in India and of its specific legislation on both national and international procedures. In particular, it examines the issue of 'public policy' as a possible reason for challenge of an arbitral award, comparing its application according to Indian law with that foreseen by the United Nations Commission on International Trade Law (UNCITRAL) Model Rules.

Mariacarla Giorgetti investigates arbitration legislation in Hong Kong, in particular, its recent changes and, in consequence, the modifications concerning the rules for appointing arbitrators. These changes are meant to make arbitration carried out at the Hong Kong International Arbitration Center a useful instrument for the settlement of disputes between Western and Chinese subjects, as it ensures, on the one hand, the Western contractor's interest within a third legal system and, on the other hand, the interest of the Chinese party to maintain a geographical and cultural proximity to the site of a future dispute between the parties.

Although arbitration is being increasingly used to resolve business and commercial disputes in India, within domestic law, none of the public environmental legislation that protects public interest provides for arbitration, conciliation, or mediation as a method for public or private environmental conflicts and issues. Charu Sharma investigates this problem, which has become particularly relevant, due to the fact that disputes are getting increasingly more complicated within the industrial, power, energy, pharmaceutical, and environmental sectors. According to Charu Sharma, the contemporary dynamics of environmental conflict demands the adoption of all kinds of dispute resolution techniques, including arbitration and existing law.

Ashok Kumar Singh's chapter deals with the law of discovery and production of documents in arbitration in India. In particular, he analyses the arbitration law followed in India to carry out international practices. He also establishes a nexus between what has already been adopted and implemented by India in its arbitration legislation and what is still left to be explored apropos discovery and production of documents.

The concluding section on 'Towards an Asian Arbitration Model' offers an informed view of the emerging trends in Asian arbitration contexts. In his analysis of legalisation of international arbitration in Asia, Shahrizal M. Zin comes to the conclusion that international arbitration will become more internationalised, and this will imply a steady growing harmonisation of national arbitration laws and increasing participation of lawyers and arbitrators involved in international arbitration. This will consequently determine greater cultural homogenisation of Asian legal consciousness, attitudes, and values.

In the final chapter, Rajesh Sharma shows that China, South Korea, and Japan have set a new and positive trend in the dispute settlement mechanism of their Free Trade Agreements (FTAs), specifically including the Code of Conduct for arbitrators in the dispute settlement system. With these new trends in action, he concludes that China, South Korea, and Japan are developing a new Asian style of dispute resolution mechanism in their FTAs, whether signed with developed or developing countries.

Vijay K. Bhatia, Maurizio Gotti, Azirah Hashim,
Philip Koh, and Sundra Rajoo

Part I

Asian perspectives on arbitration

1 International commercial arbitration in Asia

Discursive and professional perspectives

Vijay K. Bhatia

1.1 Overview

International business and trade exchanges across international borders have increased enormously over the last few years. In this context, Asia is being widely regarded as the emerging economic powerhouse, in spite of the recent economic recession in some parts of the region. As a natural consequence, this increase in international business activities has brought about an increasing number of trade disputes that are being resolved through arbitration, which is being regarded as one of the most economical and effective alternatives to litigation for settling commercial disputes in Asia and elsewhere across the globe. International commercial arbitration thus has attracted increasing research interest, both from professional (legal as well as arbitral) as well as discoursal perspectives (Bhatia et al., 2008, 2010, 2012). However, relatively little attention has been paid to arbitration in Asia, especially from the point of view of language use. Considering the number of commercial arbitration disputes attracted by some of the key arbitration institutions in Asia, especially those in China, India, Hong Kong, and Singapore, it has become necessary to identify and discuss some of the key challenges in international commercial arbitration practice in Asia, in particular focusing on the hybrid nature of arbitration practice (Bhatia et al., 2010, 2012). In order to do so, I would like to highlight some of the significant aspects of this interdiscursive practice embedded in a mixed arbitration-litigation culture.

Drawing on the analysis of some of the significant voices from the profession, key practices (both discursive as well as professional), and interdiscursive analytical insights, I would like to explore the nature and function of commercial arbitration in Asia, in particular, focusing on the judicial intervention v. arbitration supportive environment in some of the key Asian regimes, with implications for the development of arbitration as an independent institutional practice, especially in the context of a general resistance to arbitration in Asia. In order to explore the interrelations between discursive and professional arbitration practices in Asia, I would like to investigate the extent to which the integrity of arbitration principles is maintained (Bhatia, 2011) in various Asian contexts, focusing in particular on arbitration norms and practices as they are influenced by local juridical, cultural, and linguistic factors from a number of different perspectives, such as legal, discourse-analytical, and arbitration practice. For a detailed account of some of the key aspects of arbitration practices in Asia, I would primarily focus on four countries—China, India, Hong Kong, and Singapore—as these four countries attract not only business activities but also a large number of arbitration disputes. In order to have a broader coverage, I will try to extend the study to briefly cover developments in Japan and Malaysia too. Let me begin by giving a brief account of some of the key characteristics of arbitration practice in international commercial contexts.

1.2 International commercial arbitration

International commercial arbitration was originally proposed by the United Nations Commission on International Trade Law (UNCITRAL) and was established by the United Nations General Assembly by its Resolution 2205 (XXI) of 17 December 1966 'to promote the progressive harmonization and unification of international trade law'. As part of their work, the commission prepared a model law on international commercial arbitration, which was subsequently adopted by the United Nations General Assembly on 21 June 1985 and was recommended for adoption as the UNCITRAL Model Law on International Commercial Arbitration. Although the Model Law was not binding, the UN recommended its adoption and incorporation into the domestic law of individual member states. International arbitration, in principle, was intended as an alternative to litigation to resolve commercial disputes in cross-border contexts, which was also meant to lead to an integration and harmonisation of processes and procedures across legal systems and cultures.

Today, international arbitration is undoubtedly the most widely used alternative dispute resolution (ADR) mechanism to resolve commercial disputes between parties. International commercial arbitration crucially depends on the parties' agreement to resolve disputes through private adjudication by a single arbitrator or a tribunal of more than one, appointed in accordance with rules of a specific arbitration institution that the parties themselves have agreed to adopt, usually by including an arbitration clause in their contract. The practice of international arbitration has developed in a manner to allow parties from different legal and cultural backgrounds to resolve their disputes without any interference from the system of courts.

1.3 Distinctive characteristics

In arbitration, parties or their representatives, who are mostly legal professionals, present a dispute to an impartial single arbitrator or an arbitration tribunal to resolve it and order a decision, which is like a legal judgement, known as award in arbitration. Unlike other forms of ADR, namely, conciliation and mediation, which do not suggest or impose any specific decision to resolve the dispute, the arbitration decision or award is binding for the disputing parties. In arbitration, the parties have considerable input in the selection of arbitration tribunal, and also in the choice of processes and procedures they would like the tribunal to follow, including the seat of arbitration, as well as the arbitration rules within which the resolution is negotiated.

Arbitration is thus the most appropriate form of ADR mechanism when the disputing parties fail to resolve their dispute on their own and want a third party to suggest a resolution, and at the same time, when they would like to avoid the time and expense of litigation where they have absolutely no control over the decision-making process. As mentioned earlier, the decision of the arbitration tribunal is enforceable and cannot be challenged in a court of law, except on procedural grounds under a very restricted set of conditions. So, the main advantage of arbitration is that it is like litigation in effect, in that it is decided by a neutral arbitrator or arbitration tribunal, but unlike litigation, it is informal, expedient, economical, private, and confidential in nature, and at the same time, gives sufficient voice and freedom to disputing parties in the way it is actually conducted.

One of the crucial aspects of arbitration in international commercial contexts, in particular for this chapter, is the limited interference of courts allowed in most countries, especially in the context of enforcement of awards. Since arbitration is a form of private adjudication, one may get the impression that the final outcome will not have the same effect in the enforcement that is often associated with a court judgement; however, the fact is that arbitration awards have equal, if not more, enforcement value, even across jurisdictional borders. Enforceability of an award under the New York Convention on the Recognition and Enforcement of Foreign Arbitral Awards of 1958 (New York Convention) is one of the most effective instruments used in international commercial arbitration practice.

1.4 Court intervention in arbitration

The most prominent role of the courts often is at the enforcement stage, in particular, when the award is challenged by any of the disputing parties. Some of the distinct advantages of arbitration as compared with litigation, such as the time and cost of dispute resolution, as discussed in earlier sections, can turn into disadvantages, if, and when, the dispute does not end merely with the final award. The aggrieved party may challenge the award or restrict the implementation of it in a court of law, resulting in the whole exercise of arbitration being nullified, thus causing delay in resolution and increase in the cost. In order to keep the option open for anticipated challenge to an award if not to the liking of any of the parties, it is more than likely that parties invariably involve legal professionals, rather than specialists in the specific field in which the dispute is grounded, as arbitrators or counsels. In many of the Asian countries, there seems to be a general resistance to arbitration, which we turn to in the next section.

1.5 Resistance to arbitration in Asia

Michael Hwang (2007), in his address to the International Arbitration Club, raised the issue of resistance to arbitration in Asia and identified several classes of resisters to arbitration in Asia. There are those, he points out, who are unlikely to play by the rules and often use delay tactics to frustrate arbitration. They are not interested in the ultimate resolution of the dispute and would do anything to deny the disputing party the award, he suggests. Then, there are those who do not sabotage the arbitration if their client has a week defence, but who certainly believe that their clients are likely to get a better outcome in the local court, he maintains. Besides, he points out, there are also those who advise their clients not to agree on arbitration as a preferred instrument of conflict resolution. Finally, there are those who need to be persuaded by reasoned awards. This issue of scepticism is also reflected in a survey conducted by Anesa (2017), which shows that 'Indian companies express a higher level of satisfaction when the dispute is administered and resolved in arbitration centres outside India rather than within the country'. She concludes that it is necessary to investigate the reasons for this kind of scepticism towards Indian centres, which assumes greater importance in the context of increasing economic activity in recent years. In this chapter, I would now like to focus on the key aspect of commercial arbitration that illustrates the nature and integrity of this ADR mechanism in Asia, i.e., court intervention in arbitration, especially when the arbitral award is challenged to frustrate enforcement.

1.6 Challenge to enforcement of awards

The most prominent role of the courts is at the enforcement stage, especially when the award is challenged by any of the disputing parties, and within that the most controversial aspect of court intervention is the judicial application of 'public policy exception'. One of the most problematic issues in the use of public policy exception as a ground to resist enforcement or setting aside of arbitration awards is that there is no universal definition of public policy; it depends entirely on the states in which arbitration awards are enforced, particularly the principles, rules, and regulations that govern justice, moral, or other fundamental sociopolitical and economic interests of a state. The New York Convention of 1958 represents the key aspects of the global regime that regulates the recognition and enforcement of foreign arbitral awards, especially Article III, which requires all the signatory states to enforce arbitration awards in line with arbitration rules. However, Article V (2) (b) of NYC also allows states to refuse to recognise and enforce an award, if it contravenes the public policy of that state.

> Article V (2) (b) of New York Convention
>
> 2. Recognition and enforcement of an arbitral award may also be refused if the competent authority in the country where recognition and enforcement is sought finds that:
>
> a ...
> b The recognition or enforcement of the award would be contrary to the public policy of that country.
>
> (Emphasis added)

This provision is also reenacted in Article 36 (1) (b) (ii) of the Model Law, which reads as follows:

> Article 36. Grounds for refusing recognition or enforcement
>
> Recognition or enforcement of an arbitral award, irrespective of the country in which it was made, may be refused only:
>
> a ....
> b if the court finds that:
>   i ...; or
>   ii the recognition or enforcement of the award would be contrary to the public policy of this State.
>
> (Emphasis added)

Although the language used in both provisions is non-binding (notice the use of discretionary *may* in both the New York Convention, as well as in the UNCITRAL Model Law), courts can still enforce an award, even if the grounds for refusal have been proved, especially invoking the public policy exception, which continues to play a key role in setting aside or refusal to enforce arbitral awards. It is also important to understand that public policy differs from state to state, as there seems to be no universal agreement about its true nature; however, despite the uncertainty surrounding public policy, the courts in arbitration supportive jurisdictions have interpreted it narrowly and usually refrained from setting aside international arbitral awards. In fact, a pro-enforcement attitude towards arbitral awards is viewed as a key factor of public policy itself, in that the application of the public policy exception in most jurisdictions is usually on the side of enforcement, especially in most Western jurisdictions. In what follows, I consider some of the key aspects of public policy as a ground to resist enforcement of, or set aside, arbitration awards in various Asian regimes.

1.7 Judicial application of public policy exception in Asia

1.7.1 China

China's arbitration law is not based on the UNCITRAL Model Law and provides for a relatively lower level of party autonomy. The state can intervene in the validity of arbitration awards, in the selection of arbitration procedures, and certainly in the enforcement of awards through the courts in accordance with the legal provisions of the place where the arbitration takes place. Arbitration is thus considered a judicial activity as part of China's legal system (Chi, 2011). Chi (2011) compares arbitrators' procedural power under Chinese law to their international counterparts to understand the extent to which China is arbitration-friendly. China's restriction on arbitrators' procedural power reflects tension between state (judicial) power and private (arbitral) power in arbitration. As Chi (2011:280) points out, the very basis of arbitration, because of its private and autonomous nature, is the parties' agreement, which allows maximum freedom and discretion to arbitrators, which inevitably results in arbitrators encroaching on courts' judicial power, and which, at the same time, tends to create a tension between 'state (judicial) power' and 'private (arbitral) power'. Although Chinese law and Chinese institutional arbitration rules may appear to be quite similar to their international counterparts, they are quite different in a number of ways. The difference lies in their respective strategies in balancing judicial power vis-a-vis arbitral power. Chinese law emphasises judicial power at the cost of arbitral power to strengthen the state power. Public policy is also interpreted in terms of social and public interest, viewed as fundamental principles of Chinese law, sovereignty, or security of the state, or customs, traditions, or fundamental moral standards of China (Chi, 2011). For purposes of the public policy exception, the Chinese courts have generally accepted the terminology in the Civil Procedural Law of PRC in Articles 70 and 71 of the Arbitration Law of the People's Republic of China, which provides that a court may refuse the enforcement of an arbitral award, if it determines that the award is against the social and public interest of China.

> Article 70 If a party presents evidence which proves that a foreign-related arbitration award involves one of the circumstances set forth in the first paragraph of Article 260 of the Civil Procedure Law, the people's court <u>shall</u>, after examination and verification by a collegial panel formed by the people's court, <u>rule to set aside</u> the award.
>
> Article 71 If the party against whom the enforcement is sought presents evidence which proves that the foreign-related arbitration award involves one of the circumstances set forth in the first paragraph of Article 260 of the Civil Procedure Law, the people's court <u>shall</u>, after examination and verification by a collegial panel formed by the people's court, <u>rule to disallow the enforcement</u>.

The two articles also provide for appeal of an arbitral award if there is sufficient evidence that substantiates the procedural aspects of an arbitration trial, such as the limited scope or lack of arbitration agreement, inappropriate or denial of evidence, doubts about the impartiality of the entire process or of the arbitration tribunal, and so forth. But the one that is important for our discussion here is that the People's Court, in both these sections, is legally bound to refuse to enforce or set aside (note the legally binding use of *shall* in Articles 70 and 71) an award that contravenes the public interest, which includes the principles of Chinese law, fundamental interests of the society, safety, sovereignty, and good social customs of the country. It is interesting to note that Article 9 of the Arbitration Law also obligatorily (again indicated by the legally binding use of *shall*) provides that the Tribunal's award and the court's decision to enforce or refuse to enforce a 'foreign-related' arbitral award (i.e., that made in China and administered by a Chinese arbitration institution with some foreign element, such as a foreign party) is final and hence cannot be appealed by either party.

> Article 9 The arbitration award is final. After the award is given, the arbitration commission or the people's court shall not accept the re-application of the suit concerning the same dispute by any of the parties concerned.

More recently, Gao (2015) pointed out that the Supreme People's Court of China (SPC) has set up a reporting system, which required the local court to report to higher court—and ultimately up to the SPC—any cases in which the local court delivers the final decision on a refusal of recognition and thereby on the setting aside of a foreign arbitral award. He also points out that Chinese courts are now required to interpret public policy narrowly in an attempt to make sure that an award is unlikely to be refused enforcement, unless it is 'manifestly contrary to the principle of the law, fundamental interests of the society, safety of the country, sovereignty, or good social customs. There is no concept of international public policy rule or domestic public policy rule under the Chinese law' (Gao, 2015: 3). So far, there is only one case in which the court refused to recognise and enforce a foreign arbitral award in China on the ground of public policy, which, he claims, shows that Chinese courts are very serious in their application of public policy exception to refuse recognition and enforcement of arbitral awards. In that particular case, he points out, the court held that the recognition of the foreign award would violate the public policy of China, because the arbitral award re-devised the burden between the parties and effectively changed the content of a judgement already made by a PRC Court. The violation of judicial sovereignty is deemed as a violation of public policy of China.

1.7.2 India

In line with the UNCITRAL Model Law, the Indian Arbitration and Conciliation Act (1996) was introduced with the hope that there would be minimal judicial intervention in the arbitral process. However, in practice, the Indian courts have often shown a great propensity towards interfering with international arbitration, particularly at the award enforcement stage on grounds of public policy. One of the factors that created this confusion was the fact that the Arbitration and Conciliation Ordinance of India (1996) applies both to domestic as well as international arbitration. Local courts seem to be too eager to interpret various aspects of public policy exception as a ground to resist or refuse to enforce arbitration awards. An explicit lack of attention to interdiscursive and intertextual factors (Bhatia, 2017) in the construction and interpretation of arbitration law encouraged the courts to adopt more innovative interpretations. There was a seeming reluctance on the part of the courts to adequately distinguish domestic and international awards, and there were cases where a decision on a domestic award was used as precedent to resist enforcement of an international award. Article 34 (2) of the Arbitration and Conciliation Act 1996 provides that

2 An arbitral award may be set aside by the court only if

- a The party making the application furnishes proof that…
- b The court finds that-…
  - ii The arbitral award is in conflict with the public policy of India…

Since there is no further definition or specification of what public policy incorporates, in practice, there have been some unfortunate decisions. In one of the most notorious challenges to arbitral awards in India, ONGC v. Saw Pipes, the Supreme Court of India, while considering the scope of interference with an arbitration award under the Arbitration and Conciliation Act 1996, expanded the scope of challenge by interpreting the words *public policy* too widely to include anything contrary to Indian Law. Saw Pipes challenged an Indian arbitral award on the grounds that it was in conflict with the public policy of India. Despite precedents suggesting that public policy be interpreted in a narrow sense, the Court interpreted public policy in the broadest terms possible. The Court held that any arbitral award that violates Indian statutory provisions is patently illegal and hence contrary to public policy, which effectively opened the floodgates for losing parties in the arbitral process to challenge awards in courts, a situation that the 1996 Act was enacted to avoid.

The Indian Arbitration Act did not include 'error of law' as a ground for setting aside arbitral awards. The Supreme Court decision in the ONGC v. Saw Pipes case unfortunately indicated that the principle of judicial noninterference in India became seriously undermined. Fali S. Nariman (2003), a very senior lawyer and arbitrator, said that the judgement has 'virtually set at naught the entire Arbitration and Conciliation Act of 1996… To have introduced—by judicial innovation—a fresh ground of challenge and placed it under the head of "public policy" was contrary to the plain intent of the new 1996 law, namely the need of finality in alternative methods of dispute resolution without court interference'. He continued, 'if courts continue to hold that they have the last word on facts and on law—notwithstanding consensual agreements to refer matters necessarily involving facts and law to adjudication by arbitration—the 1996 Act might as well be scrapped'.

Subsequently, to repair the damage done by the Supreme Court decision in the Saw Pipes case to the integrity of arbitration as an alternative to litigation, we find two major developments. The first was the Bharat Aluminium Co. v Kaiser Aluminium Technical Services case, which rectified the anomaly, effectively reversing the damage done by the Saw Pipes v. ONGC case, by clarifying that Part I of the Act only applies to Indian-seated arbitrations. This decision limits the power of the court to set aside a foreign award. Now, although the Indian court may still refuse to enforce a foreign award, its grounds for doing so are restricted to the familiar limited circumstances in Article V of the New York Convention, provided for in Article 48 (2) (b) of the 1996 Act, which states that:

> Enforcement of an arbitral award may also be refused if the Court finds that—
>
> a …
> b the enforcement of the award would be contrary to the public policy of India.
>
> Explanation—Without prejudice to the generality of clause (b) of this section, it is hereby declared, for the avoidance of any doubt, that an award is in conflict with the public policy of India if the making of the award was induced or affected by fraud or corruption.

In the present context, it is highly unlikely that the court will be able to set aside an award on the basis that it is, in the court's opinion, legally or factually wrong. The decision in this case is of great significance and does much to allay the concerns previously held that India was not an arbitration-friendly jurisdiction.

The second development was the 246th Law Commission of India Report, which introduced 'Amendment to the Arbitration and Conciliation Act, 1996', which seeks a balance between judicial intervention and judicial restraint. It has recommended the addition of Section 34 (2A) to deal with purely domestic awards, which may also be set aside by the Court, if the Court finds that such an award is vitiated by 'patent illegality appearing on the face of the award'. In order to provide a balance and to avoid excessive intervention, it is clarified in the proposed proviso to the Section 34 (2A) that such 'an award shall not be set aside merely on the ground of an erroneous application of the law or by re-appreciating evidence'. The Commission has further recommended the restriction of the scope of public policy in both Sections 34 and 48. Under the formulation of the Commission, an award can be set aside on public policy grounds only if it is opposed to the 'fundamental policy of Indian law' or it is in conflict with 'most basic notions of morality or justice'.

1.7.3 Hong Kong

Hong Kong is a strong arbitration-friendly regime, and the government fully supports arbitration as an ADR mechanism. The Arbitration Ordinance, closely based on the UNCITRAL Model Law, provides for an economical and speedy resolution of international commercial disputes and allows maximum freedom to the disputing parties to resolve their disputes outside the court with minimum court intervention, except where the court finds public interest at stake. Among the various provisions, the Arbitration Ordinance limits court interference to cases where an award is challenged on procedural grounds, such as the incapacity of a party, lack of arbitral jurisdiction, and, more importantly, on public policy exception.

Section 84 of the Arbitration Ordinance (Singapore) states that, with the court's leave, an arbitration award, whether made in or outside Hong Kong, may, except in very limited circumstances, be enforced in the same manner as a judgement of the High Court.

> Cap 609 s 84 Enforcement of arbitral awards (ARBITRATION ORDINANCE)
>
> 1 Subject to section 26(2), an award, whether made in or outside Hong Kong, in arbitral proceedings by an arbitral tribunal is enforceable in the same manner as a judgment of the Court that has the same effect, but only with the leave of the Court.

Since Hong Kong, as part of the People's Republic of China, is a party to the New York Convention on the Recognition and Enforcement of Foreign Arbitral Awards, an award obtained in Hong Kong is enforceable in other countries that are signatories to the New York Convention. If the losing party has no assets in Hong Kong but does in another jurisdiction, an arbitration award may be more valuable than a court judgement, if the country where the assets of the losing party are situated has no reciprocal judgement enforcement arrangement with Hong Kong, but is a signatory to the New York Convention, such as the UK, the US, and Japan, which are Hong Kong's major trading partners.

The courts' approach towards the issue of public policy exception as a ground for refusing enforcement of international awards is the same as the approach adopted towards a domestic award, though it is not clearly stated in the Ordinance whether refusal on public policy grounds is only limited to procedural issues or can be extended to the substance of the award. However, in practice, this ground is only applied on procedural aspects, such as bias and misconduct of arbitrators. In principle, public policy exception can be used in matters of substantive law. The most significant case of public policy exception as a ground for refusing enforcement is that of Hebei Import & Export Corporation v Polytek Engineering

Company Limited [1999], in which public policy was narrowly construed and applied, avoiding consideration of every conceivable procedural weakness. The Court of Final Appeal held that 'contrary to public policy' means 'contrary to the fundamental conceptions of morality and justice of the forum in which enforcement is sought', which clearly underpins Hong Kong's pro-enforcement policy towards arbitral awards.

1.7.4 Singapore

Singapore originally enacted Arbitration Act 37 of 2001, but subsequently revised it in 2002 as Arbitration Act (Chapter 10), which modified the arbitration law to relax rules governing representation in international arbitration proceedings in Singapore. Singapore was criticised for decisions in the late 1980s that restricted the ability of parties to be represented by counsel of their choice. This prompted concern within Singapore that such a rule was viewed as harmful to its reputation as one of the popular options for resolving international commercial disputes in Asia. The revised version of its international arbitration law was primarily meant to eliminate any restrictions on the parties' autonomy, especially in the matters of choice of counsel to enhance its reputation as an arbitration-friendly regime. However, in the matters of setting aside international arbitration awards, Section 48 (1) was as vague as most other Asian jurisdictions.

> ARBITRATION ACT (CHAPTER 10)
>
> (Original Enactment: Act 37 of 2001) (Revised in 2002)
>
> 48—(1) An award may be set aside by the Court—
> b if the Court finds that—
>   i the subject-matter of the dispute is not capable of settlement by arbitration under this Act; or
>   ii the award is contrary to public policy.

Singapore, however, followed the recommendations in the Model Law very closely, which permitted court involvement in specific contexts, including issues such as the arbitration agreement, appointment of arbitrators, challenge procedure, competence of tribunal in matters of jurisdiction, and setting aside, recognition and enforcement of awards. Singapore courts have made sure that court intervention is in line with what is expressly envisaged in the Model Law. A recent case in point is that of PT Asuransi Jasa Indonesia (Persero) v Dexia Bank SA. The Court adopted a narrow interpretation of the public policy formulation and dismissed the attempt to use the public policy exception as a cover for a party's dissatisfaction with the outcome of its arbitration.

The Court observed that it has been accepted by the international arbitration community that the public policy exception in the Model Law is intended to comprehend only those matters that would offend the most basic notions of morality and justice and that the public policy defence should be construed narrowly. Thus, in the context of the New York Convention 1958, it has been said that, 'the convention's public policy defence should be construed narrowly. Enforcement of foreign arbitral awards may be denied on this basis only where enforcement would violate the forum state's most basic notions of morality and justice'.

More crucially, the concept of finality under the Model Law global regime is clearly emphasised in art 34, and in the case of Singapore, under Section 31 of the International Arbitration Act (originally enacted in 1994, but revised in 2002). The court is only permitted to refuse enforcement of the arbitral award on the grounds set out in art 34 of the Model Law and Section 31 of the IAA. In this case, the Court emphasised that effect must be given to 'the principle of international comity enshrined in the [New York] Convention that strongly inclines the courts to give effect to foreign arbitration awards' unless the award 'violates the most basic notions of morality and justice'.

The court simply took a mechanistic approach and submitted that if an enforcing court goes behind the award itself and descends into the merits, it would negate the finality desired in international arbitrations. To permit a court to take a less mechanistic approach is to open the door to a multitude of challenges to the recognition and enforcement of arbitral awards beyond those intended to be permitted under the Model Law regime. That would turn the clock back on the progress of international arbitration as a reliable means of resolving international disputes.

1.7.5 Japan

The Japanese Arbitration Law of 2003, which came into force on 1 March 2004, is based on the 1985 UNCITRAL Model Law, with very few variations. Moreover, there are no recent supreme court cases that define public policy under Articles 44–46 of the Japanese Arbitration Law, especially in the context of setting aside or enforcement of awards, except the one decided in 1997 (in Northcon I, Oregon Partnership v. Mansei Kôgyô Co Ltd., 51 Minshu 2573 (Sup. Ct. 11 July 1997)). Referring to this case, the IBA Sub-Committee on Recognition and Enforcement of Awards Country Report—Japan points out that the Japanese Supreme Court has defined 'public policy' in the context of enforcement of foreign judgements as follows:

> Even if the judgment of the foreign court includes content based on a system that is not adopted by our country, this by itself will not automatically mean that the condition [for enforcement, i.e., that the foreign judgment does not violate public policy] is not satisfied; but if it is incompatible with the basic principles or basic ideas of the legal system of our country, the foreign judgment shall be in violation of public policy...
>
> (Tezuka and Kawabata: 2015: 2)

More recently, however, the lower courts have indicated some explanation for the application of 'public policy or good morals' as a ground for setting aside an arbitral award.

In the case of X K.K. v. American International Underwriters, Ltd., the Tokyo District Court, on 28 July 2009, stated that since arbitration is based on the parties' agreement, and there is generally no appeal mechanism anticipated, and the award is considered final, the court may exercise its authority only as provided in the Arbitration Law. The Court made it clear that the Arbitration Law does not permit a court to set aside an arbitral award on the grounds of violation of public policy 'if it is merely the arbitral tribunal's fact finding or decision on law that is found to be unreasonable'. The court is permitted to set aside an arbitral award 'only when the legal result achieved by the arbitral award is incompatible with the public policy or good morals of Japan' (Tezuka and Kawabata: 2015: 5).

1.7.6 Malaysia

Although the Kuala Lumpur Regional Centre for Arbitration is surrounded by some of the leading arbitration centres, such as the Singapore International Arbitration Centre, the

Hong Kong International Arbitration Centre, and, of course, several others in China and India, it has been developing rapidly in the last few years and has become a prominent seat of international commercial dispute resolution in Asia. This is largely due to the government support to meet the demands and needs of the global business community and active efforts of the local professional community. Arbitration in Malaysia is governed by the Arbitration Act 2005, which draws on the UNCITRAL Model Law. Sections 38 and 39 of the Arbitration Act clearly provide that an arbitral award either from Malaysia or another foreign country is binding and enforceable. However, at the same time, Sections 37 and 39 of the Arbitration Act 2005 also give discretion (notice the use of *may*) to the court to reject enforcement or setting aside of an award on 'public policy exception'.

> Section 37(1)(b)(ii) – An award <u>may be set aside</u> by the High Court only if the High Court finds that the award is in conflict with the public policy of Malaysia; (2) Without limiting the generality of subparagraph (1)(b)(ii), an award is in conflict with the public policy of Malaysia where (a)...; or (b) a breach of the rules of natural justice occurred (i) during the arbitral proceedings; or (ii) in connection with the making of the award.
>
> Section 39(1)(b)(ii) – Recognition or enforcement of an award, irrespective of the State in which it was made, <u>may be refused</u> only at the request of the party against whom it is invoked if the High Court finds that the award is in conflict with the public policy of Malaysia.

Although the courts are given discretion to set aside or refuse to enforce an arbitration award when it is considered to be in conflict with public policy in Malaysia, the term *public policy* is not defined in the Act, except as a breach of the rules of natural justice noticed in the arbitral proceedings or in the making of the award. However, Malaysian courts have generally adopted quite a narrow approach to interpret public policy as a ground to refuse enforcement of foreign arbitral awards. In a recent case of Open Type Joint Stock Company Efirnoye ('EFKO') v. Alfa Trading Ltd., the High Court adopted a narrow interpretation of public policy and refrained from interfering in the decision of the arbitral body outside Malaysia. The case involved a Russian company as plaintiff, which was the buyer of palm oil products, with a Malaysian company as the seller. They had a series of disputes regarding breach of contractual obligations, and as a consequence, both the parties initiated separate proceedings, and the Russian party had a Russian award in their favour, whereas the Malaysian party had a Ukrainian award in their favour. The plaintiff sought to enforce the Russian award in the High Court of Malaysia under Section 38 of the Arbitration Act, whereas the defendant invoked Section 39 (i) (b) (ii) to argue that the award from the Russian Federation was in conflict with the public policy of Malaysia. The High Court, however, contended that Section 39, with regard to the contravention of public policy argument, ought not to be utilised as a valid ground to reopen settled matters in the arbitration, and hence the Court ruled in favour of the Plaintiff.

1.8 Concluding remarks

Arbitration in Asia has had a fairly chequered history. There has been a fair amount of scepticism in some countries, in particular India and China. In India, the development from arbitration-scepticism to arbitration-friendly has been hampered by the freedom exercised by the court's interpretation of public policy in various ways. In China, on the other hand, it has been the result of viewing arbitration as a judicial activity as part of China's legal system, which was played out as tension between the institutionalised judiciary and the private adjudication in arbitration. In practice, the real issue has been balancing arbitral power v. judicial power. However, both in China and India in the last decade or so, the judiciaries have taken necessary steps to ensure narrow interpretations of public policy in line with international practice. Hong Kong and Singapore, on the other hand, have both been quite arbitration-friendly states, almost in line with the international practice of interpreting public policy narrowly, clearly, precisely, and unambiguously (see Bhatia, 1993), restricting the limits of juridical interference in arbitration to those awards only that are contrary to the fundamental conceptions of morality and justice. In the case of Malaysia and Japan, the challenge to international arbitration awards is successful only when it is in breach of the principles of natural justice or incompatible with the good morals of the individual state, which is very much in line with the international practice.

As regards the interpretation of public policy where arbitration is concerned, there still seems to be a relative vacuum in international, including Asian, contexts. Bermann (2014: 70) makes an attempt to explain some of the developments when he says that a prominent feature of the public policy defence is the distinction between 'substantive' and 'procedural' public policy. Another expression that is commonly used in the context of public policy is the 'most basic notions of morality and justice'. Unfortunately, however, he points out that even the meaning of this is also rarely explained or expanded for application. 'The national reports typically cite isolated examples of judicial refusals to recognize or enforce awards on grounds of public policy, without advancing meaningful general propositions' (Bermann, 2014: 72).

1.9 Interdiscursive issues in interpretation

One of the important issues that comes up in the analysis of arbitration discourse and practice, particularly from the point of view of discursive construction and interpretation of arbitration discourse, is the important role of interdiscursive aspects of legal construction and interpretation (Bhatia, 2010). I have made an attempt to highlight the way different discourses—legislative as well as arbitral, grounded in a number of different jurisdictions, sociopolitical as well as economic contexts, and other disciplinary and cultural constraints—are frequently required to cooperate and co-construct formulation, reframing, and recontextualisation of some of the most elusive concepts, such as public policy, judicial and arbitral power, most basic notions of morality and justice, or patently legal or illegal in the context of different arbitral regimes. A very insightful illustration of this phenomenon was the interpretation of the Act of 1996, which does not provide for challenge to a foreign arbitral award specifically. Although Section 48, and more particularly Section 48(1)(e), read with other substantive provisions, makes it abundantly clear that although it is not permissible to challenge a foreign award, it could be resisted in its enforcement on the same grounds as are available while challenging a domestic award. A bare reading of Section 48(1)(e) would demonstrate that a foreign award can be challenged in a country in which it was made or the country under the law of which it was made. The Court in India did exactly that and went for interpretation to extend the same to foreign awards with disastrous consequences. Some of these misinterpretations of specific laws could have been avoided by recourse to some of the basic notions of discursive construction and interpretation.

To sum up, although Asia initially seemed to have a chequered history in terms of its use of public policy exception as justification for refusing to enforce international awards, a number of developments in recent years, particularly in China and India, have created arbitration-friendly regimes to support and take advantage of the unprecedented increase in international trade and commercial activities across the national boundaries. This can also be seen as a move towards greater harmonisation of international commercial arbitration practices across the globe, which is a welcome sign for the development of the institution of international commercial arbitration as a global practice.

References

Anesa Patrizia (2017): 'Arbitration Practice in India: A Discursive Perspective', Bhatia et al. (Eds.) *International Arbitration Discourse and Practices in Asia*, London, Routledge.

Bhatia, Vijay K. (1993) *Analysing Genre: Language Use in Professional Settings*. London, Longman.

Bhatia, Vijay K. (2010) 'Interdiscursivity in Professional Communication', *Discourse and Communication*, 21/1, (32–50).

Bhatia, Vijay K. (2011): Witness Examination as Interdiscursive Practice, in the Special Issue of *World Englishes*, 30, (106–116).

Bhatia, Vijay K., (2017): *Critical Genre Analysis: Investigating Interdiscursive Performance in Professional Communication*, London, Routledge.

Bhatia, Vijay K., Christopher N. Candlin, and Jan Engberg, (Eds) (2008): *Legal Discourse Across Cultures and Systems*, Hong Kong, HKU Press.

Bhatia Vijay K., Christopher N. Candlin, and Maurizio Gotti, (Eds) (2010): *The Discourses of Dispute Resolution*, Bern, Peter Lang.

Bhatia Vijay K., Christopher N. Candlin, and Maurizio Gotti, (Eds) (2012): *Arbitration Practice and Discourse: Issues, Challenges and Prospects*, Farnham, Ashgate Publishing Group.

Bermann, George, (2014): *Recognition and Enforcement of Foreign Arbitral Awards: The Application of New York Convention by National Courts* (Draft).

Chi Manjiao, (2011): 'Are We "Paper Tigers"? The Limited Procedural Power of Arbitrators Under Chinese Law', *Journal of Dispute Resolution*, 2, (1–24). Also available at: http://scholarship.law.Missourie.edu/jdr/vol2011/iss2/2. Accessed on 20 January 2016.

Gao, Xiaoli, (2015): *IBA Sub-committee on Recognition and enforcement of Awards Report of the People's Republic of China on Public Policy as a Ground for Refusal of Enforcement of Arbitral Awards under the New York Convention.*

Hwang, Michael, (2007): *Is There Still Resistance to Arbitration in Asia*, Address to the International Arbitration Club. www.arbitrationicca.org/media/4/92275989554120/media012232972346990why_is_there_still_resistance_to_arbitration_in_asia.pdf. Accessed on 25 January 2016.

Nariman, Fali S., (2003): Speech at the Inaugural Session of 'Legal Reforms in Infrastructure' (May 2, 2003). http://shodhganga.inflibnet.ac.in/bitstream/10603/95269/11/11_chapter%206.pd. Accessed on 20 January 2016.

Tezuka Hiroyuki and Kawabata Yutaro, (2015): *IBA Sub-Committee on Recognition an Enforcement of Awards Country Report – Japan.*

Cases

Bharat Aluminum Co. v Kaiser Aluminum Technical Services. SCI 7019 (2005)

Hebei Import & Export Corp. v. Polytek Engineering Co. Ltd. [1999] 2 HK.C. 205 (Ct. Final Appeal 1999)

ONGC. v. Saw Pipes (2003) 5 SCC 705

Open Type Joint Stock Company Efirnoye ("EFKO") v. Alfa Trading Ltd. http://kl.kehakiman.gov.my/sites/kl.kehakiman.gov.my/attachments/D-24NCC-221-2010.pdf.

P T Asuransi Jasa Indonesia (Persero) v Dexia Bank SA

Renu Sagar Power Co. Ltd. v. General Electric Co (1994) Suppl. (1) SCC 644

X K.K. v. American International Underwriters, Ltd., Haneritimes No. 1304 (Tokyo Dist. Ct. 28 July 2009). www.ibanet.org/Document/Default.aspx?DocumentUid=6B55AAFC-DD34-4144-9680-A22A4E3A1CC9.

Statutes and Laws

246 Law Commission of India Report, http://lawcommissionofindia.nic.in/reports/Report246.pdf.

Arbitration and Conciliation Ordinance of India (1996), www.wipo.int/edocs/lexdocs/laws/en/in/in063en.pdf.

Arbitration Law (No.138 of 2003) (Japan), http://japan.kantei.go.jp/policy/sihou/arbitrationlaw.pdf.

Arbitration Law of the People's Republic of China, http://english.mofcom.gov.cn/article/policyrelease/Businessregulations/201312/20131200432698.shtml.

CAP 609 Arbitration Ordinance (Hong Kong), www.legislation.gov.hk/blis_pdf.nsf/6799165D2FEE3FA94825755E0033E532/C05151C760F783AD482577D900541075?OpenDocument&bt=0. Accessed on 30 January 2016.

Convention on the Recognition and Enforcement of Foreign Arbitral Awards (New York, 1958) (the "New York Convention"), www.uncitral.org/uncitral/en/uncitral_texts/arbitration/NYConvention.html.

International Arbitration Act (Chapter 143A), http://statutes.agc.gov.sg/aol/search/display/view.w3p;page=0;query=DocId%3A%22fdb4f13d-0fdb-4083-806a-0c16554efd0b%22%20Status%3Ainforce%20Depth%3A0;rec=0.

Singapore Arbitration Act (Chapter 10), http://statutes.agc.gov.sg/aol/search/display/view.w3p;ident=c8b78a73-0c5f-4534-b60e-56e600fd50e0;page=0;query=DocId%3Ae8687d02-1aae-42ff-9afa-92c086e168c0%20Depth%3A0%20Status%3Ainforce;rec=0#pr48-he-.

UNCITRAL Model Law, www.uncitral.org/pdf/english/texts/arbitration/ml-arb/06-54671_Ebook.pdf.

2 Setting aside or non-enforcement of arbitral awards in international arbitration on the public policy ground – a regional perspective[1]

John K. Arthur

2.1 Introduction

An award in international commercial arbitration (ICA) is only liable to be set aside, or refused recognition or enforcement, on the grounds contained in Articles V(1)(a)–(e) and V(2)(a) and (b) of the New York Convention (NYC) and Articles 34 and 36 of the United Nations Commission on International Trade Law Model Law (UNCITRAL Model Law) on ICA, respectively.[2] These grounds are concerned with the structural integrity of the arbitration proceedings[3] and not the merits of an arbitral award.[4] One of the grounds upon which a court may set aside or refuse enforcement of an arbitral award is if it finds that the award is in conflict with the public policy of that State.[5]

2.2 The concept of public policy

It has been suggested that an award should only be set aside on the 'public policy ground' if it is contrary to 'truly transnational' public policy.[6] International public policy is confined to violation of fundamental conceptions of legal order in the country concerned, or norms that embody and reflect fundamental notions of morality and justice.[7] The public policy ground was defined by Sir Anthony Mason NPJ in *Hebei Import & Export*[8] in well known

1 This paper was first delivered at the ICAAD 2015 conference held on 20–21 August 2015 at the KLRCA, KL, Malaysia. An earlier version of this paper was published in the Australian Alternative Dispute Resolution Bulletin, 2015, Vol. 2, No 6–10, pp. 11–14.

2 *TCL Air Conditioner (Zhongshan) Co Ltd v Judges of the Federal Court of Australia* (2013) 251 CLR 533; (2013) 295 ALR 596; [2013] HCA 5 at [53]–[54]. The International Arbitration Act 1974 (Cth) (IAA) gives the force of law in Australia to the Model Law: Section 16 IAA.

3 *Kanoria v Guinness* [2006] EWCA Civ 222, [30] cited by the Hong Kong Court of Appeal in *Grand Pacific Holdings Ltd v Pacific China Holdings Ltd (in liq) (No 1)* [2012] 4 HKLRD 1 at 7[7] per Tang V-P (with whom Kwan and Fok JJA agreed) cited in *Cameron Australasia Pty Ltd v Aed Oil Ltd (subject to deed of company arrangement)* [2015] VSC 163 at [20] (Croft J).

4 *AKN v ALC* [2015] SGCA 18, [37] (Menon CJ), Singapore Court of Appeal.

5 Article V(2)(a) and (b) NYC; Article 34(2)(b)(ii), Article 36(1)(b) Model Law; Section 8(7) International Arbitration Act 1974 (Cth.); see also Section 37(1)(b)(ii) of the Malaysian Arbitration Act 2005; Article 66 of the Arbitration Law 1999 (Indonesia).

6 In France, traditionally, ICA awards could only be rejected on the grounds of public policy or *ordre public* if there was shown to be a contravention of international public policy: NCCP Article 15002 *Societe Impex v Societe PAZ*, Judgment of 18 May 1971, Cour de Cassation, [1972] DS Jur 37.

7 Bermann, Recognition and Enforcement of Foreign Arbitral Awards: The Application of the New York Convention by National Courts, [July 2, 2014 draft] by Prof. George A. Bermann, available at: http://www.iacl2014congress.com/fileadmin/user_upload/k_iacl2014congress/General_reports/Bermann__General_Report_Recognition__Enforcement_of_Foreign_Awards_July_2_2014__2_.pdf p 71; and see *TCL Air Conditioner (Zhongshan) Co Ltd v Castel Electronics Pty Ltd* (2014) 311 ALR 387; [2014] FCAFC 83 at [76].

8 (1999) 2 HKCFAR 111, (at p 130F); [1999] 1 HKLRD 665.

terms as meaning 'contrary to the fundamental conceptions of morality and justice of the forum'. Given the amorphous nature of public policy considerations 'should be approached with extreme caution' and construed narrowly.[9] It has been said that '(i)t is never argued at all but when other points fail'. The same case described public policy considerations as 'a very unruly horse and when once you get astride it, you never know where it will carry you'.[10] Public policy will necessarily differ from forum to forum[11] and the Model Law, like the NYC, does not prescribe a universal standard of public policy; however, a breach of natural justice has been internationally accepted as a violation of generic 'procedural public policy'.[12] It is suggested that 'most national courts have adopted the narrower standard of international public policy, applying substantive norms from international sources'.[13]

2.3 The interpretation and application of the public policy ground in the Australian/Asian region

2.3.1 Australia

In Australia, which is a signatory to the NYC and a Model Law country, the public policy ground is construed narrowly. The Full Federal Court recently held that an ICA award will not be set aside or denied recognition or enforcement as contrary to public policy (by reason of a breach of natural justice or otherwise),[14] unless there exists real unfairness or real practical injustice in the conduct of the arbitration or making of the award.[15] In reaching this conclusion, the Court had regard to the critical international instruments, in light of international and regional case law making it clear that this should be the approach in all ICA cases.[16] There are significant parallels between the Australian approach and that adopted in other countries in Asia.

2.3.2 Malaysia

Malaysia is a signatory to the NYC. The Malaysian Arbitration Act 2005 is based on the Model Law. In order to set aside an award on the public policy ground, it needs to be established that there is a 'conflict with the public policy of Malaysia in the narrow sense of something offending basic notions of morality and justice or something clearly injurious to the public good in Malaysia'.[17] It has been held that Malaysian Courts should follow an

9 Deutsche Schachtbau- und Tiefbohrgesellschaft mbH v Ras Al Khaimah National Oil Co [1987] 2 All ER 769 at 779 (Donaldson MR, with Woolf and Russell LJJ agreeing).

10 Richardson v Mellish (1824) 2 Bing 229, 252; 130 ER 294, 303.

11 Natural Justice Fallibility in Singapore Arbitration Proceedings (2014) 26 SAcLJ by K.H. Shahdadpuri at pp. 576–7, [40], [42].

12 Ibid, Shahdadpuri at n. 9.

13 ICCA Guide to the NYC, Pieter Sanders (Gen. Ed.) at p. 107.

14 Or on the other grounds in Articles 34 and 36 Model Law: see TCL case in n. 14 at [111].

15 TCL Air Conditioner (Zhongshan) Co Ltd v Castel Electronics Pty Ltd (2014) 232 FCR 361 (2014) 311 ALR 387; [2014] FCAFC 83 ("TCL case"). For a more detailed case note of the TCL case, see: Australian Alternative. Dispute Resolution Bulletin, December 2014, Lexis Nexis at pp. 134–5.

16 TCL case at [75]–[76]; See also International Relief and Development Inc v Ladu [2014] FCA 887; BC201407777 at [169] (Kenny J); Indian Farmers Fertiliser Cooperative Ltd v Gutnick [2015] VSC 724 at [20]–[24] (Croft J).

17 Majlis Amanah Rakyat v Kausar Corporation Sdn Bhd [2009] 1 LNS 1766.

approach based on 'comparative jurisprudence in the interests of maintaining comity of nations and a uniform approach to the model law, so far as that is possible, to the concept of "public policy" in relation to foreign awards.'[18]

2.3.3 Singapore

Singapore is a NYC signatory state, and the Model Law is given force of law in Singapore.[19] A court may refuse enforcement of a foreign award if it finds that 'enforcement of the award would be contrary to the public policy of Singapore'.[20] The exception is construed narrowly.[21] An award will only be refused enforcement if it would 'shock the conscience' or 'violate the forum's most basic notions of morality'.[22] There must be exceptional circumstances that violate the most basic notions of morality and justice or are injurious to the public good.[23] Singapore courts will readily pay heed to international jurisprudence on the Model Law in describing the ambit of the ground.[24]

2.3.4 Hong Kong

The NYC applies in Hong Kong.[25] The provisions of the Model Law, likewise, have the force of law in Hong Kong, subject to the Arbitration Ordinance Cap 609. The 'contrary to public policy' ground, which is narrowly construed,[26] means 'contrary to the fundamental conceptions of morality and justice of the forum'.[27] '(T)he award must be ... fundamentally (and obviously) offensive to that jurisdiction's notions of justice'.[28] '(T)here must be ... a substantial injustice arising out of an award which is so shocking to the court's conscience as to render enforcement repugnant'.[29] The conduct complained of 'must be serious, even egregious',[30] and only a sufficiently serious error that has undermined due process will suffice.[31]

18 Ibid. This approach is along the same lines as the Australian approach seen in the TCL case.

19 By its International Arbitration Act, Section 3.

20 Section 31(4)(b) IAA (Singapore).

21 AJU v AJT [2011] SGCA 41 and according to one commentator there has been no instance where the Singapore courts have refused to enforce an arbitral award on the grounds of public policy: *Public Policy and Singapore Law of International Arbitration*, by Nish Shetty, Clifford Chance; 25 March 2015; Memorandum TO Members of the IBA Recognition and Enforcement of Awards Subcommittee.

22 PT Asuransi Jasa Indonesia (Persero) v Dexia Bank SA [2007] 1 SLR (R) 597. See also, AJU v AJT [2011] SGCA 41; AQU v AQV [2015] SGHC 26; AKN v ALC [2015] SGCA 18; Coal & Oil Co LLC v GHCL Ltd [2015] SGHC 65.

23 PT Asuransi Jasa Indonesia (Persero) v Dexia Bank SA [2007] 1 SLR(R) 597.

24 Ibid PT Asuransi case at [59].

25 Upon the Government of China extending the territorial application of the NYC to Hong Kong upon resumption of sovereignty over Hong Kong on 1 July 1997: www.uncitral.org/uncitral/en/uncitral_texts/arbitration/NYConvention_status.html.

26 Shanghai Fusheng Soya-Food Co Ltd & Anor v Pulmuone Holdings Co Ltd [2014] HKCFI 894 per Hon Mimmie Chan.

27 See n. 15 prior.

28 Bokhary PJ in *Hebei Import & Export*, see n. 15 explained (at p 123H-I).

29 A v R (Arbitration: Enforcement) [2009] 3 HKLRD 389, per Reyes J.

30 Grand Pacific Holdings Ltd v Pacific China Holdings Limited (in liq) (No 1) [2012] 4 HKLRD 1 at [94] (Tang VP).

31 Ibid, Grand Pacific Holdings Ltd at [105].

2.3.5 *China*

China has been a party to the NYC since 1987.[32] Chinese courts have adopted an active and supportive policy with respect to both the domestic and international arbitration based on the law.[33] While the 'public policy' exception is not expressly included as one of the grounds in Articles 237(3) and 274(2) of Civil Procedural Law of the PRC, both provide that where an award contradicts the 'social and public interest' of China, its enforcement will be refused.[34] The *social and public interest* is a vague term, subject to interpretation,[35] but equates with *public policy* under international norms.[36] According to commentators, 'a violation of public policy seems to require proof of an affront to the higher "social public interest" of China as a whole, whether it relates to the moral order of the country or the sovereignty of the Chinese courts .... This difficult level of proof may explain why the SPC has apparently vacated only one foreign arbitral award on public policy grounds since (at least) 2000'.[37] Courts in the PRC have generally interpreted the public policy exception very narrowly[38] and have shown an almost universal reluctance to invoke 'public policy'-type grounds.[39]

2.3.6 *India*

India is a signatory to the NYC. The Indian *Arbitration and Conciliation Act* 1996 is based on the Model Law, and the public policy exception is framed in Model Law terms in Section 34 of the Act.[40] The broad interpretation of 'public policy' used for setting aside a

32 www.uncitral.org/uncitral/en/uncitral_texts/arbitration/NYConvention_status.html; See also The Public Policy Exception in Mainland China, by Dr Chen Fuyong, Deputy Secretary-General, Beijing Arbitration Commission, Beijing, 2015 (presently unpublished).

33 Ibid, Dr Chen Fuyong at n. 32 citing Judge Xiaolong Lu of the Supreme Court at the 17th ICCA Congress in Beijing: Xiaolong Lu, *The Recognitions and Enforcement of Foreign Arbitral Awards in China*, ICCA Congress Series No. 12 (Beijing 2004), van den Berg (ed) (2005).

34 Ibid, Dr Chen Fuyong at n. 32. These provisions are the result of amendments to the Chinese Civil Procedural Law which became effective on 1 January 2013. See Herbert Smith Freehills, China Disputes E-Bulletin, 6 May 2013.

35 Ibid, Dr Chen Fuyong at n. 32.

36 Ibid, Dr Chen Fuyong at n. 32.

37 The Enforcement of Foreign Arbitration Awards in China, by Henry (Litong) Chen, MWE China Law Offices and B. Ted Howes, McDermott, Will & Emery, see: www.mwe.com/info/pubs/BLR_1109.pdf. Dr Chen Fuyong refers to the case of *Hemofarm DD et al. v. Jinan yongning pharmaceutical co. Ltd.* (2004), where the Supreme Court declined to support the enforcement of the award, by reason that the award was outside the scope of the arbitration clause, violating China's judicial sovereignty and Chinese courts' jurisdiction, and further constituting a violation of China's public policy, ibid, Dr Chen Fuyong at n. 32.

38 Ibid, Dr Chen Fuyong at n. 32.

39 Ibid, The Enforcement of Foreign Arbitration Awards in China, see *Conclusion*.

40 Amendments have been made to Section 34 by the Arbitration and Conciliation (Amendment) Ordinance 2015 by an amendment to the Explanations to that section to provide: 'Explanation I. For the avoidance of any doubt, it is clarified that an award is in conflict with the public policy of India, only if, (i) the making of the award was induced or affected by fraud or corruption or was in violation of Section 75 or Section 81; or (ii) it is in contravention with the fundamental policy of Indian law; or (iii) it is in conflict with the most basic notions of morality or justice. Explanation 2. For the avoidance of doubt, the test as to whether there is a contravention with the fundamental policy of Indian law shall not entail a review on the merits of the dispute'.; and the insertion of a new sub-section: '(2A) An arbitral award arising out of arbitrations other than international commercial arbitrations, may also be set aside by the Court, if the Court finds that the award is

domestic arbitration award in India will not be applied to enforcement of an ICA award,[41] and courts are slower to invoke public policy in cases involving a foreign element than when purely municipal legal issues are involved.[42] Enforcement of an ICA award will only be able to be opposed on grounds of 'public policy', when the award is contrary to the fundamental policy of Indian law[43]; the interests of India; justice and morality;[44] or, in addition, if it is patently illegal.[45]

2.3.7 Japan

Japan is also a signatory to the NYC. The Japanese Arbitration Law[46] is based on the 1985 Model Law, with a few limited variations.[47] The Arbitration Law provides that an arbitral award may be set aside or refused recognition or enforcement if 'the content of the arbitral award is in conflict with the public policy or good morals of Japan'.[48] Japanese courts have narrowly interpreted 'public policy' in light of the purposes of the Arbitration Law. While there are no published Supreme Court cases defining the term *public policy*,[49] the lower courts have concluded that if arbitral proceedings violated the public policy of Japan, this would mean that 'the content of the arbitral award is in conflict with the public policy or good morals of Japan'.[50] The public policy exception has rarely been successful in Japan.[51]

vitiated by patent illegality appearing on the face of the award: Provided that an award shall not be set aside merely on the ground of an erroneous application of the law or by reappreciation of evidence'.

41 Shri Lal Mahal Ltd. -v- Progetto Grano Spa Civil Appeal (2014) 2 SCC 433, [22], [25] (SC).

42 Shri Lal Mahal Ltd. -v- Progetto Grano Spa Civil Appeal (2014) 2 SCC 433, [22], [25] (SC).

43 The 'fundamental policy of Indian law' was discussed in Oil & Natural Gas Corporation Ltd v Western Geco international Ltd (2014) 9 SCC 263, and was seen as a regressive step for the non-interference trend in *ONGC v Western GECO – A new impediment in Indian Arbitration*, Arthad Kurlekar: http://kluwerarbitrationblog.com/2015/01/07/ongc-v-western-geco-a-new-impediment-in-indian-arbitration/.

44 Ibid Shir Lal Mahal at n. 39 relying upon Renusagar Power Co. Ltd vs General Electric Co 1994 AIR 860, 1994 SCC Suppl. (1) 644, at [66].

45 ONGC v. Saw Pipes, 2003 (5) SCC 705; Associate Builders v Delhi Development Authority 2014 (4) ARBLR 307.

46 Law No. 138 of 2003, which came into force on 1 March 2004. It should be noted that the interpretation of the public policy ground in India is clarified and assisted by recent amendments to *Arbitration and Conciliation Act* 1996.

47 See IBA Sub-Committee on Recognition and Enforcement of Awards Country Report – Japan 30 June 2015 Country Reporters: Hiroyuki Tezuka (h_tezuka@jurists.co.jp) Yutaro Kawabata (y_kawabata@jurists.co.jp).

48 Articles 44(1)(viii), 45(2)(ix), and 46(8) of the Law; see n. 34.

49 Under Articles 44–46 of the Law, see n. 34.

50 See n. 34; and see, K.K. Kouno v. Y Inc., LEX/DB No. 25473502, (Tokyo Dist. Ct. 13 June 2011), upheld in Y Inc. v. K.K. Kouno, LLI/DB No. L06720791, (Tokyo High Ct. 13 March 2012) upheld the Tokyo District Court's judgment; in that case, the court set aside an arbitral award on the basis that it offended Japanese procedural public policy, in that the arbitrator had taken a central fact as being undisputed, although it was in fact disputed between the parties.

51 Baker and Mackenzie: 2011; Dispute Resolution Around the World – Japan; Enforcement of arbitration awards, p 17 available at: http://www.bakermckenzie.com/-/media/files/insight/publications/2016/10/dratw/dratw_japan_2011.pdf?la=en.

2.3.8 South Korea

South Korea is a Model Law country and a signatory to the NYC. South Korean courts interpret the public policy ground restrictively and narrowly, in light of the need for certainty and stability in international commercial transactions.[52] The Supreme Court has stated that the public policy exception was intended to protect only the most fundamental moral beliefs and social order in the enforcing country.[53] The Supreme Court has ruled that 'recognition or enforcement may be refused on public policy grounds only if the consequences would be against the good moral and social order of the country'. The existence of fraud in the arbitration would be valid grounds to refuse enforcement under Article V(2)(b).[54]

2.4 Conclusion

It is submitted that the approach of Australian courts – in narrowly construing the 'public policy' ground by examining the *lex arbitri* in the context of the NYC and the Model Law, in light of international and regional case law – is in accord with international, as well as Asian, practice. Its emphasis on comparative jurisprudence will cultivate a uniform approach to the interpretation of the Model Law and the concept of 'public policy' in ICA, as well as the development of an 'internationally recognised harmonised procedural jurisprudence',[55] not to mention the comity of nations.

While firm conclusions will require detailed and careful analysis,[56] it is suggested that, at least in Model Law countries in the region, the approach adopted by national courts in the interpretation of the public policy ground demonstrates a largely harmonised approach. Divergence between jurisdictions will predominantly be explained by distinct cultural and linguistic emphases, rather than substantive difference. This augurs well for legal convergence and harmonisation of law and practice in Asia.[57] An emphasis on comparative jurisprudence and the development of a uniform approach to the interpretation of the NYC and the Model Law will facilitate regional trade and commerce by leading to greater certainty and predictability in approach to curial intervention in ICA.

52 South Korea: receptive to foreign arbitration awards? Beomsu Kim and Benjamin Hughes of Shin & Kim, see: www.shinkim.com/upload_files/data/SouthKoreaAsiaCounsel-January2010(5).pdf referring to Korean Supreme Court Dec. No. 89Daka20252, 10 April 1990.

53 Korean Supreme Court Dec. No. 89Daka20252, 10 April 1990 and Korean Supreme Court Dec. No. 93Da53504, 14 February 1995 cited in Beomsu Kim and Benjamin Hughes at n. 44.

54 Korean Supreme Court, 2006Da20290, Decided on 28 May 2009.

55 Rt Hon. Sir Michael Kerr, *Concord and Conflict in International Arbitration,* (1997) 13 *Arbitration International* 122 at 125–6.

56 See for example, *The Interpretation and Uniformity of the Uncitral Model Law on International Commercial Arbitration focussing on Australia, Hong Kong and Singapore*, Dean Lewis, Wolters Kluwer, 2016 where the author provides a detailed analysis of the approach of three Model Law countries to the interpretation of Articles 2A and 34 by way of example.

57 Ibid, Dean Lewis, see n. 56, pp. 4, 12, 21ff.

3 Will the 'haves' come out ahead of the 'have-nots' in international arbitration?

The structural dynamics of justice in Chinese-African commercial arbitration disputes

Janet Ainsworth

The scholarly study of international commercial arbitration practices is of vital importance in understanding globalised law and economies. Currently, disputes in the transnational commercial context are overwhelmingly resolved through arbitration, rather than through litigation (Drahozal 2000). Those disputes frequently involve enormous sums of money, often enough to have significant impact on national economies. As long ago as 1996, the International Chamber of Commerce (ICC) reported that more than 12% of international commercial arbitrations were for awards exceeding 10 million dollars (ICC Bulletin 1997); by 2012, the ICC was reporting that almost 10% of international commercial arbitration cases were worth more than 90 million dollars (Gerbay 2014). In the two-year span from 2009 through 2010, a total of 113 international commercial arbitration awards exceeded one billion dollars (Gluck 2012). By any accounting, international commercial arbitration can have major implications, both for individual participants and for national economies. In addition, since many international commercial disputes involve state-owned enterprises or even states themselves as parties, such disputes often have implications for international relations between countries. Thus, in order to have an accurate understanding of contemporary transnational trade, finance, banking, and securities—not to mention global multilateral international politics—one must, of necessity, take into account the structure and practices of international commercial arbitration.

Unfortunately, scholarship in this area is hampered by a lack of publicly available empirical data. In contrast to litigation, which is largely public and comparatively accessible, international commercial arbitration cases are generally confidential—that is to say, secret—and what happens in these arbitrations is accessible only to the parties themselves and the arbitrators, who agree not to disclose details after the case is concluded. Indeed, this confidentiality is one of the reasons why arbitration has become such a dominant force in the regulation of commercial practice (Gerbay 2012). Parties to a dispute have a strong interest in keeping the existence of the dispute and its resolution out of the public eye. Because even the mere possibility of an expensive judgement can affect the financial viability of a commercial entity, keeping the fact of a potential or actual dispute secret to the greatest degree possible has high economic value. Moreover, the losers in arbitration do not want to advertise the fact that their business practices were found to be unlawful to their other trading partners, for fear that some of them will file similar actions that could result in further judgements against them. Confidentiality can protect business information, such as intellectual property and trade secrets, from becoming publicly available. Moreover, if the case involves allegations of incompetence or bad faith against the other party, keeping those allegations secret allows the disputant to make them in the context of the dispute, without the more severe relational damage that a public accusation would entail. In short, there are sound reasons why confidentiality of arbitral proceedings is highly valued by parties.

However valuable this is to the parties to arbitration, this confidentiality does mean that data from the vast majority of arbitration proceedings are inaccessible to researchers. There is some limited, publicly available arbitral data from arbitrations that are appealed—a tiny percentage of the overall number of arbitrations—and limited reports derived from a small proportion of arbitral cases is available in Mealey's Arbitration Reporter and in the ICC-redacted reports of arbitral awards. It is difficult for scholars to draw conclusions from these sources, however. The reported cases, by definition, are atypical arbitrations—appeals are available only in highly unusual circumstances, and the Mealey's and the ICC reports self-select for particularly noteworthy or novel awards (Ginsburg 2003). Some arbitrators have written scholarly articles about their experiences (see, for example, Brower & Brueschke 1996; Kaufmann-Kohler 2003; Rubenstein 2004), but again, we cannot know how representative their experiences are or on what assumptions they ground their analyses. What we know about arbitrations from all of these sources is therefore only the tip of a vast, submerged iceberg of secret adjudications—and we have no real way of knowing to what extent that visible tip is a fair reflection of what is happening in the unseen and unreported bulk of international commercial arbitrations. Christopher Drahozal, a leading scholar in the field, warns (2003) that the lack of empirical data in this area means that scholars must be modest in the conclusions that can be drawn from such sources.

Notwithstanding the limited data we have, there is general agreement among both practitioners and scholars (Kerr 1997; Van den Berg 1998; Borris 1999; Rubenstein 2004) that, since the 1990s, there has been an increasing convergence in transnational arbitration norms and practices. Gabrielle Kaufmann-Kohler (2003) has described this phenomenon as occurring in a number of key aspects of international commercial arbitration practice—for example, substantive choice of law procedures, evidence presentation conventions, and discovery practices have substantially converged and become regularised, regardless of where a particular arbitration is held. Principles of party autonomy in the conduct of dispute framing and resolution and increasingly rule-bounded proceedings—for example, the 1999 IBA Rules on the Taking of Evidence in International Commercial Arbitration—have furthered procedural convergence. The widening adoption of the United Nations Commission on International Trade Law (UNCITRAL) Model Law and the Arbitration Rules similarly have enhanced both procedural and substantive convergence, and the almost universal national adoption of the New York Convention on the enforcement of arbitral awards in national courts has likewise steered international commercial arbitration practices towards relative uniformity.

On balance, the convergence has been in the direction of making arbitration more like litigation—more specifically, like common law litigation (Dezalay & Garth 1996; Drahozal 2000; Rubenstein 2004). In fact, arbitration centres operating in civil law jurisdictions are often now explicitly adopting common law norms, practices, and procedures in their international commercial dispute resolution fora. Despite Dubai being a civil law jurisdiction, Dubai's International Financial Centre (DIFC), created by the DIFC Arbitration Law of 2008, is constituted as a common-law, English-language arbitration institution dedicated to resolving transnational commercial disputes (Mohtashami & Tannous 2009). Sweden, another civil law jurisdiction, boasts on the website of the Swedish Arbitration Association that its practices are 'in line with current best practices of commercial arbitration', and utilise common-law adversarial procedures, rather than civil law inquisitorial ones, 'with the parties themselves controlling the facts and the evidence to be introduced' (Swedish Arbitration Association website 2016). Far from being the speedy, informal, flexible, and cost-contained procedures envisioned in the ideology of alternative dispute resolution, modern international commercial arbitration looks and feels instead like litigation-light—in its structured formality, its evidence-taking conventions, its rule-boundedness, its discovery practices, and most especially, its facilitation of party autonomy and control over the process (Kaufmann-Kohler 2003).

It has been suggested by some scholars (e.g., Bhatia 2011) that this convergence with litigation practices has been a suborning of the arbitration process, through what is described as 'colonisation' of arbitration by litigation-trained lawyers. Recent scholarship (Kathpalia 2012), based on extensive surveys of various stakeholders in the arbitration process, suggests that international commercial arbitration's current 'litigation-light' character is likely the product of party preferences, rather than lawyer control. International commercial actors value arbitration over litigation, because it gives them quicker access to a resolution procedure, control over the selection of the fact-finding and law-applying actors, and secrecy about the existence of the dispute and of its resolution, not because they want to avoid law or lawyers. Transnational commercial disputes routinely involve millions—even billions—of dollars at stake. With the stakes so high, what parties want is maximum control over the dispute resolution process and maximum predictability concerning its unfolding. Informality and flexibility are precisely the antithesis of this party desire for predictability and control; the greater the procedural regularity, the more parties can plan effectively for what will happen; the greater the informality of the procedures, the harder it is for parties to have an advance sense of control over the process. Procedural cost containment in typical international commercial disputes is likely a minor concern for the parties; when multimillions of dollars are at stake in a judgement, spending a few hundred thousand dollars on discovery or evidence presentation would probably seem a wise investment to the parties. In short, whether normatively this is a good thing or a bad thing, one undeniable aspect of modern international commercial arbitration practices that everyone agrees on is that, factually, it is increasingly common-law litigation-like in its practices.

What this means for scholars is that theories that have been derived from the study of litigation may be a valuable resource in formulating the questions to be asked in studying international commercial arbitral norms and practices. Because the paucity of available data from international commercial disputes makes this academic field information-poor, theoretical constructs are especially useful in helping us ask the right questions to advance scholarly understanding of this important area of study.

One good example of how theory developed from empirical analysis of litigation might shed light on the data-poor world of international commercial arbitration is to consider the question that law and society researcher Marc Galanter asked more than 40 years ago (Galanter 1974)—namely, why is it that, where there are power asymmetries between litigants, the powerful tend to do better in court than the relatively less powerful actors? Or, as he put it, why do the so-called 'haves' tend to prevail in litigation over the 'have-nots'? Many scholars before Galanter had noticed the empirically demonstrable fact that the wealthy and powerful tend to win more than their fair share of lawsuits. Generally, this was explained by academics on the left as a product of hegemony—that judges were either knowingly putting a thumb on the scale for the interests of the ruling classes or that judges were the unwitting patsies of the manipulation of court proceedings by the wealthy and powerful. Either way, the standard explanation before Galanter posited a court system biased by judicial preference for the interests of the powerful.

Galanter did not dismiss out of hand the possibility of such a political bias in the court system; however, he was interested in the persistence over time of the advantages that the wealthy and powerful had in court, even in courts dominated by progressive judges that would be unlikely to be consciously acting as hegemonic tools of the privileged. Galanter argued that it is not necessary to posit a biased hegemonic court system in order to see that the structural architecture of litigation gave powerful actors structural advantages over less powerful actors in the system. As he saw it, powerful actors tended to be 'repeat players' in the litigation system, whereas less powerful actors tended to be 'one-shot players', that is, comparatively much less experienced in the litigation system, perhaps even first-time and only-time participants. Galanter showed how repeat players could use litigation to their advantage and could repel attempts by one-shot players to try to change the rules of engagement.

One of the resources that repeat players have is the ability to take the long view—after all, they know that they are repeat players and will be working in the system frequently in the future. That means that the consequences of any one case matter less to them than it does to the one-shot player—since by definition, this particular case is all there is for the one-shot player. Repeat players also accumulate knowledge about tactics and strategies from their earlier experiences, including knowledge about the practices, preferences, and predispositions of individual judges. One-shot players lack this knowledge base. Repeat players can plan for future cases—they can choose to lose this battle but win the war; or they can resist a settlement in a particular case even when settlement would be objectively reasonable, knowing that they can afford a war of attrition, whereas the one-shot player cannot. Repeat players develop inside knowledge of institutional incumbents and know what kinds of arguments and evidence are most likely to persuade them. They also have the opportunity to develop and deploy reputation to their advantage before those incumbents, whereas one-shot players are unknown to the institutional incumbents and thus have no reputational resources to use to their advantage. Ironically, even procedural due process protections designed to make the system fairer by establishing a level playing field for the parties can actually amplify the advantages of the repeat players over the one-shot players. The greater the procedural protections in a dispute resolution system, the more complex it becomes, and the more the accumulated knowledge and experience bonus of repeat players comes into play.

Further, because repeat players have the ability and incentive to take the long view, they tend to be both more active and more effective than one-shot players in influencing the adoption of favourable rules and practices for their future benefit, and in bending the interpretation of existing rules and procedures to their advantage in the present case. They have a seat at the table when rule changes are made, and they are persuasive advocates for their interests when rules get interpreted in the process of dispute resolution. As a result of all these advantages held by repeat players in litigation, Galanter argued, the structural advantages of powerful actors could explain much of their disproportionate success in court, even without resorting to the ideological explanation of courts being suborned by the ruling classes.

Galanter's theory on why the 'haves' come out ahead in litigation has been hugely influential, both in scholarly impact—as of this writing, it has been cited nearly 4,000 times in the scholarly literature—and in actual strategic attempts to achieve distributional justice on behalf of those lacking the power resources of the wealthy and well-connected. For example, the California Office of Economic Opportunity's legal services for the poor program attempted to create a California Rural Legal Assistance office (CRLA) to develop a nucleus of attorneys to represent the interests of California's migrant farm workers in court battles against agricultural big business (Galanter 1974; Menkel-Meadow 1999). The idea behind the CRLA office was to convert powerless migrant farm workers—one-shot players in their complaints of mistreatment on the job—into a collective set of repeat players, through having lawyers who would, in effect, be repeat players in the system. In vetoing the creation of this office, the governor's office said, 'What we created in the California Rural Legal Assistance Office is an economic leverage equal to that of a large corporation. Clearly that should not be the case'. In other words, the CRLA was an attempt to get repeat player status for what would otherwise have been one-shot players doomed to a high chance of failure in their lawsuits. The conservative governor's office recognised this strategy as a way of undermining the structural advantages of the 'haves,' in this case, agricultural big business, and shut it down. While Galanter's theory of the structural causes of advantage and disadvantage in the legal system does not depend on political manipulation, clearly, parties positioned like agricultural big business can use their political clout to ensure that their non-political structural advantages in the system remain intact.

Does Galanter's theory regarding the structural advantages of repeat players have relevance for non-litigation dispute resolution practices such as arbitration? American domestic arbitration practices appear to display precisely the characteristics that Galanter would predict in the context of consumer disputes with corporations, medical patient disputes with doctors and hospitals, and employee disputes with their employers. In fact, domestic non-commercial arbitration in the United States has been roundly criticised for stripping consumers (Horton & Chandrasekher 2015) and employees (Sternlight 2015) of the right to pursue their statutory and even constitutional rights in court, substituting arbitration, in which the advantages of the repeat player banks, corporations, hospitals, and employers are even greater than they would have in litigation, because in arbitration, they alone select the arbiters, and the results, even if substantively grossly tilted in favour of the repeat player entities, are almost entirely impervious to independent judicial review. The power asymmetries in these domestic arbitrations also include, as Galanter would have predicted, asymmetries of information as well, with the repeat player entities knowledgeable from earlier-occurring arbitrations of the predilections and perspectives of the arbitrators—knowledge that 'one-shot' consumers lack access to. This phenomenon, in effect, makes the basis of legal decision making the private property of repeat players alone (Gilles 2016).

The world of mandatory arbitration of consumer disputes is, of course, worlds apart from the kind of arbitration occurring in the international commercial realm. The gross power disparities between domestic consumers and major corporations, coupled with the ability of corporations to unilaterally dictate the terms of dispute resolution, appear quite unlike the world of international commercial transactions. No actor in that context is comparable in legal powerlessness to the lack of bargaining power of a consumer in the American domestic context. At first glance, then, one might be tempted to say that, even if Galanter's thesis has explanatory power in looking at mandatory consumer arbitration cases, it is unlikely to have relevance to international commercial arbitration as it exists today, since, arguably, there are no true powerless one-shot players in the modern world of global commercial transactions.

While it is certainly true that there is no equivalent of the migrant farm workers that the CRLA sought to convert from one-shot players into repeat players, that is not to say that all participants in today's world of international commercial arbitration have equal structural advantages of the kind described by Galanter in looking at repeat players in litigation. Not every participant in global commerce has equivalent experience and reputational capital to leverage in the international commercial arbitration system when disputes occur, and not every participant has the ability to capture rule interpretation and practice norms in international arbitration and bend them in their interests.

To explore this more fully, consider the example of international commercial arbitration between African commercial entities in conflict with Chinese enterprises. In the past few decades, there has been an explosion of financial dealings between China (and Chinese enterprises) and African states (and African enterprises). China has become by far the largest trade partner in Africa, with more than 160 billion US dollars in trade annually (Kuo 2016). China imports massive quantities of African raw materials, including oil, gas, and strategically important minerals, and in turn exports its manufactured goods to Africa. Besides trade, China is a major source of investment capital and financial assistance in infrastructural projects in Africa (Foster et al. 2009). These burgeoning economic ties and their implications have not gone unrecognised by commentators and scholars (see, e.g., Raine 2006; Brautigan 2009; Dollar 2016). While some of these observers see the relationship as exploitative and even neocolonial, and others instead see positive potential synergies in Chinese involvement in developing African economies, it is agreed that, regardless of whether this is a welcome or troubling development, the financial magnitude of these relations is enormous and unprecedented.

Given the magnitude of these trade and finance ties, it is unsurprising that disputes have inevitably arisen and, given the prevalence of arbitration to resolve such globalised disputes, that these disputes have generated considerable international commercial arbitration. That fact, too, has not gone unnoticed by scholars. Scholar and arbitrator Won Kidane (2011) has described what he sees as the trends in dispute resolution between Chinese and African entities from an African perspective, and he endorses the use of arbitration as a dispute resolution vehicle for these cases. Chinese legal scholar Zhu Weidong (2013) has also analyzed commercial dispute resolution in the China-Africa context, strongly advocating for arbitration as what he terms 'the best option' for settling their trade and investment disputes.

Keeping in mind the paucity of hard data on these Chinese-African trade disputes—and China-Africa arbitrations appear to be under-represented among the available reported arbitral awards—one can speculate that, if Galanter's thesis holds true in the international commercial arbitration arena, we would expect to see repeat-player structural advantages for China and Chinese enterprises in such disputes. In many cases, the Chinese parties are either state-owned enterprises or privatised entities with significant state interpenetration. In contrast, the African parties are typically either African states or African commercial entities with little previous participation in international commercial arbitration until quite recently. This is not to say that arbitration centres have been absent from Africa; there are such centres in Rwanda (the Kigali International Arbitration Centre), Nigeria (the Lagos Court of Arbitration), Egypt (Cairo Regional Centre for International Commercial Arbitration), and the Ivory Coast (Abidjan's Cour Commune de Justice et d'Arbitrage), among others. But it is one thing to create an arbitral forum and another thing entirely for it to be chosen by litigants to resolve their disputes, and there is no evidence that China and Chinese entities have made significant use of those African arbitral fora to settle trade disputes with African partners.

Indeed, there has been robust international competition among arbitral fora to be selected as the site for arbitration, with intense public relations campaigns waged by these centres to promote themselves as the most favourable and efficient places in which to resolve transnational disputes (Drahozal 2000, 2004, 2008). In the end, this arms race by arbitration centres to market themselves to potential disputants predictably appears to have been won mainly by the larger, more established centres, rather than by the newly established regional centres attempting to get a toehold in the dispute-resolution business. Again, Galanter's thesis would predict that repeat players would have a preference for the predictability inherent in using fora and participants familiar to them from earlier cases. Dislodging long-standing arbitration centres from their preferential position in the international dispute resolution hierarchy would hardly be in the interest of repeat players, since selecting a new and untried forum would forfeit their investment in reputational capital, as well as losing the predictability of dealing with familiar arbitrators and familiar processes for arbitrating. This is exactly what Christopher Drahozal (2004) found in his study of regulatory competition among arbitration centres—established centres saw a jump in the number of arbitrations attracted as competition for arbitration business became more overt, but new entrants found it difficult to attract new commercial business. This would suggest that China, as an early entrant to transnational commercial arbitration, would have an insurmountable edge over newer African arbitration centres, even if the Chinese government and Chinese commercial entities were otherwise neutral in their preference for a forum and had no 'home field' preference for China, per se. Repeat players prefer sites where they have played before, as Galanter would predict.

It has been argued (see, e.g., Rau 1998; Posner 2005) that the process of arbitration itself will mitigate the power of powerful players, at least where the parties each have some control over the selection of the arbitrator. Arbitrators who want to get repeat arbitration business, the argument goes, cannot afford to disappoint either party completely. Therefore, arbitrators looking out for their own self-interests will be tempted to compromise, to 'split the baby,' so that each party will walk away from the proceeding with a willingness to hire the arbitrator for future cases. If the 'baby-splitting' hypothesis were accurate, then arbitrators would ensure that both parties to a dispute would win at least some concessions. However, empirical studies of international commercial arbitrations (Keer & Naimark 2001; Drahozal 2008; Greenbaum 2015) have failed to bear out the 'baby-splitting' hypothesis. Instead, what researchers have found is a bimodal distribution, with most awards clustered around two poles—either what the disputant was originally seeking or nothing. This means that, contrary to the optimistic assumptions of the 'baby-splitting' hypothesis, a disputant in an international commercial arbitration is likely to face a winner-take-all result. Since arbitrators are not systematically 'baby-splitting,' the advantages accruing to repeat players are not, in fact, mitigated by alleged arbitrator self-interest.

In the context of Chinese-African commercial disputes, China is in the repeat-player disputant role, with many different African states and entities as the other disputants. That alone, as Galanter posits, would be a structural advantage for all of the reasons discussed earlier in this chapter. But that inherent structural advantage would be amplified if almost all Chinese-African trade disputes were to be heard in the same forum. As it happens, this possibility is increasingly likely. In August of 2015, 50 African nations and China entered into the Johannesburg Consensus, an agreement to develop the China-Africa Joint Arbitration Centre (CAJAC), with dispute resolution centers in Johannesburg and in Shanghai. Later that year, at the 6th Ministerial Conference of the Forum on China-Africa Cooperation, the Johannesburg Action Plan 2016–2018 was signed by the 50 attending African states and China. The Action Plan was designed as a comprehensive framework for strengthening economic and trade ties between China and African nations. Not surprisingly, it included provisions promoting the CAJAC and requiring that future trade and investment agreements between Chinese and African partners mandate that disputes be arbitrated at the CAJAC.

Although, in theory, both the Johannesburg and Shanghai CAJAC centres are of equal status, the CAJAC website itself hints that the Shanghai site is intended to be the primary arbitration centre. For example, the CAJAC website provides what it calls 'model arbitration clauses' to include in future bilateral contracts between African and Chinese participants. Two options for the site of potential arbitration are included in these 'model clauses'. The first option reads, 'Any dispute arising from or in connection with this Contract shall be submitted for binding arbitration to the Shanghai International Economic and Trade Arbitration Commission. The arbitration shall be held in the China-Africa Joint Arbitration Centre in China'. The second option reads, 'Any dispute arising from or in connection with this Contract shall be submitted to the China-Africa Joint Arbitration Centre in Johannesburg or the China-Africa Joint Arbitration Centre in Shanghai for final and binding arbitration. Please choose only one of the above institutions by ticking in front of the institution's name'. In other words, the recommended choice of forum language either uses Shanghai's CAJAC by default or gives the parties a choice between Shanghai and Johannesburg. No Johannesburg forum default choice parallel to the Shanghai forum default version is given.

Since the CAJAC system has not been in existence for long, we do not have even significant anecdotal evidence about which of the two CAJAC centres parties are choosing in their post-Johannesburg Consensus contracts. Galanter would, of course, predict that China, the repeat player, would prefer that its repeat player advantages be maximised by having the lion's share of disputes adjudicated in the Shanghai CAJAC centre. He would also suggest, however, that it probably doesn't matter whether the Shanghai centre ends up monopolising the arbitration proceedings between Chinese and African entities. A duopoly—Johannesburg and Shanghai—would provide almost as much structural repeat-player advantage as a Shanghai centre monopoly would, since China would be a repeat player in every African dispute, regardless of the centre where the proceedings were held, while the African entities, absent substantial cartelisation, would lack those structural advantages in the Johannesburg centre, as well as in Shanghai.

If Galanter's thesis that repeat players have structural advantages holds as true in international commercial arbitration, as it seems to in other dispute resolution contexts, it suggests that there may be strategic moves that less powerful disputants could adopt to mitigate the advantage that repeat players have. Some scholars (e.g., Delazay & Garth 1998) have worried that international commercial arbitration is rigged in favour of economically powerful actors, so that the interests of economically dominant countries will prevail over the interests of less developed countries engaged in globalised trade. If they are correct that obtaining favourable results in international commercial litigation turns out to be a matter of power and power alone, then nothing short of African states and commercial entities gaining sufficient economic power to compete with Chinese entities will help level the playing field for African disputants. This is unlikely to occur, at least for many years. On the other hand, if there are structural reasons that explain, in part, why dominant economic actors might have disproportionate success, those structural advantages can be mitigated through strategies such as using law firms that represent a large number of African interests collectively—a sort of legal cartelisation—or by African entities hiring advisers with longtime experience in international commercial arbitration. In short, the advantages of the Chinese repeat player might be mitigated if African entities made themselves more like repeat players than like one-shot players. This strategic move could have implications not just for making Chinese-African disputes fairer but also for trade disputes more generally between the powerful global North and the less powerful global South.

Despite all the characteristics of international commercial arbitration proceedings that are congruent with litigation practices, it must always be remembered that arbitration is not litigation. Scholars need to be alert for the differences, as well as the similarities, as international commercial arbitration continues to develop its convergent practices with litigation practices. However, given the paucity of data from which to draw out explanatory models in international commercial arbitration, theory derived from the more abundantly data-rich litigation world can help scholars test hypotheses and highlight areas of practice where we might look to see the workings of international commercial arbitration within the broader global economic regulatory framework.

References

Bhatia, V.K. (2011). Interdiscursive colonization of international commercial arbitration. *World Englishes* 30, 76–80.

Borris, C. (1999). The reconciliation of conflicts between common law and civil law principles in the arbitration process. In S.N. Frommel and B.A.K. Rider (eds.) *Conflicting Legal Cultures in Commercial Arbitration: Old Issues and New Trends.* Leiden, The Netherlands: Kluwer Law International, 1–18.

Brautigan, D. (2009). *The Dragon's Gift: The Real Story of China in Africa.* New York: Oxford University Press.

Brower, C.N. and J.D. Brueschke. (1996). *The Iran-United States Claims Tribunal.* New York: Springer.

China-Africa Joint Arbitration Centre website, www.shiac.org/CAJAC; last visited 12/26/2016.

Delazay, Y. and B. Garth. (1998). *Dealing in Virtue: International Commercial Arbitration and the Construction of a Transnational Legal Order.* Chicago, IL: University of Chicago Press.

Dollar, D. (2016). *China's Engagement with Africa.* Washington, DC: Brookings Institute.

Drahozal, C.R. (2000). Commercial norms, commercial codes, and international commercial arbitration. *Vanderbilt Journal of Transnational Law* 33, 79–145.

Drahozal, C.R. (2003). Of rabbits and rhinoceri: A survey of empirical research on international commercial arbitration. *Journal of International Arbitration* 20, 23–34.

Drahozal, C.R. (2004). Regulatory competition and the location of international arbitration proceedings. *International Review of Law and Economics* 24, 371–384.

Drahozal, C.R. (2008). Busting arbitration myths. *University of Kansas Law Review* 56, 633–677.

Foster, V., W. Butterfield, C. Chen, and N. Pushak. (2009). *Building Bridges: China's Growing Role as Infrastructure Financier for Sub-Saharan Africa.* Washington, DC: World Bank.

Galanter, M. (1974). Why the 'haves' come out ahead: Speculations on the limits of legal change. *Law and Society Review* 9, 95–160.

Gerbay, R. (2012). Confidentiality vs. transparency in international arbitration: The English perspective. *Transnational Dispute Management* 9, 1–14.

Gerbay, R. (2014). Is the end nigh, again?: An empirical assessment of the 'judicialiation' of international arbitration. *American Review of International Arbitration* 25, 23–247.

Gilles, M. (2016). The day doctrine died: Private arbitration and the end of law. *University of Illinois Law Review* 2016, 101–154.

Ginsburg, T. (2003) The culture of arbitration. *Vanderbilt Journal of Transnational Law* 36, 1325–1345.

Gluck, G. (2012). Great expectations: Meeting the challenge of a new arbitration paradigm. *American Review of International Arbitration* 23, 231–243.

Greenbaum, C. (2015). Putting the baby to rest: Dispelling a common arbitration myth. *American Review of International Arbitration* 26, 101–199.

Horton, D. and A.C. Chandrasekher (2015). After the revolution: An empirical study of consumer arbitration. *Georgetown Law Journal* 104, 57–124.

ICC International Court of Arbitration Bulletin, May 1997.

Kaufmann-Kohler, G. (2003). Globalization of arbitral procedure. *Vanderbilt Journal of Transnational Law* 36, 1313–1324.

Kathpalia, S. (2012). Is arbitration being colonized by litigation? Practitioners' views in the Singapore context. In V.J. Bhatia, C. Candlin, and M. Gotti (eds.) *Discourse and Practice in International Commercial Arbitration*. Farnham: Ashgate Publishing, 263–281.

Keer, S.E. and R.W. Naimark. (2001). Arbitrators do not 'split the baby': Empirical evidence from international business arbitrations. *Journal of International Business Arbitrations* 18, 573–578.

Kerr, M. (1997). Concord and conflict in international arbitration. *Arbitration International* 13, 121–129.

Kidane, W. (2011). *China-Africa Dispute Settlement: The Law, Culture, and Economics of Arbitration*. Leiden, The Netherlands: Kluwer Law International.

Kuo, F. (2016). What China knows about Africa that the West doesn't. *The National Interest*, May 22, 2016.

Menkel-Meadow, C. (1999). Do the 'haves' come out ahead in alternative judicial systems?: Repeat players in ADR. *Ohio State Journal on Dispute Resolution* 15, 1–60.

Mohtashami, R. and S. Tannous. (2009). Arbitration at the Dubai International Financial Center: A common law jurisdiction in the Middle East. *Arbitration International* 25, 173–186.

Posner, R.A. (2005). Judicial behavior and performance: An economic approach. *Florida State University Law Review* 1259–1278.

Raine, S. (2006). *China's African Challenges*. London: Routledge.

Rubenstein, J. (2004). International commercial arbitration: Reflections at the crossroads of the common law and civil law traditions perspective. *Chicago Journal of International Law* 5, 303–310.

Rau, A.S. (1998). On integrity in private judging. *Arbitration International* 14, 115–156.

Sternlight, J.R. (2015). Disarming employees: How American employers are using mandatory arbitration to deprive workers of legal protection. *Brooklyn Law Review* 80, 1309–1356.

Swedish Arbitration Association website, www.swedisharbitration.se; last visited 12/29/2016.

Van den Berg, A.J. (1998). *International Dispute Resolution: Towards an International Arbitration Culture*. Leiden, The Netherlands: Kluwer Law International.

Zhu, W.D. (2013). Arbitration as the best option for the settlement of China-Africa trade and investment disputes. *Journal of African Law* 57, 149–163.

Part II

Discursive practices in arbitration

4 The combination of arbitration with conciliation/mediation in the legislation of the People's Republic of China

Maurizio Gotti, Piera Pellegrinelli and Elena Signorini[1]

4.1 Introduction

Alternative dispute resolution (ADR) is divided into two main forms: arbitration, on the one hand, and conciliation/mediation, on the other hand. While in arbitration, the procedure results in an arbitration award, which is as binding as the decision of a judge of first instance, in conciliation/mediation, agreement is reached by the parties through the work of a neutral party, who helps them analyse the true interests involved in the dispute and leads them towards a resolution of the dispute, without imposing any decision (Berger, 2006). In theory, mediation and conciliation should have their own fields of application, deriving from the specific characteristics of these two instruments, the techniques and the tactics they employ, and the professional preparation of the experts working in each field. In practice, the terms 'mediation' and 'conciliation' are often used as synonyms for the same concept, that is, an informal cooperation towards the solution of a controversy, thanks to the neutral participation of a third party.

In Western legal culture, the dispute resolution field is clearly divided into three well-distinguished areas: litigation, arbitration, and conciliation/mediation, with no possibilities of mixture between these procedures. As Phillips (2005, p. 24) clearly states, 'Some arbitrators and mediators believe that mixing mediation and arbitration is heretical and even unethical'. The complexity and the risks implicit in mixing these ADR procedures derive from the different codes of behaviour that conciliators/mediators and arbitrators follow:

> The Mediator Standards allow private communication between mediator and the parties, relying on self-determination and confidentiality to ensure the parties' right to make important decisions without influence. The Arbitrator Code, by contrast, protects arbitrators from confidential information by allowing only plenary exchanges. These opposing principles cannot both be observed in med-arb.
>
> (Fullerton, 2010, p. 56)

Although the combination of arbitration with conciliation/mediation also has some advantages – one of them being that it eliminates the need to start over with a new arbitrator who is wholly unfamiliar with the dispute (Fullerton, 2010) – what particularly concerns Western legal experts about the combination of arbitration with conciliation/mediation is the

1 Although the authors have collaborated at every stage in the production of this chapter, Sections 1 and 2 were written by Maurizio Gotti, Section 3 was written by Piera Pellegrinelli and Section 4 by Elena Signorini. Section 5 was jointly written by the three authors.

problem raised if the conciliation/mediation should fail, and the fact that conciliators/mediators should return to acting as arbitrators. Probably the information divulged by the parties in the conciliation/mediation process would have never been revealed in an arbitration proceeding. Indeed, how could the arbitrators realistically ignore the confidential information that they acquired when they were acting as conciliators/mediators? This is the reason why the 'AAA [American Arbitration Association] does not promote hybrid proceedings involving the same neutral, but it nevertheless will consider a request from sophisticated commercial parties for an "arb-med" (i.e., the arbitrator serves as the mediator) or "med-arb" (the mediator switches to acting as arbitrator) process, provided there is disclosure of the ethical issues to the parties and an appropriate waiver is signed by the parties. ... The LCIA [The London Court of International Arbitration], the ICC [International Chamber of Commerce], and the World Intellectual Property Organization, a recognised agency of the United Nations, all have a model clause along similar lines' (Connerty, 2012, p. 78).

This mixed form of dispute settlement has traditionally encountered strong opposition in several Western countries, although over the last decades there has been a change in this attitude:

> Traditionally, it was an agreed doctrine within the world of arbitration that an arbitrator's duty shall not be mixed with any mediating activity or intent to reconcile. This was one of the greatest dangers widely highlighted in arbitration seminars as it was stated outright that an arbitrator who initiated conciliation or mediation was exposed to the risk of an eventual challenge. Again, the participation in international commercial arbitration of jurists with such different origins has, in practice, caused such inflexible positions to be questioned. In fact, even in continental Europe, procedural law in countries of Germanic origin included an obligation for the judge to facilitate conciliation between the parties throughout the proceedings.
>
> (Cremades, 1998, p. 162)

In the Asian context, conciliation often combines and interferes with the other two legal procedures, i.e., litigation and arbitration. This depends on the fact that conciliation has a long tradition there, and for centuries, it has been considered the best way to solve disputes. Indeed, the Western world is traditionally characterised, to varying degrees, by the litigation culture, while in Eastern countries, the emphasis is on conciliation. The latter attitude is deeply embedded in Eastern traditions, mainly aiming at promoting amicable settlement of disputes and to suppress litigation. Although radical political and economic changes taking place in the last century have certainly affected this type of culture, it still persists in many noticeable forms. Here is Taniguchi's comment on the Chinese situation:

> In China, where this type of culture originated, a strong emphasis on conciliation was maintained even under the Maoist communist regime as the means to solve a so-called 'contradiction within the people'. The judge's primary obligation was said to be not to decide cases but to 'educate' the parties so that they would be willing to terminate their dispute. This is a good example of how a strong culture can survive even a very radical political, economic and social change.
>
> (Taniguchi, 1998, p. 32)

This explains why one of the main features of the Chinese legal system is the integration between conciliation and arbitration. This concept of hybrid dispute processing is also present in the Japanese legal culture (Sato, 2008). The double possibility combined in the same procedure has been criticised, particularly by scholars mainly living in Western countries. Others, instead, who have a deeper knowledge of Eastern arbitral practices, are less critical. Here is Moser and Yuen's opinion:

> Many have argued that it is not appropriate for a single person or a tribunal to wear the hats of both conciliator and arbitrator, the point here being that an arbitrator who fails to settle a dispute by conciliation and resumes the arbitration will run the grave risk of infringing the principles of natural justice. However, many have also argued the contrary: provided that certain safeguards are put in place during the conciliation process, the two procedures can work side-by-side.
>
> (Moser and Yuen, 2005, p. 401)

It is the aim of this chapter to investigate the texts of both the PRC Arbitration Law[2] and the Law on Mediation and Arbitration of Labour Disputes[3] in order to examine, in particular, the norms concerning the combination of conciliation/mediation and arbitration in Chinese legislation. This combination has been focused on, as it clearly shows how typical traits of the Chinese legal tradition and social culture have greatly influenced the characteristics of the arbitration process in this country. Although the original texts were written in Standard Chinese (also known as Mandarin and Putonghua), here we will examine their English version.

4.2 Cultural aspects

As said before, the integration between conciliation/mediation and arbitration is due to the fact that the tradition of using conciliation to settle disputes in Asia dates back to the ancient past. Conciliation is preferred in settling disputes whenever possible, but it is neither a necessary nor compulsory step in the arbitration proceeding. If conciliation is successful, a settlement agreement will be reached, and the case will be closed by the disputing parties. If, instead, a settlement agreement cannot be reached after a reasonable period of time, the proceeding will continue according to the arbitration procedure.

In the past, a good judge was not supposed to give a judgement but to try to bring about a good conciliation. Indeed, for the Chinese, litigation is seen as a harmful way of dispute resolution, as it may result in a loss of face and friendship. Although China established a judicial system very early in its history, the Chinese emphasis on morality encouraged individuals or groups in conflict to resolve their differences by means of discussion or compromise, rather than adjudication (Jemielniak, 2015). Even the radical political and economic changes taking place in China in the past eighty years have not completely affected this culture, and a strong emphasis on conciliation has been maintained. The judge's primary obligation is said to be not to decide cases but to educate the parties, so as to induce them to terminate their dispute (Liao, 2012).

The traditional Chinese preference for mediation and conciliation over formal methods of dispute resolution has its origins in Confucian philosophy, which views social conflicts as a shameful aberration of morality and as a form of disruption of the natural order of social

2 Available at www.wipo.int/wipolex/en/text.jsp?file_id=182634.

3 Available at www.lawinfochina.com/display.aspx?id=6584&lib=law.

life. Instead, conciliation and compromise are considered virtues to be used in conflict resolution. This cultural and legal dichotomy actually reflects a conceptual dichotomy of *li* (礼) and *fa* (法), which has traditionally characterised the spirit of traditional Chinese law (Ch'ü, 1980). *Li* is a key Confucian term, with a wide range of meanings. In its broad sense, *li* refers to the rules of behaviour that regulate human needs and conduct in social and political institutions (Cao, 2004). It thus refers to ethics and moral rules pertaining to correct conduct and good manners, in line with the teaching of Confucius, according to which broad moral principles are rooted in innate human feelings about what people would, in general, instinctively feel to be right. *Fa* is a very important word in the Chinese legal vocabulary, as it indicates positive or written law, deriving its meaning from the notion of a model or standard imposed by superior authority, to which people must conform (Liao, 2010). In case of a conflict between *li* and *fa*, traditional Chinese society has commonly preferred *li*, as the use of persuasion and the appeal to reason and common sense was considered the exemplification of good conduct and behaviour (Lee and Lai, 1978).

Although this cultural dichotomy has sometimes aroused an open conflict between the two schools – Confucianism and Legalism – the purpose of both schools has always been the maintenance of social order. The difference between them lay mainly in what constituted an ideal social order and by what means such an order could be attained (Ch'ü, 1980). The Confucian school mainly emphasised teaching and moral guidance, rather than penal law, as instruments for the government of the people, as only through teaching could a proper sense of virtuous conduct be inculcated in the people. Although necessary, penal laws should principally be used to supplement and reinforce the lessons to be obtained from the teachings and guidance furnished by the ruler and his officials. The Confucian school believed that a government based on law creates contention, because its people, knowing in advance what the written law is, can find means to circumvent it and will rest their sophisticated arguments on the letter, rather than the spirit, of the law (Liao, 2010). Moreover, in case of conflict, the Confucian school recommended finding a compromise between the parties, rather than recourse to punishments or litigation, as this was considered the most appropriate way to attain the country's social aims. This was in line with the Confucian belief in the cosmic or immanent order of the world; a disturbance of the social order meant a violation of the total cosmic order, because the sphere of man and nature is inextricably interwoven to form an unbroken continuum (McKnight, 1992).

Another cultural element that has to be taken into consideration when dealing with business relations and disputes in China is the concept of 'face' (Goffman, 1955) – that is, 'the public self-image that every member of a society wants to claim for himself/herself' (Brown and Levinson, 1978, p. 66). According to Goffman, facework can either be positive or negative: positive facework refers to the need a person feels for appreciation and approval, inclusion, and respect, which is expressed in interactions by means of such speech acts as compliments and promises. Negative facework reflects, instead, the degree to which a person protects his/her own freedom and privacy from interference. People are very careful in identifying and meeting the different face needs of their interlocutors and adopt appropriate strategies to address them to their advantage. As Brown and Levinson (1978) have shown, linguistic expressions may be more or less face-threatening. Face is an important issue in the field of arbitration, as the use of language has relevant consequences for the outcome of a business transaction or a dispute-resolution process; indeed, when the parties' faces are threatened, there is a greater tendency not to cooperate or to withhold important information.

The terms *mian*[4] (面) and *lian* (臉) are commonly used in Chinese business communication to refer to the figurative use of English 'face'. Chinese *mian* and *lian*, as salient sociological constructs of Chinese society, are inextricably linked to almost all business transactions involving Chinese people (Lee-Wong, 2000). Indeed, the importance of *mian* and *lian* to Chinese business discourse is well established (Chu, 1996; Irwin, 1996; Blackman, 1997; Backman, 1999). In her seminal paper, Hu (1944, p. 45) distinguishes the meanings of the two words for 'face' as follows: *mian* pertains to the reputation achieved 'through getting on in life, through success and ostentation'. This is the type of face that is non-moral. In contrast, *lian* is the 'respect of the group for a man with a good moral reputation'. Moreover, *lian* is often used in situations predominantly concerning successful social performance. Indeed, the loss of *mian* and *lian*, although clearly separable, can be seen as constituting a certain progression in terms of seriousness of the particular event that has damaged one's face: the loss of *mian* would generally represent damage to social image that is less serious, and the loss of *lian* would be perceived as damage to social image that is more serious (Hinze, 2005). Ho (1974, pp. 242–243) provides the following example:

> [A] professor who reveals his ignorance in a subject in which he professes expert knowledge 'loses *mianzi*', but if in addition to being ignorant he is caught plagiarising, then he loses not only his *mianzi* in his role as a professor, but also his *lian* as a respectable person.

The importance of the two concepts of *mian* and *lian* in contemporary Chinese society is great, as clearly highlighted by Hinze (2005, p. 186):

> Given the fact that, in Chinese society, a person's identity is inextricably linked to those with whom he or she is closely associated, the importance of *mian* and *lian* in Chinese social relationships cannot be overstated. One can quite easily imagine that, in a society where concepts like *lian* and *mian* are collective properties that are experienced vicariously, such concepts would inevitably feature prominently in the daily flow of social relationships.

This explains why *mian* and *lian* lie at the core of business transactions in China. Indeed, face is a crucial factor in business there (Gu, 1990; Yeung, 1997). In Chinese social life and in the business context, human relationships play a pivotal role: 'There are no separate rules that divide the conduct of business from that of personal affairs, in which the key factor is proper human relations. And of course, proper human relations in Chinese terms means personal relations primarily based on Confucianism' (De Mente, 1996, p. 196). For a Chinese businessman to maintain face is very important, because a loss of *mian* would result in a loss of authoritativeness, while a loss of *lian* would result in a loss of trust and credibility within the business community. Moreover, business relations should also tend towards the achievement of harmony and avoidance of conflict, in line with the Confucian teachings and tradition. Every effort to find a possible solution to a dispute is thus seen as the preferred way to avoid the loss of face of the parties involved in the dispute.

4 In modern Chinese, out of preference for disyllable words, *mianzi* is often used instead of *mian*. The orthographic representation of the word *mianzi* is composed of two characters, *mian* and *zi*. *Mian* is the part from which the word derives its meaning. *Zi* is a polysemous morpheme. Its most common meaning is 'son', but when compounded with *mian* (as *mianzi*), it is a nominalising suffix (Hinze, 2005).

4.3 Mediation in the legislation of the People's Republic of China

China has had a long and successful use of mediation to resolve disputes (McLaughlin, 2010). As seen above, the importance of mediation in China stems from Confucian thought: according to Confucius, the natural hierarchy of things, the set of moral rules to ensure man to live in harmony with the cosmos (*li*) is placed on a higher plane than the written law (*fa*). This view is held in all types of relationships, including economic ones. This explains the importance of mediation in the Chinese system as an alternative method of resolution of disputes (Cohen, 1966; Harpole, 2007; Liebman, 2007). In China, there are three different types of mediation: the mediation run by a private body, mediation in a lawsuit, and mediation in arbitration.

4.3.1 Mediation run by a private body

In China, there are several private institutions that assist the parties in a commercial dispute, in exchange for compensation for administrative expenses. In 1987, the China Council for the Promotion of International Trade (COOIC) created the Conciliation Center in Beijing (CCPIT), which has given rise to other forty mediation centres that work under the general supervision of the CCPIT/CCOIC. According to available statistics, by the end of 2003, this network of mediation centres had handled more than 4,000 domestic and international cases, with a success rate of over 80% (Wenying, 2005). Mediation run by this network of centres follows a set of common rules that govern the organisation of the mediation process (for example, the acceptance of cases, the arbitrator's choice, the place of mediation). The CCPIT/CCOIC centres have a panel of mediators, and before 2005, the parties were obliged to choose among them. Since 2005, however, the parties have been free to choose one or more mediators not included in the panel. The CCPIT/CCOIC centres also have a code of conduct for mediators (in force since 2005). Under this code, the mediator must be independent and impartial, and if the mediator fails to resolve the dispute, he or she cannot serve as an arbitrator in any arbitration following the same dispute, unless it is agreed by the parties.

Extrajudicial conciliation is generally entrusted to the people's committees of conciliation, established by the committees of urban residents and by the village committees, as organisations with popular participation deal with population control and the management of services for residents. In addition to these committees, there are a great number of figures of conciliators and mediators who work in a more or less official capacity (Thireau and Hansheng, 2001). The relevant legislation is the People's Mediation Law, which came into force on 1 January 2011. The aim of the law is 'to improve the people's mediation system, regulate the people's mediation activities, timely solve disputes among the people and maintain social harmony and stability'. The term 'people's mediation' refers to a process, by means of which a people's mediation commission persuades the parties involved in a dispute to reach a mediation agreement on the basis of equal negotiation and free will.

People's mediation commissions observe the following principles: mediate on the basis of free will and equality of the parties concerned; abide by laws, regulations, and policies of the state; respect the rights of the parties concerned; and refrain from stopping the parties concerned from protecting their rights, through arbitration, administrative means, or judicial means, in the name of mediation. People's mediation commissions may not charge fees for the mediation of disputes among people. The state encourages and supports the people's mediation work. The local people's governments at or above the county level guarantee the funds needed for the people's mediation work, and commend and reward people's mediation commissions and people's mediators that make outstanding contributions according to the relevant state provisions.

The parties involved in a dispute may apply to a people's mediation commission for mediation, and a people's mediation commission may also voluntarily offer to mediate. However, no mediation may be made if one party has expressly refused to settle the dispute by mediation. Typically, the solution found by the mediators is better accepted by the parties with respect to judicial decisions: the greater speed and effectiveness of mediation make it a valuable support for the work of judges (Wall, 1991; Wei, 2005). This implies, as a result, a decrease in legal action and in associated costs.

4.3.2 Mediation within the civil trial

The practice of combining trial and mediation in China's judicial system is widely used. The courts frequently emphasise the use of mediation, and the Code of Civil Procedure (2012) contains provisions that provide for the use of mediation. The people's courts may mediate the disputes according to the principles of voluntariness and lawfulness; if a mediation agreement cannot be reached, the courts will render judgements without delay (Article 9). In this case, it is usually the judge himself who acts as a mediator. This solution deserves to be criticised, because it compromises the integrity and effectiveness of the procedure, given the authority of the judge-mediator to make the final decision if the mediation is unsuccessful.

Chinese judicial mediation is different from that practised in the Western world: Chinese courts regularly use mediation, and, in case of failure, an ordinary trial almost always follows, most likely solved by the same judge who has previously led the mediation proceeding. In Western countries, by contrast, mediation is separate and distinct from ordinary judgements and arbitration, and the mediator, besides not being the same person who handled the mediation attempt, acts with rules that are different from those typical of a civil trial. The difference stems from the starting point, which appears to be diametrically opposed: Chinese judges depart from the situation and decide whether to proceed with mediation, arbitration, or an ordinary trial (starting from the specific case); Western legal systems generally identify the general and abstract rule to be applied to the concrete case (Huang, 2006).

The Chinese Code of Civil Procedure expressly recognises the right of the parties to use mediation (Article 49): the parties must exercise their litigation rights according to the law, observe litigation procedures, and carry out legally effective written judgements or orders and mediation statements. Chapter VIII is entirely devoted to mediation (Article 93–99). In handling civil cases, the people's court may distinguish between right and wrong and mediate disputes according to the principle of parties' voluntariness and based on clear facts (Article 93). When a people's court conducts mediation, a single judge or a collegial bench may preside in the mediation. Mediations are conducted locally whenever possible. When a people's court conducts mediation, it may employ simplified methods to notify the parties and witnesses to appear in court. Article 94 eliminates unnecessary formalities in the mediation process that could hinder the success of mediation: this choice deserves to be welcomed. Mediation is based on a free choice by the parties, without being liable for any coercion, as 'a mediation agreement must be based on voluntariness of both parties, and shall not be reached through compulsion' (Article 96). The content of the mediation agreement may not contravene the law. When a mediation agreement is reached, the people's court draws up a written mediation agreement. Once the mediation agreement is signed and exchanged by both parties, it becomes legally binding (Article 97). When the parties concerned reach a mediation agreement by themselves during the process of litigation, the people's court may, according to the application of the parties concerned, confirm the mediation agreement in accordance with the law and work out a mediation document.

Mediation enjoys considerable success in China, in light of the international trend to use ADR to resolve disputes and because it is a useful tool that allows judges to avoid mistakes. The success of mediation no longer requires the delivery of a judgement, which, if affected by errors of fact or law, exposes the judge to possible sanctions, which could jeopardise the benefits accrued, career advancements, salary, and honorary titles (Diamant, 2000; Benjamin, 2008).

4.3.3 Mediation in arbitral proceedings

Mediation can be adopted in an arbitration process. Arbitration, in fact, is not an obstacle to the possibility for the parties to conciliate. Article 49 of the Arbitration Law of the People's Republic of China, promulgated on 31 October 1994, states that 'after the parties have applied for arbitration, they may reach reconciliation on their own initiative. Whereas a reconciliation agreement has been reached, a request may be made to the arbitration tribunal for an award based on the reconciliation agreement or the application for arbitration may be withdrawn'. The rule of law identifies the subjects to whom the power to find a conciliatory solution is delegated; more precisely, the arbitral tribunal is required to act only when an agreement is reached, by adopting a decision that will incorporate the terms of the agreement identified by the parties. In this case, unlike what commonly happens in arbitration proceedings, the role of the arbitral tribunal is 'passive'. It is worth appreciating the lack of interference between the arbitral tribunal – which manages the arbitration procedure – and the stage of mediation, left to the parties, who are free to choose how to conduct the mediation in the manner they consider most appropriate.

When an agreement is reached through reconciliation, the arbitration tribunal will compile the reconciliation document or make an award based on the results of the agreement. The document of reconciliation and the arbitral award are equally binding from a legal point of view. According to Article 52, the document of reconciliation becomes legally binding immediately upon receipt by the parties concerned. If any of the parties concerned have gone back on their word after receiving the document of reconciliation, the arbitration tribunal will make a timely ruling.

Originally, the arbitration rules of the most important centre for international arbitration of China – the China International Economic and Trade Association Commission (CIETAC) – did not contain any provisions regarding the use of mediation. Only in 2005, an article (Article 40) was introduced stating that the arbitral tribunal could act as conciliator when a party so desires and the other party agrees. If conciliation failed, the dispute would be referred to arbitration. This solution aroused some concern, given that the involvement of the mediator-arbitrator weakened the effectiveness of the mediation, because the parties had less incentive to share confidential information with the mediator-arbitrator (which could be used in the subsequent arbitration). In the present version of the Arbitration rules, adopted on 4 November 2014 and in force since 1 January 2015, Article 47 better regulates the relationship between conciliation and arbitration. When both parties wish to conciliate, or when one party wishes to conciliate and the other party's consent has been obtained by the arbitral tribunal, the arbitral tribunal may conciliate the dispute during the arbitral proceedings. It is still the primary choice of the parties to ask the arbitral tribunal to reconciliate the parties, save the possibility for the parties to find a conciliatory solution alone.

The wording of the provision is clear in giving the arbitral tribunal the widest powers of mediation: the aim – namely the reconciliation of the parties – should not be threatened by formalism. The limit to the power of the arbitral tribunal to identify the most appropriate mode of mediation, with reference to the specific case, lies in the possibility of the parties, at any time, to abandon this way when they no longer consider it viable. When the parties have reached a settlement agreement through conciliation by the arbitral tribunal or by themselves, they may withdraw their claim or counterclaim, or request the arbitral tribunal to render an arbitral award or a conciliation statement in accordance with the terms of the settlement agreement. If the conciliation is not successful, the arbitral tribunal will resume the arbitral proceedings and render an arbitral award. In case of unsuccessful conciliation, neither party may invoke any opinion, view, or statement, and any proposal or proposition expressing acceptance or opposition by either party or by the arbitral tribunal in the process of conciliation as grounds for any claim, defense, or counterclaim in the subsequent arbitral proceedings, judicial proceedings, or any other proceedings.

Mediation is not entrusted only to the arbitral tribunal: on this issue, the new version of the Arbitration Rules responds to the criticisms that had been made with regard to the choice made in 2005. If the parties wish to conciliate their dispute, but do not wish to have conciliation conducted by the arbitral tribunal, CIETAC may, with the consents of both parties, assist the parties to conciliate the dispute in a manner and procedure it considers appropriate. It is therefore possible – after obtaining the unanimous agreement of the parties involved – that the mediation is conducted by someone other than the arbitral tribunal. In such case, CIETAC plays an assisting role, helping the parties to pursue the path of mediation.

When the parties have reached a settlement agreement by themselves through negotiation or conciliation before the commencement of an arbitration, either party may request CIETAC to constitute an arbitral tribunal to render an arbitral award in accordance with the terms of the settlement agreement. Unless otherwise agreed by the parties, the Chairman of CIETAC will appoint a sole arbitrator to form such an arbitral tribunal, which will examine the case in a procedure it considers appropriate and render an award in due course. The specific procedure and time period for rendering the award is not subject to any other provisions of the CIETAC Rules.

4.4 The Law on Mediation and Arbitration of Labour Disputes

Labour disputes are a predominant social problem in China today. The consequences of Western-style economic development and the choice for a market-oriented economic reform have produced an increase in violations of workers' rights (Széll, 2010). To prevent labour disputes, China's government has made concerted efforts to protect workers against abuse in the workplace and solve conflicts (Jing, 2008). Since 1992, the authorities have promulgated a series of labour regulations to monitor labour relations and regulate labour-dispute resolution. The result is a system relying on multiple instruments for settling labour disputes that includes both political and administrative structures in the form of government labour consultation with trade unions, labour arbitration, and labour litigation in court.

Granting the request of the International Labour Organization, China has created a tripartite consultation mechanism that prevents disputes from becoming intractable. Indeed, 'when a labor-related dispute occurs, parties involved may go through three steps to seek a resolution: mediation, arbitration and litigation' (Article 77 Labour Act 1994). In this way, the ADR mechanisms are incorporated into the Chinese global system (Esplugues and

Barona, 2014). This system works at various levels in order to achieve different aims: mediate widespread labour disputes, promote collective labour contracts, and conduct consultations on labour issues by involving all major players within employment relations. What particularly favours the effectiveness of China's consultation system in settling labour disputes is its tripartite nature. As Shen (2008, p. 264) aptly remarks, 'the Chinese government and the ACFTU [All-China Federation of Trade Unions] always associate tripartite consultation with collective labour contracts, and often refer to the tripartitism and collective bargaining'. Labour tripartitism is based on such methods as labour inspection, negotiation, and consultation.

The aim of this section is to investigate the different roles played by mediation for settling labour disputes; in particular, the analysis will focus on the combination of conciliation/ mediation and arbitration in Chinese norms and other informal processes that are used in labour dispute settlement. The recourse to mediation is on the increase:

> The rising star in the ADR firmament is mediation. Because of its enormous flexibility and the strong support that it receives from national and international institutions, mediation is taking the lead as the main device to solve or manage any kind of dispute.
> (Esplugues and Barona, 2014, p. 41)

However, some clarification should be made about the terms used to describe this process, since some linguistic peculiarities may create difficulties in our analysis. For example, this occurs with the terms *consultation* and *negotiation*, which are sometimes used interchangeably with the words *mediation*, *coordination*, and *conciliation*. The term *mediation* in not clearly defined in Chinese statutes (Esplugues and Barona, 2014) and the English translation of Chinese laws sometimes renders the same terms as either *mediation* or *conciliation*, thus creating confusion. As Esplugues and Barona (2014, p. 83) specify, 'it has to be kept in mind that the Chinese term 'mediation' does not fully correspond to mediation as known in most Western jurisdictions'. Moreover, there are different lexical elements used to refer to the various ways for resolving disputes mentioned in Chinese legislative texts. One of these, for example, is *negotiation*. This term is often found in legal texts and it is sometimes difficult to understand clearly if it is used to denote the initial approach to conflict resolution or as an alternative tool to the three methods indicated above, i.e., *mediation, conciliation*, or *arbitration*. The term *negotiation* has its origins in rhetoric, and, in fact, more than a specific means of settling disputes, it seems to identify the operating procedures that the parties, duly accompanied by a third neutral party, put in place to resolve a conflict. A negotiation has a lot in common with a mediation, as they are both non-adversarial approaches requiring the assistance of a third party to resolve a conflict. This third party is not a decision maker, and when the process is successful, its outcome will be accepted by the parties themselves. The term *negotiation* is explicitly mentioned in the text of the Regulations of the People's Republic of China on the Settlement of Labor Disputes in Enterprises of 1993; for example, in Article 6, it is introduced to identify an alternative to other methods of dispute resolution:

> In case of a labor dispute, the parties shall first find a solution through negotiations. If the parties are unwilling to go for negotiations or negotiations fail, the case may be referred to the mediation committee of the enterprise in which the dispute has occurred; if mediation fails, the case may be referred to the labor dispute arbitration committee for arbitration.
> (Art. 6)

A negotiation has been commonly defined as a 'process of (labour) disputes settlement where the disputing parties negotiate or consult with for a purpose of reaching a settlement or a compromise themselves' (Mo, 2000, p. 25). Instead, in this text, the term *negotiation* seems to be used with a different meaning. In the fourth paragraph of Article 7 and in Article 9, of the same Regulation of 1993, it is used in a vaguer and 'non-technical' way, and not as a measure of 'help' towards the resolution of the dispute as outlined instead in Article 6 cited above:

> The number of members to the mediation committee shall be determined through negotiations between workers' congress and the enterprise director or manager, at the proposal of the former.
>
> (Art. 7)

> In an enterprise without any trade union organization, the establishment and composition of the mediation committee shall be determined through negotiations between the workers' representatives and the enterprise representatives.
>
> (Art. 9)

In Article 6, instead, a negotiation is mentioned as the resource that the parties may have at their disposal, characterised by the cooperative spirit of those who agree to find a solution to a common problem. In this process, there is usually a third party who accompanies the parties and helps them overcome the psychological obstacles that stand in the way of obtaining a result, by using negotiative strategies, techniques, and tactics designed to favour successful communication and the achievement of a common goal, satisfactory to both.

In the Chinese system, the use of practices of compromise and mediation allows people to restrict the exasperated competition between individuals: according to the Confucian system (already discussed in the preceding sections), the optimal resolution of a difference is through moral persuasion and agreement, and 'not under duress' (Laeuchli, 2005). Therefore, in case of conflict, the sides will normally seek a solution through negotiation or other means of resolving disputes, such as mediation. The legislator, however, does not specify the details of this procedural stage. Indeed, the drafting of regulations in China has been quite heterogeneous (Széll, 2010), and in legal texts issued after 1993, we no longer find any reference to negotiation.

Similar considerations to those now made for negotiation may be extended to the mode of 'consultation' that is mentioned both in Article 77 of the Labour Act of 1994[5] and in Article 5 of the Law of the People's Republic of China on Labor Disputes Mediation and Arbitration of 2007,[6] identified as an instrument to be used as an alternative to the three classical methods of ADR. However, as previously mentioned, these legislative texts, too, have certain linguistic peculiarities that make it difficult to understand the real intention of the lawmaker, as it is not clear whether the two terms (*negotiation* and *consultation*) are used as synonyms or, indeed, represent distinct methodologies. Nevertheless, they are

5 The Labour Law of The People's Republic of China was adopted at the Eighth Meeting of the Standing Committee of the Eighth National People's Congress on 5 July 1994 and promulgated by Order No. 28 of the President of the People's Republic of China.

6 The Labor Dispute Mediation and Arbitration Law of the People's Republic of China was adopted at the 31st meeting of the Standing Committee of the Tenth National People's Congress of the People's Republic of China on 29 December 2007 and became effective as of 1 May 2008.

considered part of the Chinese labour tripartitism system, and they are 'widely used in handling labor relations due to the fact that a negotiation or consultation may not break but improve employment relationships between parties who will have to deal with each other again, or even to help them learn how best to handle conflict with other parties in the future' (Shen, 2007, p. 95).

4.4.1 Relations between mediation and arbitration

With reference to mediation, this process is a type of self-regulation of workers and employers specifically mentioned in Chapter X (Articles 77–80) of the Labour Act of 1994, which deals with labour disputes. In that text, mediation is presented as a first instrument that the parties can adopt to meet their own expectations. Various PRC state institutions at all levels overwhelmingly push civil parties into mediation before going into arbitration. As Howson asserts,

> This push into mediation results in a compromise settlement where employer (with significantly greater leverage) and employee both win a little and lose a little, and employees enjoy something much less than pure rights protection or adequate monitoring of oppressive employers.
>
> (Howson, 2010, p. 323)

As regards the nature of mediation, this is not presented as a judicial or administrative process, as it is considered private. This interpretation is confirmed by the composition of the Enterprise Mediation Committee (EMC), which only includes representatives of the three parties involved (workers, employers, and the trade union).

While mediation is completely voluntary, arbitration is often seen as a mandatory step before legal action is taken. This concept is often made explicit, so as to keep such provocative disputes away from formal legal institutions. Indeed, if the text of 1994 emphasises the power of the parties to choose among the different procedures available, in the later text of 2007, the lawmaker has determined the almost-obligatory passage between them, providing for the transition to the next procedure only in case of failure of the previous phase. As Esplugues and Barona specify,

> Mediation is a mandatory proceeding preceding labor arbitration, which must in turn precede a trial before court.
>
> (Esplugues and Barona, 2014, p. 93)

This insertion of mediation into the arbitration system explicitly mentioned in the law of 2007 was inspired by the principle 'one mediation, one arbitration and two court cases (*tiao yi, yi cai, liang sheng*)' (Zou, 2012). Under this approach, the management of labour disputes has been developed precisely in distinct phases: the first with mediation, the second with arbitration (in case mediation has failed), and the third and final phase in court (with the two trials [two tests] system), to be followed in case arbitration has failed.

The confirmation of this cascading system – only when previous proceedings are concluded negatively do the parties move on to the next step – is confirmed by the fact that the process of arbitration is accessed prior to the process of litigation. In fact, in the wording of the rules devoted to arbitration, one can detect a sort of 'strong advice' to refer the matter to arbitration before resorting to court action. Arbitration is thus considered a prerequisite for litigation (Brown, 2010). Similarly, mediation is considered a prerequisite for arbitration, and this is the reason why Article 42 of the Law of the People's Republic of China on Labor Disputes Mediation and Arbitration of 2007 encourages the arbitration panel to mediate before continuing with the arbitration process. Some scholars consider this process of mediation within arbitration proceedings as a distinct subcategory of mediation (cf. Esplugues and Barona, 2014).

In case of a positive outcome of the mediation, the arbitrators will issue a *statement of mediation*, declaring that an agreement has been reached. This declaration of mediation will become effective after both parties have signed it. The documents issued within the two mediation processes have different efficacy. Indeed, the agreement reached by mediation is not binding for any party concerned, and parties eventually can still file a claim for arbitration. Instead, the mediation agreement achieved through the arbitration procedure is binding and enforceable in court (Lu, 2008). In case of no appeal within fifteen days, or in the event of failure to implement the arbitration decision within the time limit by either party, the other party may apply to the court for the application of the mediation agreement (Esplugues and Barona, 2014). Moreover, while the arbitral decision may be challenged before the court within fifteen days, the document resulted from mediation cannot be contested (Section 2, Article 27–30, Law 2007). This greater degree of efficacy explains why a large percentage of disputes are settled by mediation conducted by arbitrators (Yang, 2015).

4.5 Conclusion

The analysis of the texts of both the PRC Arbitration Law and the Law on Mediation and Arbitration of Labour Disputes has enabled us to find a clear confirmation in both texts of the possibility of combining the process of conciliation/mediation with that of arbitration. While in Western legal culture this mixed form of dispute settlement has traditionally encountered strong opposition, in the Chinese context, this possibility is not only not contrasted but it is also explicitly admitted. This depends on the fact that conciliation and mediation have a long tradition there, and find their origins in Confucian philosophy, which views social conflicts as a shameful aberration of morality and as a form of disruption of the natural order of social life.

Another cultural element that has clearly influenced the adoption of this mixed form of dispute resolution is the great importance of the concept of 'face' in business relations. Indeed, this concept has great relevance in the field of arbitration, since when the parties' faces are threatened, there is a strong tendency not to cooperate or to withhold important information. Therefore, in line with the Confucian teachings and tradition, every effort to find a possible solution to a dispute is seen as the preferred way to avoid the loss of face of the parties involved in the dispute.

This analysis points to a more general development of the ADR movement also in other contexts, as it favours negotiation between the parties and therefore promotes a greater level of privatisation of justice. To enhance this movement, however, it is necessary to guarantee the adherence to the basic principles on which mediation is based: voluntariness, equality, confidentiality, neutrality, and impartiality of mediators, as well as the enforceability of the settlement reached. Only in applying these principles will the mediating practice grant free access to a reliable way to resolve both commercial and labour disputes.

References

Backman, M., 1999. *Asian eclipse: Exposing the dark side of business in Asia*. Singapore: John Wiley & Sons.

Benjamin, L. R., 2008. Mediating the mediation debate. Conflict resolution and the local state in China. *Journal of Conflict Resolution*, 52(5), pp. 737–764.

Berger, K. P., 2006. *Private dispute resolution in international business: Negotiation, mediation, arbitration*. The Hague: Kluwer Law International.

Blackman, C., 1997. *Negotiating China: Case studies and strategies*. Sydney, NSW: Allen & Unwin.

Brown, R., 2010. Comparative alternative dispute resolution for individual labor disputes in Japan, China, and The United States: Lesson from Asia? *St. John's Law Review*, 86, pp. 543–577.

Brown, P. and Levinson, S., 1978. Universals in language usage: Politeness phenomena. In: Goody, E. ed. *Questions and politeness: Strategies in social interaction*. Cambridge: Cambridge University Press. pp. 256–289.

Cao, D., 2004. *Chinese law: A language perspective*. Aldershot: Ashgate.

Chu, C.-N., 1996. *The Asian mind game: A westerner's survival manual*. St Ives: Stealth.

Ch'ü, T., 1980. *Law and society in traditional China*. Westport, CT: Hyperion.

Cohen, J. A., 1966. Chinese mediation in the eve of modernization. *California Law Review*, 54(3), pp. 1201–1226.

Connerty, A., 2012. The 2012 revision of the CIETAC arbitration rules: A look at the most significant changes. *Dispute Resolution Journal*, May/July, pp. 73–78.

Cremades, B. M., 1998. Overcoming the clash of legal cultures: The role of interactive arbitration. *Arbitration International*, 14(2), pp. 157–172.

De Mente, B. L., 1996. *Chinese etiquette and ethics in business*. Lincolnwood, IL: NTC Publishing Group.

Diamant, N. J., 2000. Conflict and conflict resolution in China: Beyond mediation centered approaches. *Journal of Conflict Resolution*, 44(4), pp. 523–551.

Esplugues, C. and Barona, S., 2014. *Global persperctives on ADR*. Cambridge: Intersentia.

Fullerton, R., 2010. Med-Arb and its variants: Ethical issues for parties and neutrals. *Dispute Resolution Journal*, May/October, pp. 52–61.

Goffman, E., 1955. On face-work: An analysis of ritual elements in social interaction. *Psychiatry: Journal for the Study of International Processes*, 18, pp. 213–231.

Gu, Y., 1990. Politeness phenomena in modern Chinese. *Journal of Pragmatics*, 14(2), pp. 237–257.

Harpole, S. A., 2007. The combination of conciliation with arbitration in the People's Republic of China. *Journal of International Arbitration*, 24(6), pp. 623–633.

Hinze, C., 2005. Looking into 'face': The importance of Chinese *mian* and *lian* as emic categories. In: Bargiela-Chiappini, F. and Gotti, M. eds. *Asian business discourse(s)*. Bern: Peter Lang. pp. 169–210.

Ho, D. Y., 1974. Face, social expectations, and conflict avoidance. In: Dawson, J. L. M. and Lonner, W. J. eds. *Readings in cross-cultural psychology: Proceedings of the inaugural meeting of the International Association of Cross-Cultural Psychology held in Hong Kong, August, 1972*. Hong Kong: Hong Kong University Press. pp. 240–251.

Howson, N. C., 2010. Review of 'Understanding Labor and Employment Law in China' by Ronald C. Brown. *Law and Politics Book Review*, 20(8), pp. 319–328.

Hu, H. C. (X. J.), 1944. The Chinese concept of 'face'. *American Anthropologist*, 46(1), pp. 45–64.

Huang, P., 2006. Court mediation in China. Past and present. *Modern China*, 32(3), pp. 275–314.

Irwin, H., 1996. *Communicating with Asia: Understanding people and customs*. St Leonards, NSW: Allen & Unwin.

Jemielniak, J., 2015. Exploring Med-Arb and Arb-Med discourse in China: Challenges and prospects. In: Bhatia, V. K. and Gotti, M. eds. *Arbitration discourse in Asia*. Bern: Peter Lang. pp. 155–182.

Jing, L., 2008. China's new Labor Contract Law and protection of workers. *Fordham International Law Journal*, 32, pp. 1083–1131.

Laeuchli, U. M., 2005. *Negotiations and other ADR with the Chinese.* At www.mediate.com//articles/Laeuchli.cfm.

Lee, L. T. and Lai, W. W. 1978. The Chinese conceptions of law: Confucian, legalist and Buddhist. *The Hastings Law Journal*, 29, pp. 1307–1329.

Lee-Wong, S. M. 2000. *Politeness and face in Chinese culture.* Frankfurt am Main: Peter Lang.

Liao, M., 2010. A comparative study of Chinese and American criminal sentencing discourse. *ESP Across Cultures*, 7, pp. 105–128.

Liao, M., 2012. Courtroom discourse in China. In: Tiersma, P. and Solan, L. eds. *The Oxford handbook of language and law.* Oxford: Oxford University Press. pp. 395–407.

Liebman, B., 2007. China's courts: Restricted reforms. *The China Quarterly*, 191, pp. 620–638.

Lu, H., 2008. New development in China's labor dispute resolution system: Better protection of workers' rights? *Comparative Labor Law and Policy Journal*, 29, pp. 247–273.

McKnight, B. E., 1992. *Law and order in sung China.* Cambridge: Cambridge University Press.

McLaughlin, J. T., 2010. Planning for commercial dispute resolution: The view from the People's Republic of China. *Alternatives to the High Cost of Litigation*, 28(7), pp. 140–143.

Mo, J., 2000. Probing labour arbitration in China. *Journal of International Arbitration*, 17(5), pp. 19–83.

Moser, M. and Yuen, P., 2005. The new CIETAC arbitration rules. *Arbitration International*, 21(3), pp. 391–403.

Phillips, G., 2005. Same-neutral Med-Arb: What does the future hold? *Dispute Resolution Journal*, May/July, pp. 22–30.

Sato, Y., 2008. Hybrid dispute processing in Japan: Linking arbitration with conciliation. In: Bhatia, V. K., Candlin, C. and Engberg, J. eds. *Legal discourse across cultures and systems.* Hong Kong: Hong Kong University Press. pp. 53–74.

Shen, J., 2007. The labour dispute arbitration system in China. *Employee Relation*, 29, pp. 520–539.

Shen, J., 2008. Labour disputes and their settlement in China: A systematic review of the post reform research. *The International Journal of Comparative Labour Law and Industrial Relations*, 24(2), pp. 263–288.

Széll, G., 2010. Changing labour relations in China. *Indian Journal of Industrial Relations*, April, pp. 554–565.

Taniguchi, Y., 1998. Is there a growing international arbitration culture? An observation from Asia. In: Jan van den Berg, A. Gen. ed. ICCA (International Council for Commercial Arbitration) *International Dispute Resolution: Towards an International Arbitration Culture.* Dordrecht: Kluwer Law International, pp. 31–40.

Thireau, I. and Hansheng, W., 2001. *Disputes au village chinois. Formes du juste et recompositions locales des espaces normatifs.* Paris: Éditions de la MSH.

Wall, B. 1991. Community mediation in the People's Republic of China. *The Journal of Conflict Resolution*, 35(1), pp. 3–20.

Wei, D. 2005. The reform of grass roots tribunals and the application of the law in rural China – The case of the district of Weicheng, in the city of Xianyang, Shaanxi Province. *China Perspectives*, 61, September-October. www.chinaperspectives.revues.org/527.

Wenying, W., 2005. The role of conciliation in resolving disputes: A P.R.C. perspective. *Ohio State Journal on Dispute Resolution*, 421, pp. 436–440.

Yang, Y., 2015. *Mediation over arbitration institutionalization of labor dispute settlement in China.* Ann Arbor: University of Michigan. At http://sites.lsa.umich.edu/accountability-and-development/wp-content/uploads/sites/251/2015/04/Yang-Poster-2015.pdf.

Yeung, L. N. T., 1997. Polite requests in English and Chinese business correspondence in Hong Kong. *Journal of Pragmatics*, 27(4), pp. 505–522.

Zou, M., 2012. Labour Law with Chinese characteristics? Chinese Labour Law at a critical point in history. At www.ilera-directory.org/15thworldcongress/files/papers/Track_4/Wed_W2_ZOU.pdf.

5 Arbitration practice in India

A discursive perspective[1]

Patrizia Anesa

5.1 Introduction

Today, International Commercial Arbitration (ICA) is a widely adopted Alternative Dispute Resolution (ADR) method used to resolve international disputes of a commercial nature. It is a particularly attractive tool for international companies, especially given that the enforcement of awards at an international level, and not only at a domestic level, is a key feature of the New York Convention (Moses, 2008). The private aspect of the process allows parties from different linguistic and legal cultures to resolve their disputes, while limiting the potential for intervention by the courts. Some Asian countries, such as Singapore and Hong Kong, have assumed a leading role in international arbitration, and the growing economic role of powers, such as China and India, together with the increasing attention to the arbitral field by linguists and legal scholars make the investigation of Asian arbitration discourse even more urgent.

More specifically, this study aims to offer new insights into arbitration in India, making use of the results obtained from a questionnaire[2] and structured interviews conducted with experts in the field operating in the Indian subcontinent. It also offers a comparative analysis with similar studies carried out by experts in other Asian countries, such as Singapore (Kathpalia, 2012), as well as in some Western countries, such as Italy (Belotti, 2012a,b). Moreover, the results obtained from legal experts in the field operating in India (especially arbitrators) are compared with industry perspectives as illustrated in the Pricewaterhouse-Coopers report (2013) on corporate choices in international arbitration, and, with a more specific focus on the Indian context, in the study by Rajarao and Patel (2013), on corporate attitudes and practices towards arbitration in India.

Arbitration professionals can offer precious information in order to understand how ICA is developing in India and to investigate to what extent its integrity is maintained. The approach adopted is in line with Bhatia's interpretation of interdiscursivity (Bhatia, 2007) and his idea that an insightful study of arbitration practice needs to go beyond the purely textual level. Thus, "one needs to determine the extent to which arbitration interdiscursively 'appropriates' generic forms and conventions from litigation, particularly in terms of the intentions, purposes, processes, procedures, and the shared expertise expected on the part

1 I am grateful to my respondents who gave their time for this project so enthusiastically. I am particularly indebted to Nishant Nigam and Vijay Gupta and the other anonymous experts who took part in the project for sharing their precious thoughts with me.

2 The questionnaire used is an adaptation of the questionnaire designed for the project "International Commercial Arbitration Practice: A Discourse Analytical Study," coordinated by the City University of Hong Kong. It is principally based on the questionnaires utilized by Belotti (2012a,b) and Kathpalia (2012). Some of the questions are also loosely drawn from Kachwaha's guide on arbitration (2013).

of the participants involved" (2007, p. 397). Consequently, the contribution that professionals operating in the arbitration field can make in order to reach a wider understanding of arbitration discourses beyond the textual level cannot be underestimated.

5.2 Arbitration in India

India's increasing business activity on a global scale has inevitably generated a growing number of commercial disputes, both at domestic and international levels. It has been argued that the rate of economic growth "has, in many instances, outpaced the rate of growth of dispute resolution mechanisms" (Sarma, Oinam, and Kaushik, 2009, p. 1) and that the increase in caseloads has become unmanageable. In an interview[3] in 2013, Law Minister Ashwani Kumar said that over 30,000,000 cases were pending in Indian courts. This situation has inexorably led to the acknowledgment that ADR is crucial for the Indian legal system.

Among the most widely used ADR methods are Arbitration, Mediation, and Conciliation. Another common ADR system in India is the *Lok Adalat*, which is based on Gandhian principles and aims at a cordial resolution of disputes. *Lok Adalat* (which means "People's Court") has ancient origins, but its modern institutionalised form may be said to have started in 1982 in Gujarat (Khan, 2006). The 1987 Legal Services Authorities Act gave a statutory status to *Lok Adalats*. It has now spread throughout the country and has contributed to lightening the burden on the Indian court system. A variety of other hybrid means of dispute resolution have also spread, such as Mini-trial, Medola, Med-Arb, Ombundsman (see Khan, 2006), neutral evaluation, and fast track arbitration.[4]

Arbitration is consistently gaining popularity as a means of dispute resolution throughout the world. The PricewaterhouseCoopers (2013) survey conducted among international corporations highlights the fact that arbitration is particularly popular in the Energy and Construction sectors. In India, according to Kachwaha (2013, p. 1), the main fields in which arbitration is used are "[s]hipping, construction, joint venture agreements and cross border commercial contracts." However, he also points out that "for disputes related to loans and borrowings, arbitrations are not ordinarily used, as the lender typically depends on the built-in securitization mechanism rather than a private dispute resolution forum."

From a legal perspective, India has adopted the United Nations Commission on International Trade Law (UNCITRAL) Model Law for international commercial arbitration and the UNCITRAL Rules of Arbitration, and its institutional framework has been modified accordingly. India is also a signatory to the New York Convention on the enforcement of arbitration awards, thus guaranteeing the enforcement of awards in most countries in the world. Over the past few decades, India has adopted a series of measures to support the use of arbitration, and the New Arbitration and Conciliation Act of 1996 sets forth the principles of autonomy of the parties and maximum judicial support with minimum judicial intervention by the courts.

Several arbitral institutions have been established in India over the years, and among the most renowned we find: the Indian Council of Arbitration, the International Centre for ADR (ICADR), the Council for National and International Commercial Arbitration,

3 *The Times of India*, 7th March, 2013. http://timesofindia.indiatimes.com/india/Over-3-crore-cases-pending-in-courts-in-India-Govt/articleshow/18847570.cms.

4 Fast track arbitration may be defined as "time-bound arbitration, with stricter rules of procedure, which do not allow any laxity or scope for extensions of time and the resultant delays, and the reduced span of time makes it more cost-effective" (Sarma, Oinam, and Kaushik, 2009, p. 13).

the Indian International and Domestic Arbitration Centre, and the Indian Institute of Arbitration & Mediation. However, a survey conducted among Indian companies (Rajarao and Patel, 2013, p. 13) illustrates that the most popular arbitration centres are often located outside India, namely in Singapore – e.g., the Singapore International Arbitration Centre (SIAC) and the Industrial Arbitration Court (IAC) – and in the UK – e.g., the International Chamber of Commerce (ICC) and the London Court of International Arbitration (LCIA). The reasons for such choices are related to costs, the international reputation, and credibility generally associated with these centres and the perception of neutrality, impartiality, and independence. The same survey also shows that Indian companies express a higher level of satisfaction when the dispute is administered and resolved in arbitration centres outside India, rather than within the country. Consequently, it seems decisive to investigate the reasons behind this relative level of scepticism towards Indian centres, especially in the light of the crucial importance assumed by economic, financial, and commercial growth in India and the relative need for efficient and trustworthy dispute resolution methods.

5.3 Method

While acknowledging the inherent limits of a small-scale survey, the main objective of the study is to gain new insights into the role that arbitration assumes in both Indian and international commercial arbitration involving Indian parties, with particular attention given to the discursive, cultural, and linguistic aspects that characterise the way in which the proceedings are conducted and the documentation is produced. The study also focuses on the differences emerging in Indian arbitration, compared with other Asian and Western countries.

The ethnographic data derive from a questionnaire given out and interviews conducted with six experts in the field currently operating in India. The respondents are all experienced professionals. In particular, when asked what professional category would best describe their activity, three responded "advocates" and three said "engineers", and regarding their specific experience in the arbitral field, four usually act as arbitrators and two mainly as counsellors and consultants. The professionals contacted could decide whether to answer a specifically designed questionnaire to be returned to the researcher or to be directly interviewed by the researcher. Four parties opted for the first option and two for the second. The questions included are both close-ended (Yes-No, multiple choice, Likert scale) and open-ended.

The questionnaire and interviews include a preliminary part about the participants' role, professional category, and experience. This information is particularly useful to observe any differences in the perception of arbitration across professional categories and roles. The main sections concern the following:

- an overview of arbitration practices in India, especially in relation to other countries,
- its main features,
- the role of arbitrators,
- arbitration clauses,
- awards,
- evidence and hearings,
- language,
- reasons for preferring arbitration and areas of concern.

5.4 Results

5.4.1 Overview

The use of arbitration in India is now widespread over the whole country and is seen by all participants as undergoing constant growth. Indeed, with India becoming a hub for foreign investment, more and more companies are entering into agreements and commercial transactions with Indian entities, and experts strongly believe that these processes will also determine an increase in the number of disputes emanating from such relationships. Nowadays, contracts show a tendency to include an arbitration clause, and it is thus predictable that dispute resolution through arbitration will continue to grow. One of the respondents involved in this study confidently stated that arbitration is the best remedy available. The generally positive attitude with which arbitration is greeted by parties and professionals also allows us to predict that the proportion of disputes settled through arbitration is likely to increase.

Nowadays, in India, parties are more aware of different dispute resolution mechanisms, and all respondents agree that arbitration is definitely more popular than other methods. Other forms, such as mediation and conciliation, are sometimes "thought of as mere replacements for the good old 'negotiation' practice which was used prior to proceeding legally" (R1). At the same time, "mediation and conciliation are becoming more regulated and are often encouraged in a more formal manner in order to avoid going to arbitration or the courts" (R1). As far as Online Dispute Resolution is concerned, this system exists in India, but at the same time, it is very rarely used. It is generally stated that this situation derives from a lack of clear laws regarding this procedure, which is not yet very well established or regulated.

Respondents generally agree that as regards arbitration in India when compared to other countries, the situation is quite complex. While arbitration in India is constantly growing, some respondents argue that the arbitration mechanism in India is yet to get fully in line with best practices in international arbitration. Moreover, other countries, such as Singapore and Hong Kong, maintain a leading role in Asia, given their tradition and international recognition in the field. In particular, a considerable number of Indian parties still prefer to recur to internationally renowned centres, such as the SIAC. Indeed, the SIAC statistics confirm that in 2009–2011, India contributed the highest number of filings (84); in 2012, 49 cases involving Indian parties were filed (SIAC 2012); and in 2013, India was the top nationality (excluding Singapore) by number of new cases filed at SIAC (85) (SIAC 2013).[5]

Some of the reasons determining the attractiveness of Singaporean centres to Indian parties are illustrated by Choo (2012):

- Neutrality: according to the Corruption Perception Index 2011[6], Singapore is perceived as the least corrupted Asian country.
- Convenience and connectivity.
- Similarities between the Singaporean and the Indian legal system.
- Use of the English language.
- State-of-the-art arbitration facilities and services.

5 SIAC Reports are available at www.siac.org.sg/2013-09-18-01-57-20/2013-09-22-00-27-02/annual-report.

6 www.transparency.org/cpi2011/results/#CountryResults.

It is also generally believed that European countries are more organised and professional than India, which ultimately leads to higher levels of efficiency in proceedings and to the end result being less costly and generally concluded within the time frame stipulated by the parties. However, respondents point out that arbitration in India is becoming more and more popular. In particular, an expert clearly states:

> India is slowly but steadily becoming a hub in the Asian region for arbitration. Though it has a long way to go to even catch up with Singapore and Hong Kong, yet Institutions such LCIA and ICC showing interest in the Indian market have lent the much needed support to the system here.
>
> (R1)

Indeed, Singapore and Hong Kong represent the fulcrum of Asian International arbitration, with institutions such as the Hong Kong International Arbitration Centre (HKIAC) or the SIAC. At the same time, however, respondents believe that renowned international institutions, such as the LCIA or the ICC through its arbitration body (the International Court of Arbitration), have given substantial support to the Indian arbitration system in order to lead it to adopt international best practices. In particular, LCIA India was established in New Delhi in 2009 and has since organised series of conferences, seminars, and workshops, involving professionals, students, and others interested in arbitration processes. Indeed, according to Zaiwalla, "LCIA India has undoubtedly brought along with it the tried and tested experience of the LCIA, which is now recognized as one of the leading international arbitration institutions in the world" (Zaiwalla, 2010, p. 660).

5.4.2 *Features of arbitration*

5.4.2.1 *Advantages and disadvantages*

Traditionally, the main advantages attributed to arbitration are time and cost-effectiveness, flexibility, freedom on the part of the parties to decide on some of the aspects of the procedure, confidentiality, and enforceability of the award (Moses, 2008; Tay, 1998). Respondents confirm that, in India, arbitration is one of the preferred ADR forms, and they state that one of the principal advantages of arbitration is flexibility, which in business is generally greeted very positively, in particular because it allows freedom in choice of place, time, and procedures. Indeed, parties generally choose their own judges and time frame, as well as the manner in which the proceedings are to be held. All this saves time, which is considered crucial in the commercial world. It is also generally believed that the achieved outcome does not contain irregularities, having been pronounced by a person or tribunal chosen by the parties themselves, thus leading to a higher level of satisfaction.

However, in terms of cost and time effectiveness, responses have not been completely homogeneous. There seems to be strong consensus that arbitration proceedings are generally concluded in a shorter time than litigation, but while some state that arbitration is considerably faster, others point out that the difference is not very significant. In fact, Sarma, Oinam, and Kaushik (2009) remark that "[a]rbitration in India is rampant with delays that hamper the efficient dispensation of dispute resolution" (2009, p. 14). From a legal perspective, this situation partially derives from the fact that while the 1940 Act set a fixed time for the completion of proceedings, the 1996 Act does not. This is because the latter Act guarantees the autonomy of arbitration, and it was felt that no intervention from courts would automatically lead to timely proceedings. Thus, it was not deemed necessary to stipulate a time frame. However, court intervention is still relatively common in Indian arbitration (Biswas, 2014), which leads to longer dispute settlement times.

Regarding costs, two respondents state that arbitration is clearly cheaper than litigation, but the others pointed out that it is not always cost-effective. Tay (1998) illustrates that arbitration may be cheaper, especially when based exclusively on the analysis of documents, and tends to be faster when conducted by a technical professional, rather than a lawyer. In fact, arbitration costs include a series of items, such as arbitrator's fees, administrative costs, lawyers' fees, expert witnesses' fees, and rent for arbitration venues. There are, of course, considerable differences between *ad hoc* and institutional arbitration. The former is characterised by great flexibility and fees, which are generally decided by the arbitrator upon the parties' consent and can vary from Rs[7] 1,000 to Rs 50,000 per hearing, depending on the arbitrator and the type of claim (Sarma, Oinam, and Kaushik, 2009, p. 16). On the contrary, in the case of institutional arbitration, different centres clearly indicate the types of costs that the parties may bear. For instance, the Rules of Arbitration of the Indian Council of Arbitration[8] establish:

- A registration fee of Rs 1,000.
- Administrative Fee and Arbitrator's Fee, which vary according to the amount under dispute in each case. For instance, fees can range from Rs 8,000 (when the amount is up to Rs 500,000) to Rs 68,000, plus Rs 2,500 per crore[9] of part thereof (for amounts exceeding Rs 100,000,000).
- Arbitrators are also entitled to special fees for the study and preparation of material.
- The ICA is also entitled to a Special Fee of Rs 500 per hearing.

In other countries, similar differences also exist between *ad hoc* and institutional arbitration, as shown by studies that point out that the costs of arbitral institutions tend to be kept under control, and thus are lower than *ad hoc* proceedings (see Belotti, 2012b, p. 250 on the Italian situation).

In particular, cost is internationally considered one of the main areas of concern. In a Singaporean study, the majority of respondents (88%) indicated that the recent exponential growth of arbitration costs is a major concern (Kathpalia, 2012, p. 270). In a study by Ali (2010) based on respondents from different countries, especially mainland China and Hong Kong, only 36% of people identified the costs as an advantage of arbitration, whereas the forum's neutrality was chosen as the strongest advantage by 88% of respondents. Also, at a corporate level, costs represent one of the main areas of concern, as confirmed by the PricewaterhouseCoopers survey (2013). The increase of costs may be determined, as Nottage (2012, p. 14) observes, by the growth of international firms dealing with international commercial arbitration, which work on a billable hour system, thus aiming to prolong the procedure, rather than settling the case as fast as possible.

In terms of informality, the respondents generally agree that arbitration is normally more informal than litigation. Indeed, parties choose not only their own arbitrator but also the procedure to be followed during the proceeding. For instance, parties may agree that no

7 1 Indian Rupee = 0.02 USD approximately.

8 Data derived from the Rules of Arbitration of the Indian Council of Arbitration. Available at: www.intracen.org/Rules-of-Arbitration-of-the-Indian-Council-of-Arbitration/.

9 Crore = unit equal to ten million.

oral evidence will be admitted and that only documentary evidence will be admissible during the proceeding. On the contrary, the parties do not have the same liberty before a Court of Law.

As regards confidentiality (a characteristic that is traditionally attributed to arbitration), it has been argued that most proceedings are strictly confidential, and the only public evidence is the award (To, 2008). As Azzali (2008) points out, there is a difference between privacy and confidentiality of arbitration. The former implies that strangers are precluded from attending proceedings, while the latter implies that information cannot be disclosed. In some cases (especially dealing with intellectual property and trade secrets), confidentiality may play an important role in the choice of arbitration (Dessemontet, 2001, p. 299). In other cases, it is not considered a predominant feature. The respondents agree that, in India, confidentiality is also a key feature of international arbitration, simply because "confidentiality in contemporary times is an important aspect of almost everything we do" (R1). Hence, it is an essential element, especially as the parties involved have a lot at stake in terms of their data, trade secrets, reputation, and goodwill. Moses (2008) also mentions that companies place great importance on keeping certain information confidential that could potentially damage their credibility. Even though some scholars have argued that arbitration proceedings are not confidential *per se*, the respondents confirm that it entirely depends on the wishes of parties and the appreciation of such a request by the arbitral tribunal. In particular, one respondent affirms that confidentiality is an emerging concept in India and, thus, is slowly gaining importance with Indian parties. Moreover, proceedings are often held in private, avoiding undue public exposure.

Some of the advantages of arbitration also throw into evidence another aspect. For instance, while being generally considered an advantage in comparison with litigation, the cost of arbitration in India is also seen by one of the respondents as one of its main disadvantages. Moreover, sometimes the dispute does not end merely with the final award. The aggrieved party may choose legal recourse to challenge the award or restrict the implementation of said award before a Court of Law. Consequently, the whole exercise of arbitration may be nullified and deemed futile, and thus this process may cause an exponential growth in terms of costs and length of the proceedings. Moreover, the professional background of the arbitrator in a specific field is one of the key elements of arbitration. However, this aspect is sometimes associated with the risk of a lack of legal expertise on the part of a technical professional. In this regard, Tay (1998, p. 20) states: "An expert lacking a judicial approach is worse than any non-technical judge." However, in practical terms, this risk could easily be avoided, in that, parties enjoy a certain level of freedom in the choice of the arbitrator and thus can select an arbitrator with both technical and legal expertise.

5.4.2.2 *Litigative colonisation of arbitration?*

Worldwide, it has also been stated that arbitration has recently been particularly influenced by litigative procedures (Kerr, 1997; Nariman, 2000), thus affecting the very nature of the arbitral system. Respondents confirm that this tendency is also present in India, and one expert states, "There is such a tendency and that emanates from the fact that most Arbitrators at least in India are from the legal field – such eminent lawyers or retired judges from the high Courts or the Supreme Court. Hence, they are not able to break from the shackles of procedure and rules" (R1). Similarly, Sarma, Oinam, and Kaushik (2009, p. 15) affirm that "the parties usually approach arbitration with a similar mindset as for Litigation." Agarwal (2008) also confirms that arbitrators are often retired judges who tend to treat arbitration following traditional litigative procedures, for instance, allowing frequent adjournments, thus hampering the time effectiveness of litigation.

Nariman (2000, p. 262) argued that international commercial arbitration had become "almost indistinguishable from litigation, which it was at one time intended to supplant – with law, more law, legalese and more legalese," and the literature often mentions the fact that arbitration is being colonised by litigation. However, one respondent disagrees with such a statement, especially in light of recent developments that have given arbitration more freedom from the clutches of legal proceedings, and interestingly, he points out that this type of "colonisation" would "kill the main purpose of resolving the dispute through arbitration" (R2). In his opinion, it is crucial to give arbitration more freedom and, at the same time, more authority.

5.4.3 Arbitrators

As regards arbitrator selection, generally the choice of the arbitrator(s) can be based on professional qualifications and experience, as well as personality and cost (Paulsson, Rawding, and Reed, 2011). Arbitrators often display specific knowledge of a particular field of business, thus being seen as insiders. According to our respondents, in India, a large number of arbitrators are selected on the basis of their compatibility with the parties. However, merely being compatible is not the only criterion to be taken into account. Competence is also highly valued. In particular, the qualifications and prior experience that the arbitrator possesses also play a major role in an individual being chosen as an arbitrator. Finally, the selection has to be in line with the contractual clause.

Among the qualities that arbitrators are supposed to display, one respondent also observes that they should be calm and composed. Impartiality is also identified as an important characteristic, which should not just be a formal requirement but must be the guiding principle in the actions of all arbitrators. In addition, arbitrators ought to be well qualified and ready to consider what is being presented to them. Hence, they should be receptive to various contentions and views. As happens at an international level, in India, there are no specific limitations on who may act as an arbitrator, but parties commonly prefer a person who possesses some sort of legal knowledge in addition to the specific qualification or expertise he or she may have.

Parties are usually aware of the background of an arbitrator and choose with knowledge of the pros and cons of their choice. As Bhatia points out, the choice of legal experts as arbitrators may favour "the importation of typical litigation processes and procedures into arbitration practices" (Bhatia, 2007, p. 397). However, appointing a lawyer as an arbitrator is not generally seen as something that may affect the amicability of the procedure, a question that is perceived as particularly important, in that arbitration is generally considered more amicable than litigation but still adjudicatory in nature.

Indian arbitrators also belong to other professional categories. For instance, when dealing with engineering contracts, they are often experienced engineers, and the Indian Council of Arbitration[10] has a specific roster for engineers available to serve as arbitrators. The same applies for other specific professional categories, such as chartered accountants and maritime experts. Each expert has a different *forma mentis* and adopts a different *modus operandi*, which may influence the way the proceedings are conducted and how documents

10 See www.icaindia.co.in/htm/membership/memberscouncil/engineers.pdf.

are drafted. Consequently, the "mixture of discourses" that characterise and construe arbitration (Bhatia, 2007, p. 397) is also given by the influence of litigative practices on arbitration and is boosted by the co-presence of people with different professional backgrounds.

5.4.4 Arbitration documentation

5.4.4.1 Arbitration clauses

As mentioned above, commercial contracts nowadays tend to include an arbitration clause. With reference to the characteristics that such a clause should contain, one respondent points out, "I feel that an arbitration clause in cross border agreements should be a three-step procedure providing for negotiation, mediation and eventually arbitration as a method for dispute settlement" (R1). Similarly, two other respondents have stated that different methods for dispute resolution should not be seen as mutually exclusive, and a number of attempts should be made in order to try to resolve issues in the most effective way in terms of both time and cost. Thus, an exhaustive arbitration clause should also contemplate a possibility for negotiation and mediation as methods to resolve disputes.

Moreover, the clause should unambiguously state the law governing the contract, the seat of arbitration, and whether we are dealing with institutional or *ad hoc* arbitration. The language in which the arbitration proceedings will be conducted should also be clarified. Multinational corporations often develop a "standard" arbitration clause, which is usually in line with current practices and conventions. This approach avoids the time-consuming praxis of writing clauses anew and guarantees the use of consolidated writing principles. Standard arbitration clauses tend to affect arbitration processes only when the arbitration clause has, for some reason, become obsolete, that is, the clause was drafted far in advance of the proceedings actually taking place. In such a scenario, the arbitration clause does not cover various exigencies that may have emerged in the meantime, due to a change in the law or other circumstances (R1 and R2).

5.4.4.2 Awards

All participants in the survey stated that the language chosen does not influence the structure and the form of the award and its main characteristics.

In other contexts, it has been shown that the arbitrator's professional background may affect the discursive features of awards (Gotti and Anesa, 2011). However, Indian professionals believe that, in India, this type of influence is generally lower. For example, one respondent states that, in India, "the professional category merely influences the use of terminology and the ease of it while writing the award" (R1). It is generally believed that what is affected is principally the lexical level, in that the use of some specific terminology may or may not be present, rather than the syntactic, textual, or discursive aspects of the award, or its macrostructure. Some preliminary research (Anesa, 2015) shows the presence of a certain level of informality and several linguistic inaccuracies in some types of Indian awards, regardless of the arbitrator's professional background. Further investigation is thus needed in order to gain new insights into the discursive features of Indian awards and to unveil if and to what extent they show processes of differentiation across professional cultures.

On a practical note, challenges to awards are not generally based on vague linguistic formulations, but rather on issues such as the misconduct of the arbitrator. Indeed, none of the respondents has ever experienced an award challenged on vague linguistic formulations, and they have stated that, in their experience, most awards are challenged on the fact that the arbitrators exceeded their jurisdiction. However, the number of applications challenging arbitration awards is seen by most respondents as an indication that arbitration is becoming, to some extent, more similar to litigation. Indeed, one respondent states that a lot of arbitrations end up in court, thus inevitably reducing the difference between arbitration and litigation (see Section 4.2.2).

5.4.5 Evidence and hearings

The colonisation of arbitration by litigative procedures seems to be confirmed by the fact that, according to the respondents, hearings are conducted in a manner that is not considerably different from a regular court hearing. However, not all respondents totally agree. While some state that the same procedure is followed both in court as well as in arbitration, others observe that although the general structure may be similar, arbitration hearings present fewer formalities. It has been pointed out that in some Western countries, the practice of adopting time-limited hearings is sometimes present, but this is not yet the case in Asian countries (Kathpalia, 2012, p. 271). No Indian respondent has adopted such a procedure, which would be an exception in the Indian context.

Considering witness examination, some respondents state that the procedure is largely the same as in the litigative system. More specifically, witness examination is usually conducted after the witness has filed a written statement of what the witness wishes to state under oath. The written statement helps to save time for the tribunal, as the said statement is taken on record in its entirety. Thereafter, the counsel or advocate of the opposite party cross-questions or cross-examines the witness on the statement, which is recorded before the tribunal. The arbitrator very seldom questions the witness, as that could be construed as a bias towards a certain party in the arbitration. As for the selection of expert witnesses, they are generally selected based on their knowledge and their specialisation regarding the matter, at the request of the parties. The language generally used in examinations is English, unless the person who is being cross-examined does not understand English, and in that scenario, the local language is generally used. Interpreting and translation services are used, but very seldom.

Arbitration practices tend to undergo a process of standardisation. Thus, especially in the case of institutional arbitration, proceedings tend to be conducted according to international conventions. Indeed, no respondents, even those also operating internationally, were able to identify any specifically Indian traits, as procedures tend to be quite homogeneous and uniform, despite the cultural background of the participants.

5.4.6 Language

All respondents confirmed that English, being widely used as a lingua franca in trade and commerce and in general in international communication, is predominantly the language of arbitration in India, as happens in other Asian countries (see Kathpalia, 2012), although there are generally no specific guidelines on the language to be adopted.

From the experience of the respondents, in a multilingual international arbitration setting, the contract itself generally stipulates that English will be the language in which arbitration will be conducted. Thus, the most common language used in arbitration proceedings and in documents is English. However, with regard to documentation, some respondents have sporadically seen French and German being used. English is generally preferred, even if it is not the first language of the parties, and this confirms its predominant role as a lingua franca in arbitration proceedings. Language is not considered a particularly important factor in the selection of the arbitrator. However, most parties in international arbitration where English is the given language prefer arbitrators who are well versed in English.

5.5 Conclusions

This study shows that Indian arbitrators consider flexibility, free choice of arbitrator and procedure, and speed as main advantages of arbitration. The main area of concern is that of cost, although a certain level of heterogeneity is present in the respondents' answers regarding this point. The time frame within which arbitration takes place may also be of concern, especially because the challenge of awards may prolong the time for dispute resolution.

As regards the phenomenon of "arbitigation," mentioned by Kerr (1997) and, in general, the influence of litigative procedures on arbitration (e.g., Nariman, 2000), respondents have highlighted that this process is taking place in India, too, like in most countries. In particular, the significant presence of retired judges in India may contribute to the phenomenon. Although harmonisation of practices and procedures is generally desirable, changing the mindset of the professionals involved cannot happen in the short term, as they are "so deeply rooted in their individual legal culture and jurisdictional practices that they find it difficult to switch hat, as it were, when they operate in arbitration" (Bhatia, Candlin, and Gotti, 2012, p. 315). However, the respondents highlight that this process happens in particular in the conduction of proceedings, rather than in the writing of Indian awards (Anesa, 2015). The issue as to whether arbitration and litigation should be placed along a continuum of dispute resolution methods or whether they are considerably different in nature and thus irreconcilable remains open. However, given the widespread use of arbitration across the world, it is important to investigate its integrity and discursive features in order to understand how efficiency can be improved.

Among the respondents, there seems to be awareness that ideal arbitration practice should also, at least theoretically, incorporate a mediation attempt, thus contributing to the amicable character of the procedure. On the other hand, it is generally believed that the specificity of arbitration should be maintained, and the process could not be seen as merely amicable. In fact, the question of amicability is not considered relevant, since arbitration, unlike other ADR procedures, is not meant to be a win-win situation, as it has an adjudicatory nature. In particular, some respondents have pointed out that a higher level of autonomy of arbitration may contribute to an increasing level of trust towards this method.

In conclusion, following Kathpalia, it can be argued that "arbitration is not likely to be supplanted by litigation even though it is being influenced by it" (2012, p. 275). Arbitration, as the respondents have confirmed, is widely used, and it is plausible to predict that its use will increase, especially in countries like India, where the caseload of courts is not easily manageable. In this context, arbitration will continue to represent a precious alternative to litigation, even though efficiency concerns need to be addressed.

References

Agarwal, A., 2008. Resolving Business Disputes in India by Arbitration: Problems due to the Definition of 'Court'. *IIMA Working Papers.* Available at: www.iimahd.ernet.in/publications/data/2008-12-03Agarwal.pdf.

Ali, S., 2010. Barricades and Checkered Flags: Comparing Views on Roadblocks and Facilitators of Settlement among Arbitration Practitioners in East Asia and the West. *Pacific Rim Law and Policy Journal* 18(2), 244–278.

Anesa, P., 2015. Discursive Peculiarities of Indian Arbitral Awards. In Bhatia, V.K., and Gotti, M. (eds) *Arbitration Discourse in Asia*. Bern: Peter Lang, pp. 305–326.

Azzali, S., 2008. Confidentiality vs. Transparency in Commercial Arbitration: A False Contradiction to Overcome. *Transnational Notes*. Available at: http://blogs.law.nyu.edu/transnational/2012/12/confidentiality-vs-transparency-in-commercial-arbitration-a-false/.

Belotti, U., 2012a. *Dispute Resolution Narratives. A Linguistic Analysis of Arbitration Practices*. Bergamo: CELSB Libreria Universitaria.

Belotti, U., 2012b. Arbitration in Italy: A Two-headed Janus? In Bhatia, V.K., Candlin, C.N., and Gotti, M. (eds) *Discourse and Practice in International Commercial Arbitration (Issues, Challenges and Prospects)*. Farnham: Ashgate, pp. 239–261.

Bhatia, V.K., 2007. Interdiscursivity in ritical genre analysis. *Proceedings of the 4th International Symposium on Genre Studies*, University of Southern Santa Catarina, Tubarão, Santa Catarina, Brazil, pp. 391–400.

Bhatia, V.K., Candlin, C.N., and Gotti, M., 2012. Contested Identities in International Arbitration Practice. In Bhatia, V.K., Candlin, C.N., and Gotti, M. (eds) *Discourse and Practice in International Commercial Arbitration: Issues, Challenges and Prospects*. Farnham: Ashgate, pp. 301–318.

Biswas, T.K., 2014. *Introduction to Arbitration in India*. Alphen aan den Rijn, The Netherlands: Kluwer Law International.

Choo, J., 2012. Indian arbitration users and the Singapore appeal. *Singapore International Arbitration Blog*. Available at: http://singaporeinternationalarbitration.com/2012/04/14/indian-arbitration-users-and-the-singapore-appeal/.

Dessemontet, F., 2001. Arbitration and Confidentiality. *The American Review of International Arbitration* 7(1), 299–318.

Gotti, M. and Anesa, P., 2011. Professional Identities in Italian Arbitral Awards: The Spread of Lawyers' Language. In Bhatia, V.K., and Evangelisti Allori, P. (eds). *Discourse and Identity in the Professions*. Bern: Peter Lang, pp. 189–212.

Kachwaha, S., 2013. *Arbitration Guide: India*. IBA Arbitration Committee 2013. Available at: www.ibanet.org/Document/Default.aspx?DocumentUid=1CF8C452-D4C3-4043-90F6-6F39B1B628B2.

Kathpalia, S. 2012. Is Arbitration Being Colonized by Litigation? Practitioners' Views in the Singapore Context. In Bhatia, V.K., Candlin, C.N., and Gotti, M. (eds). *Discourse and Practice in International Commercial Arbitration: Issues, Challenges and Prospects*. Farnham: Ashgate, pp. 263–281.

Kerr, M., 1997. Concord and Conflict in International Arbitration. *Arbitration International* 13, 121–143.

Khan, S.A., 2006. Lok Adalat: An Effective Alternative Dispute Resolution Mechanism. New Delhi: S.B. Nangia.

Moses, M.L., 2008. *The Principles and Practice of International Commercial Arbitration*. New York: Cambridge University Press.

Nariman, F.S., 2000. The Spirit of Arbitration: The Tenth Annual Goff Lecture. *Arbitration International* 16(3), 261–278.

Nottage, L., 2012. Addressing International Arbitration's Ambivalence: Hard Lessons from Australia. In Bhatia, V.K., Candlin, C.N., and Gotti, M. (eds) *Discourse and Practice in International Commercial Arbitration: Issues, Challenges and Prospects*. Farnham: Ashgate, pp. 11–43.

Paulsson, J., Rawding, N., Reed, L., 2011. *The Freshfields Guide to Arbitration and ADR. Clauses in International Contracts*. The Hague, The Netherlands: Kluwer Law International.

PricewaterhouseCoopers, 2013. *Corporate choices in International Arbitration Industry perspectives*. Available at: www.pwc.com/gx/en/arbitration-dispute-resolution/assets/pwc-international-arbitration-study.pdf.

Rajarao, V., and Patel, D., 2013. *Corporate Attitudes & Practices towards Arbitration in India*. Available at: www.pwc.in/en_IN/in/assets/pdfs/publications/2013/corporate-attributes-and-practices-towards-arbitration-in-india.pdf.

Sarma, K., Oinam, M., and Kaushik, A., 2009. Development and Practice of Arbitration in India. *CDDRL Working Papers*, 103. Available at: http://iis-db.stanford.edu/pubs/22693/No_103_Sarma_India_Arbitration_India_509.pdf.

Tay, C.T.S., 1998. *Resolving Disputes by Arbitration: What You Need to Know*. Singapore: Singapore University Press.

To, C., 2008. Confidentiality in Arbitration. In Bhatia, V.K., Candlin, C., and Engberg, J. (eds) *Legal Discourse across Cultures and Systems*. Hong Kong: Hong Kong University Press, pp. 75–107.

Zaiwalla, S., 2010. LCIA India: Will It Change the International Arbitration Scene in India? *Journal of International Arbitration* 27(6), 657–665.

6 A contrastive corpus-based analysis of Italian and Singaporean arbitration practice narratives

Ulisse Belotti

6.1 Introduction

Disputes are considered almost inevitable in international trade and cross-border investment. In theory, a dispute may be resolved in two different ways. A party may decide to take legal action against the counterpart and leave the whole matter to the decision of a court judge, or one may decide to settle the dispute through alternative forms of dispute resolutions, be they conciliation, mediation or arbitration. Furthermore, a party may decide to try some form of amicable settlement and then, if this proves to be unsatisfactory, to opt for litigation. Indeed, litigating cross-border business disputes in national courts presents an array of problems connected to different legal systems, such as common law and civil law. As far as international trade is concerned, arbitration has turned out to be the most popular way of resolving disputes, even though evidence shows that it has become too similar to litigation (Nariman 2000; Stipanovich 2008).

This work sets out to investigate arbitration practitioners from two very different cultural and professional backgrounds, in Italy and Singapore. Therefore, two corpora of interviews of Italian and Singaporean arbitration practitioners were collected in order to analyse the state of the art of arbitration in the two countries and investigate the linguistic realisations that these experts, mainly counsels and arbitrators, have employed using English as either a lingua franca, for the Italian respondents, or as a mother tongue, for the Singaporean interviewees.

Indeed, narrative is considered a universal mode of verbal expression, and narrative analysis has been employed to investigate different domains such as literature (Voloshinov 1973; Banfield 1982), news reporting (Fairclough 1992; Waugh 1995) and academic discourse (Swales 1990; Thompson and Ye 1991; Hunston 1993).

As far as arbitration discourse is concerned, researchers have investigated a variety of features, such as the linguistic and discoursal characteristics of international arbitration laws in different countries, cultures and sociopolitical backgrounds (Bhatia *et al.* 2003a,b). Moreover, insights into the influence that litigation practices and discourse have had over arbitration as a method of resolving international commercial disputes have been provided by recent research (Bhatia *et al.* 2010; Bhatia 2011; Gotti 2012).

While written arbitration discourse has received consistent scholarly investigation, oral arbitration narratives have experienced less attention. A notable exception is represented by Hafner (2011), who investigated the influence of different legal cultures on arbitration, drawing on a comparative analysis of the discourse of professional reasoning in International Chamber of Commerce arbitral awards, through interviews with arbitration stakeholders. As regards Italy, oral narratives from arbitration practitioners have been collected and investigated by Belotti (2012a,b), while insights into arbitration practice in Singapore have been provided by Belotti and Giorgetti (2015) and Kathpalia (2010), who analysed the relationship between international commercial arbitration and litigation through a survey, which was distributed to arbitrators and arbitration practitioners.

6.2 Methodology and data

Two corpora of arbitration practice narratives, one collected in 2008 from Italian arbitration practitioners (CERG 2008 henceforth) and one collated in 2014 from Singaporean arbitration professionals (AAD 2014 henceforth), were compared to address the following research questions:

1. How do arbitration practitioners from different legal and cultural backgrounds determine the most critical aspects of arbitration practice?
2. How differently do Italian and Singaporean arbitration practitioners use metaphors and direct speech acts to deliver arbitration-related issues?

It seems relevant to point out that, although the two corpora were collected at different times and in two different countries, they were based on the same questionnaire[1].

The corpus collected in Italy between October 2008 and March 2009 comprises 12 interviews with arbitration practitioners, all nonnative speakers of English but using English as a lingua franca, with the exception of one professional whose native language is American English. CERG 2008 amounts to 580 minutes of recorded interviews, which were transcribed (288,648 words) using SoundScriber (2004). The corpus collected in Singapore in July 2014 consists of eight interviews with arbitration professionals, all native speakers of English (Singapore variety), with the exception of one who claimed that his native language is Tamil, acting as either arbitrators or counsel to parties. AAD 2014 amounts to 260 minutes of recorded material (44,354 words), which was transcribed using the same transcription software and conventions (See Appendix 1) as those used for CERG 2008.

6.3 Critical aspects of arbitration practice

This section of the chapter explores some of the most critical issues of international commercial arbitration highlighted by the respondents from both corpora with a particular emphasis on cross-examination, arbitration clauses and the cost of arbitration.

6.3.1 Cross-examination

Although the main purpose of International Commercial Arbitration (ICA) is to resolve disputes arising from parties from different countries, the way in which the resolution of disputes is initiated, developed and presented is different depending on whether the parties are from a common law or a civil law system. One of the most outstanding differences between the two systems lies in how witness testimony is managed. In civil law systems, it is the judge's role to read the documents presented by the parties well in advance of the hearing. These documents may include written statements of the witnesses or 'witnesses may appear at the hearing to give an unprompted narrative and to be questioned by the

1 The two corpora and the questionnaire are available upon request to ulisse.belotti@unibg.it.

judge' (Elsing and Townsend 2002: 4). It is also up to the judge to ask questions, even though counsels to the parties are allowed to provide the judge with further questions. On the other hand, in common law systems, it is generally accepted that the best evidence comes from cross-examination, the stage in which common law lawyers do their best to destroy the credibility of the opposing party's witnesses. When a dispute involves parties from these two very different legal systems, problems are likely to occur, particularly in terms of the counsels' skills to cope with cross-examination. As far as our corpus[2] is concerned, the majority of arbitration practitioners from Singapore focused on cases in which the practitioners from civil law traditions were regarded as naïve, if not incompetent to manage cross-examination, as exemplified in the following extracts.[3]

1 So in an arbitration you have so many levels of sophistication and lack of experience so you have these problems ... you have these problems which are are different to as multi-lingual multi-cultural multi-disciplinary which is ...so the very sophisticated arbitrator ...presiding arbitrator will say now not only that cross-examination but there's going to be a very specialized form of cross-examination in the form of hot tubbing ... then you have a very inexperienced say civil lawyers on one side ...often they matter even common lawyers and they have no idea what they heard about hot tubbing and they read about it but they don't know exactly what to do ...you know ... and ... and so this is a big problem because we don't all come from the same source of education ...knowledge and experience so it is truly an international problem ...

(AAD 2014: I2)

2 [...] I mean the question you ask me leads a real life example that I had where the counsel for the claimant was a common law practitioner ...the counsel for the respondent wasn't but they had agreed to this procedure but I think the counsel for the respondent ...she ...didn't understand what cross-examination was and she was so disadvantaged because every time she asked the questions the witness just said ya but she didn't seem to understand what she was supposed to get out of the witness then ultimately they lost but I think they were very disadvantaged they agreed to a process which they didn't really understand what it entailed so I think it's it's a problem...

(AAD 2014: I3)

In (1) and (2), both respondents clearly underline the fact that counsels from civil law systems, if not adequately trained in conducting cross-examination, may be totally unsuited to cope with cross-examination in general, not to mention specialised forms, such as 'hot-tubbing'.[4] These interviewees also pointed out that this situation may affect the whole arbitration procedure, as it becomes not just '*a problem*' but '*an international problem*'. From the Italian perspective, respondents see cross-examination differently. Some agree that specific training in cross-examination is deemed necessary in order to use it appropriately, as

2 Throughout the chapter, AAD 2014 refers to the interviews based on the questionnaire administered to Singapore arbitration practitioners, and CERG 2008 refers to the interviews based on the questitionnaire administered to Italian arbitration practitioners; the numbers refer to the individual interviews.

3 The stretches of spoken language used in this study have been reported verbatim, preserving misstatements, omissions, false starts, repetitions and errors of grammar.

4 Hot-tubbing, often used after cross-examination, is a method of giving evidence where both experts give evidence simultaneously and the tribunal chairs a discussion between them.

indicated in extract (3). Others simply point out the fact that cross-examination is not an issue in civil law systems where live testimony is seen with considerable scepticism, if not totally ignored. Moreover, live testimony can pose further risks, including the fact that it can be challenged in a court, as exemplified in excerpt (4).

3 I think that eh... there could be some advantages in ... in the long run... but eh ...the immediate effect would probably create general confusion again because it's... it's very delicate to give certain tools to people who do not have a specific background and so in ...in the short run it it could eh... add complexity to the system rather than ...than ...bringing benefits

(CERG 2008: I4)

4 Ehm... well well in civil law proceedings cross examination is sometimes not not even eh... known because eh ...the lawyer cannot cross examine directly he can ask the judge to examine ehm ...often in our system questions have to be put and answered this happens also in the common law system because (slight intake of breath) for instance... we in Italy we do not know yet the system of asking questions in writing and answer answer in writing this is common in eh... in common law countries which surprises the civil lawyers because (subvocalizing) you must have the witness there ok... but then cross examination is something different ... you collect the deposition of a witness (slight intake of breath) what happens is that the deposition can be ...let's say challenged in open court

(CERG 2008: I2)

Under the Italian arbitration law, it is typical that an arbitrator or a panel of arbitrators renders an award after considering written documents if the dispute is on matters of law, for example, on how a contractual provision should be interpreted. Conversely, if the dispute is more complex and it is on matter of facts, oral testimony is admitted, provided it is requested by both parties. Indeed, arbitration practitioners from common law and civil law systems who practise in multiple jurisdictions face the challenge of having to adjust to these varying rules, and the situations may get even more complicated, because there are no written rules of cross-examination for arbitration proceedings (Cymrot 2007).

This may inevitably lead to the conclusion that a harmonisation of such different jurisdictional systems, although highly attractive by the arbitration community, 'is unlikely to take effect any time in the near future' (Bhatia 2011: 115). As a matter of fact, reasons against such harmonisation rest on robust arguments. For example, the preparation of witnesses for testimony is prohibited in civil law jurisdictions, but considered usual practice in common law jurisdictions (Moses 2012) where witnesses are carefully instructed, if not rehearsed, on how to behave and what to say in the course of a cross-examination, thus putting arbitration practitioners from civil law tradition in a much weaker position than their common law colleagues. However, some of the interviewees from CERG 2008 indicate that arbitration procedure is flexible enough to 'define a set of procedures that are unlikely to be challenged as unacceptable or unfair from either side of the increasingly less divisive common law-civil law divide' (Elsing and Townsend 2002: 7), as exemplified in the following excerpt:

5 But I think it is also ...well ... it's a matter of training because handling witnesses is not an easy matter at all eh ... being eh... effective in cross-examining a witness it's ...is difficult and it's also a question of legal culture I mean we face a lot of eh... well let's say it's a bit schizophrenic in this respect because the laws tell ...

tell you that you cannot prepare the witness that a witness has to be neutral that has to be eh...well eh... impartial ...examined only ...well ...by the judge or the arbitrator ...

INTERVIEWER: *Which is typical of the ...our system for example.*
Ya, exactly and so ...
INTERVIEWER: *We cannot ask questions directly to witnesses ...you have to go through the judge who makes questions to the witness.*

That's exactly the point... I mean ...there is a a particular crime which is 'subornazione di testimone' [*subornation of perjury* my translation] which is still a ...a ... still a problem for us to face eh... what happens is that well in doing cross-examination ... probably I'm anticipating a little bit next question but in cross-examination ehm... it's customary to prepare the witness otherwise well you have your own witness which ... who has to be cross-examined by the other party you have to prepare him otherwise eh... probably the... the whole matter would be ... in favour of the other party.

(CERG 2008: I7)

In (5), the speaker talks about the problems connected to a practice that is rooted in the common law tradition, but unknown or prohibited in civil law jurisdictions. The problem mentioned here, i.e., *the subornation of perjury*, refers to the practice of inducing someone to make false statements while under oath. Here, the respondent, being unable to remember or produce the required phrase in English, uses the Italian noun phrase *subornazione di testimone*, something which, under the Italian law, is a crime.

6.3.2 Arbitration clauses

Given that international commercial arbitration lies in its consensual nature, the parties to an international contract have substantial freedom in designing the manner in which the arbitral proceedings are conducted. The first and most important opportunity for the parties to take control of their arbitration is in the drafting of the arbitration clause that may be very detailed or simply refer to a generic commitment of resolving the disputes arising between the parties. Problems are likely to occur when parties decide to amend model arbitration clauses or replicate standard clauses without paying too much attention to how they work and the way they interact with the jurisdiction and governing laws. This is due to the fact that arbitration clauses are often left behind as the final step to be agreed upon, after the more substantive provisions have been negotiated at length.

In fact, this may result in arbitration clauses that are pathological (Townsend 2003; Liu 2006), especially when drafters are not fully aware of the risks connected to both ready-to-use standard model clauses and homemade arbitration clauses.

This section of this chapter investigates how arbitration practitioners from Italy and Singapore see the most critical aspects of arbitration clauses. Indeed, the majority of Italian practitioners (10 out of 12) identified the seat of arbitration as the most critical aspect of arbitration clauses, followed by the appointment of arbitrators and the applicable law, while the Singaporean arbitration professionals indicated that pathological arbitration clauses are the result of a number of reasons, such as poor or incomplete knowledge of the arbitral procedure, the fact that these clauses are crammed with unnecessary information or lack something that is considered to be essential or even that arbitration clauses are often homemade or the result of copy-and-paste techniques.

6.3.2.1 *Poor or incomplete knowledge of the arbitral procedure*

When arbitration clauses are drafted by lawyers who are more qualified as litigators than arbitrators, it is almost inevitable that these clauses are influenced by the litigative background of the drafters themselves, and this may affect the content of the clauses, as exemplified in extract (6), in which the proposition *many of whom may not have ever seen the inside of an arbitration chamber* clearly signals that badly drafted arbitration clauses are likely to be drawn up by corporate lawyers with no experience in arbitration. In excerpt (7), the Italian respondent addresses the issue of applicable law. Although the choice of the law to be applied by the arbitrators to determine the substantive issues may not affect the validity of an arbitration clause, it is advisable that the parties agree upon the applicable law, because if parties fail to include the applicable law, this very likely leads to an increase in the cost and the duration of the arbitration procedure itself.

> 6 Yes (.) yes we've had quite a few instances that we encountered (.) very badly drafted clauses and you know invariably it's put down to the eh (.) lawyers who are involved at the drafting stage of the contract (.) how much or how little they know about the arbitral process (.) and in fact I think that's probably one of the great weaknesses because the people who actually conduct the arbitrations and experience the ups-and downs and the difficulties (.) are the dispute resolution lawyers but the lawyers who draft them are the transactional or corporate lawyers (.) *many of whom may not have ever seen the inside of an arbitration chambers* (laughs)
>
> (AAD 2014: I4)

> 7 (small intake of breath) uhm … well I think the real critical points are mm… two… I would say… one is the applicable law and the second is eh …where the arbitration is held ehm … I have seen in my life arbitration clauses in which there is no choice of law and this creates problem (slight intake of breath) because mmm… there is always a fight … by the two sides normally …very often on which kind of ahm…of law to apply because each of them try to eh… bring the question debate on their bet… the better known ground … their own law … and the place again because eh… place influences the …very often … the procedural rules mm for better or for worse …and so it is important to choose a really neutral place … or a favourable place if you can.
>
> (CERG 2008: I2)

A further critical aspect of arbitration clauses, which was identified by both Italian and Singaporean arbitration professionals, concerns the practice of using arbitration clauses previously employed in similar situations. This 'cut-and-paste' technique may save time, but may also result in problematic cases, as exemplified in the following extracts.

> 8 But I think ehm the common problem that we see is people do a cut and paste approach (.) so *they don't think about* what dispute they're dealing with *they don't think* about the value of the claim *they don't think about* the subject matter *they don't think about* the location of the parties ahm *they don't think about* which institutional rules may be better for them ehm… they simply say … ok this company A and company A uses SIAC and we will always use SIAC and may not be the case and may not be favourable for you …so I think that's the common problem we see (.)
>
> (AAD 2014: I6)

9 I mean when the parties write an arbitration clause they have to think... *is this going to work in practice for what are our interests...* because very often there are a lot of mistakes done by parties who are not familiar with the difficulties of international arbitration and perhaps they take an arbitration clause from a prior document without realizing that in...that specific case it doesn't work ...you may have a situation for instance where you have multi-party arbitration you have more than one party to the contract and then a classic traditional arbitration clause thought toward for two parties only may not work anymore you may choose an arbitration institution eh... the rules of which are not consistent with that specific contract and so on ...

(CERG 2008: I5)

In both (8) and (9), the focus is on the fact that an arbitration clause should be drafted and agreed upon according to the specific needs of the parties and the scope of the arbitration itself, since an all-purpose arbitration clause is practically nonexistent. When arbitration clauses are simply copied from preexisting documents, serious problems may arise as envisaged in (8), where the parties showed no attention to details considered essential or used an arbitration clause for a traditional two-party dispute when more than two parties were involved in the dispute, as indicated in (9). From a linguistic point of view, it is worth pointing out that the critical claim *they don't think about* is repeated five times in (8) without any hedging devices. This grammatical parallelism serves the function of both providing cohesion to the narration itself and making it clear that some arbitration clauses are drafted without carefully considering the most important aspects of arbitration. In (9), the stretch of direct speech *is this going to work in practice for what are our interests* is embedded in the narrative so that the parties' interests are clearly voiced.

6.3.2.2 'Homemade' arbitration clauses

Pathological arbitration clauses may include serious pitfalls, such as 'equivocation, inattention, omission, overspecificity, unrealistic expectations' (Townsend 2003: 30–33). In addition, arbitration clauses may be 'ambiguous, negligent, lacking in essential or necessary elements, too elaborated' (Gómez Domínguez 2007: 120). Problems may also arise when counsels to parties, instead of relying on clauses drafted by well-established arbitral institutions (e.g., ICC, AAA, LCIA, SIAC and so forth), decide to draft their own clause, which often results in faulty clauses, as exemplified as follows.

10 Well (.) I mean it really depends on whether that clause is properly drafted (.) I mean if it works (.) then ...the reason the clients wonna go with that ...is that they are comfortable with it (.) they are familiar with it (.) they know what to do if a dispute arises (.) and to some extent it is tried and tested (.) I mean my surprise ... ahm... in dealing with a lot of these cases is that (.) despite the ease of adopting a standard template on the web site which you can take from SIAC or ICC (.) people still try and draft their own piece of arbitration agreements and that's where the problems arise...

INTERVIEWER: *Home-made*

Ya home-made and I don't understand why they don' just grab something off (.) I mean clients come to us and say (.) *look why didn't you grab something off the web site from ICC because that's tried and tested you know it works why do you need to come up with some funky or unusual things* (.) *unless you have some unique circumstance which requires that* (.) but even then most standard templates can address those issues.

(AAD 2014: I3)

11 Eh... the ...the poor drafting ... they are very ...very... poorly drafted eh... they are poorly drafted and that the ...let's say the beginning of the end ... once the arbitration clause is poorly drafted then it's *when the nightmare starts* because they .eh... either it's very difficult to start an arbitration either because the arbitration clause is very complicated or because it's not valid (chuckle) eh... or once they make to start an arbitration they find out that the way they drafted the arbitration clause leads the parties to a very expensive arbitration proceedings to a...a an excess of power recognized to the arbitrators in terms for example of time extension eh... so the ...the... it's really the poison ... might be the poison ... *the poison pill* in the ...in the ...in all the story so ...that's why ...the reason eh... that I believe ehm... are eh... of the poor drafting of arbitration clauses ...one ...is probably psychological ehm...because the arbitration clause is included in the contract when they sign the contract ...*when they get married* so they don't want psychologically ... *they are not inclined to think of the divorce* of any problem so psychologically they pay less attention to the dispute clauses eh... in US it's ...(subvocalizing) called midnight clause that is another issue they get to the final eh ...dispute clause at the end of exhausting eh...negotiation about real issues ... what they think are real issues and they are real issues when they finally settle all the real issues they come to the dispute clause ...eh ...they say ok but ...you know... we are getting married and this one issue ...the second issue is poor culture and knowledge ...they don't know much ...lawyers eh... they don't know much about arbitration ... I would say worldwide ...there are jurisdictions that they know more others that they know less eh... but basically arbitration is very still ...a very specific eh... branch and so ...it's not ...let's say common knowledge of ...of ... eh... a lawyer ...of a jurist ... so they sometimes they do not know how to draft ...they underestimate ...that's why ... this is another reason they should use institutional arbitration ...they can just copy the arbitration clause... period!

(CERG 2008: I10)

These two extracts show how differently the same issue can be addressed. The Singaporean respondent (10) focuses on the importance of relying on trustworthy arbitral institutions in order to avoid arbitration clauses, which may include '*funky or unusual things*'. Here, the adjective *funky* is likely to have been used to mean a clause that is inappropriate. On the other hand, the Italian interviewee (11), while delivering the idea that arbitration clauses are often poorly drafted, tries to provide reasons, relying on what Cameron (2007) and Koller (2003) call 'metaphor cluster', i.e., a set of metaphors used in close textual contiguity, even though they do not share the same cognitive basis.

In the first metaphor, '*it's when the nightmare starts*', the target is represented by arbitration procedure, and the source is the 'nightmare' that signals that poorly drafted arbitration clauses may spoil the whole arbitration process. The respondent, talking about the risks connected to the excessive power that an arbitration clause may grant arbitrators, states that this may be a '*poison pill*' for the whole procedure. Here, the meaning of the source is to be interpreted in the sense that a poorly drafted arbitration clause is deemed to compromise arbitration itself. In addition, the speaker mentions the fact that the initial phase, in which companies decide to set up a business relationship, entails not just trade agreements but it may also enjoy the magic atmosphere of a just married couple. In this metaphorical expression, the target is represented by the parties and the source by marriage, so that when the personified parties *'get married'*, it is very unlikely that '*they are inclined to think of the divorce*'. Indeed, the way in which these arbitration practitioners made use of metaphors shows a different way of addressing the same problem. The Singaporean respondent addressed the question in a way that may be defined as rational and concise. Conversely, the Italian speaker's words and flow of argumentation reveal that he was psychologically involved, and this involvement is testified by the use of a cluster of metaphors. This is not directly connected with the professional culture of the two interviewees, but it is reasonable to assert that this psychological involvement is a manifestation of specific cultural traits. If we assume, in Trompenaars and Hampden-Turner's words (1998: 6), that 'culture is the way in which a group of people solves problems and reconciles dilemmas', the stretch of discourse in (11) clearly displays the features of someone from an affective culture, in which an active involvement in a spoken narrative plays a relevant role.

6.3.3 The cost of arbitration

Arbitration costs, which include arbitrators' fees/expenses and administrative fees and also lawyers' and experts' fees and expenses, are on the rise in international commercial arbitration, thus producing a growing source of concern (Aksen 2007; Stipanovich 2008). However, according to the results from the survey on arbitration conducted in 2013 by Queen Mary University of London (School of International Arbitration) and PricewaterhouseCoopers, costs are not the principal preoccupation of commercial parties in deciding to arbitrate. Nevertheless, parties want to know not only how much arbitration will cost but also 'whether any, some, or all of those costs will either be recoverable from, or payable to, the other side depending on the arbitration's outcome' (Smit and Robinson 2010: 270). According to Bühler (2005: 179), arbitration costs may be kept under control in four ways, i.e., 'the drawing up of the procedural time table, the provision of guidance on what issues to brief, the awarding of legal costs prior to the final award and the awarding of costs related to document production'. As far as the CERG 2008 corpus is concerned, only two respondents out of 12 think that arbitration costs are lower than those connected with litigation are. The majority of the Italian interviewees maintain that arbitration proceedings often take years and are therefore expensive, and this is mainly because parties are bound to pay both their lawyers and the panel of arbitrators, as exemplified in the following extracts.

12 Yes arbitration is always more expensive definitely … you have to pay eh. at least your lawyers and the panel …the panel of arbitrators who basically are lawyers.
(CERG 2008: I3)

13 Ehm… yes… well I. I… would think that for medium-small cases …eh… international arbitration is definitely more expensive than transnational litigation ehm… and and… (subvocalizing) unless I mean there are there are (subvocalizing) really specific agreements between the parties and … maybe with …eh ad-hoc arbitration if the parties already have somebody in mind and so there there can be (subvocalizing) some patterns where arbitration even in small cases is more cost effective than transnational litigation but eh… otherwise eh… the cost is really an issue and I do believe that …yes …for for big cases ehm… I I think that the money is is worth the

service at the end ehm…even though eh …you see more and more cases where you have arbitration and parallel proceedings and in that case then it becomes really questionable whether it's it's better value for money because you would end up paying both things at the same time.

(CERG 2008: I4)

Given that party costs account for the majority of the costs connected with international arbitration, some respondents turned their attention to the role played by arbitral institutions in keeping costs under control. Indeed, costs in arbitrations conducted under the auspices of arbitration institutions are more likely to be foreseen. Under particular circumstances, international arbitration may be even less expensive than litigation, as one of the Italian interviewees pointed out.

14 If you really draft a good arbitration clause …if you pick up the right arbitral institution and for example you adopt a sole arbitrator clause with an institution that is not too expensive … (throat clearing) you have some … way to… to keep costs under control that it's still eh… less expensive than any …any litigation.

(CERG 2008: I12)

As regards the Singaporean arbitration context, Kathpalia (2012) investigated the relationship between international commercial arbitration and litigation through a survey that was distributed to arbitrators and legal practitioners. Kathpalia found that Singaporean practitioners expressed concern over a number of issues, including, among others, the escalation of costs. One of the findings in Kathpalia's work (2010: 270) was that 'a significant number of respondents (63 percent) indicated that ICA is as expensive as transnational litigation for medium/smaller cases but better value for more complex cases'. The idea that arbitration is less expensive in complex cases is not shared by most respondents in our corpus, as exemplified in the following two extracts:

15 No (.) again it really depends on the jurisdiction .(.) because you see the emergence of really efficient courts ah.(.) with specialist judges …I think you are really getting more value for money in those courts (.) a clear example is…in the London Commercial Court (.) even in the Singapore court you get your action from start to ending in nine months (.) I mean …it's really very quick ahm…efficiency (.) top legal brains (.) fraction of the cost (.) you don't have to pay the arbitrators their fees (.) the judges are paid by the state so …why not↑ …

(AAD 2014: I3)

16 […] I mean …some people have the idea that it should be … cheaper it goes back to the idea that arbitration should be less formal… faster and cheaper but I don't think that is necessarily the case …certainly not for the kind of high value disputes that that people see now… in arbitration and I think actually … to be perfectly honest… that arbitration for high value cases is probably more expensive than litigation going on in court.

(AAD 2014: I1)

One of the respondents argued that it is not just a matter of comparing small/medium cases with more complex cases in arbitration, but comparison should be made between arbitration and litigation costs.

17 […] when we compare the cost of ah… international arbitration (.) we always have to compare it against litigation costs (.) if you had gone to court and that immediately begs the question which court (chuckle)…so for example if …you're comparing a three tribunal member arbitration going on in Geneva for two weeks and you're comparing THAT against …let's say a high court hearing for two weeks in Malaysia↑ …I'm pretty sure that Geneva (laughs) arbitration is going to come out as more expensive but if you would compare it against eh… a court of a different country (.) you know …let's say we are all in the English commercial courts with very expensive English commercial Queen's Counsels and juniors arguing it … then perhaps the Geneva ah. arbitration would be a better value (.) ahm but (.) let me see what I can say (.) which is objective (2) no matter which national court we are comparing international arbitration against (.) the SAVING that international arbitration makes in terms of costs (.) is the REDUCTION in the appeals… and so ah… with international arbitration you get your (.).I adopt the phrase .your first instance decision which is your award …right … but once you get that award it's more or less unshakable the the you know … you don't have all these appeal mechanisms (.) but if you had (.) you're comparing to a national court (.) you may get your first instance decision shall we say relatively cheaply (.) BU:T depending on the system the layers of appeal that you have to get at the end of it ah … you know it could end up costing a lot more and I think that's what we can say OBJECTIVELY without having to go into detail exactly which court am I comparing against…

(AAD 2014: I5)

The same problem was addressed from a different perspective by another respondent, who compared litigation and arbitration not just in terms of overall costs but also in terms of recoverability of the money spent by the parties.

18 In the Singapore context …your recoverability of legal cost is much better in arbitration than it is in litigation so if you're looking at it from that perspective yes you may be paying your lawyers five million dollars in legal fees but at the end of the day if you win … ahm… you may get four million dollars or four and half million dollars from the arbitrator so that's quite good recovery …whereas in litigation …at least in the Singapore context… if you pay five million dollars you may get back one million dollars.

(AAD 2014: I6)

6.4 Metaphors

If we assume that the human conceptual system is fundamentally metaphoric, we can say that metaphors are 'pervasive in human beings' language, thought and action' (Lakoff and Johnson 2003: 3). Indeed, this 'pervasiveness' is apparent not only in ordinary language (Cameron and Deignan 2006) but also in languages for specific purposes (Richardt 2005), such as in the discourse of science (Lakoff and Johnson 1980; Fahnestock 1999; Vereza 2008) and in specialised communication, including a variety of domains such as medical prose (Salager-Meyer 1990) and economics (Kermas 2006). Indeed, metaphors in the legal domain have received limited scholarly attention, and studies have mainly explored the role that metaphors may play in conflict resolution (Smith T. 2005, 2009; Chiu *et al.* 2011) and in augmenting legal reasoning and individuals' awareness of the nature of the law (Hibbitts 1994; Winter 2008). In the Italian context, metaphors have been investigated in normative texts (Morra *et al.* 2006), whereas very limited attention has been paid to spoken legal language. Recent research has focused on 'why litigation and even arbitration as a dispute resolution mechanism would serve as good a metaphor-if not a better one-for translation' (Hungpin 2014: vii). As far as our corpus is concerned, I have identified numerous groups of metaphors, each arranged around a target domain that is represented by arbitration and the source domain expressed by a variety of terms. A comparison between the Italian and Singaporean corpora shows that some of these terms, such as WAR, FIGHT, GAME, have been used by arbitration practitioners from both jurisdictions, while others are corpus-specific. For the purpose of this study, metaphors will refer to any figure of speech in which an implied comparison is made between two seemingly dissimilar things that are thought to have something in common.

6.4.1 Arbitration is war/fight

The word *fight* is quite frequent in both corpora (12 occurrences in CERG 2008 and 17 in AAD 2014) and is part of an array of noun phrases, such as *a ground for fight*, or verbal phrases, such as *fight a battle.* More specifically, the term *fight* does not occur in isolation but it is often associated with nouns and phrases belonging to the same domain, such as *enemy, tactical manoeuvre, attack, sabotage* (CERG 2008), *war, hired guns, fight hard* (AAD 2014) and others, which are often used to refer to warfare situations.

> 19 I think that's because the dispute has to do with the (.) amount involved and the importance (.) of the result (.) has therefore made the tussle over the decision more critical and when it is more critical (.) more resources are put in (.) and *we (.) the front-line soldiers*...so to speak (.) *are under more pressure to fight it out more vigorously* and so that's why it is related to the concept that the question you asked about whether or not is becoming more like litigation (.) invariably (.) invariably I mean unless the matter involved isn't large or that it is primarily eh (.) trade association in a sort of dispute over grain supply ... oil supply and it's going to be resolved by arbitrators who come from the association (.) those cases (.) you can imagine (.) can move pretty fast... (.) I mean if the stakes are (.) fifty million ...a hundred million dollars at stake (.) right↓ and if it goes both either way (.) the swing is in the larger (.) you can imagine. (.) *they will fight it out with all vigour.*
>
> (AAD 2014: I4)

In extract (19), talking about the duration of arbitration, one of the interviewees maintains that if the amount at stake is huge and the resources invested are also relevant, then counsels who are involved in the arbitration process are likely to come under pressure to be on the winning side. This situation is illustrated by the metaphor COUNSEL IS A SOLDIER, in which the counsel represents the target domain and the 'soldier' represents the source domain. Here, the concept delivered by the source domain is augmented by the noun phrase *front-line,* meaning that counsels involved in such stressful situations are forced to do their best (*fight it out more vigorously*) because they are in the same position as that of soldiers first in line for battle. The same concept is reiterated when the speaker, after mentioning multimillion disputes, asserts that parties/counsels (*they*) are highly determined (*with all vigour*) to win.

Although arbitrators are obliged to make decisions according to applicable substantive law, most arbitration laws and rules allow that decisions may be made according to the principle of '*amiable compositeur*' (also *ex aequo et bono*), provided that the parties involved agree that the arbitrator(s) can render a decision based on the principles of reasonableness and fairness. When asked about the fact that the appointment of lawyers might affect the 'amicability' of the arbitration procedure, both Italian and Singaporean respondents agreed that efforts to solve problems in an 'amicable manner' have nothing to do with arbitration itself, as clearly indicated in the following extracts:

20 In the common law system it's a very adversarial system so there is an amicable part but it comes before the arbitration once you're in arbitration *you have war* (.)

(AAD 2014: I7)

21 I don't I don't agree with the main statement I mean eh... you find sometimes arbitration clauses that say before resorting to arbitration the parties must make en effort to settle in an amicable way before as a condition to arbitration but once you are in an arbitration by definition you are in a situation where *the parties are one against the other and they have to fight a battle* which is a legal battle so they need lawyers ehm...

(CERG 2008: I5)

In (20) and (21), the speakers from common law and civil law, respectively, besides following a similar line of reasoning, adopt the same adverbial clause '*once you're in arbitration*' (20) and '*once you are in an arbitration*' (21) to introduce the metaphorical expressions '*you have war*'(20) and '*they have to fight a battle*'(21). Here, the target is represented by arbitration, while the source is war/battle. Indeed, the underlying idea is that after the arbitration procedure has commenced, parties and their counsels find themselves in an environment in which points of law and facts are harshly discussed.

The issue of '*amiable compositeur*' is also strongly criticised by all Singaporean arbitration practitioners, who, talking about the future prospects of arbitration, maintain that disputes should not be decided according to the 'fair and just' principle, as exemplified as follows.

22 I mean ...there used to be a notion that arbitration you know ... aligned with the concept of amiable compositeur (.) is that *you split the baby into two* (.) if I have a claim of fifty million ...you have a claim of twenty-five (.) maybe we'll lump it together and see how we ought to divide it up or something (.) but that's not justice (.) that's just positioning (.) and each side having his own grievance (.) rightly or wrongly ...right↑ ...justice is the requirement to go <u>INTO</u> the merits of what has happened by the governing law that they have decided to be judged (.) and so justice requires a judgment (.) and an assessment of what has happened and an assessment of who is the wrongful party and an assessment of what ought to be the reparation or compensation to the innocent (4) so to that extent (.) that is the ...the twin-similar purpose of both ...ah forms of tribunal.

(AAD 2014: I4)

23 I don't think that a good arbitration lawyer will shy a way from settlement and that's in the interest of the client (.) I think you can still use your skills as a litigator ah (.) to do certain things *to push enough buttons* to make certain applications eh that will assist in an amicable resolution eventually (2) eh so I think having those legal skills are good (.) because you don't want someone again with no disrespect (.) who has no experience in legal issues (.) to take over a process and then just decide on sort of (.) you know ... *let's cut the baby in half* (.) may not be the best cases (.) in cases (.) especially when you're dealing with high value disputes (.)

(AAD 2014: I6)

These two practitioners, on highlighting the negative aspects of resolving disputes according to the principle of '*amiable compositeur*', use two metaphorical expressions *'you split the baby into two'* and *'let's cut the baby into two'*, which clearly refer to the well-known passage from the Old Testament.[5] In arbitration, 'splitting the baby' is looked at as a very undesirable result, since the parties want the decision maker to pick a winner and a loser. From a linguistic point of view, these two metaphorical expressions provide an interesting example of idiom variation.

a *You split the baby in two* (22)
b *Let's cut the baby in two* (23)

If we consider the original phrase '*split the baby*', we see that the two speakers modified the phrase in two different ways. In (a), the respondent added the subject *you* and the prepositional phrase *in two,* while the speaker in (b) not only added the prepositional phrase *in two* but also included an internal modification, since the original verb *split* was substituted with the verb *cut.* What clearly stands out is that both speakers knew the original phrase, which was modified the very moment they uttered the phrase, thus showing a certain degree of creativity (Pitzl 2012: 47) that allowed them to deliver the meaning they had in mind. This 'creative idiom' serves the functions of both summarising and emphasising what has been said before, i.e., the concept of '*amiable compositeur*'.

Interestingly, the same pattern has been used by one of the CERG 2008 respondents, who maintained that lawyers, trained as litigators, are sometimes involved in arbitration proceedings, with the result that they tend to argue on points of law as if they were in a court.

> 24 [...]...of course ...lawyers bring ehm... to arbitration their ehm... mental structure of going to court where they argue on points of law and of course [subvocalizing] as arbitrators we often are ...confronted with lawyers or things to be in courts ... they want just writs ...*split the legal hair into sixteen parts* whilst it it is not really the... really the idea and the aim of the original arbitration.
>
> (CERG 2008: I2)

In (24), the interviewee claims that lawyers, hired as either arbitrators or counsel to the parties in arbitration proceedings, tend to keep their 'mental structure' of advocates, suggesting the idea that an advocate, even though wearing the hat of a counsel or an arbitrator, still remains an advocate with all the consequences that this may entail. Here, the idiom *split the legal hair into sixteen parts* is conceptually the same as the original English idiom 'split hairs'. That lawyers are hair-splitters is a popular commonplace and is founded on the belief that lawyers complicate the law and often complicate it unnecessarily. At a closer look, we see that the interviewee has changed the original idiom 'split hairs', not only by using *hair* in the singular form but also by including the adjective *legal,* followed by the

5 Two prostitutes carry a baby come before King Solomon and ask him to solve their dilemma. Each claims that the baby is hers. Solomon suggests they divide the baby in two, so that the women can each have a half. One woman agrees; the other says 'Give her the living child, and by no means put him to death'. Solomon declared that woman the mother, since she was putting the safety of the baby first, as a true mother would do.

prepositional phrase *into sixteen parts*, in which the single hair may be split. In this way, the idiom becomes metaphorical, because the expression *legal hair* clearly refers to the object of the dispute, and the *sixteen parts* is a metaphor of how the whole matter is treated, delivering the idea that lawyers tend to argue about details that may be ignored.

From a linguistic point of view, 'split hairs' and the newly coined expression *split the legal hair into sixteen parts* are different surface realisations of the same conceptual metaphor. The analysis supports the view that the Italian speaker, using English as a lingua franca, knows the original English idiom, but instead of employing it as it is, he modifies it so as to highlight the fact that lawyers involved in arbitration focus on the legal details of the dispute (*they just want writs*) and tend to minimise the business problem.

6.4.2 Arbitration is an animal

Metaphors are not just a figure of speech but they are also a part of a more complex process that entails the creation of new meaning through what Fauconnier and Turner (2003: 39) call 'conceptual blending'. Every time a speaker uses a metaphor, the speaker creates an imaginary space in which the target and the source do not mean what they each meant separately, but, through a blending process, a new concept comes to the surface. Indeed, humans often use animal metaphors to express the relationship with the environment and nature at large (Goatly 2006). As far as our corpus is concerned, arbitration practitioners used metaphors to frame spaces in which arbitration or issues related to arbitration are conceived in terms of animals, as in the following example.

25 […] But it's not you know it's not a *zebra ah(.) that you know …a.a…zebra that comes with stripes (.) the zebra sometimes comes without stripes* (.) unless you make sure in your clause …you see… all our dealings are private (.) you know (.) the arbitration will be a private process and bla…bla…bla and all that.

(AAD 2014: I2)

Although zebra stripes are still a mystery, it is generally believed that the white stripes are a sort of camouflage that helps zebras hide from lions, known to be colour-blind. In reality, stripes help zebras to blend with grass and bushes, making them much more difficult to be spotted. Here, the respondent intimates that failing to include a provision on privacy in the arbitration clause may result in unexpected situations in which privacy may be compromised. This is because those who are involved in drafting arbitration clauses tend to replicate what has been done in previous situations without paying too much attention to privacy. In excerpt (25), in order to deliver the idea of unexpected situations, the speaker says that a *zebra ah (.) that you know …a .a… zebra that comes with stripes.* The initial part of the metaphor clearly refers to arbitration clauses that are expected to be carefully drafted, i.e., having all necessary details; thus, the target is represented by a well-drafted arbitration clause, and the source is '*a zebra that comes with stripes*'. Unfortunately, it may happen that arbitration clauses are not drafted as they should, a situation in which *the zebra sometimes comes without stripes.* On the other hand, Italian arbitration practitioners adopted a more traditional stance, as in the following example.

26 […] I think that it is less and less frequent this kind of approach because they finally understood that that's not eh… the right approach *because arbitration is a*

> *very nice animal but has to be handled with care* and has to be adapted to every … to a case by case eh …on a case by case basis …
>
> (CERG 2008: I10)

In (26), the speaker mentions the fact that some multinational companies tend to employ the same arbitration clause over and over again, as if conditions and situations were the same. Since it is unlikely that such a situation occurs, the interviewee personifies the target (arbitration), which is '*a very nice animal*', meaning that it is an animal you may rely on even though it '*has to be handled with care*'.

6.5 Quoted direct speech

This section seeks to examine how quoted direct speech acts are embedded in the narratives and the functions they serve. From a quantitative point of view, CERG 2008 comprises 36 instances of direct speech acts, while AAD 2014 contains 64 occurrences. In both corpora, these occurrences are irregularly distributed in all sections of the questionnaire. As far as the respondents are concerned, the data show that 5 out of 12 respondents in CERG 2008 and 7 out of 8 in AAD 2014 quoted direct speech in their narratives.

Moreover, one of the CERG 2008 interviewees and one of the AAD 2014 respondents used reported speech 16 and 33 times respectively, showing that this rhetorical device is particularly suitable as a frame for the construction of language reports. Data in both corpora also show that narrators incorporated reported speech into narratives by using not only reporting verbs (*say*, *tell*, *advise*, *ask*, *persuade*) but also signalling devices, such as discourse markers and silent or filled pauses.

Drawing on Thompson (1996) and Clark and Gerrig (1990), I will analyse the stretches of language in which the interviewees make use of direct speech acts in order to include somebody else's ideas and comments. In particular, two of the aspects identified by Thompson (voice, message, signal and attitude) will be investigated, i.e., voice and message.

6.5.1 Voice

If we take the five groups of 'voices' identified by Thompson (1996: 507), i.e., self, specified other(s), unspecified other(s), community and unspecifiable other(s), we see that in our corpora that the vast majority of instances of 'voices' belong to the 'specified other(s)' group. If we consider the frequency with which these referents are referred to, both corpora comprise a similar number of occurrences. For example, parties are referred to eight times in CERG 2008 and seven times in AAD 2014, arbitrators seven times in both corpora and counsels six times in CERG 2008 and three times in AAD 2014.

What marks a difference between the two corpora is that AAD 2014 comprises instances of 'multiple voices' in the same language report, as in the examples that follow.

> 27 We were involved in that where the arbitrator having after deciding the award (.) one of parties then *wrote* in saying *by the way (.) we didn't deal with the question of interest* and so the arbitrator *said ok and here's my decision on interests (laughs)* so he wrote another award without giving the other side an opportunity to … to take their position (.) …that was set aside (.) that part of it at least.
>
> (AAD 2014: I4)

In (27), the speaker mentions a situation in which one of the parties contends that the award did not take 'the question of interest' into account. The quoted speech acts clearly refer to what one of the parties decided to do after the award was rendered. In addition, the respondent adds a further voice, that of the arbitrator who rendered a decision on this issue. Another example of 'multiple voices' is provided by the stretch of narrative as follows (28), in which the interviewee, talking about the characteristics an arbitrator should have, plays the roles of both the arbitrator and the parties involved in the arbitration process. Instead of a single point of view, the speaker is able to present different perspectives, thus becoming 'polyphonic', in Bakhtin's words (1973: 4).

28 [...] the claimant wants X the respondent wants Y and the arbitrator goes back and says *why don't the two of you eh... try to agree* and then you go back and say *look we're telling you we <u>CAN'T</u> agree please <u>DECIDE</u>* and the arbitrator again comes back and says *why don't the two...* why do they do that↑ and the answer is fear ...because the arbitrator is ...is fearful ... and he thinks you know *if the two sides agree I cannot be criticized because they agree but if I would have to decide it immediately at least one person is not happy and then I will be criticized* so I think the first characteristic is eh... <u>DECISIVENESS</u> (.) that people are paying you money to decide please don't take their money and not give the service ...<u>DECIDE↑</u>

(AAD 2014: I5)

6.5.2 *Specified other(s)*

Parties and arbitrators are the two 'voices' that are more frequent in both corpora, and this is highly expected, given the fact that the questionnaire was addressed to arbitration professionals about facets of the whole arbitration procedure. The extract that follows is largely representative of both the CERG 2008 and AAD 2014 corpora.

29 I mean the short answer is (.) by quite a lot ...ya ...and the arbitrators ...you know (4) when you sit as an arbitrator you ...you ... a very connoisseur about goes with procedural order number one this famous *PO* (.) one procedural order number one (.) and arbitrators go round sharing the drafts ... procedural order number one to see ah... you know ... *is there anything I missed out that might be useful to put into my procedure* of (.) number one ...but one of the eh... items in procedural order number one you are likely to see and it certainly appears in mind↑ ah... is *do the parties wish me to decide this dispute in accordance with law↑ or do the parties wish me to decide eh...eh... this dispute right... eh... you know ... along a mediator role ...* right ...as you have eh ...articulated (.) and in every instance the parties say *we wish you to decide this in accordance with law* (.) I suspect to the general relief of the arbitrator but the arbitrator is relieved because he is a <u>LAWYER↑</u> and so he is much more eh comfortable deciding the thing according to to law (.) then you know in this sort of brave new world which really doesn't have ...a lot of rules ...right

(AAD 2014: I5)

In (29), the respondent addresses the issue of lawyers being appointed as arbitrators and how this has affected the original aim of arbitration, i.e., to resolve disputes amicably and through the active participation of the parties involved. From a linguistic point of view, we see that the first quoted speech *is there anything I missed out that might be useful to put into my procedure* is not introduced by a reporting verb, but by the discourse marker *you know*. In addition, the noun phrase *procedural order number one* is repeated four times, and this grammatical parallelism signals involvement on the part of the speaker with the arbitration procedure that has become so deeply standardised as to make it indistinguishable from a court procedure. Indeed, the repetition of the same lexical unit performs the pragmatic function of both keeping the narration going and creating coherence. It is also worth pointing out that the speaker makes use of the acronym PO (procedural order), assuming the interlocutor's shared knowledge of the arbitration procedure. Commenting on the fact that arbitration procedures give way to more formal procedures, one of the CERG 2008 interviewees asserted that the increase in the number of new arbitrators had inevitably led to situations in which these new arbitrators would request more guarantees, thus favouring the process of judicialisation of arbitration itself, as exemplified in the following excerpt, in which the narrator animates one of these 'new' arbitrators.

> 30 The qualities getting lower and so the reaction is to find I think guarantees … parachutes like …ok so *I wa:nt the right to be HEARD* (.) *I want to use the right to be HEARD* (.) *I want the RIGHT to give you* so this is [throat clearing] probably the noble reason of this *processualizzazione* (*judicialization* my translation).
>
> (CERG 2008: I10)

Here, the verbal phrase *I want* is repeated three times. On uttering this lexical unit, the speaker expands the meaning of the verbal form *I want* by adding *to use* in the second sentence and refines the same meaning by adding the verbal phrase *to give you* to the third sentence. It is also worth noting that the past participle *HEARD*, uttered twice, and the noun *RIGHT* are pronounced more loudly than their surrounding speech. Thus, emphasis is put on *heard* and *right*, meaning that these new arbitrators are likely to find themselves in situations in which something you should be allowed to have by law is to be strongly and openly requested. In addition, the speaker uses the metaphorical word *parachutes* as a source domain, the target domain being the guarantees that these new arbitrators expect to be given. The aim of keeping the flow of narration going is also indicated by the use of the term *processualizzazione*, uttered in Italian as if the narrator were more eager to deliver the exact meaning of what he had in mind, rather than to offer a tentative translation of the Italian term *processualizzazione* into English. Moreover, this excerpt offers an interesting example of an 'unquote' (Golato 2000: 31), which occurs when the boundaries of a quotation are clearly marked by the use of a conjunction (*so* in this case), which signals both the beginning of the quotation and a switch from the reported speech to the narrative, serving the pragmatic function of allowing the speaker to exit the quotation frame.

6.5.3 Message

According to Thompson (1996: 512), a message may be reported in five different ways, i.e., via a quote, echo, paraphrase, summary and omission. For the purpose of this study, only quotes will be investigated.

6.5.3.1 Quotes

The issue of context seems to be particularly important, not only because it provides essential information on the place, the time and the professional status of the interviewees but also because it furnishes notice about the narrator's native/nonnative speaker status. As far as CERG 2008 is concerned, we know that the direct speech acts were originally uttered in Italian and that the frame shift had undergone two different phases. Indeed, we know very little about this original frame, and we can only provide a description of the context in which the words were uttered, but not the actual words that were used. Then, this original frame shifted into a secondary frame, that of the reported speech, in which the Italian respondents converted the speech acts uttered in Italian into direct speech acts in English, using English as a lingua franca, as in the following example:

> 31 [...] I remember when ah... having to draft an arbitration clause in the old system e::hm there would be no one excluding (1.2) no lawyer really in his senses excluding the appeal because (.) *beh if we lose what happens we cannot appeal ehm.*
>
> (CERG 2008: I2)

In (31), the quotation is introduced by the discourse markers *beh* [*well* my translation], which signals that the speaker, while presenting the problems connected with the drafting of an arbitration clause, focuses on the possibility of having to face an unfavourable award. The use of the discourse marker *beh* introduces the uneasy situation in which an appeal cannot even be considered unless it is clearly provided for in the arbitration clause. The second discourse marker *ehm*, placed at the end, defines the boundary of the reported speech and allows the speaker to exit the quotation itself. Indeed, quotations may be differently embedded into the narrative flow as with 'partial quotes' (Thompson 1996: 513), which occur when one or more quotes appear within paraphrases and summaries.

> 32 [...] I have been discussing this kind of problems with in-house counsels of a multinational ...and *they tell me* eh (.) when we have (1.5) *because they have very often trans-national matters* (.) disputes and *they say* well (.) first we try negotiation (1.5) direct (.) then we try mediation negotiation with the facilitator *as you know* (.) mediator who tries to put the parties together without having the possibility to impose or to even suggest a solution (.) *then of course* we resort to arbitration because eh (1.2) there is a clause already in a contract in this case because the choice of a a jurisdiction eh (1.7) or a jurisdictional court would be often eh:m (.) either risky or not accepted by the other party of course we are a multinational a German company would say ok *let's come to Germany and and fight out but the Chinese would say no excuse me I don't come into your tent to be devoured* (laughs) ...
>
> (CERG 2008: I2)

In (32), the narration begins with a quotation introduced by the reporting verbal phrase *they tell me,* interrupted by the parenthetical clause *because they have very often trans-national matters,* which serves to clarify the context in which the original words might have been uttered. Then, the quotation is resumed by the reporting verbal phrase *they say,* and after that, the narrator switches from quoting direct speech to summarising the role and function of mediation within the arbitration process. This shifting is signalled by the discourse marker *as you know,* which serves to include the hearer in what is being reported. Next, the narrator switches again to reported speech, and this switching is signalled by the adverbial clause *then of course.* After that, and quite unexpectedly, the narrator drops the direct speech and provides a summary in which the advantages of having an arbitration clause included in the contract are indicated. After giving this summary, the respondent switches again to direct speech introduced by the adverbial clause *of course,* followed by the pronoun *we*, which initiates the direct speech act. Indeed, this stretch of language shows that the narrator's attempt to report the two parties' positions is likely to have involved considerable reshaping of the original speech acts. One party is reported to have said: *let's come to Germany and fight out* and the other to have replied: *no excuse me I don't come into your tent to be devoured.* Although it is very unlikely that both parties used metaphors such as *fight out* and *to be devoured* in their spoken interaction, it appears to be very likely that the narrator tried to metaphorically describe a situation in which one of the parties was inevitably bound to lose.

As regards AAD 2014, all respondents but one confirmed that they were native speakers of English, and this is perfectly in line with the recent history of Singapore (Chew 2014). What Italian and Singaporean interviewees have in common is that they used quotations to give a general picture of what the reported people meant. In other words, what the narrators have provided is not just a description of what was said, but what Clark and Gerrig (1990: 767) call a 'strip of depicting behaviour', as in the following example:

> 33 [...] where you have some aged arbitrators who'll say *fine (.) before even open a sheet of paper ...let's talk about how much you are going to pay me for this process* (.) whether as for an institution (.) they do that to an extent but the institution has a lot of procedural safeguards built in (.) where they determine upfront for example SIAC has got a fee calculator on the website (.) you can tell upfront *ok these are the maximum fees you'll be paying so you know upfront ...ok this is what we are going to do...*
>
> (AAD 2014: I6)

In (33), the respondent, talking about the costs that parties may have to face, compares ad hoc and institutionalised arbitration. The first quotation, which mentions the arbitrators' request in terms of fees, is complemented by a summary illustrating how arbitral institutions usually operate in determining these fees. The summary is followed by another quotation showing the advantages for parties when they decide to apply to an arbitral institution.

Excerpts (32) and (33) show that quotations and summaries may coexist in the same narration and that the interplay between these two different options enables the narrator not only to provide the information requested but also to give some 'colour' to what has been narrated.

6.5.4 Functions

Thompson (1996: 512) states that quotations serve two main functions, i.e., to 'indicate a higher degree of faithfulness to an original (or possible) language event' and to 'present the reported language event more vividly to the hearer by simulating the original event'. Although these two functions have been largely employed by the respondents in our corpus, it seems relevant to point out that four more functions have been identified in our corpus, i.e., demonstrating the validity or the likelihood of what narrators are reporting, providing internal or embedded evaluation, adding credibility to the narrative and shifting responsibility from the narrator to the person(s) quoted. From a quantitative point of view, both CERG 2008 and AAD 2014 show a similar distribution, since '*demonstrating the validity or the likelihood of what narrators are reporting*' appears to be the most frequent (8 and 16 instances, respectively), followed by '*shifting responsibility from the narrator to the person(s) quoted*' (five and eight instances, respectively) and '*providing internal or embedded evaluation*' (two and four instances, respectively), while '*adding credibility to the narrative*' is the least frequent of all (two and one instances, respectively). Given the limited occurrences of the last two functions, we will provide examples of the most frequent ones.

6.5.4.1 Demonstrating the validity or the likelihood of what narrators are reporting

One of the reasons why speakers include quoted direct speech acts in their narrative is that they want to add liveliness to what they are saying. This may also give the impression of authentic recollection of an event, even though it would be inadvisable to assume that these direct speech acts report 'verbatim' the actual words used.

34 [...] so the aim as a counsel is to make the witness appear as a <u>LIAR</u> to the tribunal (.) so you'd ask questions like *'are you lying now' or 'were you lying then' 'you're not being honest' 'you're not being truthful'* (.)

(AAD 2014: I3)

35 [...] We really had one ... he challenged one of arbitrators and the ...the judge in Milano decided that he ... should have challenged before the institution ... that was our position ...*we told him ...you can challenge ...but you can challenge here not in state court* ...that what the state court judge decided and that was a good ... good ...decision.

(CERG 2008: I10)

In (34), the speaker's narration is about the role that a counsel is expected to play when cross-examining, i.e., to make a witness appear unreliable to the members of an arbitration tribunal. In order to show the validity of what he is saying, he inserts direct speech acts that reproduce what he is likely to have asked the witness. Under certain circumstances, it is reasonable to suppose that the words uttered were so memorable that they stuck in the speaker's memory, thus enabling him to repeat them almost verbatim. A different situation is illustrated in (35). Here, one of the parties decided to challenge one of the arbitrators in a state court, even though the arbitrator was appointed by an arbitral institution. The speaker, after mentioning the judge's decision in favour of the arbitral institution, puts in the stretch of direct speech '*we told him...you can challenge ...but you can challenge here not in state court*', which serves to demonstrate that the party should have challenged the arbitrator in the arbitral institution, i.e., *here*, and not in a state court.

6.5.4.2 Shifting responsibility from the narrator to the person(s) quoted

36 [...] but the tribunal called us and the hearings were in three weeks (.) he said *if you want a block of three weeks (.) the earliest we can give you is (.) March 2015* and this is last year that they were telling us *(.) unless you are prepared to come to London (.) we can see ...it's actually a sole arbitrator ...ahm...because I need to be there* (.) so everybody had to go to London (.) and we had spent ... eh did the hearing there because he was too busy (.)

(AAD 2014: I7)

37 [...] As I said they sometimes have a strong impact because sometimes it is not even a question of a policy of a company but is a question of laziness of the people involved in negotiation they take a precedent and they say *this worked two years ago why shouldn't it work now* eh ...

(CERG 2008: I5)

In (36), the respondent mentions the problem of arbitrations taking much longer than expected. Indeed, delays in concluding arbitration procedures may be caused by various factors, including the fact that the most renowned arbitrators are very busy people. Here, responsibility for a delay is clearly shifted to arbitrators who impose conditions such as *if you want a block of three weeks ...the earliest we can give you in ...March 2015* or *unless you are prepared to come to London*. A critical situation is portrayed in (37), where the speaker, talking about standard arbitration clauses employed by multinational companies, maintains that those who are involved in business transactions, generically referred to as *people involved in negotiation*, sometimes arrive at important decisions using procedures that, successfully employed in the past, are supposed to be effective in similar situations (*they say... this worked two years ago why shouldn't it work now*), denoting that important aspects, such as the drafting of arbitration clauses, are sometimes treated carelessly.

6.6 Conclusions

Our findings show that all respondents from both CERG 2008 and AAD 2014 are well aware of the fact that arbitration is significantly affected by both the procedures and the language of litigation, thus making arbitration similar to litigation, even with differences determined by the legal systems and the overall attitude towards arbitration.

For example, in Italy, legislation on arbitration, even though recently amended, has not shown it to be arbitration-friendly, and this has confined Italy to the fringe of the international arbitration market, as recent statistics have shown (Bonsignore 2010). In Singapore, instead, legislation has given arbitration a favourable position, thus making this small city state a leading hub for international commercial arbitration.

A factor that should be taken into account is that the professionals involved in arbitration from both countries are largely legal practitioners who have mainly acted as litigators, thus transferring their professional culture into a practice, which was meant to be different.

From a linguistic point of view, this study has shown similarities and differences in the language used by the interviewees. As far as CERG 2008 is concerned, findings show that the majority of respondents, mainly NNSs of English, employ an array of rhetorical devices, such as metaphors, borrowings, code-switching and quoted reported speech. As regards AAD 2014, we have seen that the Singapore respondents made use of metaphors and quoted direct speech, but did not employ any borrowing and code-switching devices, and this is likely to be due to the respondents' NSs of English condition. The picture that emerges from this research is that the narrators of arbitration practices from both corpora make quite an extensive use of reported speech and that the quoted speech acts in the corpus are not a verbatim reproduction of the direct speech acts uttered either in Italian or in English, but that they have undergone significant reshaping and reworking of the original speech acts. The analysis also supports the view that quoted reported speech has served an array of functions, such as demonstrating the validity or the likelihood of what is being reported, shifting responsibility from the narrator to the person(s) quoted and intensifying the reported events by animating different actors, i.e., arbitrators, counsels and parties.

Indeed, the level of involvement was found to vary according to the respondents' different attitudes. Some of the interviewees from both corpora who were deeply involved in the narrating process used quoted reported speech quite extensively, adding liveliness to their narratives, while others just provided the requested information.

From a lexical viewpoint, one of the most salient differences between the two corpora lies in the fact that CERG 2008 interviewees used a consistent number of Latin words, phrases and even maxims, while there is no trace of Latinate forms in AAD 2014. The most obvious explanation for this is that Italian arbitration practitioners are so deeply 'rooted' in legal culture, which is mainly litigation-oriented that, when narrating their personal experiences in arbitration, they tend to use lexical items that are typical of litigation language. It is well known that this kind of language is conservative in nature, and legal texts tend to be produced and reproduced according to established formats and formulas, which contributes to making legal language stable and in line with the conventions of the community of legal practitioners. Moreover, the use of Latin words and formulas serves the pragmatic function of delivering specific legal content in a limited number of words.

In conclusion, it can be argued that, given the limited number of interviewees, these results do not allow us to draw definitive conclusions, even though this study may contribute to starting a more comprehensive comparison between such different cultural and professional arbitration environments.

Acknowledgements

The author would like to acknowledge the assistance given by the following Italian and Singaporean advocates and arbitration practitioners, whose precious collaboration has made this study possible:

Adv. Stefano Azzali
Adv. Prof. Massimo Benedettelli
Adv. Gabriele Bonivento
Adv. Raja Bose
Adv. Cecilia Carrara
Adv. Roberto Casati
Adv. Giovanni De Berti
Adv. Samuel Chacko
Adv. William McGurn
Adv. Steven Y.H.Lim
Prof. Angelo Lucchini
Adv. Stefano Modenesi
Adv. Micael Montinari
Adv. Alberto Nanni
Adv. Kah Cheong Lye
Adv. Cristina Pagni
Dr Stefano Pavletič
Adv. Paul Sandosham
Adv. Kabir Singh
Adv. Francis Xavier
Adv. Jimmy Yim
Adv. Paolo Gnignati

Appendix 1: Transcription conventions

The audio recorded materials in the corpus have been transcribed according to the following conventions.

Symbol	*Represents*
(.)	Micro-pause (<0.2 s)
(1.8)	Timed pause
<?>	Unintelligible speech
a::nd	Colons represent lengthened vowel sound
RIGHT	Underlined, capitalized word shows emphatic stress, enunciated louder than surrounding speech.
↑ ↓	Indicate rising/falling intonation
< >	False start
o </>	Incomplete word (complete of)
Items in brackets indicate non-transcribable vocalisations or other actions	(Chuckle)
	(Slight intake of breath)
	(Breath intake)
	(Throat clearing)
	(Subvocalising)

References

Aksen, Gerald 2007. Reflections of an international arbitrator. *Arbitration International* 23/2, 255–259.

Bakhtin, Michail 1973. *Problems of Dostoevsky's Poetics*. Ann Arbor, MI: Ardis.

Banfield, Ann 1982. *Unspeakable Sentences. Narration and Representation in the Language of Fiction*. Boston: Routledge and Kegan Paul.

Belotti, Ulisse 2012a. Arbitration in Italy: a two-headed Janus? In Bhatia, Vijay K. *et al.* (eds) *Discourse and Practice in International Commercial Arbitration. Issues, Challenges and Prospects*. Farnham: Ashgate, 239–261.

Belotti, Ulisse 2012b. *Dispute Resolution Narratives. A Linguistic Analysis of Arbitration Practices*. CERLIS Series, Vol. 2. Bergamo: CELSB Libreria Universitaria. Online at http://hdl.handle.net/10446/27256.

Belotti, Ulisse and Maria Carla Giorgetti 2015. Critical aspects of arbitration practices. Narratives from Singapore. In Bhatia Vijay K. and Gotti, Maurizio (eds) *Arbitration Discourse in Asia*. Bern: Peter Lang, 183–224.

Bhatia, Vijay K. 2011. Witness examination as interdiscursive practice. *World Englishes* 30/1, 106–116.

Bhatia, Vijay K., Candlin, Cristopher N., Engberg, Jan, and Trosborg, Anna (eds) 2003a. *Multilingual and Multicultural Contexts of Legislation. An International Perspective*. Frankfurt am Main: Peter Lang.

Bhatia, Vijay K., Candlin, Cristopher N., Gotti, Maurizio (eds) 2003b. *Legal Discourse in Multilingual and Multicultural Contexts. Arbitration Texts in Europe*. Bern: Peter Lang.

Bhatia, Vijay K., Candlin, Cristopher N., and Gotti, Maurizio (eds) 2010. *The Discourses of Dispute Resolution*. Bern: Peter Lang.

Bhatia, Vijay K., Candlin, Cristopher N., and Gotti, Maurizio (eds) 2012. *Discourse and Practice in International Commercial Arbitration. Issues, Challenges and Prospects*. Farnham: Ashgate.

Bonsignore, Vincenza 2010. La Diffusione della Giustizia Alternativa in Italia nel 2008: I Risultati di una Ricerca. In *Terzo Rapporto* 125 *sulla Diffusione della Giustizia Alternativa in Italia*. ISDACI, Unioncamere, Camera di Commercio di Milano, Camera Arbitrale di Milano 2010. Online at http://blogconciliazione.com/upcontent/uploads/2010/02/Ebook-Terzo-Rapporto.pdf, Accessed June 2009.

Cameron, Lynne 2007. Patterns of metaphor use in reconciliation talk. *Discourse and Society* 18, 197–222.

Cameron, Lynne, and Deignan, Alice 2006. The emergence of metaphor in discourse. *Applied Linguistics* 27/4, 671–690.

Chew, Phyllis Ghim-Lian 2014. The role of English as a lingua franca in institutions of hugher education in Singapore. *The Asian Journal of Applied Linguistics* 1/1, 28–35.

Chiu, Sheng-hsiu and Chiang, Wen-yu 2011. FIGHT metaphors in legal discourse: what is unsaid in the story? *Language and Linguistics* 12/4, 877–915.

Clark, Herbert H. and Gerrig, Richard J. 1990. Quotations as demonstrations. *Language* 66, 764–805.

Cymrot, Mark A. 2007. Cross-examination in international arbitration. *Dispute Resolution Journal* 62/1, 52–65.

Elsing, Siegfried H. and Townsend, John 2002. Bridging the common law civil law divide in arbitration. *Arbitration International* 1/1, 1–7.

Fahnestock, Jeanne 1999. *Rhetorical Figures in Science*. New York: Oxford University Press.

Fairclough, Norman 1992. *Discourse and Social Change*. Cambridge: Polity Press.

Fauconnier, Gilles and Turner, Mark 2003. *The Way We Think: Conceptual Blending and the Mind's Hidden Complexities*. New York: Basic Books.

Goatly, Andrew 2006. Humans, animals, and metaphors. *Society & Animals* 14/1, 15–37. Online at https://doi.org/10.1163/156853006776137131. Accessed June 2014.

Golato, Andrea 2000. An innovative German quotative for reporting on embodied actions: Und ich so/under so 'and I'm like/and he's like'. *Journal of Pragmatics* 32, 29–54.

Gómez Domínguez, Luis Alfonso 2007. Causes and consequences of faulty arbitration clauses. Estudios Socio-Jurídicos, Bogotá (Colombia), 9/2, 111–141.

Gotti, Maurizio 2012. The judicialization of arbitration discourse in the Italian context. In Bhatia, Vijay K. *et al.* (eds) *Discourse and Practice in International Commercial Arbitration. Issues, Challenges and Prospects*. Farnham: Ashgate: 129–146.

Hafner, Cristoph A. 2011. Professional reasoning, legal cultures, and arbitral awards. *World Englishes,* 30/1, 117–128.

Hibbitts, Bernard J. 1994. Making sense of metaphors: visuality, aurality and the reconfiguration of American legal discourse. *Cardozo Law Review* 16/2, 229–356.

Hungpin, Pierre Hsieh 2014 *The Mediator, the Negotiator, the Arbitrator or the Judge? –Translation as Dispute Resolution*. Thesis for the MA degree in Translation Studies. School of Translation and Interpretation – Faculty of Arts – University of Ottawa. Online at www.ruor.uottawa.ca/bitstream/10393/30562/1/Hsieh_Hungpin_Pierre_2014_thesis.pdf, Accessed 19 February 2015.

Hunston, Susan 1993. 'Projecting a sub-culture. The construction of shared worlds by projecting clauses in two registers'. In Graddol, David *et al.* (eds) *Language and Culture*. Clevedon: BAAL and Multilingual Matters.

Kathpalia, Sujata 2012. Is arbitration being colonized by litigation? Practitioners' views in the Singapore context. In Bhatia, Vijay K. *et al.* (eds) *Discourse and Practice in International Commercial Arbitration. Issues, Challenges and Prospects*. Farnham: Ashgate Publishing Limited, 263–281.

Kermas, Susan 2006. Metaphor and ideology in business and economic discourse in British and American English. In Flowerdew, John and Gotti, Maurizio (eds) *Studies in Specialized Discourse*. Bern: Peter Lang, 109–129.

Koller, Veronika 2003. Metaphor Clusters in Business Media Discourse: A Social Cognition Approach. Doctorial Thesis. Vienna University.

Lakoff, George and Johnson, Mark 2003. *Metaphors We Live By*. Chicago: The University of Chicago Press.

Morra, Lucia, Rossi, Piercarlo, and Bazzanella, Carla 2006. Metaphor in legal language. In Wagner, Anne and Cacciaguidi-Fahy, Sophie (eds) *Legal Language and the Search for Clarity*, Bern: Peter Lang, 141–174.

Moses, Margaret L. 2012. Ethics in international arbitration: traps for the unwary. *Loyola University Chicago International Law Review* 10/1, 73–80.

Nariman, Fali S. 2000. The spirit of arbitration: the tenth annual Goff lecture. *Arbitration International*, 16/3, 261–278.

Patocchi, Paolo M. and Schiavello, Giuseppe 1998. Arbitrato irrituale: how it should be handled in a non-Italian jurisdiction? A discussion from a Swiss perspective. LLP; riprinted from *The Arbitration and Dispute Resolution Law Journal*, June 1998: 132–151.

Pitzl, Marie-Luise 2012. Creativity meets convention: idion variation and re-metaphorization in EFL. *Journal of English as a Lingua Franca*, 1/1, 27–55.

PricewaterhouseCoopers 2013. Corporate choices in international arbitration. Industry perspective. Online at www.pwc.com/gx/en/arbitration-dispute-resolution/assets/pwc-international-arbitration-study.pdf, Accessed July 2015.

Richardt, Susanne 2005. *Metaphor in Languages for Special Purposes: The Function of Conceptual Metaphor in Written Expert Language and Expert-Lay Communication in the Domains of Economics, Medicine and Computing*. Bern: Peter Lang.

Salager-Meyer, Françoise 1990. Metaphors in medical English prose: a comparative study with French and Spanish. *English for Specific Purposes* 9, 145–159.

Smit, Robert H. and Robinson, Tyler B. 2010. Cost awards in international commercial arbitration: proposed guidelines for promoting time and cost efficiency. *The American Review of International Arbitration* 20, 267–284.

Smith, Thomas H. 2005. Metaphors for navigating negotiations. *Negotiation Journal* 21, 343–364.

Smith, Thomas H. 2009. When experts educate, what do their metaphors say? Complex metaphor structure in the professional conflict resolution literature. *Iberica* 17, 175–195.

SoundScriber 2004. Regents of the University of Michigan. Online at www-personal.umich.edu/~ebreck/sscriber.html, Accessed June 2005.

Stipanovich, Thomas J. 2008. Arbitration: the "new litigation". Online at http://microlib.cc.utexas.edu, Accessed January 2012.

Swales, John 1990. *Genre Analysis. English in Academic and Research Settings*. Cambridge: Cambridge University Press.

Thompson, Geoff 1996. Voices in the text: discourse perspectives on language reports. *Applied Linguistics* 12/4, 365–382.

Thompson, Geoff and Ye, Yiyun 1991. Evaluation in the reporting verbs used in academic papers. *Applied Linguistics* 12/4, 365–382.

Townsend, John M. 2003. Drafting arbitration clauses: avoiding the 7 deadly sins. *Dispute Arbitration Journal* 58/1, 28–36.

Trompenaars, Fons and Hampden-Turner, Charles 1998. *Riding the Waves of Culture*. New York: McGraw-Hill.

Vereza, Solange 2008. Exploring metaphors in corpora. A study of '*war*' in corpus generated data. In Zanotto, Maria Sophia *et al.* (eds) *Confronting Metaphor in Use. An Applied Linguistic Approach*. Amsterdam/Philadelphia: John Benjamins Publishing Company, 163–180.

Voloshinov, Valentin Nikolaevich 1973. *Marxism and the Philosophy of Language*. New York: Teachers College Press.

Waugh, Linda R. 1995. Reported speech in journalistic discourse. The relation of function and text. *Text* 15, 129–173.

Winter, Steven L. 2008. What is the 'colour' of law? In Gibbs, Raymond W., Jr. (ed.) *The Cambridge Handbook of Metaphor and Thought*. Cambridge and New York: Cambridge University Press, 363–379.

7 Arbitration discourse in Vietnam

Challenges and opportunities[1]

Patrizia Anesa and Net Le

7.1 Introduction

Over the past two decades, many Asian countries have made considerable efforts to promote the use of Alternative Dispute Resolution (ADR) to settle international disputes and to ensure that their jurisdictions are in line with international standards in the field of arbitration (D'Agostino 2014). Admittedly, regions such as Hong Kong and Singapore still dominate the arbitration scene, but in other countries in the Asia-Pacific area, interest in arbitration is increasing.

This chapter focuses on the developments that international arbitration has undergone in Vietnam. This country has considerably modernised its arbitration legislation and consolidated the activity of its arbitration centres with the aim to satisfy the expectation of both Vietnamese and foreign parties. More specifically, the focus of this study is twofold. First, it aims at delineating the main legal aspects that typify arbitration in Vietnam, illustrating the general legal framework within which arbitration develops. Second, it investigates the opinions and perceptions of professionals operating in the field in order to identify the main prospects and challenges. Data have been collected through interviews with Vietnamese arbitrators.[2]

Thus, the legal perspective is combined with a cultural one, which we hope will allow the analysis of arbitration discourse to delineate the fundamental elements that characterise arbitration in Vietnam beyond the purely technical legal aspects.

7.2 Arbitration in Vietnam

7.2.1 Background

Arbitration in Vietnam has undergone substantial transformation in recent years. First of all, a legal regime that supports and favours the use of arbitration has been implemented (see Section 3). Moreover, the activity of the arbitration centres present in the country has considerably intensified. Namely, the centres operating in Vietnam are as follows: ASEAN International Arbitration Centre, Can Tho Commercial Arbitration Centre (CCAC), Financial Commercial Arbitration Centre (FCCA), Ho Chi Minh City Commercial

1 Although this chapter has been jointly written, Patrizia Anesa's contribution mainly concerns Sections 7.1, 7.2, 7.4, 7.5. Net Le's contribution mainly concerns Section 3. Both authors are responsible for Section 6.

2 We would like to express our deepest gratitude to the professionals who have kindly agreed to be interviewed for the purpose of this project, namely: Vu Xuan Phong, Nguyen Dang Trung, Hoang Nguyen Duc, Dinh Thi Quynh Nhu, and Tuan Anh Phan. We are also indebted to Vietnam International Arbitration Centre and Pacific International Arbitration Centre for the precious assistance received during the data collection process.

Arbitration Centre (TRACENT), Indochina Trade Arbitration Centre (ITAC), Pacific International Arbitration Centre (PIAC), Vietnam Financial Banking Arbitration Centre (VIFIBAR), and Vietnam International Arbitration Centre (VIAC). Among them, VIAC[3] is by far the most renowned institution, with a volume of disputes amounting to almost one billion USD in 2015.

In particular, such centres have gradually moved towards the promotion of arbitration by implementing rules that are in line with the United Nations Commission on International Trade Law (UNCITRAL) Model Law. For instance, VIAC amended its rules of arbitration in 2012 and PIAC in 2014 (to a great extent replicating those of VIAC).

It is interesting to note that these centres often list several international arbitrators on their webpages, together with the languages they speak, in order to attract foreign parties who would prefer their arbitration to be conducted in a language other than Vietnamese.

Arbitration centres also support research activities and encourage publications and participation at international conferences on arbitration, with the aim to promote Vietnam centres as potential seats of arbitration.

VIAC is the best-known centre and was formally established in 1993 as a merger between the Foreign Trade Arbitration Committee (set up in 1963) and the Marine Arbitration Committee (created in 1964). Its activity is constantly growing, as illustrated in Figure 7.1.

Figure 7.2 presents the distribution of disputes. In 2015, international disputes represented around 37% of the cases dealt with by VIAC. Although domestic disputes clearly represent the majority, attempts have been made to make Vietnam a more attractive seat for international arbitration.

The nationalities of those parties involved in international disputes at VIAC in 2015 are summarised in Table 7.1. The prevalence of Asian parties is manifest, with Chinese distinctly constituting the prevailing nationality. However, different continents are represented, and, interestingly, European countries such as Italy, Switzerland, or the Netherlands are also becoming involved.

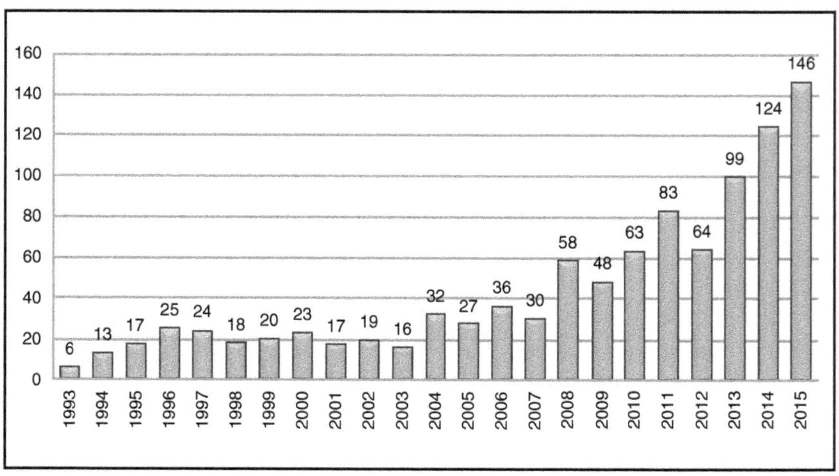

Figure 7.1 Number of disputes in VIAC (1993–2015).
Source: http://eng.viac.vn.

3 See www.viac.org.vn for more information.

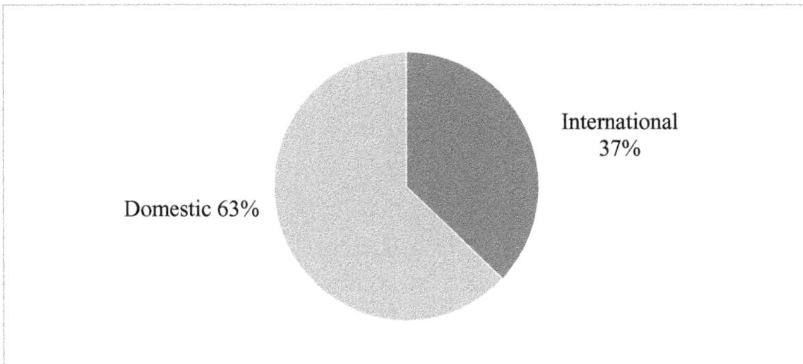

Figure 7.2 International/Domestic disputes filed at VIAC.
Source: https://vietnamarbitration.wordpress.com/.

Table 7.1 Nationality of parties involved in 2015

Nationality	*Number of disputes*
China (including Hong Kong)	23
Taiwan	5
Singapore	3
India	2
Korea	2
Russia	2
Japan	2
US	2
Philippines	2
Switzerland	1
UAE	1
Italy	1
Australia	1
Bermuda	1
Cambodia	1
Netherlands	1

Source: https://vietnamarbitration.wordpress.com/.

VIAC also has a mediation centre. Before entering into the content of the disputes, the parties are encouraged to settle the dispute through negotiation or mediation. At any time, the parties can negotiate, even during the arbitration, as this is seen as a convenient way to settle the dispute. As one of the respondents to our interview stated, "The decision is up to the parties. It is just something that is encouraged" (R1[4]). If parties cannot successfully negotiate, then they proceed with arbitration. Indeed, Article 27 of the VIAC Rules recites:

> The Arbitral Tribunal shall, at the request of the parties, conduct a mediation. If the mediation is successful, a minutes of successful mediation shall be drafted.[5] The minutes shall be signed by the parties and the Arbitrators or the Sole Arbitrator.

4 Respondent 1.

5 Inaccuracies or non-standard forms present in the original texts cited (documents or interviews) have been preserved.

> In such a case, the Arbitral Tribunal shall make the Decision recognizing the successful mediation. The Decision of the Arbitral Tribunal shall be as valid as an Arbitral Award.

Respondent 1 also clearly points out, "We don't interfere. We encourage," to emphasise the voluntary aspect of opting for mediation.

7.2.2 The future of arbitration

In Vietnam, professionals, trainees, and students are developing a deeper knowledge of arbitration procedures and a higher awareness of the importance of ADR methods. Currently, arbitration is not usually taught as a subject in Vietnamese universities, but it is commonly part of other, more general courses.

The future of arbitration in Vietnam is defined as "bright" by one of the respondents (R3). Indeed, Vietnam has developed important business and trade relationships at international level, for example, with other Asian countries, America, and Africa. Consequently, more business inevitably leads to more disputes.

One fundamental agreement that has recently been signed by Vietnam is the TPP (Trans-Pacific Partnership), whose aim is the liberalisation of trade between the partner countries. Signatories include Canada, the United States, Mexico, Peru, Chile, Japan, Vietnam, Malaysia, Brunei, Singapore, Australia, and New Zealand. The TPP represents the largest trade agreement ever signed, and the free trade area involved makes up 40% of the global economy.

Analysts point out the considerable advantages of this partnership for the Vietnamese economy. The estimation is that it will lead to an increase in Vietnam's GDP of 8%–10%. Indeed, the export of Vietnamese products is likely to increase as the agreement establishes the elimination or reduction of tariffs. This will be particularly beneficial for the agricultural and textile sectors. The agreement also sets forth the liberation of trade in services, which will help to boost a sector that still has a considerable amount of growth potential within the Vietnamese economy.

Analysts also predict that this agreement will be particularly valuable for Vietnam, in that it also includes specific anti-corruption and good governance clauses. Both aspects are indeed crucial, as they have often represented a deterrent to foreign investment.

Thus, the intensification of commercial exchanges, the implementation of political reforms, and the consequent growth of foreign investment will increase the need for international arbitration. (Note: The recent turn of events in which President Trump has abandoned this 12 nation Trans-Pacific Partnership will have geopolitical and possibly international trade agreements implications.)

7.3 The legal framework

Traditionally, the Vietnamese legal culture is considered particularly hybrid, in that while the codification is largely inherited from the French system, culturally there exists a general "reluctance to bring a dispute into court," which is probably linked to the Taoist tradition (Le et al. 2016: 2).

Vietnam is signatory to the New York Convention on the Recognition and Enforcement of Foreign Arbitral Awards of 1958, subject to the reciprocity reservation (it will only enforce awards of other signatory states) and the commerciality reservation (it will only enforce awards which are deemed commercial under national law). It is not signatory to the Washington Convention of 1965.

Arbitration is considered relatively new in Vietnam (Lien 2013: 569). From a legislative perspective, the first step towards the use of arbitration was the promulgation of Decree No. 116-CP in 1994, followed by the Ordinance on Commercial Arbitration (the Ordinance) in 2003. This text replaced all previous relevant legislation on arbitration, and its principles are based on the UNCITRAL Model Law.

Arbitration in Vietnam is currently governed, in particular, by the 2011 Law on Commercial Arbitration (LCA), which covers the following issues:

- jurisdiction of arbitration;
- arbitration institutions and proceedings;
- court involvement in arbitration;
- establishment and operation of foreign arbitration in Vietnam;
- enforcement of arbitral awards.

The 2014 Resolution Guiding the Implementation of Certain Provisions of Law on Commercial Arbitration by the Supreme People's Court aims to guarantee the accurate and consistent enforcement of the regulations of the LCA. More precisely, the scope is to guide the implementation of certain provisions of the LCA on the power, sequence, and procedures of the Court over arbitration, and registration of ad hoc arbitral awards (Article 1).

The LCA governs both domestic and foreign arbitration. The latter concerns disputes settled by a tribunal established under foreign law (Article 3.11). This approach clearly follows the UNCITRAL Model Law.

As regards the possibility of acting as an arbitrator, it has been claimed that the requirements, which include full legal capacity, education, and experience, may allow a vast range of people to act as arbitrators, but, on the other hand, it is also feared that this may lead to poor quality in the conduct of arbitration. However, the statistics from VIAC prove otherwise, and most arbitral awards are successfully enforced (Le 2015). VIAC has a roster of reputable lawyers, economists, and public officers, which includes many foreign lawyers and engineers.

One respondent to our interviews has stated that approximately 80% of arbitrators have a legal background, with a degree in law. Others may come from other fields and have experience in business and economics. As arbitration becomes more popular, it is plausible to presume that, in the future, more professions will be involved in arbitration.

The LCA has contributed to attracting foreign arbitrators and lawyers, as branches and representative offices of foreign arbitration institutions are now permitted to operate in Vietnam. Before the introduction of the LCA, only Vietnamese nationals could be appointed as arbitrators, which was somehow antithetical to the nature of international arbitration. Moreover, unlike in litigative procedures, in arbitration, a foreign lawyer is not required to be admitted to the Vietnamese National Bar. Thus, it may well be argued that "with the increase in disputes applying foreign laws, involvement of foreign lawyers will become essential in arbitral proceedings in Vietnam" (Nguyen and Nguyen 2015).

7.4 Arbitration discourse in practice

7.4.1 The arbitration agreement

Another important aspect treated in the LCA is related to the arbitration agreement, which may be in the form of the arbitration clause or as a separate agreement. The LCA establishes that the agreement must be made in writing, for example, by telegram, fax, telex, email, or other form prescribed by law. More precisely, before 2010, many arbitration agreements were deemed void for mistyping the name of the arbitration centre or unclear intention of the parties in a common written agreement. Under Article 16, an arbitration agreement can even be a draft attached to an email sent to a party, which has been accepted electronically. Alternatively, in a contract that has an arbitration clause but where the name of the arbitration institution is not defined and the parties do not agree on the institution nor on *ad hoc* process, the claimant has the right to bring the case to the institution at its request (Article 43.5). The law also mandatorily requires that courts must reject jurisdiction when there is an arbitration agreement (Article 6).

As regards the arbitration clause, more and more contracts include one, which can be standardised to some extent, but at the same time reflects the specificities of the case. The respondents of the interviews also confirm that they tend to encourage the use of an arbitration clause in the process of drafting contracts. The arbitration clause is sometimes defined by the parties themselves, but this could create difficulties for the arbitrators, for example, if the arbitration seat is not defined (R3). Thus, general standardised clauses tend to be used. For instance, the Model Arbitration Clause recommended by VIAC in drafting a contract is the following:

> *Any dispute arising out of or in relation with this contract shall be resolved by arbitration at the Vietnam International Arbitration Centre (VIAC) in accordance with its Rules of Arbitration.*
>
> or
>
> *Any dispute arising out of or in relation with this contract shall be resolved by arbitration at the Vietnam International Arbitration Centre at the Vietnam Chamber of Commerce and Industry (VIAC) in accordance with its Rules of Arbitration.*

It also suggests considering the addition of elements, such as the number of arbitrators, the place of arbitration, and, in the case of disputes involving a foreign element, the governing law and the language of the proceedings. The Model Clause recommended by PIAC is rendered linguistically in exactly the same way as that of VIAC.

7.4.2 Awards

Following a well-established generic structure, awards must include the following elements:

- Date and location of issuance of the award;
- Names and addresses of the claimant and respondent;
- Full names and addresses of the arbitrators;
- Summary of the statement of claim and matters in dispute;
- Reasons for issuance of the award, unless the parties agree it is unnecessary to specify reasons for the award;
- Result of the dispute resolution;
- Time limit for enforcement of the award;
- Allocation of arbitration fees and other relevant fees;
- Signatures of the arbitrator(s) (Nguyen and Dang Vu 2014).

Awards tend to follow a standard rhetorical structure. Especially in the case of institutional arbitration, the centre generally provides model layouts that are followed in the drafting process. The main differences can be found in the style of writing, which depends on the individual preferences of the arbitrators and, in the case of awards drafted in English, on the specific language competence of the drafters, but the style of writing can be different.

7.5 The experts' perspective

This section investigates more specifically the perceptions of arbitrators operating in Vietnam. The semi-structured interviews loosely followed a specifically compiled questionnaire.[6] Five experts agreed to meet us in Ho Chi Minh City in December 2015 to share their views on the topic.

7.5.1 The arbitration context

According to the respondents, international arbitration in Vietnam generally involves the countries with which Vietnam has strong business relationships, such as China or India. This form of dispute resolution is certainly growing in popularity but not dramatically. Indeed, some of the expressions regularly used by the respondents are "gradually," "step by step," "little by little," and "one day at a time" to indicate that the process is taking place slowly, but consistently. Professionals affirm that, at the moment, the majority of companies, which are small-medium-sized enterprises, are still not very familiar with arbitration, but the situation is slowly changing.

The use of arbitration is still regarded with some scepticism. This is generally attributed to a general wariness towards a method of dispute resolution that companies may not be familiar with. Indeed, when corporates explore different options, they may not possess the adequate legal knowledge to evaluate the advantages of arbitration (R3).

However, nowadays, companies are starting to show interest, and in a short time, such interest will become a choice when they may actively consider options other than litigation. Indeed, given the backlog of cases in courts, arbitration will certainly become a more attractive choice. Currently, Singapore and Hong Kong remain the preferred seat for arbitration, but companies also want to explore other options, which may be less costly and more convenient, and Vietnam may, in the future, represent a more enticing alternative.

In Vietnam, *ad hoc* arbitration is not very common, as it is somehow less institutionalised and hence is often attributed to a lower level of trustworthiness. Thus, people tend to prefer institutional arbitration. All respondents confirm that institutional arbitration is the preferred form of arbitration, especially in international contexts, and in general, well-established institutions like VIAC are involved. However, one respondent underlines that arbitration is still not very popular in Vietnam, and so providing statistics about a clear preference between *ad hoc* or institutional arbitration may not be so revealing at present.

7.5.2 Advantages of arbitration and areas of concern

7.5.2.1 Positive aspects

Among the main advantages attributed to arbitration, the respondents have primarily identified confidentiality, as well as freedom to choose the arbitrators and other aspects of the

6 See Belotti (2012a: 137–143) for the questionnaire developed within the project "International Commercial Arbitration Practice: A Discourse Analytical Study," coordinated by the City University of Hong Kong. See also Belotti (2012b), Kathpalia (2012), Anesa (2015), and Anesa and Belotti (Chapters 5 and 6, this volume).

procedure. This is in line with the main positive aspects which emerge in the literature: "Parties tend to prefer the private nature of the proceedings and the ability to decide on important issues, including the arbitrators, choice of law, venue and language" (Le 2015).

In particular, people tend to emphasise the crucial role played by confidentiality: "In arbitration you should keep secret any information" (R5), stated one respondent. Instead, in court, everybody can access the material related to a case: "To go to court is very dangerous ... you are in the court today and tomorrow you are in the newspaper" (R5).

Costs are clearly another important decisional element, and professionals are well aware that the cost of arbitration proceedings is not to be quantified only in terms of arbitration fees:

> From my perspective and so from a business perspective, confidentiality is how to minimize business disruption ... the cost is not how much we have to spend for the arbitrator but how to resolve the case and how we can reduce the risks associated to that case ... it's much larger.
>
> (R3)

If one takes into consideration that the amount of resources spent in litigative procedures is huge, arbitration appears as an opportune choice. "All things considered, arbitration is cheaper than litigation," stated one respondent, who also pointed out that different centres may have different fees, however (R4).

Moreover, a dispute in court can last as long as 3–4 years, whereas the average arbitration is much shorter, generally a few months. Indeed, respondents have identified the average duration as 5–6 months. Respondents show considerable concerns towards the backlog in Vietnamese courts, which hinders the carrying out of justice: "In America they have this saying, justice delayed is justice denied" (R5). Thus, arbitration may represent a precious alternative.

Among the reasons to opt for arbitration, companies also appreciate the involvement of the parties in the choice of the place, language, and, above all, the arbitrator, who can, of course, be a foreign arbitrator. One respondent stated that "arbitration is free" to emphasise the freedom of choice that the parties enjoy.

In particular, the freedom to choose the arbitrator is considered particularly important, because a judge in litigative procedures "could also be incompetent" (R4), whereas in arbitration, people have a chance to choose who will make the final decision. The choice of the arbitrator is indeed crucial. Given the lack of trust in the justice system and the general perception that it lacks neutrality and fairness, being permitted to choose an arbitrator is particularly significant. The impartiality of arbitrators also plays a crucial role from a corporate perspective. Generally, three arbitrators are appointed, which avoids the possibility of impartiality implied in selecting only one arbitrator.

Preferring international arbitration to litigation also offers the possibility to select the *lex causae* (i.e., the law that governs the merits of a dispute). This refers to disputes with a foreign element. Choosing the substantive law represents a considerable advantage for the parties in order to minimise risks.

Another advantage of arbitration is that the award is final, conclusive, and enforceable. Thus, the decision cannot be appealed. A request for setting aside an award can be accepted only under specific circumstances, namely: there was no arbitration agreement or it was invalid; inconsistency of the composition of the arbitral panel according to the agreement; lack of jurisdiction of the arbitration tribunal; breach of the arbitrators' obligations; or the award is contrary to the public interest of the Socialist Republic of Vietnam.

In other words, as lack of trust in the justice system is palpable, a higher level of involvement of the parties is welcomed. The outcome of arbitration is seen as more predictable and less erratic than court judgements. Historically, the lack of legal certainty has been an area of concern for investors, and arbitration may be linked to a reduction of risks for foreign investment. Thus, the presence of an effective arbitration system is crucial in order to encourage investment.

7.5.2.2 Areas of concern

The main areas of concern regard the enforcement of awards, which is particularly problematic from a corporate perspective. Indeed, lack of enforceability leads to time wasting, which is not compatible with business activity. In particular, the main concerns lie in the enforcement of foreign awards on the part of the courts. Many scholars have highlighted that this process is often slow and the result unpredictable (see, for example, Nguyen and Duong Vu 2014: 680; Le et al. 2016). Indeed, although Vietnam is signatory to the New York Convention, not all awards are necessarily enforced.

Le et al. affirm that the enforcement may be refused in the following cases:

> (i) the underlying contract (including the arbitration provision) was invalid due to the fact that the signatory to that contract was not duly authorized to sign it; (ii) the dispute should not be resolved by arbitration under the laws of Vietnam, or the recognition and enforcement of the award is contrary to the "basic principles of the laws of Vietnam," a concept which has had a vague expression in law; or (iii) upon an analysis of the factual content of the case, the judge believes the award should not have been granted
>
> (Le et al. 2016: 11)

It has also been noted that the scope of the grounds for setting aside arbitral awards is wider than in international law and practice, and it may represent a limitation to the use of arbitration (Nguyen and Dang Vu 2014).

Confidentiality, although generally seen as one of the main advantages of arbitration, can also represent an area of concern. Indeed, the LCA clearly establishes that the arbitral tribunal must keep all material and information confidential, unless a competent state authority requires otherwise. However, "whether the parties themselves are under such obligation is not clear. Similarly, the confidentiality of the award and subsequent enforcement procedures by the parties themselves is also unclear" (Nguyen et al. 2014: 467).

As regards costs, it has been pointed out that the presence of a foreign arbitrator can increase them. However, "every arbitration institution tries to protect costs" (R2), in the sense that since costs can be a problematic area of arbitration, centres tend to indicate an indication of fees on their websites according to case type, so that parties can easily estimate the approximate costs before filing the case.

Other aspects of arbitration may be interpreted quite differently, as they may be interpreted in turn as positive or problematic aspects. For instance, in terms of amicability, arbitration is not generally seen as amicable *per se* by the professionals interviewed, but rather as less formal than litigation. The procedure itself may be defined as relatively amicable, but not the decision: "At the end of the day there is also a winning and a losing party" (R1).

In arbitration, a first negotiation should generally be attempted, but in practice, this requirement is not always fulfilled. "In Vietnam a lot of times parties do not know about it and so mediation is skipped," stated R2.

One of the respondents conducted a survey with local businesses, which included 250 participants. Interestingly, 80% of businesses showed some kind of misunderstanding about arbitration. Indeed, another expert affirmed that "a lot of times people are not clear about the procedure" (R5), meaning that they are not familiar with the technical aspects of arbitration, and thus are not well positioned to consider the most advantageous dispute-resolution system. A deeper knowledge of arbitration would enable them to make more informed choices.

The general lack of trust in the justice system often affects people's perceptions of arbitration procedures. One respondent pointed out that, especially in the larger districts, there are a lot of pending cases in court, above all civil cases, and so companies "don't want to use arbitration because in their mind it's like the court," and they affirm: "We are business, we don't have a lot of time" (R1). Arbitration is thus not discerned very clearly from litigative procedures. Another respondent confirmed: "In Vietnam people do not want to cooperate with the authorities, with the court, with the arbitrators," and stated that "to go to the court is unlucky and people want to stay away from there" (R2). Plainly, he also affirmed: "In the last 20 years, whenever I go to the court, people think I am a criminal. They do not separate criminal court and civil courts." This is also one of the reasons why "to invite witnesses is very difficult" (R2), as people often prefer not to be involved in any way in a dispute.

7.5.3 The language of arbitration

The language of arbitration in disputes without a foreign element is Vietnamese. On the other hand, in the case of disputes with a foreign element, the parties can agree on the language of arbitration. If an agreement cannot be reached, the language is decided by the arbitration panel. Accordingly, Article 21 of the VIAC Rules and Article 21 of the PIAC are identical and recite as follows:

1. For disputes without a foreign element, the language of arbitration shall be Vietnamese.
2. For disputes with a foreign element and disputes to which at least one party is an enterprise with foreign invested capital, the language of arbitration shall be as agreed by the parties. Otherwise, the Arbitral Tribunal shall determine the language or languages to be used in the arbitral proceedings, taking account of the relevant circumstances including the language of the contract.
3. If a document is made in any language other than the language of arbitration, the Arbitral Tribunal or the Centre, where the Arbitral Tribunal has not yet been constituted, may request a party or the parties to provide the translation thereof.

(Article 21. Language of arbitration)

Respondents to the questionnaire highlighted that the language chosen often depends on those spoken by the parties, who will in turn appoint an arbitrator with knowledge of that language. In turn, arbitrators may also "decide whether to accept the appointment based also on their knowledge of the procedural language" (Faienza 2014).

Normally, Vietnamese is employed, but in international cases, the parties can of course decide, and English is often used as a lingua franca in international disputes. VIAC arbitrators also stated that English is generally employed, followed by French and Russian in a minority of cases.

As Faienza remarks, "The language in which the proceedings will be held becomes of great importance for the characteristic purpose of arbitration itself: the consensual resolution of disputes" (Faienza 2014). However, this fundamental choice is somehow considered of secondary importance, and professionals confirm that sometimes, the procedural language is chosen without appropriate reflection, and parties may even waive the right to choose it.

Choice of the procedural language is particularly significant, first of all because it generally determines the language used for all communications. Instead, a failure to define the procedural language in the agreement may at times lead to the parties using different languages during the initial phase, which may potentially generate misunderstandings and delays (R1).

If not agreed upon by the parties, the arbitral tribunal determines the language of arbitration. In this case, international doctrine and praxis indicate that the principle of equal treatment must be applied. Moreover, in order to guarantee efficiency, the nationality of the arbitrator is also an important factor for the final choice (R1).

Discussing the notion of the agreement between the parties regarding choice of language, Faienza poses a crucial question: "When is the choice of the parties absent? Is an 'implicit agreement' of the parties, a sort of *facta concludentia* (i.e. the use of the same language for the contract, the arbitration agreement, the correspondence etc.), allowed?" (Faienza 2014). The author suggests that "a positive answer to this question could be possible. However, a sort of *kompetenz-kompetenz* rule[7] is applicable: the arbitral tribunal is not only entitled to determine the language, but also to verify the existence and the extent of the agreement concerning this choice" (Faienza 2014).

Failure to choose the language in the arbitration agreement may have considerable negative consequences, and seems to go against the nature of the procedure itself. Indeed, by definition, arbitration allows the parties the freedom to choose most aspects of the procedure and thus to choose a language that can be tailored to suit their common needs. Moreover, choice of an appropriate language is fundamental in order to guarantee efficiency, reduce costs (which arise, for instance, from the need for interpretation and translation services), and allow for fairness.

By and large, it can be stated that if the language of the contract is that spoken by the parties, it generally becomes the language of arbitration, and therefore it is not necessary to specify it in the arbitration clause. However, it is normally advisable to include the choice of language in the arbitration agreement, and parties considering two languages of arbitration should be aware that this choice can increase costs considerably (R1).

7.6 Conclusions

In Vietnam, the rapid intensification of interaction with foreign companies and institutions is leading to a constant increase in the need for arbitration, both at domestic and international levels. The progress of VIAC in terms of the number of disputes is remarkable, even when compared to some advanced arbitration centres in the region, such as SIAC of Singapore and KLRCA of Malaysia. However, despite the modernisation of the legal framework and attempts made to promote the use of arbitration in Vietnam, some aspects still have to be improved. The opinion of one of the professionals well summarises the situation. He or she points out that many foreign enterprises have invested in Vietnam, and it is felt that they

7 In essence, the kompetenz-kompetenz doctrine provides that the arbitral tribunal shall decide itself whether it has jurisdiction to decide a dispute brought before it (Landolt 2013).

"have to be encouraged to choose Vietnam as a seat … as Vietnam is gaining experience"; but, at the same time, "of course we have to do more" (R2).

Professionals show a maturing awareness of the importance of arbitration as an international dispute resolution method, and recent reforms have strengthened confidence in the arbitration process. In particular, among the main advantages to preferring arbitration over litigation, confidentiality is assigned a high level of importance, as is the freedom to choose some of the aspects of proceedings. Costs, of course, play a role, especially in terms of saving resources and minimising business disruption.

Arbitration centres in other Asian countries continue to be the preferred seat. This happens because of a number of factors that are traditionally associated with Vietnam, such as "low awareness of arbitration by the business community, weakness of state structures that support arbitration, poor capacity of arbitration centres and arbitrators, and unclear and inconsistent legal framework" (Lien 2013: 587). In general, the main criticisms are directed at the uncertainty of timing and result, as well as the relative lack of clarity as regards the recognition and enforcement of foreign arbitral awards (Hogan Lovells 2015: 6).

Given the globalisation of business and the exponential growth of transnational agreements, it is clear that the choice of a dispute-resolution method cannot be based purely on historical and traditional factors, but has to pursue objectives, like the optimisation of resources, time and cost efficiency, and flexibility.

In conclusion, it may be argued that margins for improvement are still present, particularly concerning the transmission of information and communicating with companies about ADR procedures. However, reforms are being implemented and several promotional tools adopted. Given the economic, social, and legal factors discussed above, it can easily be argued that the use of arbitration will continue to grow in this country, and if the present momentum endures, Vietnam is likely to become an important alternative to the more established institutions operating in Asia.

References

Anesa, Patrizia (2015) Discursive peculiarities of Indian arbitral awards. In Bhatia, Vijay K. and Gotti, Maurizio (eds) *Arbitration Discourse in Asia*. Bern: Peter Lang, pp. 305–323.

Belotti, Ulisse (2012a) *Dispute Resolution Narratives. A Linguistic Analysis of Arbitration Practices.* Bergamo: CELSB Libreria Universitaria.

Belotti, Ulisse (2012b) Arbitration in Italy: a two-headed Janus? In Bhatia, V.K., Candlin, C.N., and Gotti, M. (eds) *Discourse and Practice in International Commercial Arbitration (Issues, Challenges and Prospects)*. Farnham: Ashgate, pp. 239–261.

D'Agostino, Justin (2014) Arbitration in Asia at full gallop (10 February 2014). Available at: http://kluwerarbitrationblog.com/2014/02/10/arbitration-in-asia-at-full-gallop/. Accessed: 12/06/2016.

Faienza, Valentina (2014) The choice of the language of the proceedings: an underestimated aspect of the arbitration? *Kluwer Arbitration Blog*. Available at: http://kluwerarbitrationblog.com/2014/05/06/the-choice-of-the-language-of-the-proceedings-an-underestimated-aspect-of-the-arbitration/. Accessed: 03/06/2016.

Hogan Lovells (2015) Arbitration in Vietnam. Client Note. Available at: www.hlaseanhorizon.com/_uploads/pdfs/SNGLIB01-120843-v11-Client_note_-_Arbitration_in_Vietnam.pdf. Accessed: 15/08/2016.

Kathpalia, Sujata (2012) Is arbitration being colonized by litigation?—practitioners' views in the Singapore context. In Bhatia, V.K., Candlin, C.N., and Gotti, M. (eds) *Discourse and Practice in International Commercial Arbitration: Issues, Challenges and Prospects.* Farnham: Ashgate, pp. 263–281.

Landolt, Phillip (2013) The inconvenience of principle: separability and Kompetenz-Kompetenz. Journal of International Arbitration, 30/5, pp. 511–530.

Le, Net (2015) Arbitration procedures and practice in Vietnam: overview. *Practical Law: Arbitration Global Guide 2014/15*. 1–8. Available at: https://vietnamlawinsight.files.wordpress.com/2016/06/vietnam_arbitration_1-608-8005.pdf. Accessed: 01/07/2016.

Le, Net; Vinh Nguyen, Thi Kim & McDonnell, Joseph (2016). Enforcement of contracts in Vietnam and the risks of bilateral investment treaty (BIT) disputes. *The Gakushuin Journal of International Studies*, 3, 1–18.

Lien, Bui Thi Bich (2013) Arbitration in Vietnam. *JurisNet*, 569–593. Available at: https://www.academia.edu/7447828/Chapter_15_ARBITRATION_IN_VIETNAM. Accessed: 16/08/2016.

Nguyen, Corinne & Duong Vu, Anh (2014) Arbitration in Vietnam. *Journal of International Arbitration* 31/5, 675–682. Available at: http://eng.viac.vn/uploads/38452-JOIA%2031-5_Corinne%20Nguyen%20&%20Anh%20Duong%20Vu.pdf. Accessed: 02/08/2016.

Nguyen, Manh Dzung & Dang Vu, Minh Ha (2014) Arbitration Guide. Vietnam. International Bar Association. Available at: www.ibanet.org/Document/Default.aspx?DocumentUid=4DCE3539-D1B4-4251-B850-0B6C61DC0105. Accessed: 03/08/2016.

Nguyen, Manh Dzung; Le, Quang Hung & Nguyen, Ngoc Minh (2014) Vietnam. *Law Business Research Ltd*. 463–471. Available at: http://dzungsrt.com/wp-content/uploads/doc/A2014-Vietnam-Chapter.pdf. Accessed: 15/07/2016.

Nguyen, Manh Dzung and Nguyen, Thi Thu Trang (2015) Vietnam. *Global Arbitration Review*. Available at: http://globalarbitrationreview.com/chapter/1036916/vietnam. Accessed: 30/07/2016.

8 Perceptual, cultural and linguistic challenges facing Japan as a site of international arbitration

Richard Powell

8.1 Introduction: economic giant, arbitral dwarf?

Despite decades of glacial economic growth (World Bank, 2016[1]), relegation into third place among the world's economies (BBC, 2011), and per capita GNI underperforming the Asian city states of Hong Kong and Singapore (World Bank, 2016[2]), Japan remains an economic giant in Asia and indeed globally, with a GDP more than twice the size of India's and nearly a third bigger than Germany's. Moreover, it is hardly an economic loner, having signed free trade agreements with 15 countries and with the Association of Southeast Asian Nations (ASEAN), embarked upon negotiations with six more, including a trilateral partnership with China and Korea (MOFA, 2016), and ratified the now-threatened Trans-Pacific Partnership trade agreement before any other participant. In the field of international arbitration, however, Tokyo lags behind established international arbitral sites in Europe and North America and newer ones closer to home in Asia.

The reasons Japan has not experienced the "dramatic growth in arbitration caseloads in institutions established in other parts of Asia" (Nakamura & Nottage, 2012:4) remain complex, multifaceted, and largely elusive, with cultural, institutional, economic, local, and global factors all part of the discussion. Running through most of the professional and academic commentaries, however, is the view that Japan *should* be a bigger international arbitral player than it is. Discussing updates to arbitral procedures on an influential business law platform, one barrister involved in international dispute resolution in Asia, Australia, and Britain remarks that in view of Japan's economic and legislative infrastructure, "it is surprising that its arbitration system is one of the least utilised in Asia" (Watkin, 2014). Frequently linked to this puzzled frustration are suggestions, seldom supported with specific evidence, that limited arbitral activity is somehow associated with declining national confidence because of weak economic growth, the aging (and since 2000, shrinking[3]) of the population, parochial education, or a conservative and inward-looking legal culture.

1 Typically between around 0% and 2%, after posting growth as high as 7% in the late 1980s (World Bank, 2016).

2 $41,000 and $52,090, respectively, according to the World Bank's Atlas method for reducing currency fluctuation effects: Japan's $38,840 remains considerably higher than any large Asian polity and is similar to many European states.

3 The Guardian (2016.2.26) *Japan's Population Declines for First Time Since 1920s-Official Census* (www.theguardian.com/world/2016/feb/26/japan-population-declines-first-time-since-1920s-official-census).

Four years after Japan implemented a new arbitration Law (2003[4]), as part of a series of reforms designed to deregulate and expand the judicial system, an American-born Keio University law professor argued that "the reputation of Japan as a place that is 'open for business' and possessed of the infrastructure necessary to protect the legitimate interests of foreign investors is at stake" (McAlinn[5], 2008:7). While lacking sufficient data to evaluate the extent to which Japan has actually opened its doors, this chapter outlines the legislative and administrative infrastructure now in place to support arbitration in Japan, and it then sets out to explore professional and academic discourses that compare its marginalisation in international arbitration with perceptions of the country as administratively inflexible, culturally introverted, or linguistically challenged. Perceptions are not everything, but their potential influence on the practice of dispute resolution should not be ignored, given that arbitration is one of several choices for dealing with international cases.

8.2 International influences on Japanese law

Japan has long turned to the outside when contemplating legal reform. Indeed, Colombo (2014:747) claims no developed country has been more willing to look to foreign law, adding that it has also been a leading exporter of legal models, especially in post-socialist Southeast Asia (ibid:749). Its first arbitral legislation, the *Kōjisaikoku Tetsuzuki oyobi Chūsai Tetsuzuki ni kansuru Hōritsu* (Public Notice and Arbitral Procedures Law, hereafter "the 1890 Law"[6]), was adopted from German law and implemented during an era of rapid industrialisation, when legal ideas from France were being adopted wholesale, though often embodied subsequently in more authoritarian forms inspired by Germany (Dean, 1997:149). The continental civil law orientation remains strong, evinced by limited documentary disclosure during litigation (Marckwald, 2014), lack of requirement for consideration in contracts (Ogano, 2017), and a German-style propensity on the part of judges to encourage conciliation and settlement (Nakamura & Nottage, 2012:1). However, certain features of common law were introduced after the Pacific War under the influence of the United States, including a shift from family obligations towards individual rights and the inclusion of some adversarial procedures for trials (Dean, 1997:143–148). More recently, case law has been accorded increased weight (Masuda, 2016; Ogano, 2017).

Further Americanisation of the judicial system has come with a spate of reforms in the last two decades designed to enhance public engagement with, legal processes and expand the size of the legal profession and the size of legal practices. In 1996, the Civil Procedure Code was amended to make litigation easier. In 2004, law schools were established to accept students from a variety of academic backgrounds and pass up to 30% of them for bar admission, a sharp increase from previous rates of between 1% and 3% (Steele & Haruyama, 2016:2). The stated aim is to triple entry into a profession hitherto producing one lawyer per 6,300 citizens, compared with 1 per 290 in the United States,[7] a difference that is

4 *Chūsai Hō*/仲裁法, enacted as Law 138 of 2003 and implemented in 2004.

5 Professor McAlinn passed away in May 2016.

6 公示催告手続及ビ仲裁手続ニ関スル法律. Accessed 2017.2.02 from: Houko.com, www.houko.com/00/01/M23/029.HTM.

7 Comparisons with the US are, however, questionable, not only on sociocultural grounds (e.g, differential crime rates and attitudes to litigation) but also institutionally, inasmuch as Japan's civil law tradition limits the number of professionals regarded strictly as "lawyers" (*bengoshi*), but includes prosecutors, scriveners, and others who might be included in the category of lawyer in some common law jurisdictions. Nevertheless, the number of lawyers in Japan is comparatively low among developed countries.

especially marked in non-urban areas (Hashimoto, 2007:1), as half the nation's legal practitioners are in Tokyo (Onishi, 2008). While not going as far as American-style juries, in 2009, a system of lay assessors (who collaborate with professional judges on verdicts) was introduced for criminal trials, in an attempt to make the judiciary less bureaucratic and remote (Hashimoto, 2007:1).

Most of the legal reforms have drawn, to some extent, on overseas developments, and some have been specifically designed to increase cross-border legal activity. In 1996, measures for the registration and employment of foreign lawyers (*Gaikokuijn Bengoshi ni yoru Hōritsu Jimu no Toriatsukai ni kansuru Tokubetsu Sōchihō*) were modified to increase the range and independence of their activities on Japanese soil, with further amendments in 2003 strengthening the basis for setting up joint legal practices. The 2001 Justice System Reform Council Report that ushered in the new law schools (JSRC, 2001) noted the need to "internationalise training" (Klaphake, 2010) and produce a bar and a judiciary with a more international outlook, better language skills, and more specialised knowledge of growth areas, such as intellectual property (Hashimoto, 2007:2). In 2008, Hong Kong-born Peter Tam and Korean Park Han Young became the first foreigners without Japanese permanent residence to start the bar entry training course, having passed the bar on their first attempt (Nakai, 2008).

Meanwhile, the courts seem increasingly willing to take note of international agreements, even where Japanese domestic law is silent. For example, in a society that was relatively homogeneous until recently and remains reluctant to curb freedom of expression, domestic laws to control racial discrimination are weak,[8] but a Brazilian-born plaintiff successfully relied on Japan's ratification of the Convention on the Elimination of All Forms of Racial Discrimination when seeking compensation against a shop that had banned local Brazilians in the wake of shoplifting incidents (Yamanaka, 2002).

Recent revisions in Alternative Dispute Resolution (ADR) institutions and practices can be seen very much as part of reforms aimed at expanding international, as well as domestic, dispute resolution. The 1996 amendments to rules for foreign lawyers registered in Japan included a provision (Article 5) for them to act as advocates in international arbitrations. Another amendment in 2003 (Article 52) extended this right to foreign-based lawyers hired overseas by parties pursuing arbitration in Japan. Alongside expanding the legal profession, reducing the costs of litigation, and introducing lay assessors, recommendations issued by the Justice System Reform Council included the strengthening of collaboration with foreign lawyers and revitalision of the Japan Arbitration Center for Intellectual Property and the ADR functions of the Japan Patent Office, "while carefully watching international movements" (JSRC, 2001).

8.3 Development of Japanese arbitration

If the United States is taken as the point of comparison, as is increasingly the case among Japanese proponents of legal reform, then Japan has traditionally leaned more towards alternatives to litigation for resolving disputes. Despite being an early adopter of modern arbitral mechanisms with the 1890 Law, however, arbitration has not figured predominantly among them.

8 A hate speech law enacted in 2016 to address harassment of Japanese Koreans relies more on admonishment than punishment.

The 1890 Law was incorporated into a new Code of Civil Procedure and was more or less a translation of a German model (Eastman, 2004). Its 21 articles largely address filing and notification procedures and remained intact until an amendment to provisions about registration, just as the new law was being brought in. This does not necessarily mean arbitral procedure was stagnant, however, as it appears courts exercised sufficient discretion to interpret the law in line with changing international developments (Nakamura & Nottage, 2012:5). Nevertheless, arbitration seems to have operated at low volume, and the first internationally oriented arbitral institution did not appear until the Japan Shipping Exchange (JSE/*Nippon Kaigunshūkaijo*) in 1921. Comprehensive reforms were discussed in the 1990s, but, as this was a period of widespread bankruptcy and corporate restructuring following the collapse of Japan's bubble economy, priority was given to modernising insolvency laws (Nakamura & Nottage, 2012:6). In place of new legislation, reciprocal agreements with other countries were put in place, but according to Keio University's Masuda Susumu, China and Japan regularly rejected each other's decisions.[9]

The 2003 Law entirely replaced the 1890 Law and was applied retroactively to agreements in force at the time of implementation in 2004. It encompasses the main 1985 United Nations Commission on International Trade Law (UNCITRAL) provisions, including the requirement for written evidence of consent for arbitration and the limitation of court intervention to a narrow range of circumstances, such as the need to dismiss arbitrators or set aside awards. Among grounds for challenging awards in the local courts, Article 3 refers to cases where requisite notice about the appointment of arbitrators was not given or when the details of an award go beyond the dispute at stake or the scope of the arbitral clause in question.

The 2003 Law also includes innovations, such as recognition of consent to arbitration expressed electronically (Article 13) and provision for Japanese courts to appoint arbitrators if Japan may be the arbitral site and one party has their main place of business there (Article 8). Whereas UNCITRAL rules specifically envisage international disputes, by default, the new Japanese legislation appears to cover both cross-border and domestic arbitrations. In the absence of specific provisions about choice of venue, Nakamura and Nottage (2012:7) find some ambiguity about whether parties could opt for foreign arbitration laws for proceedings conducted in Japan, while concluding that they probably cannot.

Following on the heels of the 2003 legislation was a new Law to Promote the Use of out-of-court Dispute Resolution Procedures[10] (the "2004 ADR Law"), covering mediation and more informal conciliation, as well as arbitration, and enabling the Ministry of Justice to accredit institutions offering ADR services.

In the case of commercial arbitrations, especially those with international dimensions, the highest profile body is the Japanese Commercial Arbitration Association (JCAA/ *Nihon Shōji Chūsai Kyōkai*/日本商事仲裁協会). Touting itself as Japan's only permanent commercial arbitral body (JCAA, 2017), it was established in 1953 as the independent heir to the International Commercial Arbitration Committee, set up in 1950 by the Japanese Chamber of Commerce and Industry. In addition to Tokyo, there are offices in Kobe, Nagoya, Osaka, and Yokohama. It provides arbitration services under UNCITRAL-compliant rules published bilingually and disseminates information through a bilingual website, which

9 Personal communication, 2016.2.24.

10 "Law Promoting Out-of-Court Dispute Resolution Proceedings," *Saibangai Funsōkaiketsu Tetsuzuki no Riyō no Sokushin ni kansuru Hōritsu* 裁判外紛争解決手続の利用の促進に関する法律, Law 151 of 2004, effective 2007.4. Accessed 2017.2.20 from: http://law.e-gov.go.jp/htmldata/H16/H16HO151.html.

has carried a regular *Newsletter* in English since 1996 (before which, there were English quarterly bulletins). Since 1952, cooperation agreements have been concluded with some 50 overseas ADR institutions, covering matters such as exchange of information and assistance in sourcing arbitrators and mediators (ibid). It has a record of updating its rules in line with both domestic and international developments. In 2004, it amended provisions for commercial arbitrations in line with the 2003 Law (McAlinn & Nottage, 2004) and in 2014, introduced procedures similar to those at the Hong Kong and Singapore International Arbitration Centres (HKIAC and SIAC) for joining third parties and appointing emergency arbitrators (Watkin, 2014).

JCAA charges a request fee of ¥54,000, or approximately $480. By way of comparison, HKIAC charges a registration fee of HK$8,000 (approximately $1,000) (HKIAC, 2017) and SIAC a filing fee of S$2,000 ($1,400) (SIAC, 2017). JCAA's published administrative fees range from ¥216,000 ($1,900) for claims up to ¥5 million ($45,000) to ¥15,120,000 ($134,000) for claims over ¥5,000,000,000 ($44 million). These details are publicised not only on JCAA's own website but also by the Japan External Trade Organization, established in 2003 but descended from a series of similar bodies going back to the 1950s to promote Japanese trade (JETRO, 2017).

Alongside arbitration, JCAA further offers mediation, which it describes as "more economical and expeditious... than litigation or arbitration" (JCAA, 2017), and enacted new International Commercial Mediation Rules in 2009, after studying practices at the Singapore Mediation Centre, the International Chamber of Commerce, and elsewhere (JCAA, 2009).

As mentioned above, the Japan Shipping Agency has been involved in arbitrations since 1921. It routinely includes arbitration clauses in contracts it supervises and refers disputes to arbitration under the rules of the Tokyo Maritime Arbitration Commission (TOMAC), charging a filing fee of ¥100,000 (approximately $900) (JSE, 2017). These rules are published in both Japanese and English, and there is a bilingual website.

Another body overseeing arbitrations of a commercial nature is the Japan Intellectual Property Arbitration Center, which also has a bilingual portal. Founded in 1998 as the Industrial Property Rights Center, it has expanded its operations since changing its name in 2001, but mostly handles fewer than ten cases a year and deals far more in mediation than arbitration (JIPAC, 2017). Japan signed up to the World Intellectual Property Organization Treaty in 2011.

It is not hard to find information about arbitration on influential Japanese forums nowadays, and indeed several key bodies publicise it to the point of promotion. *Nichibenren*, the Japan Federation of Bar Associations, regularly announces events, including a training programme organised by the Association for Overseas Technical Scholarship in 2006 that invited 22 arbitration specialists from 11 Asian countries; a symposium on "best practices in arbitration" run by the International Bar Association's Asia-Pacific Arbitration Group; and, most recently, a seminar on international trade conflicts and arbitration in Nagoya, at the end of January 2017 (JFBA, 2017).

In the smaller domestic arena, one recent development that has attracted some public interest is sports arbitration. Traditionally, the judiciary has been reluctant to intervene in the internal affairs of sports bodies, and indeed, in 1994, the Tokyo District Court refused to hear a case brought by a racing driver fighting a fine imposed by his governing authority (Dogauchi, 2006:301). However, an increase in doping scandals, the desire to deflate media speculation about well-known competitors, and awareness of athletes' need for prompt resolutions, given their short careers and fleeting chances for global glory, led, in 2003, to the inauguration of the Japan Sports Arbitration Agency (JSAA) under directors reflecting a balance among former competitors, administrators, and legal experts (ibid:302). To act, it requires there be an arbitration clause in standard contracts between athletes and their governing bodies (ibid:305). The fee to file an application is ¥50,000 ($450) (JSAA, 2017). The Agency's website and awards, so far, are only available in Japanese. One contributor to JCAA's *Newsletter* (Ogawa, 2010) has advised that all awards be made public, unless special circumstances obtain, presumably because of widespread interest in sports stars and antipathy towards faceless administrators.

With a limited budget and staff, JSAA focuses on selection disputes (Dogauchi, 2006:305), a topic that gained wide publicity in 2006 when swimmer Chiba Suzu filed a claim with the Court of Arbitration for Sport (CAS). Although proceedings were held under Swiss rules, Japan was chosen as the venue. Chiba's argument that she was unfairly excluded from the Sydney Olympics was rejected, but CAS nonetheless awarded her ¥650,000 in recognition of the opacity of selection criteria in Japanese swimming (ibid:302).

The handful of cases undertaken so far by JSAA itself include a weightlifting coach, who was suspended when an athlete under his supervision was found to have taken drugs, and a horse rider, who was dropped from selection for the Athens Olympics. In the first, the claimant's suspension was overturned, as the arbitrators concluded that administrative procedures had not been carried out correctly, but in the second, to the disappointment of certain quarters in the media, the athlete failed to win reinstatement, even though compensation was ordered in view of the unsatisfactory selection processes (Dogauchi, 2006:306).

A recent dispute that galvanised public attention came from a double skuller with considerable international success behind him, who failed to gain selection for the London Olympics. In a technically complex case that demonstrated the need for experts from both legal and sporting fields, the arbitrators decided that the conduct of the races held to decide Olympic selection had produced "remarkably irrational results"[11] and ordered the trials rerun.

The overview presented in this section should serve to show that after a century of relative inactivity, Japan has made strides in the last two decades to develop a comprehensive arbitral infrastructure up to international standards in both commercial and non-commercial areas, publicising arbitration not only locally but also to a wider audience, even attracting media attention. Against this background, we should consider why it has not emerged more prominently on the international arbitral stage, or at least what reasons commenters have proposed for its backstage position.

8.4 Arbitration and internationalisation

As arbitration offers the prospect of circumventing procedural and cultural differences between national legal systems, its association with international dispute resolution and the global expansion of trade and travel is deep and enduring. Japan continues to hold very few domestic arbitrations (2006:0, 2007:3, 2008:0, 2009:1, 2010:6 at JCAA, according to London lawyer Mike Goodrich, 2012), and the inclusion of a provision in the 2003 Law for consumers and employees to cancel arbitration proceedings has been seen as a concession to the general public's lack of confidence in the medium (Godwin, 2008:2). Many local bar

11 "著しく合理性を欠く結果". 2012 AWARD JSAA-AP-2011-003, published on JSAA's website: www.jsaa.jp/award/AP-2011-003.html.

associations have arbitration centres, but in practice, these nearly always refer disputes to mediation or conciliation (Nakamura & Nottage, 2012:30). Goodrich (2012:1–2) concludes that there has never been a strong arbitration culture within Japan, and consequently, such arbitral growth as has occurred is largely due to heightened recognition among Japanese corporations of international applications. One young Japanese lawyer recommending arbitration to those embarking on a legal career (Inoue, 2014) emphasises its value in dealing with companies based in unfamiliar jurisdictions, especially in "emerging countries where the justice system is not fully developed."[12] Among Japanese and Japan observers alike, the yardstick for measuring arbitral achievement is very much an international one.

Ad hoc arbitrations are rare in Japan, with most cases supervised either by JSE or JCAA (Sawada, 2014). In recent years, JSE has handled no more than 10–20 cases per annum (Nakamura & Nottage, 2012:30). JCAA has seen a gradual rise from under 10 p.a. from the 1950s through the mid-1990s to between 10 and 21 p.a. since the late 1990s (ibid:5). While these numbers compare favourably with Malaysia's KLRCA (ranging from 1 to 11 cases p.a.), they are a shadow of the figures posted by Hong Kong (240–448) and Singapore (67–119) for the decade since 1998 (compiled by HKIAC and republished in JCAA, 2008a). Not only were HKIAC and SIAC much busier, but their work volume also rose steadily, whereas JCAA's merely inched up. Masuda (2016) bemoans JCAA's inability to attract even 10% of Hong Kong's international arbitration levels, and Nakamura and Nottage (2012:38) see little prospect of a dramatic increase.

Even if we see the glass as half full rather than half empty, international enthusiasm has hardly built up behind the new Law. Much of the discussion of the figures acknowledges reasons for low levels pre-2004 but questions the reluctance of international arbitration to come to Japan's door since then.

Seventeen years ago, Californian lawyer Charles Ragan criticised Japanese arbitration to lingering effect, citing delays borne of discontinuous hearings and arbitrators reluctant to expedite matters; burdens upon foreign parties forced to translate from Japanese; lack of English proficiency; and a bar on participation by foreign advocates (in McAlinn, 2008:9). For Tokyo-based Peter Godwin (2008:1), most of these are "as irrelevant as they are old," and some were not even fair when voiced as they overlooked JCAA reforms that mitigated problems in the 1890 Law. Hence, the key challenges facing Japanese arbitration were cultural and perceptual (ibid:2), since "there is no longer any reason why an international commercial arbitration conducted in Japan should not look identical to one conducted in any one of the major arbitration centres" (ibid:4). Similarly, the "further internationalisation" urged upon JCAA by Goodrich (2012:2) depends on convincing foreign parties about the "level playing field" for dispute resolution that now exists in Japan, with the government to share blame for failing to promote Tokyo in the way that Hong Kong and Singapore have promoted their own jurisdictions. Describing inadequacies in the pre-2003 legal framework, Masuda (2016) recalls a time when even Japanese lawyers hesitated to recommend their country as an arbitral site, but feels any such reluctance nowadays is misguided.

While Godwin compresses cultural and perceptual obstacles facing Japanese arbitration into the same clause, they should be considered separately, inasmuch as each type of barrier may relate somewhat differently to actual practice. Perceptions, such as the anachronistic idea that foreign lawyers cannot do advocacy in Japanese arbitrations, can be shown to be inaccurate: according to Nakamura and Nottage (2012:23), 58 foreign lawyers, as well as

12 "司法制度が十分発達していない新興国".

38 non-Japanese lawyers registered to practise as *gaikokuho jimu bengoshi*, were involved in JCAA arbitrations between 2006 and 2010. But culturally based differences may be harder to resolve or even identify.

One example of where culture (legal or social) could be relevant is the persuasiveness of JCAA's declaration that Japanese courts have always enforced arbitral awards when required to do so (JCAA, 2017). On paper, this is undoubtedly the case, but those more familiar with jurisdictions like Hong Kong and Singapore might point out that there have been relatively few Japanese cases so far on which to test out this commitment.

There are also a number of innovations in Japan's arbitral legislation that deviate from mainstream UNCITRAL practices and clearly lean toward preexisting cultural norms there. Misgivings about them cannot necessarily be dismissed as failures of perception.

A case in point is Article 38 of the 2003 Law, which gives arbitrators the power to operate as mediators. Godwin (2008:2) plays down this mixing of roles by arguing that this merely reflects the historical propensity of Japanese judges and arbitrators alike to encourage amicable settlements, and he stresses that the new legislation requires all parties' written consent before arbitral hats can be replaced by mediatory headwear. But Nakamura and Nottage (2012:29) point out that there is nothing to prevent disputants waiving formal requirements and agreeing orally to mediation, while Sato (2008) describes deep-seated preferences not only for mediation but also for more informal conciliation, and a general lack of clarity about distinguishing different approaches. McAlinn and Nottage (2004:33) fear that "those with advisers especially from the English law tradition are likely to be very cautious about a situation ... involving just one of the arbitrators 'caucusing' (or meeting separately) with each party...."

An anti-cultural turn among scholars of Japanese law increasingly rejects, or at least demands scepticism of, explanations about legal preferences that refer to social norms rather than socioeconomic or technical factors. The classic culturalist example is the idea that Japanese litigate less than Americans because they are less confrontational or less "modern" (Kawashima, 1963, in Ginsburg & Hoetker, 2006:3). From this, a preference for conciliation or mediation over litigation and arbitration alike might seem natural. But Colombo (2014:735) reminds us that cultural arguments can be shallow, contradictory, or attenuated by the cultural limitations of their proponents, such as the tendency of common-law-based scholars to find idiosyncrasy in practices that are far from unusual in the civil law world.

In the case of litigation patterns, Ginsburg and Hoetker (2006:55) see little significance in cultural factors and, in any case, argue (2006:4–6) that it is difficult, methodologically, to compare the volume of suits across jurisdictions. Rises in Japanese court cases since the 1980s may well reflect reforms making the courts more accessible, but showing that litigations have increased does not equate to showing that people have become more "litigious." They do, however, find some evidence that arbitration in Japan is associated with litigation, rather than contrasted with it, given that the two have historically risen or fallen in tandem (ibid, 2006:48).

Onishi (2008) gives us examples of lawyers in rural Japan being used as mediators, which would appear to support the blurring between formal and informal dispute resolution that has been reported there. However, institutional factors, such as the shortage of lawyers, might adequately explain the multiple roles of attorneys; indeed, in towns that don't have a lawyer at all, citizens turn toward local officials to solve disputes (ibid).

While there can be little objection to treating culturalist arguments cautiously, however, those who oppose them should face similar scrutiny. Against the idea that Japanese society is historically biased against arbitration, Nakamura and Nottage (2012:4) mention the boom in cases in places like Hong Kong and Singapore, where "Asian" conciliatory norms are supposedly the rule. They thereby selectively emphasise a shared Asian context, while ignoring the fact that these are common law jurisdictions with very close links to the United Kingdom and, increasingly, the United States. In Singapore, English is not only the exclusive language of law but has also become the first language of most citizens. In Hong Kong, English may still be very much a minority language, but it dominates the legal profession, even after the introduction of Cantonese for proceedings, and indeed elitism and exonormativity are part of the legal culture. Ng (2009:4) remarks that a barrister from London would still feel "right at home" in a Hong Kong courtroom.

Arguments involving culture, whether positive or negative, are at bottom notoriously unsatisfactory, because of lack of agreement about what is meant, the term covering both shallow and easily changed social practices and also deeply ingrained cognitive ones. This fact is unlikely to rule culture out of discussions about perceptions, preferences, and practices, however.

The crucial role of persuasion and perceptual adjustment is a perennial feature of discourse on internationalisation, or ***kokusaika***, across a range of domains in Japan. In economics, ***kokusaika*** emerged during the country's rise to industrial prominence in the 1980s, less as a term for describing this emergence than as a rallying cry for the Japanese to counter allegations of aggressive and unfair trade practices with self-explanations that, according to Kubota (1998), typically presented Japanese culture to the outside world in essentialist terms. In education, the aims of internationalisation have tracked subsequent economic reversals in shifting from cultural defensiveness to calls to seize neo-liberal capitalism, with the targets of persuasion being both external, such as the East Asian students that universities hope to recruit in order to stimulate ideas and offset demographic aging (Howe, 2009), and also internal, such as vested interests who fear loss of cultural and linguistic identity if core values and practices change. In the legal domain, ***kokusaika*** has been constructed as a justification for a wide range of reforms, from encouraging commercial lawyers to be more competitive (Hashimoto, 2007:2) to strengthening domestic security through cross-border collaboration (JSRC, 2001).

Masuda (2016) estimates that fewer than 10% of Japan's 35,000 lawyers are involved in any cross-border practice, further noting that there are only 386 registered foreign lawyers in the country. Steele and Haruyama (2016) conclude that the Justice System Reform Council's proposals for a more international bar have largely been unfulfilled, and they come up with an interesting explanation involving the law school exams. Citing evidence that fewer than 5% of successful examinees choose the elective question on public international law, considerably lower than those electing the questions on insolvency or labour law, they see a dichotomy between an educational policy that purports to encourage internationalisation and an educational system that discourages it. While the international law question is not obviously much more difficult, the 2012 pass mark of 21.7% being not far below that for insolvency (28.8%) or labour law (25.5%), few examinees excel in it, the highest score of 68% falling well below the top mark of 82% for insolvency (ibid:6–7). The Ministry of Justice notes that most exam-takers find it challenging, not only for the deep level of knowledge required but also the breadth, which may range from UN agreements to maritime law (ibid:8). Consequently, the ratio of students passing it has fallen, as has the ratio who choose it (ibid:9).

Hence, Steele and Haruyama (2016:13) report a lack of interest in international law on the part of students, but rather than stray into culturalist explanations, they suggest practical reasons for this. Examinees, regardless of their academic and professional interests, are likely to avoid studying for the international law question, as they know they are unlikely to score high marks (although, this in itself could be mitigated by a mechanism giving credit for those electing questions later deemed to have been more difficult). They perceive the question to be unpredictable, because of the range of potential topics, and therefore difficult to prepare for strategically (ibid:10). Cram schools, therefore, steer students towards safer topics and, indeed, provide fewer lecturers for international law than for topics students are more likely to choose (ibid:11). All of this is reinforced by a poorer range of study materials in international law and the fact that firms feel that insolvency and labour law are more useful in employment (ibid:12).

Despite raising bar exam pass rates from 3% to nearly 30% over the last decade, reforms in legal education appear to have failed to relieve pressure on examinees sufficiently to encourage law students to pursue international topics. For Steele and Haruyama (2016:14), competition forces students to work backwards, choosing topics that they see as easier to pass, and "those topics are perceived to be domestically focused."

8.5 The language factor

Internationalisation is associated in many parts of Asia with the ability to use English, and in Japan, this association may verge on conflation. The Dean of Waseda University's School of International Liberal studies has sought to counter misunderstandings that the School is primarily a place to learn English, rather than somewhere to learn through English (Pinnington, 2017). Even "international" programmes with few courses taught in English or few overseas students minimally put a strong emphasis on testable proficiency in the language, such as the Kokusai Course at Nihon University's College of Economics, which imposes higher English levels on entrants than other departments and prevents students from continuing if they fail to perform well enough on language tests. A new school of medicine to open in 2017 under the International University of Health and Welfare in Narita plans to teach all its courses in English (Oshimi, 2017). Language in general, but most particularly English, is consistently part of discussions about the internationalisation of Japanese law, and it is thus no surprise to find it featuring prominently in discourses about arbitration.

In studies on arbitration in general, the importance of language choice seems largely to have been overlooked, and perhaps this is yet another result of the colonisation of what was once a civil law-oriented tradition by anglophone common law advocates (Bhatia, 2011). Powell and Azirah (2011) have argued that the lower formality and greater flexibility of arbitration might actually disadvantage some second-language speakers of English, who overestimate their proficiency or are reluctant to lose face by admitting to deficiency, until proceedings have commenced and it is too late, or too expensive, to arrange for unanticipated language support. Mizutani (2011) reminds those contemplating arbitration that translation and interpreting are time-consuming and expensive and may also result in lack of clarity; hence, parties should think "about the language of the arbitration, the language that most of the evidence will be in and … what linguistic abilities would best assist an arbitrator." Discussing the United Nations Convention on Contracts for the International Sale of Goods, McAlinn (2010) notes that six languages (Arabic, Chinese, English, French Russian, and Spanish) are considered equally authentic and advises parties to decide in advance which version they want the arbitrator to treat as official. It was precisely such confusion over the authentic version of a treaty that led to an arbitration in 2015, where linguistic experts outnumbered the lawyers (Sehil v Turkmenistan, analysed by Sharma, 2016).

Another reason for paying greater attention to language issues may lie in scholarship on arbitration, if Colombo's (2014:736) warning about the West's overdependence on literature on Asian law in European languages is heeded. In conducting research for this chapter, however, even though some interviews were done in Japanese, the bulk of relevant literature by non-Japanese and Japanese scholars alike was found to be in English, presumably reflecting the strong linkage between English and international arbitration and the low number of domestic arbitrations. Beyond literature on ADR, it is also the case that Japanese case law and statutes are increasingly available in English. While there is considerable room for improvement, the Supreme Court has greatly raised the quality, quantity, and timeliness of the English translations of decisions posted on its website. Meanwhile, English texts for some 400 statutes have been made available on the Japanese Law Translation platform www.japaneselawtranslation.go.jp.

As there was nothing in Japan's 1890 Law about language or translation, it is possible that not much thought was given to international disputes, but it is equally valid to note that the use of foreign languages was not ruled out. Under the 2003 Law, whose authoritative text is the Japanese original, parties are free to agree on the language(s) to be used in proceedings (Article 30), but if they fail to do so, this is to be decided by the arbitrator. Similarly, JCAA rules, published in Japanese and English and, since 2008, in Chinese (JCAA, 2008b), make language choice a matter for the parties, taking both the needs and costs of translation into consideration. According to information posted by the Association (cited in Nakamura & Nottage, 2012:17), most parties do not specify a language in advance. While tribunals have a tendency to prefer English, it accounted for 31% of cases between 2000 and 2009, whereas Japanese was used for 58%, with 11% of cases using both languages.

Under the Japan Shipping Exchange's TOMAC rules 30 and 31, Japanese is to be used for domestic proceedings, English for international ones, with interpreting support for oral hearings to be arranged and funded by the party relying on it (JSE, 2017). Under JIPAC's (2017) rule 29, the tribunal reserves the right to have translations of "foreign languages" and interpreting of parties, if deemed necessary after hearing their opinions.

One interpreter[13] informed me that she, and any interpreter she had observed, employed the same protocols whether working in a trial or an arbitration, with the possible exception of feeling somewhat freer to add explanatory information in the latter, knowing that proceedings were not being recorded. On the other hand, another informant[14] found trials and mediations very different, inasmuch as the latter relied mainly on *chuchotage*, which is normally employed in trials only when translating proceedings for the benefit of defendants.

Japan is generally thought of as a country of few proficient English speakers, but there is little evidence of this being a barrier to international arbitration. In considering possible reservations some parties might have about Japan, Watkin (2014) lists expense, a reputation for dispute-aversion, competition from an efficient court system, and even lack of government promotion of arbitration, but does not mention language. Anticipating an expansion of arbitral activity in the wake of the Australian-Japan Free Trade Agreement (which, unlike similar agreements between Australia and China and Australia and Korea, specifies both Japanese and English for proceedings, rather than the latter alone), Marckwald (2014) merely advises advocates to plan for the cost and time needed for translations. In dismissing

13 Takeda Kayoko, p.c. 2016.10.10.
14 Yoshida Rika, p.c. 2017.2.24.

the current relevance of Ragan's 1991 complaints about the costs of translation, McAlinn (2008:9–10) insists that "Nobody would seriously contest today that an international arbitration must be conducted in Japanese … or that the Arbitral Award must be written in Japanese." Masuda (2016) concedes that the JCAA had been criticised in the past for favouring Japanese, but believes there is no resistance to English now and that there are enough Japanese advocates competent in it.

Language concerns seem more likely to be voiced on the Japanese side. A Kobe University professor, charged with supervising international arbitration moots (Saitō 2016:7), laments that, "Despite the enormous efforts by the students, the Japanese teams have remained in the bottom ranks over the last ten years" and feels the gap with English second-language speakers elsewhere will only widen. Sophia University's Morishita (2012) observes, from the bilingual Intercollegiate Negotiation Competition, that Japanese entrants suffer the further advantage of being represented largely by undergraduates, as those at law school are consumed with the still-formidable bar exam. After taking Chūo Law School students to debate with students in an Alternative Commercial Dispute Resolution programme at Chulalongkorn University, Smith (2010) noted discrepancies between the Japanese and the Thais, not only in English but also in negotiating skills. In recognition of language demands, Keio University recently began an English-medium LLM. One law professor there believes that a reason for continuing to push for higher English proficiency is to increase international employment prospects for students set to enter a stagnant domestic market.[15]

8.6 Conclusion

This account set out not so much to evaluate Japan as a site for international arbitration as to explore how professional and academic commenters explain the gap between the country's modern arbitral infrastructure and its low profile in Asian and global ADR. While certain features of Japanese arbitration, such as a readiness to segue into mediation or negotiation, may raise eyebrows in some jurisdictions, and many Japanese doubt their own ability to perform in English with skilled negotiators, the consensus is that there are no obvious disadvantages to holding proceedings in Japan, and there are enough local advocates to participate in it (at least, as long as cases remain relatively few, anyway). Cultural and perceptional arguments inevitably come to the fore but are largely speculative.

Masuda suggests Japanese firms' willingness to go along with foreign partners' preference for non-Japanese advocates may overlook the availability of Japanese advocates sufficiently proficient in English and lead to more arbitrations taking place overseas.[16] For one young Japanese arbitrator, however, the preference for English, and hence foreign advocates, is a rational choice in a field still relatively unknown domestically.[17] A bilingual New Zealand lawyer in the Tokyo office of a large multinational practice[18] concludes that reasons for foreign partners resisting Japan as a venue may amount to little more than their attachment to more familiar and established sites elsewhere in Asia. Japanese parties may try to insist on JCAA, not least because it gives the side faced with travelling to Japan added incentive to settle, and even if the non-litigious Japanese is now something of a myth, there is still a preference in business for cultivating long-term relations and thus avoiding the conflict of litigation

15 Masuda Susumu, p.c. 2016.3.6.
16 ibid
17 Ochiai Takafumi, Atsumi & Sakai, p.c. 2017.3.7
18 Kyle Hill of Hogan Lovells, p.c. 2017.2.4

and arbitration. If the other party resists, a compromise might be reached, whereby JCAA rules are adopted but a site outside Japan conceded. This view is of a piece with Nakamura and Nottage's (2012:5) perception of the Japanese as being ready to cede territory, but not necessarily bargaining power. Home advantage may simply not be as important to firms as it seems to be to academics hoping to see Tokyo centre stage in global arbitration.

References

BBC (2011.2.14) China overtakes Japan as world's second biggest economy. Accessed 2011.2.15 from: www.bbc.com/news/business-12427321.

Bhatia, Vijay (2011) Interdiscursive colonisation of arbitration practice. *World Englishes*, 30.1, 76–80.

Colombo, Giorgio Fabio (2014) Japan as a victim of comparative law. *Michigan State International Law Review*, 22.3, 731–753.

Dean, Meryll (1997) *The Japanese Legal System*. London: Cavendish.

Dogauchi, Masato (2006) The activities of the Japan Sports Arbitration Agency. In Ian Blackshaw, Robert Siekmann & Janwillem Soek (eds.) *The Court of Arbitration for Sport, 1984–2004*, 216–234. The Hague: Asser Press.

Eastman, Richard (2004) New law, new changes: an update on the Japanese arbitration and ADR scene. Portal of Metropolitan Corporate Counsel, 2004.12.1. Accessed 2017.2.20 from: www.metrocorpcounsel.com/page/about-mcc.

Ginsburg, Tom & Glenn Hoetker (2006) The unreluctant litigant? An empirical analysis of Japan's turn to litigation. *The Journal of Legal Studies*, 35.1 (January), 31–59.

Godwin, Peter [Herbert Smith, Tokyo] (2008) Japanese arbitration in the wake of the 2004 reforms: time to recognise the end of the Ragan myth. *Newsletter* #21, Japan Commercial Arbitration Association. Accessed 2017.2.12 from: www.jcaa.or.jp/e/arbitration/docs/news21.pdf.

Goodrich, Mike [White & Case LLP, London] (2012) Japanese arbitration rules – much work done; much still to do. *Newsletter* #27, Japan Commercial Arbitration Association. Accessed 2017.2.12 from: www.jcaa.or.jp/e/arbitration/docs/news27.pdf.

Hashimoto, Hidetoshi (2007) Legal reform in Japan: the establishment of American style law schools and reinstitution of jury system. Paper presented at *44th Annual Meeting of International Studies Association Conference*, February 28 to March 3, 2007, Chicago, IL. Accessed 2010.12.10 from: www.allacademic.com//meta/p_mla_apa_research_citation/1/7/8/5/6/pages178567/p178567-1.php.

HKIAC (2017) Portal of Hong Kong International Arbitration Centre. Accessed 2017.2.20 from: www.hkiac.org.

Howe, Edward (2009) The internationalization of higher education in East Asia: a comparative ethnographic narrative of Japanese universities. *Research in Comparative and International Education*, 4.4, 384–392. doi:10.2304/rcie.2009.4.4.384.

Inoue, Aoi (2014) *Kokusai Chūsai no naniga omoshiroi no ka* [What is interesting about international arbitration?] *Asahi Judiciary* online law and economics journal, 2014.5.29. Accessed 2017.1.27 from: http://judiciary.asahi.com/corporatelaw/2014052900004.html.

JCAA (2008a) Why and how investment arbitration should be in the Australia–Japan FTA. *Newsletter* #20, Japan Commercial Arbitration Association. Accessed 2017.1.10 from: www.jcaa.or.jp/e/arbitration/docs/news20.pdf.

JCAA (2008b) *Newsletter* #21, Japan Commercial Arbitration Association, accessed 2017.1.10 from: *http://www.jcaa.or.jp/e/arbitration/docs/news21.pdf*

JCAA (2009) *Newsletter* #21, Japan Commercial Arbitration Association, accessed 2017.1.10 from: *http://www.jcaa.or.jp/e/arbitration/docs/news22.pdf*

JCAA (2017) Portal of the Japan Commercial Arbitration Association. Accessed 2017.2.10–15 from: www.jcaa.or.jp.

JETRO (2017) Portal of the Japan External Trade Organization (*Nihon Bōeki Shinkōkikō*/日本貿易振興機構). Accessed 2017.2.18 from: www.jetro.go.jp/world/qa/04C-070308.html.

JFBA (2017) Portal of *Nichibenren* (日本弁護士連合会), Japan Federation of Bar Associations. Accessed 2017.1.30 from: www.nichibenren.or.jp.

JIPAC (2017) Portal of Japan Intellectual Property Arbitration Center (*Nihon Chiteki Zaisan Chūsai Sentā*/日本知的財産仲裁センター). Accessed 2017.2.18 from: www.ip-adr.gr.jp.

JSAA (2017) Portal of the Japan Sports Arbitration Agency (*Nippon Supōtsu Chūsai Kikō*/日本スポーツ仲裁機構). Accessed 2017.2.16 from: www.jsaa.jp.

JSE (2017) Portal of Japan Shipping Exchange Inc. (*Nippon Kaigunshūkaijo*/日本海軍集会所). Accessed 2017.2.20 from: www.jseinc.org.

JSRC (2001) Justice System Reform Council Opinion (*Shihō Seido Kaikaku Shingikai Iken-sho - 21 seiki no Nihon o sasaeru Shihō Seido*/司法制度改革審議会意見書 – 21世紀の日本を支える司法制度) [Judicial System Reform Council Opinion: a justice system to support Japan in the 21st century]. Accessed 2010.4.30 from: www.kantei.go.jp/jp/sihouseido/report/ikensyo/.

Klaphake, Jay (2010) A foreigner-friendly field of dreams? *The Japan Times*, 2010.3.30. Accessed 2010.4.04 from: http://search.japantimes.co.jp/cgi-bin/fl20100330zg.html.

Kubota, Ryuko (1998) Ideologies of English in Japan. *World Englishes*, 17(3), 295–306.

Marckwald, Duncan (2014) Dining on international arbitration in Japan-what are you eating? Portal of *Corrs Chambers Westgarth*, Australian Commercial Law Partnership. Accessed 2017.2.12from:www.corrs.com.au/thinking/insights/dining-on-international-arbitration-injapan-what-are-you-eating/.

Masuda, Susumu (2016) International dispute resolution: new developments in Japan. Lecture co-hosted by *Asian Law Centre*, Melbourne University and Herbert Smith Freehills, Melbourne, 2016.2.23.

McAlinn, Gerald (2008) Facilitating arbitration in Japan: making the JCAA a regional center for ADR. *Newsletter* #20, Japan Commercial Arbitration Association. Accessed 2017.1.5 from: www.jcaa.or.jp/e/arbitration/docs/news20.pdf.

McAlinn, Gerald (2010) Choice of law under the United Nations Convention on Contracts for the International Sale of Goods. *JCCA Newsletter* #25, Nov 2010, accessed 2017.1.6 from: www.jcaa.or.jp/e/arbitration/docs/news25.pdf.

McAlinn, Gerald & Luke Nottage (2004) Changing the (JCAA) rules: improving International Commercial Arbitration in Japan. *Zeitschrift für japanisches Recht*, 18, 23–36. Accessed 2017.2.15 from: www.zjapanr.de/index.php/zjapanr/article/view/602/627.

Mizutani, Michelle (2011) Strategies for International Arbitration: how to achieve successful outcomes and reducing cost. JCCA *Newsletter* #26 June 2011. Accessed 2017.2.17 from: www.jcaa.or.jp/e/arbitration/docs/news26.pdf.

MOFA (2016) Portal of the Japanese Ministry of Foreign Affairs. Accessed 2017.1.20 from: www.mofa.go.jp/policy/economy/fta/.

Morishita, Tetsuo (2012) The challenge of intercollegiate negotiation competition – a unique moot competition of arbitration and negotiation in Japan. *JCAA Newsletter* #26. Accessed 2017.2.19 from: www.jcaa.or.jp/e/arbitration/docs/news26.pdf.

Nakai, Daisuke (2008.11.28) Foreigners break ground in Japanese legal system. *The Asahi Shimbun* (online). Accessed 2008.11.30 from: www.asahi.com/english/Heraldasahi/TKY200811280071.html.

Nakamura, Tatsuya & Luke Nottage (2012) Arbitration in Japan. *Sydney Law School Legal Studies Research Paper* No. 12/39. Accessed 2017.1.20 from: https://papers.ssrn.com/sol3/papers2.cfm?abstract_id=2070447.

Ng, Kwai Hang (2009) *The Common Law in Two Voices. Language, Law and the Postcolonial Dilemma in Hong Kong*. Stanford, CA: Stanford University Press.

Ogano, Shōichi (2017) *Nihonhō no genjō to kadai-keiyaku no seiritsu to kōsokuryoku wo chūshin ni* [Current situation and themes focusing on the formation and binding force of contracts in Japan]. *Eibeihō ni okeru keiyakuhō no genjō to kadai ni kannsuru sinpojiumu* [Symposium on current situation and themes in common law contracts], Waseda University, Tokyo, 2017.2.4.

Ogawa, Kazushige (2010) Sports Disputes Resolution in Japan – the activity and role of Japan Sports Arbitration Agency. *Newsletter* #24, Japan Commercial Arbitration Association. Accessed 2017.2.10 from: www.jcaa.or.jp/e/arbitration/docs/news24.pdf.

Onishi, Norimitsu (2008) Lawyers in Japan: low supply, iffy demand. *New York Times*, 2008.7.29. Accessed 2009.9.30 from: www.nytimes.com/2008/07/29/world/asia/29japan.html?ex=1217908800&en=d53964a851b45c4c&ei=5070&emc=eta1.

Oshimi, Takayuki (2017) The development of certification for healthcare interpreters in Japan. Paper presented at *First International Conference on Legal and Healthcare Interpreting*, University of Hong Kong, 2017.2.24–25.

Pinnington, Adrian (2017) Waseda University School of International Liberal Studies. www.waseda.jp/fire/sils/en/about/message/ and also personal communication.

Powell, Richard & Azirah Hashim (2011) Language disadvantage in Malaysian litigation and arbitration. *World Englishes*, 30.1, 92–105.

Saitō, Akira (2016) Catch the global headwinds: Japanese students encounter the International Arbitration Moot. *JCAA Newsletter* #36. Accessed 2017.2.19 from: www.jcaa.or.jp/e/arbitration/docs/JCAA%20No36.pdf.

Sato, Yasunobu (2008) Hybrid dispute processing in Japan: linking arbitration with conciliation. In Vijay Bhatia, Christopher Candlin and Jan Engberg (eds.) *Legal Discourse across Cultures and Systems*, 53–74. Hong Kong: Hong Kong University Press.

Sawada, Toshio (2014) Practice of Arbitral Institutions in Japan. *Arbitration International*, 4.2, 120–140. doi:10.1093/arbitration/4.2.120.

Sharma, Rajesh (2016) Is there any role for linguists among lawyers in arbitration? *Contemporary Asian Arbitration Journal*, 9.2, 249–271. Accessed 2016.11.11 from: https://ssrn.com/abstract=2879778.

SIAC (2017) Portal of Singapore International Arbitration Centre. Accessed 2017.2.20 from: www.siac.org.sg.

Smith, Malcolm (2010) A small experiment in international negotiations: Chuo Law School, Japan, and Chulalongkorn Law Faculty, Thailand. *Zeitschrift für japanisches Recht*, 10.19, 216–220. Accessed 2017.2.23 from: www.zjapanr.de/index.php/zjapanr/issue/view/23.

Steele, Stacey & Aya Haruyama (2016) Japanese bar examination questions and student preferences: why do more law students choose insolvency law over public international law and why does it matter? *Zeitschrift für japanisches Recht*, 21/42, 1–29.

Watkin, Damian (2014.3.12) Arbitration in Japan. Grasping the nettle? *Mondaq*. Accessed 2017.2.25 from: www.mondaq.com/x/299016/Arbitration+Dispute+Resolution/Arbitration+In+Japan+Grasping+The+Nettle.

World Bank (2016) Economic indicators. Accessed 2016.12.20 from: http://databank.worldbank.org/data/download/GDP.pdf.

Yamanaka, Keiko (2002) Ana Bortz's Law Suit and Minority Rights in Japan. *JPRI (Japan Policy Research Institute) Working Paper* No. 88, September 2002. Accessed 2008.9.20 from: www.jpri.org/publications/workingpapers/wp88.html.

Part III

Professional practices in arbitration

9 Internationalisation through institutional arbitration

The Malaysian success story

Sundra Rajoo

Introduction

The past decades have seen international arbitration confirm its position as the preferred means of resolving cross-border commercial and investment disputes. Arbitration has been widely regarded as providing significant advantages over national court litigation, including neutral expert decision makers, internationally enforceable awards, confidentiality, and procedural flexibility.

Arbitration clauses are now included in most international commercial contracts as a matter of a prerequisite. As the arbitration of cross-border transactions has increased in popularity in recent years, arbitration has also become more international.

With the rise in cross-border trade and the increase in international arbitration, the arbitration segment struggled to fit in the role of the national courts. Due to the hitches associated with the impact of national courts in international arbitration, a delocalisation theory was developed. It is based on parties' agreement, otherwise the award could not be eligible for enforcement and is detached from the procedural rules of the place of arbitration, the procedural rules of any specific national law, the substantive law of the place of arbitration, and the national substantive law of any specific jurisdiction.

It is usually emphasised that arbitration is chosen because of freedom and flexibility of this method of dispute resolution, and that is why the parties should not be bound to the peculiarities of mandatory laws of the place of arbitration. Moreover, internationalisation and institutionalisation of arbitration could be attractive, since the parties would avoid facing the risk of having an unenforceable award due to unforeseen non-compliance with local procedural law.[1]

Today, the New York Convention and the United Nations Commission on International Trade Law (UNCITRAL) Model Law stand as the cornerstone of internationalisation and an indispensable element of international commercial arbitration. The 1958 New York Convention is the most successful multilateral instrument in the field of international trade law. It is the centrepiece in the mosaic of treaties on arbitration laws that ensure acceptance of arbitral awards in arbitration agreements. Courts around the world have been applying and interpreting the Convention for over 50 years, in an increasingly unified and harmonised fashion.

The UNCITRAL Model Law has had much success in international trade, given that it is promoted not only by the United Nations towards its member states but also by individuals

1 Shirlow, Esme (2016) UNCITRAL's 2016 Notes on Organizing Arbitral Proceedings: Evolutions and Fragmentations in International Arbitration. Available at: http://kluwerarbitrationblog.com/2016/09/07/uncitrals-2016-notes-on-organizing-arbitral-proceedings-evolutions-and-fragmentations-in-international-arbitration/.

and corporations that seek the many benefits of arbitration in the resolution of their disputes, and who so provide an arbitration clause in their contract, or who may otherwise have a full arbitration agreement. The two have served as a momentous tool towards the arbitration scene as we see it today.

In Malaysia, both domestic and international arbitration proceedings are presently governed by the Arbitration Act 2005, last revised in 2011. Repealing and supplanting the Arbitration Act 1952, the underlying rationale of the 2005 Act was, in effect, to bring Malaysian arbitration in line with modern international practice. As such, the Act adheres most faithfully to the Model Law regime, reprising most of its broad precepts and differing only in respect of certain definitions and concepts, as well as, in Part III of the Act, expanding on areas not covered by the Model Law, including the consequences of the failure of an arbitrator to act. Notably, the 2005 Act limits the grounds for resisting enforcement of an arbitral award to the narrowly defined circumstances contemplated in the Model Law and moreover, "[a] comparison of the index to Part II [the core] of the new Act (ss. 6 to 39) shows that it follows section by section and in the same order the subject headings of ss. 3 to 36 of the Model Law."[2]

Apart from the Model Law, there are significant instruments that have made major contributions to the goal of harmonisation of arbitration law, such as institutional arbitration rules, international associations' guidelines such as those of the International Bar Association, customary law and practice, and the liberalisation of national legislations. The global trend towards decreasing the role of domestic courts in transnational commercial disputes has made the arbitration system more autonomous.

The need for internationalisation

The landscape of international trade today warrants the internationalisation of arbitration. In 2014, exports from World Trade Organisation members totalled US$18 trillion in 2014.[3] The main powers in trade and international commerce have also faced very volatile challenges. For example, China overtook Japan as the leading Asian exporter in 2004, 3 years after its accession to the World Trade Organisation. China surpassed the United States in 2007 and Germany in 2009 to become the world's leading exporter. In fact, the Asian economy today looks at the many challenges and opportunities led by China through its "One Belt One Road" Initiative.

In view of the current climate in global economy, internationalisation is mandatory and not optional. The internationalisation of arbitration is required to provide solutions all over the world. Also, arbitration has to be a cost-effective, flexible, quick, final, enforceable, and predictable way of dispute resolution. It is necessary to explore the ways for the advancement of international arbitration, parallel to the global developments and trends in technology, trade, finance, and business practice. The international business practice requires an efficient and dynamic dispute settlement mechanism that is adaptable to fast-changing technology, international trade, and business practice. It has been argued that the tendency to keep transnational commercial disputes out of the courts, and thereby beyond the reach of local laws, is nearly universal.

Apart from procedural grounds, the narrative and conservative approaches to arbitrability and public policy issues by the local courts have caused inconsistent court decisions. The

2 Davidson, William Stanley Waker and Rajoo, Sundra (2005) The New Malaysian Arbitration Regime, Comments Off On The New Malaysian Arbitration Regime 2005 – MLJ August 2006.

3 World Trade Organisation (2015). International Trade Statistics 2015. [online] Available at: www.wto.org/english/res_e/statis_e/its2015_e/its15_toc_e.html.

effectiveness of the New York Convention to some extent depends on national laws, since the procedure on enforcement of awards should be in accordance with the rules of the country where the award is relied upon.

The Convention is further criticised to lack efficient and universal enforcement procedures. Consequently, there is a lack of consistency in the challenge and enforcement process, due to the impact of national laws and courts. The rising criticisms on diverse local approaches at the post-award stage of arbitration have aroused new discussions.[4] It is argued that internationalisation that disrupts and transforms the boundaries and hierarchies is crucial in international trade and commercial and finance law. Therefore, the internationalisation of arbitration law is believed to be an exclusive solution to the issue of a lack of harmonisation.

There has been a search for more fair, efficient, predictable, and harmonised mechanisms in international arbitration. The harmonisation of the challenge process and enforcement of international arbitration awards is particularly important in order to have a more secure legal environment. These questions lead to a search for a universal system of international commercial arbitration and an alternative solution for true internationalisation of the arbitration process.

The Kuala Lumpur Regional Centre for Arbitration approach and experience

This universal system of international commercial arbitration and an alternative solution is necessary and has come through due to the fair implementation of relevant multilateral treaties such as the New York Convention. The internationalisation of arbitration has succeeded, as the common practices in arbitration remain the same in different jurisdictions.

As a matter of fact, because of the internationalisation of arbitration in the jurisdictions, in both common and civil law countries, there has been a proliferation of "safe seats." This basically shows that arbitration has been much more effective and reliable in the last decades, as the countries have made efforts to implement proper mechanisms and provisions, based on the experience of other places.

The jurisdictions have harmonised their arbitration frameworks and their arbitral institutions to offer more accurate arbitration proceedings. On this note, the Kuala Lumpur Regional Centre for Arbitration (KLRCA) has adopted the UNCITRAL Rules, which proves the commitment to follow the well-established arbitration principles. However, should arbitration be the same in every single part of the world, the scheme would not improve. In that regard, it is crucial to balance the internationalisation of the principles with innovation at the same time. In innovation, the arbitral institutions play a key role. As think tanks, the institutions are able to give support and feedback to the governments and lawmakers on the arbitration cases they deal with. This may eventually end up with the implementation of new state policies to improve the arbitral framework.[5]

As daily users of arbitration, the institutions are able to note the needs of the stakeholders much faster. Therefore, the role of the institutions is essential for innovation. For instance, on arbitration rules, KLRCA did pass a set of "Fast Track Rules," whose main achievement is the establishment of a deadline to finish proceedings with an award. This has been widely

4 Eskiyörük, Serhat (2013) Towards a Transnational Dispute Resolution. [online] Available at: www.trans-lex.org/bibliopdfs/serhat_eskiyoruk.pdf.

5 Kim, Jongi (2014) "International Arbitration in East Asia: From Emulation to Innovation" *The Arbitration Brief* 4(1), 1–30.

welcomed in the entire sector, as having an arbitration dispute completed within 160 days is very attractive.[6]

Further, and considering innovation as an important task within arbitration, KLRCA also considers it relevant to maintain a regionalist approach to the services provided. As a regional centre set up in Malaysia, KLRCA has always maintained an eye on its users. In this sense, KLRCA realised that, as Malaysia is a hub for Islamic finance, a specific set of rules designed for that sector might be useful.

Having that in mind, KLRCA worked towards a solution and looked for a Shariah-compliant product that would fulfil the expectations of the users. As a result of that, the KLRCA I-Arbitration rules were launched, providing a Shariah-compliant scheme for disputes that relate to Islamic transactions. The milestone was recognised worldwide and received the congratulations of the arbitration society when the Award for Innovation from the Global Arbitration Review was given to KLRCA.[7] These achievements obtained in Malaysia did eventually reach the practitioners worldwide and have helped to improve the arbitration scenario. The involvement in the development of new rules by the institutions is necessary, as improvements are needed to serve different contexts.

Beyond its success, international arbitration is facing many challenges today. There is an increased concern over its judicialisation, its time and cost, and various ethical issues. What can be done to overcome these challenges and to make sure that arbitration will continue to offer the qualities and advantages that have been the key to its success?

Prominent institutions do also compete in this field, and their amendments and proposals do shed light on this world of arbitration. This competition is enriching, but, at the same time, there are challenges to be addressed. The changes carried out in arbitration need to be put forth and accepted by the arbitral community in order to ensure successful implementation.[8]

There is always a need in arbitration to be able to adapt ourselves to the given circumstances. All the changes also need constant capacity building to be able to be implemented. The proposals have to be explained to the users in advance to avoid a wrong execution of the new rules. With any change or new endeavour, eliminating initial doubt can only be successfully carried out by engaging the right people in a precise manner. On the other hand, being able to overcome challenges as an institution also provides opportunities. In this sense, the possibility of being able to develop a cooperative network with other arbitral institutions throughout the world is worth the efforts undertaken.

As an institution, the KLRCA has always worked towards developing relationships with its other collaborating institutions. As a matter of fact, KLRCA has signed various memorandums of understanding with different arbitral and education institutions, in order to create a big network that could easily raise awareness on the different relevant aspects. As such, the goal of this network is to improve the international arena with the expertise and knowledge that come out of the different participants. Being able to work together as a group increases the chances to have a louder voice in the international field.

6 Lim, Jonathan (2015) Are All Institutional Rules Now Basically The Same? [online] Available at: http://kluwerarbitrationblog.com/2015/04/10/are-all-institutional-rules-now-basically-the-same/.

7 Gadelshina, Elvira R. (2013) What Plays the Key Role in the Success of an Arbitration Institution? [online] Available at: www.financierworldwide.com/what-plays-the-key-role-in-the-success-of-an-arbitration-institution/#.WJmXG2-GO6J.

8 McIlwrath, Michael (2013) Can Arbitration Keep Up? Singapore Ratchets Up Forum Competition. [online] Available at: http://kluwerarbitrationblog.com/2013/10/31/can-arbitration-keep-up-singapore-forum-competition/.

In the same way, institutions might also make the best of their positions. For instance, leading practitioners usually deal with arbitral institutions and give feedback to them on the application of rules and hot topics in the world.[9] However, without the assistance of the institutions, many attorneys might not even be heard. The arbitral institutions do receive the comments from the community, and, because of its responsibility as think tanks, they can actually endeavour to look for developments, changes, and amendments.

Still, opportunities for arbitral institutions to grow also come with different initiatives. As the arbitral framework is in constant change with new options and solutions, training is always welcomed. The institutions play a very important role in this aspect, as, linked to the idea referred to above, they have the capacity building required.

Recently, the KLRCA has developed training courses for Sports Arbitration, as this is a niche area that has been receiving a lot of attention in the last few years. The same is true with adjudication, since training courses have been provided yearly since the enactment of the Construction Industry Payment and Adjudication Act in Malaysia (CIPAA). Because of this, the Alternative Dispute Resolution (ADR) scheme has gained in consistency in Malaysia, since leading practitioners worldwide have been engaged in the exchange of knowledge.

All this, being put together, will eventually modify the ADR world. The opportunity given to the institutions to assist, not only in arbitration, is huge, and if the institutions do actually focus on the relevant topics and fields, improvements will eventually come.

Road ahead and conclusions

The challenge lies with the next step to be taken. Given that arbitration is a mechanism that is preferred by international investors, as such the investment and cross-border legal consumers generally tend to allot the cases to legal practitioners with a distinct multi- or cross-jurisdictional practice experience. Other than creating such awareness, it is equally important to ensure that effort to build capacity is implemented.

Arbitral institutions should initiate groundbreaking work to build capacity and knowledge amongst policymakers, negotiators, the judiciary, and parliamentarians, and even strive to take it further. Arbitral institutions should be constantly engaged with other arbitral institutions to reach the true mark of internationalisation.[10]

To truly reach an international stature, the obligation also lies in the arbitral institutions to introduce innovative ADR mechanisms to face a variety of questions and issues arising from today's complex web of international trade and business. Innovation also means taking traits peculiar to a particular region and addressing them.[11] One such example of innovation can be seen in the KLRCA I-Arbitration Rules as explained before. Such evolutions include the rise of hybrid regime arbitration. But, in the end, internationalisation cannot be achieved by arbitral institutions working in isolated silos. Internationalisation can only be achieved through groundbreaking innovation and hand-in-hand capacity to help build an ADR mechanism that is successful and sustainable.

9 Liu, Joe and Bao, Chiann (2017) GAR Chapter: Innovation in Asia. [online] Globalarbitrationreview.com. Available at: http://globalarbitrationreview.com/chapter/1036901/innovation-in-asia.

10 Melnitzer, Julius (2017) Focus: How Do Global Arbitration Bodies Compare? [online] Lawtimesnews.com. Available at: www.lawtimesnews.com/201502164487/focus-on/focus-how-do-global-arbitration-bodies-compare.

11 Rogers, Catherine (2017) Innovative New Criteria for Appointment of Arbitrators at Commercial Arbitration Centre of Lisbon. [online] Kluwer Arbitration Blog. Available at: http://kluwerarbitrationblog.com/2015/07/10/innovative-new-criteria-for-appointment-of-arbitrators-at-commercial-arbitration-centre-of-lisbon/.

10 Arresting the crisis of confidence in arbitration – a Malaysian perspective

Lam Wai Loon

Introduction

Is there a crisis in arbitration? Whilst, according to KLRCA's (Kuala Lumpur Regional Centre for Arbitration) Statistics on Arbitration Cases Registered, there was a marked increase in the number of arbitration cases registered with KLRCA since 2010, we see a decrease in the number of cases registered with KLRCA after 2013. Based on the statistics,[1] there were a total of 22 cases handled by KLRCA in 2010, 52 cases in 2011, 135 cases in 2012 and 156 cases in 2013; but in 2014, the number dropped to 112; and in 2015 (up to the end of July), only 63 cases were registered with KLRCA.

I submit that the decline is likely due to two reasons. The first reason is the improved efficiency in the speed of case disposal by the judicial court system in recent years, which now makes arbitration proceedings seem to take much longer, with higher costs than court proceedings, and therefore less attractive, compared to court proceedings. The second reason is the enactment of the fairly new legislation called the Construction Industry Payment and Adjudication Act 2012, also popularly known as 'CIPAA', which came into force on 15 April 2014. CIPAA introduces the statutory adjudication regime, which provides for an interim, speedy and relatively cheap method of resolution of construction payment disputes in Malaysia. CIPAA allows the claimant to commence an adjudication proceeding for a payment claim under a construction contract during or after the completion of the project works, separately or concurrently with arbitration or court litigation on the same subject matter.

Courts have become more efficient in terms of speed of resolution of disputes, since the transformation exercise of the Malaysian judicial system led by our previous Chief Justice Tun Zaki bin Tun Azmi in 2009 and continued by his successors. Cases are being disposed of faster, and this has, in turn, cut down the legal costs incurred by litigants in court proceedings. Today, commercial and civil cases are generally completed within 9–12 months from the date of filing, with only a small percentage of cases dragged longer than 12 months. This has invariably further raised the expectation of users of arbitration – an alternative dispute resolution (ADR) that has long held itself out as a more efficient and cost-effective alternative to litigation.

David Rivkin and Samantha Rowe – in their article titled 'The Role of the Tribunal in Controlling Arbitral Costs', featured in Volume 82 of the *CIARB Arbitration Journal* – made this pertinent comment on the need for a speedier and cheaper resolution of disputes by arbitration:

1 Information and data as at July 2015 provided by the Director of the Kuala Lumpur Regional Center for Arbitration, Professor Datuk Sundra Rajoo.

> A two-year proceeding and excessive legal and arbitration fees are unacceptable in this era of the 24-hour news cycle and tightened belts. Resolution, closure and certainty are the order of the day.[2]

The improvement in efficiency and effectiveness in the resolution of cases by our judicial court system has, at the same time, brought about growing dissatisfaction and erosion of confidence in arbitration among users of arbitration. But, this phenomenon is not peculiar to Malaysia only. Voices of such 'dissatisfaction' and 'crisis of confidence' in international arbitration are growing louder in recent years.

Sundaresh Menon, the Chief Justice of Singapore, at the London CIArb Centenary Conference in 2015, made this observation:

> Murmurs of disaffection among users of arbitration have been mounting in recent years, and it is unlikely to be a coincidence that commercial courts around the world are gaining prominence at the same time.[3]

The decrease in arbitration cases could also be due to the introduction of CIPAA, which provides for an interim summary procedure for the resolution of construction payment disputes. It is worthy of note at this juncture that construction arbitrations represent a significant percentage of the total number of arbitrations in Malaysia.

Based on the KLRCA's Statistics on Adjudication Cases registered with the KLRCA, there were a total of 29 cases registered with the KLRCA in 2014. As of the end of July 2015, there have been 90 adjudication cases registered with the KLRCA.[4]

According to the analysis of statistics provided by other jurisdictions, such as Singapore, the United Kingdom and Australia, which have similar statutory adjudication regimes in their jurisdictions, the introduction of the statutory adjudication regime in their jurisdictions has contributed to a significant drop in construction arbitration and litigation cases. In Singapore, there was a drop of about 30%–40% in construction arbitration and litigation cases since the introduction of the statutory adjudication regime; in the United Kingdom, a drop of about 70% was seen; and in the New South Wales, Australia, a drop of about 90% was seen.[5]

A decline in the number of arbitration cases registered with KLRCA in the years 2014 and 2015 – and, at the same time, a marked increase in adjudication cases – reinforced the adverse impact on arbitration brought about by the introduction of the statutory adjudication regime.

The main causes of the crisis of confidence in arbitration

What are the main causes of the crisis of confidence in arbitration? In 2010, the White and Case Survey[6] identified two of the main reasons in users' disappointment in arbitration, namely, 'excessive or failure to control the process' and delay caused by the arbitrator, and

2 Volume 82 of the CIARB Arbitration Journal, p. 123.

3 'Safeguarding the Future of Arbitration', by Daniel Waldek and Herbert Smith Freehills. kluwerarbitrationblog.com/2015/08/04/safeguarding-the-future-of-arbitration/.

4 Information provided by the Kuala Lumpur Regional Centre of Arbitration.

5 See Chow Kok Fong's Security of Payment and Construction Adjudication, 2nd Ed (LexisNexis, 2013).

6 2010 White & Case Survey, p. 26.

these ultimately traced back to lack of control by arbitrators in arbitration proceedings being the main culprit.

The 2010 White and Case Survey also made this observation:

> It was pervasive throughout the questionnaire results and the interviews that parties prefer pro-active arbitrators who take control of proceedings. This is seen as an effective mechanism to limit cost and delay and reduce risks of later challenge.[7]

There may be many reasons for lack (or perceived lack) of control by arbitrators in arbitration proceedings, but they may be grouped into three main categories. The first is the lack of courage on the part of the arbitrator. The second is the lack of skill and quality required of an efficient and effective arbitrator, and this may be due to the arbitrator's lack of experience, insufficient appreciation of the extent of his powers or perceived lack of power. The third is the arbitrator's unwillingness to take charge or control of the proceedings, and this may be due to internal politics, the arbitrator's overemphasis on party autonomy and his trying to please both parties or counsel or reluctance to offend any of the parties or counsel in the proceedings.

What are the other possible responses to the crisis?

In their article 'The Role of the Tribunal in Controlling Arbitral Costs', David Rivkin and Samantha Rowe advocated the view that arbitrators must control the proceedings to avoid excessive costs and delay in the proceedings before them. The authors argued that:

> Arbitrators who simply sit back and let the parties control the agenda are letting those same parties down. Moreover, they are letting the system down ....

In fact, it is clear that parties want active intervention. They want an arbitrator to save the parties from themselves, or sometimes from their external counsel.[8]

Michael Schneider, when mounting his criticism on the IBA Guidelines on Party Representation, argued that, instead of implementing various rules on counsel conduct, what we instead need are arbitrators willing to intervene as necessary to ensure efficiency of proceedings; and he said 'we need arbitrators with courage to discipline parties'.[9]

But, is having proactive arbitrators the solution to the crisis? I respectfully submit that it is not. Whilst the promotion of 'proactiveness' of arbitrators is laudable, it would unfortunately not be the solution to the crisis; the ability of arbitrators to apply 'proactive' measures effectively and efficiently in arbitration proceedings to bring about the benefits in terms of cost and time would depend on the individual arbitrator's experience, confidence, ability and willingness to control the proceedings, and it is an unfortunate fact that there are not many arbitrators who possess the qualities required to achieve the objective of a cost- and time-efficient arbitration.

To build a sustainable future for arbitration and regain the confidence of the users, I submit that we shall not only rest our hope on the arbitrators, parties and counsel to do the

7 2010 White & Case Survey, p. 32.

8 P. 123.

9 ASA Bulletin, Volume 31, 2013, President's Message, pp. 497–501.

right thing, but we must also have a legal framework that provides a clear guidance as to what the arbitrators and the parties or their counsel should do, which matches the current expectation of the users.

In recent years, we see a coherent effort by various leading arbitration institutions like the United Nations Commission on International Trade Law (UNCITRAL), the London Court of International Arbitration (LCIA), the International Centre for Dispute Resolution (ICDR), Singapore International Arbitration Centres (SIAC) and Hong Kong International Arbitration Centres (HKIAC) to amend their arbitration rules to allow for more power to the arbitrator to control the proceedings to ensure a fair, expeditious, economical and final determination of the dispute, departing from the previous regime, which focuses more on the parties' consensus on the procedure or running of the proceedings. By examining the amendments, we see an enlargement of power of the arbitrator and, at the same time, a circumscribed parties' autonomy. The intention of these institutions for making the amendments is clear. However, despite these amendments, the users' discontent remains.

We have, in the past, left the procedure for the running of the proceedings to the parties under the philosophy of party autonomy; it did not work. We have then shifted our emphasis to giving more power to arbitrators and promoting creative methods and procedures in conducting arbitral proceedings, but the problems on costs and delay in arbitration persist. Perhaps, it is time for a major overhaul to our arbitral legal framework, as well as the mindset of the stakeholders, and let the rules and the legal framework dictate clearly how the arbitration proceedings should be properly run. We need an arbitral legal framework that would rejuvenate the confidence of users in arbitration, instil confidence in arbitrators in the management of arbitration proceedings and ensure consistency in the efficiency of arbitration, both in terms of time and cost. In other words, we need an arbitral legal framework that provides a clear guide on the proceedings for both the arbitrators and the parties or their counsel to follow, aimed at reducing time and cost in arbitration. In this respect, we should, perhaps, consider having a legal framework that provides for certain mandatory rules, amongst others:

- a Fixed timelines for submission of pleadings, documents, factual witness statements, expert reports and final submissions. Variation of any such fixed timeline can only be made with the permission of the arbitrator, upon an application by either or both parties;
- b Expressly conferring discretion to arbitrator to direct the order of proceedings, bifurcate proceedings, exclude cumulative or irrelevant testimony or other evidence and direct parties to focus on their presentations on issues, the decision of which could dispose of all or part of the case;
- c It is mandatory for parties to agree on issues for determination after the close of submission of case/defence by the parties, but before the commencement of hearing;
- d A fixed timeline for arbitrator to deliver his or her decision, with corresponding penalty of reduction of entitlement in arbitrator's fees due to delay;
- e Notwithstanding the arbitration agreement, disputes involving claim of less than a certain amount shall be referred to a sole arbitrator, unless otherwise agreed by the parties subsequent to the referral to arbitration.

In addition, we should also consider implementing arbitration-annexed mediation as part of the management of the arbitration cases. One must not forget that one of the main attractions of court litigation is the success of their court-annexed mediation. Based on the statistics provided by our Chief Justice for the year 2013, there were 251 cases registered with the first instance courts in Johor Bahru, with 47.6% of the cases settled through court-annexed mediation; in Kuala Lumpur, 571 cases were registered, with 28.3% cases settled and in Kuantan, 80 cases were registered, with 25% cases settled.

The same success story is also seen in other jurisdictions in Asia. In New South Wales, Australia, in 2013, there were a total of 671 cases filed, with 55% cases settled through court annexed mediation; and in 2014, 486 cases were filed, with 51% cases settled.

In Hong Kong, in 2014, 632 cases were filed at first instance courts (excluding family cases and land tribunal matters), with 65% cases either fully or partially settled. At the District Court level, 397 cases were filed, with 65% cases either fully or partially settled.

In Singapore, statistics based on both civil and criminal cases registered – but excluding family cases – in 2013 show that 7,292 cases were sent for mediation, with 92% success rate. In 2014, 6,420 cases were sent for mediation, with 89% success rate.

Finally, in Thailand, in 2011, a cumulative total of 163,926 cases were filed, with 79% cases settled through mediation. In 2012, a cumulative total of 180,607 cases were filed, also with 79% cases settled through mediation.

Seeing the success of court-annexed mediation, perhaps we should also move to implement our own arbitration-annexed mediation, with express power to be given to the arbitrator to direct parties to attempt mediation at any stage of the arbitral proceedings. The power of the arbitrator should include the power to forfeit a winning party its costs award if the losing party demonstrated that its opponent had 'unreasonably' been uncooperative or refused to mediate.

Conclusion

Some, particularly the purists in arbitration, may argue that these suggestions would destroy the notion of party autonomy, which forms the very important ingredient and pillar of success and popularity of arbitration, but I believe that in the current climate, if we are to continue to give more prominence to the notion of party autonomy than it should deserve, it will not be too long to see the demise of arbitration in the hearts of the users.

11 Critical evaluation of arbitration in India

Rizul Jai

Discourage litigation, persuade your neighbors to compromise whenever you can. Point-out to them how the normal winner is often a loser in fees, expenses, cost and time.

Globalisation and modernisation have led to tremendous growth and expansion of cross-border trade, commerce and investment, with a proportionate rise in the number of commercial disputes. Arbitration is the by-product of globalisation. Arbitration is a leading method for resolving disputes arising from commercial agreements and other domestic and international relationships. The significant increase in international trade and economic development in India during the last three decades has led to an increased number of commercial disputes, thereby further burdening the judicial system struggling with huge pendency of cases. As a result, Alternative Dispute Resolution (ADR), including arbitration, has become crucial in dealing with domestic as well as international disputes.

India has a history of settlement of disputes by arbitration from time immemorial. In ancient times, people often voluntarily submitted their disputes to a group of wise men of a community—called the panchayat—for a binding resolution.[1] Mahatma Gandhi advocated *panchayati raj* as the foundation of India's political system; it would have been a decentralised form of government where each village would be responsible for its own affairs. The term for such a vision was Gram Swaraj (village self-governance).[2] The Panchayat (village council) in villages would settle disputes between parties. The Panchayats have now got a Constitutional recognition under the Constitution (73rd Amendment Act 1992). The Indian Constitution also stipulates settlement of disputes by arbitration as a Directive Principle of State Policy [Article 51(d)].[3]

History of arbitration in India

Prior to the Arbitration and Conciliation Act, 1996, hereinafter referred to as 'the 1996 Act', the law governing arbitration in India consisted mainly of three statutes:

i The Arbitration (Protocol and Convention) Act, 1937 ('1937 Act')
ii The Indian Arbitration Act, 1940 ('1940 Act') and
iii The Foreign Awards (Recognition and Enforcement) Act, 1961 ('1961 Act').

1 K Ravi Kumar, 'Alternative Dispute Resolution in Construction Industry', International Council of Consultants (ICC) papers, www.iccindia.org. at p. 2. K Ravi Kumar is assistant executive engineer, Salarjung Museum, Hyderabad.

2 https://en.wikipedia.org/wiki/Panchayati_raj_(India).

3 Article 51(d) of Directive Principles of State Policy, Constitution of India.

The Arbitration Act 1940 was the general law governing arbitration in India, and it resembled the English Arbitration Act of 1934. The Arbitration Act, 1940, dealt with only domestic arbitration and, during its tenure, intervention of the Court was required in all the three stages of arbitrations in India, i.e., prior to the reference of the dispute to the arbitral tribunal, during the proceedings before the arbitral tribunal and after the award was passed by the arbitral tribunal. Before an arbitral tribunal took notice of a dispute, Court intervention was required to set the arbitration proceedings in motion. The existence of an agreement and of a dispute was required to be proved. During the course of the proceedings, the intervention of the Court was necessary for the extension of time for making an award. Finally, before the award could be enforced, it was required to be made effective by the rule of the Court. Thus, the implementation and operation of the Arbitration Act 1940 was ineffective.[4]

Purpose of the Arbitration and Conciliation Act 1996

The Government of India, in consonance with the Model Law by the United Nations Commission on International Trade Law (UNCITRAL) on International Commercial Arbitration, 1985 and UNCITRAL Conciliation Rules 1980, drafted the Arbitration and Conciliation Act, 1996 with the primary concern to have cost-effective and speedy arbitration. Amongst the main objectives of the new Act, as set out in the Statement of Objects and Reasons, are 'to minimize the supervisory role of courts in the arbitral process' and 'to provide that every final arbitral award is enforced in the same manner as if it were a decree of the Court'. The Honourable Supreme Court of India, in Fuerst Day Lawson Ltd v. Jindal Exports Ltd,[5] observed that the object of the Act is to provide speedy and alternative solution to dispute and avoid protraction of litigation. The Supreme Court further remarked, in Food Corporation of India v. Indian Council of Arbitration,[6] that the legislative intent is to minimise the supervisory role of the court in the arbitral process and quick nomination or appointment of the arbitrator, leaving all contentious issues to be decided in arbitration.

Scheme of the Act

The 1996 Act contains two significant parts—Part I and Part II thereof. Part I contains the provisions for domestic and international commercial arbitration in India, irrespective of the nationalities of the parties. Part II provides for the enforcement of foreign awards to which the New York Convention or the Geneva Convention applies.

The 1996 Act contains two unusual features that differ from the UNCITRAL Model Law. First, while the UNCITRAL Model Law was designed to apply only to international commercial arbitrations,[7] the 1996 Act applies both to international and domestic arbitrations. Second, the 1996 Act goes beyond the UNCITRAL Model Law in the area of minimising judicial intervention.[8]

4 www.nishithdesai.com/International Commercial Arbitration June 2015 Law and Recent Developments in India by Nishith Desai Associates 2015.
5 (2001) 6 SCC 356; AIR 2001 SCC 2293.
6 Food Corp Of India v. Indian Council of Arbitration, (2003) 6 SCC 564; AIR 2003 Supreme Court 3011.
7 Article 1 of the UNICITRAL Model Law.
8 S K Dholakia, 'Analytical Appraisal of the Arbitration and Conciliation (Amendment) Bill, 2003', ICA's Arbitration Quarterly, ICA, New Delhi, 2005 vol. XXXIX/No. 4 at p. 3. S K Dholakia is a Member of ICC International Court of Arbitration and Senior Advocate, Supreme Court of India.

Now, in view of the intent and object, this chapter is an attempt to critically examine and analyse how the Courts in India have interpreted the provisions of the Arbitration and Conciliation Act, 1996, to achieve these objects. This chapter is also an attempt to define the areas and to what extent the judicial intervention by the Courts in India is justified.

Judicial intervention in arbitration In India

The new Arbitration and Conciliation Act, 1996, was incorporated with the legislative intent to have an efficacious and speedy mechanism for the resolution of disputes and to reduce the judicial intervention to the minimum, due to which the earlier Arbitration Act, 1940 suffered serious infirmities. Section 5 of 'the 1996 Act' provides that no judicial authority shall intervene where so provided in this part. Section 8 of the 1996 Act provides for reference of a dispute to arbitration during pendency of a suit, thereby making it a mandatory duty for the judicial authority, i.e., court to stay legal proceedings if started, where the subject matter has been referred to an arbitral tribunal.[9] The 1996 Act provides for the following situations where a judicial authority may intervene during the arbitral process:

a For any interim measure of protection or injunction or for any appointment of receiver etc.[10] (Section 9);
b For Appointment of arbitrators, in the event when one of the party fails to appoint an arbitrator or two appointed arbitrators failed to agree upon the third arbitrator[11] (Section 11);
c In the event terminating the mandate of the arbitrator due to inability to perform his functions or failure to proceed without undue delay[12] (Section 14(2)) and
d For assistance in taking evidence[13] (Section 27).

Appointment of arbitrators

Section 11 of the Act provides for the appointment of arbitrators of any nationality. Parties are free to agree on the procedure to appoint arbitrators. Subsections (4)–(12) deal with appointment of arbitrators by the Chief Justice or any person or institution designated by the Chief Justice when the parties fail to appoint an arbitrator or where the arbitration is to be held with three arbitrators, and the two appointed arbitrators fail to agree on the third arbitrator within the stipulated time. If one of the parties does not appoint an arbitrator within 30 days or if two appointed arbitrators do not appoint a third arbitrator within 30 days, or the persons or institutions designated by the parties fail to act, the party can request the Chief Justice of India to appoint an arbitrator.[14] The Chief Justice of India can authorise any person or institution to appoint an arbitrator. In case of an international commercial dispute, the application for the appointment of arbitrators has to be made to the

9 Section 8 of the Arbitration & Conciliation Act 1996.
10 Section 9 of the Arbitration & Conciliation Act 1996.
11 Section 11 of the Arbitration & Conciliation Act 1996.
12 Section 14(2) of the Arbitration & Conciliation Act 1996.
13 Section 27 of the Arbitration & Conciliation Act 1996.
14 Section 11(4) of the Arbitration & Conciliation Act 1996.

Chief Justice of India only. In case of other domestic disputes, application has to be made to the Chief Justice of the High Court, within whose jurisdiction the parties are situated.[15]

Two of the most heavily criticised judicial interventions are as follows:

A Whether Chief Justice carries out a judicial function in determining the appointing of an arbitrator, as opposed to a **purely administrative function** and

B Whether the liberal attitude towards **'public policy'** under Section 34 of the 1996 Act effectively allows courts to set aside awards, which are based on 'errors of law'.

A Judicial function vis-à-vis administrative function

The Honourable Supreme Court of India has dealt with the nature of the appointment of arbitrators by the courts as being judicial or administrative.

i The scope and effect of the provisions of Section 11 of the 1996 Act had been the subject matter of several decisions rendered by the Supreme Court. In Ador Samia (P) Ltd Vs Peekay Holdings Ltd,[16] a Bench of two learned Judges of the Supreme Court held that the Chief Justice or any person or institution designated the Chief Justice acts in administrative capacity under Section 11 of the Act, and hence an order passed in exercise of such power does not attract the provisions of the Article 136 of the Constitution.

ii A two-judge Bench referred the case in Adur Samia (P) Ltd Vs Peekay Holdings Ltd for reconsideration to the Bench of three learned Judges. A three-judge Bench in Konkan Railway Corporation Ltd. Vs Mehul Construction Co.[17] affirmed the view taken by the two-Judge Bench in Adur Samia (P) Ltd Vs Peekay Holdings Ltd., holding that the order passed by the Chief Justice or the designate under Section 11 of the Act was an administrative order not amenable to the jurisdiction of the Court under Article 136.

iii Subsequently, a Bench of two judges, in Konkan Railway Corp. Ltd Vs Rani Construction (P) Ltd.,[18] referred to a larger Bench of the said decision of three-judge Bench for reconsideration. Thereafter, a Constitution Bench consisting of five learned judges in Konkan Railway Corp. Ltd. Vs Rani Construction (P) Ltd.[19] affirmed the decision of the three-judge Bench in Konkan Railway Corp. Ltd. v. Mehul Construction Co.,[20] holding inter alia that the order of the Chief Justice or the designate under Section 11 nominating an arbitrator is not an adjudicatory order and that neither the Chief Justice nor the designate acts as a tribunal, and hence any order passed by them cannot be a subject matter of appeal by Special Leave under Article 136. The Constitution Bench also held that the Chief Justice or the designate is not required to perform any adjudicatory function, and that the order nominating an arbitrator would be amenable to challenge under Section 12 read with Section 13 of the Act. Since the exercise of the power is purely

15 Section 11(12) of the Act.
16 (1999) 8 SCC 572.
17 (2000) 7 SCC 201, Indian Kanoon.org.com.
18 (2000) 8 SCC 159.
19 (2002) 2 SCC 388.
20 (2000) 7 SCC 201.

administrative in nature, it does not contemplate a response from the other party, and hence a notice to the opposite party is not necessary.

iv Subsequently, the decision of the Constitution Bench has been reconsidered by the larger Bench consisting of seven judges in SBP Co. v. Patel Engineering Ltd.[21] The Court overruled the decision in Konkan Railway Corp. Ltd. Vs Rani Construction (P) Ltd.[22] rendered by five learned judges and held that the power exercised by the Chief Justice of the High Courts or the Chief Justice of India under Section 11(6) of the Act is judicial power and not an administrative power and that such power, in its entirety, could be delegated only to another judge of that Court. The Honourable Supreme Court has held that the power exercised by the Chief Justice of India or the Chief Justice of the High Court under Section 11(6) is judicial power and not an administrative power. The Honourable Court has sanctioned further court interventions in the arbitral process. It was further held that the Chief Justice, while discharging this function, is entitled to adjudicate on contentious preliminary issues, such as the existence of a valid arbitration agreement, and the Chief Justice's findings on these preliminary issues would be final and binding on the arbitral tribunal.

v In 2014, the Supreme Court delivered several landmark rulings pertaining to the appointment of an arbitrator. The Court examined the scope of intervention to be exercised by courts when parties have chosen to arbitrate in Enercon (India) Ltd. & Ors. v. Enercon GmBH & Anr.[23] This judgement is a significant step in the right direction to bring Indian arbitration law in line with international jurisprudence and will aid International Commercial Arbitration—India in being perceived as an arbitration-friendly jurisdiction.

  The Court held that an arbitration agreement is valid so far, as the intention of the parties to resolve the disputes by arbitration is clear; any allegation of non-conclusion of the main contract is immaterial. Sections 8, 10, 11 and 45 of the Arbitration and Conciliation Act are mere machinery provisions for the Court to support and aid arbitration. The seat of arbitration would be the country whose law is chosen as the curial law (law of arbitration) by the parties. The courts of the seat of arbitration have the exclusive jurisdiction to exercise supervisory powers over the arbitration process. The courts of the venue of arbitration cannot have concurrent jurisdiction in this regard. The decision to uphold a poorly drafted arbitration clause is another welcome indicator of the Supreme Court's willingness to uphold the intention of the parties to arbitrate, despite irregularities in the main contract.[24]

B Public policy

Section 34 of the 1996 Act provides for manner and grounds for challenge of an arbitral award in harmony with the UNCITRAL Model Rules, which provide grounds for setting aside an arbitral award. One of the grounds is that the award is in conflict with the 'public policy' of the state.

21 (2005) 8 SCC 618.
22 (2002) 2 SCC 388.
23 (2014) 5 SCC 1.
24 http://hsfnotes.com/arbitration, Herbert Smith Free Hill Dispute Resolution.

i Section 34(2)(a) entitles the court to set aside an award only if the parties seeking such relief furnishes proof as regards the existence of the grounds mentioned therein. The grounds are as follows:

a Incapacity of a party;
b Invalid arbitration agreement;
c Lack of proper notice of appointment of arbitrator or of the proceedings or otherwise unable to present his case;
d The arbitral award dealing with the dispute not falling within the terms of submission to arbitration and
e Composition of the tribunal or the arbitral procedure not being in accordance with the agreement of the parties.

ii Section 34(2)(b)(ii) provides that an arbitral award may be set aside by the court if the arbitral award is in conflict with the public policy of India. Section 34 provides that an arbitral award may be set aside by a court on certain grounds specified, which are, however, left to be found out by the court itself. The grounds are as follows:

a The subject matter of the dispute not capable of settlement by arbitration, that is to say, the disputes are not arbitrable and
b The award is in conflict with the public policy of India. All these grounds are common to both domestic as well as international arbitral awards.

The Honourable Supreme Court, on a number of occasions, held that a suit can be filed in a court in India, challenging a foreign award passed by an arbitrator in a matter concerning international commercial transactions if the award is against 'public policy' and in contravention of statutory provisions. It is always in the domain of the judiciary to interpret the public policy at a given point of time.

In the historic ruling of Renusagar Power Co. v. General Electrical Corporation,[25] the Supreme Court, in addition to the narrower meaning to the expression 'public policy', held that an award could be set aside if it is patently illegal. It observed that this would mean that 'public policy' in Section 7(1)(b)(ii) has been used in a narrower sense, and, in order to attract public policy exception, the enforcement of the award must invoke something more than the violation of the law of India. Applying the said criteria, it must be held that the enforcement of a foreign award would be refused on the grounds that it is contrary to public policy if such enforcement would be contrary to the following:

i fundamental policy of Indian law; or
ii the interests of India; or
iii justice or morality.

In Oil and Natural Gas Corporation Limited v. Saw Pipes Limited ('Saw Pipes'),[26] the Supreme Court opined that an award that, on the face of it, is patently in violation of statutory provisions cannot be said to be in public interest and is likely to adversely

25 (1994) AIR 860, (1994) SCC Suppl. (1) 644.
26 (2003) 5 SCC 705.

affect the administration of justice, and hence, it is required to be set aside as being patently illegal. While interpreting the phrase 'public policy of India', the Supreme Court, in the case of ONGC v. Saw Pipes Ltd.,[27] examined the scope and ambit of jurisdiction of the Court under Section 34 of the Act. It was held that if the award is (a) contrary to the substantive provision of law, (b) the provisions of the Act or (c) against the terms of the contract, it would be patently illegal, which could be interfered under Section 34.

The Supreme Court further held that the phrase 'public policy of India' used in Section 34 is required to be given a wider meaning and stated that the concept of public policy connotes some matter that concerns public good and public interest. The award that is patently in violation of any statutory provisions cannot be said to be in the public's interest.

The above judgement of the Honourable Supreme Court has caused concern amongst the legal fraternity, jurists and experts. In the Saw Pipes case, the scope of public policy was widened to include challenge of award when such an award is patently illegal. Some arbitrators have viewed the judgement in the Saw Pipes case with concern. The main attack on the judgement is that it sets the clock back to the same position that existed before the 1996 Act, and it increases the scope of judicial intervention in challenging arbitral awards.[28] The Parliament, when enacting the 1996 Act and following the UNCITRAL Model Law, did not introduce 'patent illegality' as grounds for setting aside an award.

In 2014, the Supreme Court, for the first time, defined the term 'fundamental policy of Indian law', in Oil and Natural Gas Corporation Ltd. v. Western Geco International Ltd. ('Western Geco').[29] The Court observed that the phrase 'fundamental policy of Indian law' had not been elaborated by the Court. Interpreting it in this case, the Court held that the phrase included, inter alia, the following three principles:

- i Disregarding orders of superior courts
- ii Judicial approach
- iii Principles of natural justice
- iv Rational and reasonable decision

However, at the end of 2014, the Supreme Court, in Associate Builders v. Delhi Development Authority,[30] dealt with some of the key issues involving the challenge of an arbitral award in an arbitration seated in India. The Supreme Court discussed and clarified some of the earlier rulings on the scope of 'public policy' in Section 34 of the Act. The Supreme Court observed that the grounds for interfering with an arbitral award are limited to those mentioned in Section 34 of the Act and held that merits of the award can be looked into only under the broad head of 'public policy'.

27 (2003) 5 SCC 705.

28 Ashok H Desai, 'Challenges to an Award – Use and Abuse', ICA's Arbitration Quarterly, ICA, 2006, vol. XLI/No. 2, p. 4. Ashok H Desai is a Senior Advocate of the Supreme Court of India.

29 (2014) 9 SCC 263.

30 (2014) 13 SCALE 226.

The Supreme Court relied on landmark judgements like Renusagarl42,[31] Saw Pipes,[32] McDermott International,[33] Western Geco International Ltd[34] and others to lay down the ground of 'public policy' and observed the following:

- i 'Fundamental Policy of Indian law' would include factors such as (a) disregarding orders of superior courts; (b) judicial approach, which is an antithesis to an arbitrary approach; (c) principles of natural justice and (d) decision of arbitrators cannot be perverse and irrational, insofar as no reasonable person would come to the same conclusion.
- ii An arbitrator is the sole judge with respect to quality and quantity of facts, and therefore, an award is not capable of being set aside solely on account of little evidence or if the quality of evidence is of inferior quality.
- iii The Supreme Court further held that when a court is applying the 'public policy' test to an arbitration award, it does not act as a court of appeal, and consequently, 'errors of fact' cannot be corrected unless the arbitrators' approach is arbitrary or capricious.
- iv The Supreme Court described 'Interest of India' as something that deals with India in world community and its relations with foreign nations.
- v The Supreme Court held that the expression 'award against justice and morality' would include the following: (a) with regard to justice, the award should not be such that it shocks the conscience of the court; (b) with regard to morality, there can be no universal standard; however, the Supreme Court observed that both the English and the Indian courts have restricted the scope of morality to 'sexual immorality' only and (c) with respect to an arbitration, it would be a valid ground when the contract is not illegal but against the mores of the day; however, it held that this would only apply when it shocks the conscience of the court.
- vi The Supreme Court further held that 'Patent Illegality' would include (a) fraud or corruption; (b) contravention of substantive law, which goes to the root of the matter; (c) error of law by the arbitrator; (d) contravention of the Act itself; (e) where the arbitrator fails to consider the terms of the contract and usages of the trade as required under Section 28(3) of the Act and (f) if the arbitrator does not give reasons for the decision.

This decision by the Honourable Supreme Court is an important step, in line with the pro-arbitration decisions of the Supreme Court in the last couple of years. It is a welcome decision, insofar as 'public policy' had been clarified in order to provide guidance on the level of interference sought to be made under Section 34 of the Act. This marks a rare occasion where the Supreme Court has discussed 'morality' in a challenge under Section 34 of the Act.

A new and narrower definition of the term 'public policy' is required in the era of globalisation to encourage foreign investors to carry out healthy commercial relationships in India.

31 (1994) SCC Suppl. (1) 644.
32 (2003) 5 SCC 705.
33 (2006) 11 SCC 181.
34 (2014) 9 SCC 263.

Conclusion

Arbitration in India is developing and evolving. The main purpose of the Act was to provide a speedy and efficacious dispute resolution mechanism to the existing judicial system, which is overburdened with the enormous backlog of cases. Arbitration as a wing of the ADR mechanism is expanding and becoming more popular than litigation. The scope of the 1996 Arbitration Act has been widened to include allegations of fraud and other malpractices as being arbitrable. The Supreme Court of India, in Swiss Timing Limited v. Organising Committee, Commonwealth Games 2010,[35] Delhi, has now held that the allegations of fraud can be determined by arbitration where an arbitration agreement exists between the parties. This sets a new, pro-arbitration tone to the issue of arbitrability of allegations of fraud in Indian-seated arbitrations. It was held in this case that arbitration and criminal proceedings may continue simultaneously. The judgement has reflected a progressive approach in dealing with arbitrable disputes, sending a message across the globe that India is safe as far as intertrade and commerce agreements are concerned.

Earlier, ad hoc arbitration had been the preferred choice of dispute resolution in India, and it still remains. The entry of professional institutes in the market has brought about class facilities, credibility, quality service and effective case management.[36] Mediation and conciliation centers have been set up in High Courts and District Courts. There have been special conciliators appointed for the settlement of family dispute in family courts. In Delhi, special evening courts are set up to conduct mediation for suits for recovery up to a certain limit. The settlement of disputes by arbitration has gained momentum in India. According to the EY report called 'Emerging trends in arbitration in India', published on 18 October 2013, there has been a 200% growth in the number of disputes that have been referred to arbitration. Thus, there is expansion and growth of arbitration under minimal supervision and interference by the judiciary, giving freedom to the contracting parties to dissolve their disputes through mediation and negotiation and not by litigation. The Government of India has under its consideration, proposals for making arbitration the preferred mode for the settlement of commercial disputes by making it more user-friendly, cost-effective and expeditious. In 2014, the Law Commission of India in its 246th Report recommended various amendments in the Arbitration and Conciliation Act, 1996, so that India may become a hub of International Commercial Arbitration.

35 Arbitration Petition No. 34 of 2013.

36 Report by EY-'Emerging Trends in Arbitration in India' 18.10.2013. Mumbai.

12 Arbitration rules in Hong Kong

Mariacarla Giorgetti

12.1 Introduction

The panorama in Hong Kong has recently changed and, with it, the rules for appointing arbitrators. It must be remembered, in fact, that the recent reform of arbitration in Hong Kong has not only introduced the new *Arbitration Ordinance (Chapter 609),* effective from 1 June 2011, but it has also reformed the *Arbitration (Appointment of Arbitrators and Umpires) Rules (Chapter 609B).* This provision has produced a single regime for both internal and international arbitration, largely based on the United Nations Commission on International Trade Law (UNCITRAL) Model Law.

If we bear in mind also the significant role of the *Appointing Authority,* entrusted by the *Ordinance* to the Hong Kong International Arbitration Center (HKIAC), it becomes necessary to examine the relevant HKIAC regulations: the *HKIAC's Administered Arbitration Rules* and the *HKIAC's Domestic Arbitration Rules.* Following the 2011 reform, the *Administered Rules* are now applicable both to internal and international cases. The *Domestic Rules,* however, as can be read in the introduction to the *Domestic Arbitration Rules (2012)* themselves, are reserved for internal cases and cannot be applied in any case where the place of arbitration is outside Hong Kong. It should be clear, nevertheless, that the application of the *Domestic Rules* to internal cases is only possible when the parties expressly opt to apply these rules in order to obtain a formal and convenient procedure in an *ad hoc* arbitration procedure in Hong Kong.

We will begin, therefore, by analysing the regulations contained in the new *Arbitration Ordinance* and *Arbitration (Appointment of Arbitrators and Umpires) Rules.* It may be useful to clarify, first of all, the role of the latter within the legislative panorama of Hong Kong.

12.2 The appointment rules

12.2.1 Introduction

The *Arbitration (Appointment of Arbitrators and Umpires) Rules* (hereafter: *Appointment Rules*) were first introduced in 1997, with L.N. 270 of 1997. They came into force on 16 May of the same year, to the effects of the now-repealed *Ordinance* (Chapter 341). The *Appointment Rules* were later amended by the well-known 2011 reform, implemented by L.N. 38 of 2011, which introduced the new *Ordinance* (Chapter 609).

Doubts arose as to whether the repealing of the old Ordinance (Chapter 341), from which the Appointment Rules derived, had the effect of repealing the Appointment Rules, as well. L.N. 38 of 2011, while reforming the Appointment Rules and introducing Chapter

609B, stated quite clearly that these Rules were to be considered as still in force, since they were not inconsistent with the *Arbitration Ordinance* (Chapter 609), and given that, under *Section* 110 of this Ordinance, they had the same effect for all purposes as if they had been made to the effects of Cap. 609. This, however, proved to be an interim measure. A revised version of the *Appointment Rules* was issued in 2013.

12.2.2 Function and content

Having clarified their origin, it is now necessary to specify their function and the current regulatory context to which they refer. As can be seen from the title, these rules were specifically introduced with the aim of providing clear guidelines to be followed when appointing arbitrators in the cases as of *Sections* 13, 23 or 24, as can be read in the provision of *Section 5*, which describes the area of application of the *Appointment Rules.*

Before examining the methods of appointment introduced with the *Appointment Rules*, it is necessary to take a look at the content of the said *Sections* 13, 23 and 24 of the *Ordinance*, since these enable us to get a better picture of the situation. *Section* 13, entitled "*Article 6 of UNCITRAL Model law (Court or other authority for certain functions of arbitration assistance and supervision)*," refers expressly to the regulations contained in Article 6 of the Model Law. Under certain circumstances, it is necessary for a Court or other authority to intervene in order to assist parties that have met some sort of difficulty. One such case may be a failure to agree upon the number or the appointment of the arbitrators, in accordance with *Sections* 23 and 24, which will be analysed below.

Section 13 indicates which authority is to assume this function, and it does so by referring to Article 6 of the Model Law, which merely remits to each single state, and so to the Courts or other authorities specified at the moment of implementation, the rules for putting the Model Law into effect.

For Hong Kong, therefore, *Subsection 2* of the said *Section* 13 is to be observed. This means that Article 6 is to be interpreted as a reference to the HKIAC. This, in turn, provides a systematic key to the interpretation of the *Arbitration Ordinance*, which underlines the role of the HKIAC as the *Appointing Authority* of reference. Extremely relevant, in fact, is the power of the HKIAC to intervene as a supporting body. In the event of inertia or disagreement between the parties, it therefore becomes, as we shall see later, the effective manager of the entire arbitration procedure. It thereby runs the risk of creating occasions of undue interference in the parties' free choice. It is also true, however, that the identification of the HKIAC as *Appointing Authority,* as well as the supporting and supervisory body, provides users with a procedure that is swifter and more certain. This may increase its attractiveness to foreign parties.

The most significant subsection proves to be *Subsection* 2, since the others are basically provisions reconciling the articles of the Model Law with the *Sections* of the *Ordinance.* They state the limits of the areas of intervention of the Courts or of the HKIAC in their functions of support and supervision.

Section 23 makes express reference to the regulations contained in Article 10 of the UNCITRAL Model Law. It is entitled, in fact, "*Article 10 of UNCITRAL Model Law (Number of Arbitrators).*"

The principle for determining the number of arbitrators, in both the *Ordinance* and the Model Law, is the freedom of the parties.

Section 23, or more precisely Article 10, paragraph 1 of the Model Law, states, in fact, that "the parties are free to determine the number of arbitrators." To the effects of *Subsection* 2 of *Section* 23, moreover, this freedom "includes the right of the parties to authorize a third party, including an institution, to make that determination." In most practical cases, the *Subsection* described above indicates the HKIAC as the proper institution, not only to act as *Appointing Authority* but also to decide the number of arbitrators. Its decisions in this sense, therefore, give shape to the ensuing arbitration proceedings.

The choice of the number of arbitrators is by no means a secondary matter. The procedure will certainly be swifter if it is decided to entrust the dispute to a single arbitrator rather than a tribunal of three or more. The reference under Subsection 2 of Section 23 to "institutions" as a possible third party responsible for choosing the number of arbitrators already implies a strongly central role for the HKIAC. This centrality is spelt out even more clearly in the third *Subsection*. This *Subsection*, in fact, states that, if the parties are unable to decide the number of arbitrators, the decision shall be referred to the HKIAC.

Section 24, too, attributes a position of pre-eminence and centrality to the HKIAC in appointing arbitrators. It also states clearly, however, that the freedom of the parties is the cardinal principle. It refers specifically, on this matter, to the regulations contained in Article 11 of the UNCITRAL Model Law.

Subsection 1 of *Section* 24 restates, as we have said, Article 11 of the Model Law. Paragraph 2 of this article guarantees the parties' faculty to decide freely the procedure for appointing the arbitrators. Paragraph 1 states that these may be of any nationality.

The Model Law's statement on the nationality of arbitrators is of fundamental importance in terms of international arbitration, since it is an essential tool with which to combat local protectionism and arbitral partiality. This is all the more important when we consider how close Hong Kong is to Mainland China, where a strongly protectionist stance is still to be found among the local governments.

12.2.3 Procedures for cases where parties are unable to agree

Remaining with Article 11, paragraph 3 envisages two standard procedures for cases where the parties are unable to agree: one for arbitration that is to take place before a tribunal of three arbitrators (Article 11, paragraph 3 (a), UNCITRAL Model Law), the other for cases where there is to be a single arbitrator (Article 11, paragraph 3 (b), UNCITRAL Model Law).

The first of these procedures disposes the appointment of one arbitrator by each of the parties. The arbitrators thus appointed should then appoint the third arbitrator. The procedure also takes into account cases where there is difficulty over the appointments. The second part of (a) of paragraph 3 of Article 11 states that "if a party fails to appoint the arbitrator within thirty days of receipt of a request to do so from the other party, or if the two arbitrators fail to agree on the third arbitrator within thirty days of their appointment, the appointment shall be made, upon the request of a party, by the court or other authority specified in article 6." The reference to Article 6, as we have seen, is to be interpreted, in compliance with *Section* 13 *Subsection 2,* as meaning the HKIAC.

The standard procedure for the appointment of a panel of three arbitrators is therefore perfectly in line with international standards. The only slightly unusual feature is the brief term of thirty days. This certainly emphasises the intention to make this a speedy procedure, and in this, it echoes the Model Law, the reference for international arbitration and for Hong Kong specifically. The second procedure is similar to the first. It envisages that "if the parties are unable to agree on the arbitrator, he shall be appointed, upon request by a party, by the court or other authority specified in article 6."

These procedures apply not only where the parties have not established any procedure for appointing the arbitrator(s) but also, *de facto*, to the effects of paragraph 1 (4) of Article 11 of the Model Law, where the parties have established a procedure, but have then failed to appoint the arbitrator(s) for the following reasons:

a A party fails to act as required under such procedure, or
b The parties, or two arbitrators, are unable to reach an agreement expected of them under such procedure or
c A third party, including an institution, fails to perform any function entrusted to it under such procedure,

In such critical situations, the body referred to previously, "the court or other authority specified in article 6," intervenes at the request of one of the parties. It is required to take the necessary measures, unless the agreement on the appointment procedure provides other means for securing the appointment.

Paragraph 1 (4) certainly underlines the need for a rapid solution to any procedural *impasse*. But it also reiterates a strongly felt desire to safeguard the freedom of the parties. It reminds us indirectly that intervention by the Court or by any other authority as of Article 6 is to be considered a last resort. Any solution already envisaged by the parties to resolve problems arising at the phase of appointing the arbitrators will automatically prevail.

Paragraph 1 (5) states, first of all, that any decision that the Court or the authorities as of Article 6 may take over the appointment of the arbitrators – to the effects of paragraphs 3 or 4 – may not be appealed against. This is of fundamental importance, since it avoids the risk of holding up the arbitration procedure while any appeals are heard. The swiftness of the procedure is therefore preserved.

12.2.4 Arbitrators' qualification

Paragraph 1 (5) furthermore states that the Court or other authority as of Article 6 must, when appointing arbitrators, take into account any qualification required of the arbitrators in the agreement between the parties. This preserves at least a minimum of autonomy for the parties. The method of appointment as of paragraphs 3 and 4 nevertheless strongly limits the freedom of the parties.

In addition to this, the final part of paragraph 1 (5) emphasises the need to appoint arbitrators who are independent and impartial. In particular, when a single arbitrator or a neutral arbitrator is to be appointed, the necessity is emphasised that this arbitrator should not be of the same nationality as the parties. This latter specification, concerning impartiality and independence, is of fundamental importance in the eyes of the Hong Kong legislator, especially considering the closeness of Hong Kong to Mainland China and the doubts some might have concerning impartiality in this part of the world.

Section 24 does not merely reiterate the regulations of the Model Law, however. It also deals with cases where the arbitration panel consists of more than three arbitrators and differentiates between panels of odd and even numbers. As we have seen, Section 23 allows the parties to opt for arbitration panels with as many arbitrators as they wish.

Subsection 2 of *Section* 24 considers the case of an arbitration panel with an even number of arbitrators. Paragraph (a) makes it clear that, unless the parties have freely established some other appointment procedure to the effects of Article 11, paragraph 2 of the Model Law, each party must appoint the same number of arbitrators. This Solomon-style principle recalls the concepts of the "equality of arms" and the "protection of the right of reply" so dear to proceduralists and, more generally, to all lawyers with a clear concept of the "due process," which, as far as Italy is concerned, is enshrined in Article 111 of the Constitution.

In arbitration, the notion of the "due process" is essentially wide ranging and may vary to meet different concepts of the arbitration process. It is clear that a strongly contractual vision will tend to preserve the freedom of the parties and will take a more relaxed attitude towards the stringent demands of a highly formal arbitration procedure. Those who see arbitration as essentially a form of trial, given its status as an alternative to resolving disputes in courts, will concentrate their attention on those elements that are essential and unchallengeable if the procedure is to be deemed a trial, even a trial defined broadly as arbitration. One of these essential elements will certainly be the concept of "due process."

If we take a look at *Section* 24, *Subsection* 2, paragraph (a), we find that the Hong Kong legislator, while attentive towards the freedom of the parties, tends towards a more proceduralist view, one that will align arbitration with "due process."

Paragraph (b) of the second *Subsection* of *Section* 24, on the other hand, deals with the resolution of pathological cases where, even though a procedure is established for the appointment of an arbitration panel with an even number of arbitrators,

1 one of the parties fails to act in accordance with the agreement between the parties, or
2 in the case as of paragraph (a), one of the parties fails to appoint its appropriate number of arbitrators to the effects of that paragraph within thirty days of receiving intimation to do so by the other party.

If such circumstances occur, paragraph (b) of *Subsection* 2 evokes once again the HKIAC, which, at the request of one of the parties, will proceed to make the necessary appointments.

Subsection 3 of *Section* 24, on the other hand, disciplines cases where the arbitration panel consists of an odd number of arbitrators but greater than three.

12.2.5 The role of the parties

Paragraph (a) of *Subsection* 3 begins by referring to paragraph 2 of Article 11 of the Model Law. It thereby confirms once more the procedure freely chosen by the parties as the first criterion for appointing arbitrators. It then sets out a standard procedure for cases where the parties have not envisaged a specific procedure for appointing an arbitration panel with an odd number of arbitrators.

In the case of this standard procedure, it is insisted again that both parties must appoint the same number of arbitrators. This confirms the intention of the Hong Kong legislator to adopt a basically proceduralist standpoint, considering arbitration as a form of trial rather than a contractual matter.

Since there is an odd number of arbitrators and since it is envisaged that each party shall appoint the same number of arbitrators, it is obviously necessary to appoint a further arbitrator in order to create an odd-numbered panel. The appointment of this further arbitrator is not left to the parties, however, as might have been supposed in the light of what we have seen so far. Instead, it is to be made by the HKIAC. This latter provision implies a basic diffidence, perhaps justified, concerning the capacity of the parties, or the arbitrators appointed by them, to decide quickly the appointment of the neutral arbitrator who will provide the odd number of arbitrators.

It is certainly possible to sympathise with this diffidence towards the parties and the need for swiftness that has resulted in ruling out the possibility for the appointed arbitrators themselves to choose the neutral member. If we try to imagine the thought of the Hong Kong legislator expressed in dialogue, it would be something like this: "It's hard enough to get two to agree, let alone more! And after all, we know that two don't always reason better than one, and when there are a lot of them they will never agree."

As we know, merely factual considerations of this kind, drawn from experience, should not be elevated to legal policies. Their introduction into the arbitration procedure clearly harms the freedom of the parties and affects the nature of the arbitration itself. But then, we also know that arbitration is not an ordinary trial under another name and that arbitrators are not judgės!

The Hong Kong legislator, in fact, under the guise of a formal respect for the freedom of the parties, has actually adopted an ultra-interventionist approach. On the one hand, he or she loses no opportunity to grant the Courts, and thus public power, the faculty to intervene in the arbitration. On the other hand, he or she has tended to regulate each eventuality down to the smallest detail, so that nothing is left to chance and everything is carefully formalised.

This attention to the certainty of rights and procedures is undoubtedly praiseworthy. It indicates a system that is foreseeable and therefore theoretically trustworthy. But, arbitration with its wings too strongly clipped risks losing its attraction for foreign parties. It is fairly unlikely, in fact, that both parties will have already determined, at the moment when the arbitration starts, the entire procedure in its smallest details. It is more than likely, on the other hand, that they will have a general agreement for a flexible procedure, which will give them time to assess how best to handle the dispute in the light of the concrete case.

A procedure that is too formalised will lack that flexibility that is the essence of arbitration. A regulation, in fact, is not intended to discipline every conceivable concrete case and must not presume to do so. A regulation must provide a rule.

Subsection 4 of *Section* 24 is a regulation for resolving all cases where, even though a specific procedure has been envisaged, the parties have not succeeded in appointing the arbitrators. It states that for "any other case (in particular, if there are more than 2 parties)," paragraph 4 of Article 11 of the Model Law will be applied. Intervention by the Court or other authorities specified under Article 6 (in other words, the HKIAC) is the default procedure in every case. The *Subsection* we have just analysed is further evidence of the hyper-interventionist approach adopted by the Hong Kong legislator.

Finally, *Subsection* 5, *Section* 24 states specifically that any appointment made by the HKIAC, for whatever reason, "has effect as if it were made with the agreement of all parties." This *subsection* represents the formal investiture of the HKIAC as the *Appointing Authority* for the purposes of the *Arbitration Ordinance*, thereby confirming all that has been said so far. Paragraph (b) of *Subsection* 5 specifies, moreover, that the HKIAC's appointments are "subject to article 11(5) of the Model Law," which we have previously discussed.

Now that we have clarified the discipline contained in the *Ordinance*, let us return to our analysis of the procedure set out in the *Appointing Rules*. These rules introduce the figure of the *Appointment Advisory Board*. Part II of the Rules (Rules 3, 4 and 5) are dedicated to this body, which must be consulted, even though its opinions are not binding.

Rule 5 states, in fact, that before making a definitive decision on "the appointment of an arbitrator" or on "the number of arbitrators that is appropriate for any particular dispute," "the HKIAC must consult with at least three members of the Appointment Advisory Board with whom the HKIAC is able to communicate, and must consider their advice, but is not bound by it."

So what does "three members ... with whom the HKIAC is able to communicate" mean in practice? How is this Board structured?

Rule 3 states that the HKIAC *Council* must set up this consultative body. Each person or organisation, as of *Rule* 3, *Subrule 3*, must appoint a single member. The members thus appointed may not act as arbitrators during their term of office. The list of persons or organisations given under *Rule* 3, *Subrule 3*, includes all the principal fields where arbitration might be applied:

- Magistrates (*the Chief Justice of Hong Kong*)
- Lawyers (*the Chairman of the Hong Kong Bar Association*)
- Legal Doctrine (*the President of The Law Society of Hong Kong*)
- The Chambers of Commerce (both of Mainland China and of Hong Kong)
- Engineers (*the President of The Hong Kong Institution of Engineers*)
- Surveyors (*the President of The Hong Kong Institute of Surveyors*)
- Architects (*the President of The Hong Kong Institute of Architects*)
- Shipowners (*the Hong Kong Shipowners Association*)
- Insurers (*the Hong Kong Federation of Insurers*)
- Builders (*the President of the Hong Kong Construction Association*).

Rule 4 is divided into 5 *Subrules*. The first two indicate the temporal limits of the term of office of a member of the *Appointment Advisory Board*, while the third deals with the appointment of new members, in the case that a position falls vacant before the term of office has expired. The fourth *Subrule* also establishes that the Board must have at least six members in order to function regularly. The fifth Subrule establishes that no member of the Appointment Advisory Board may be appointed as arbitrator by HKIAC "during his or her term of office."

Regarding temporal limits, it is stated that the maximum term of office for a member of the Board is three years. Two years must lapse before the same person can be reappointed. Nothing is said about a maximum number of times a person can be reappointed, so presumably no such maximum exists.

As has already been said, the *Appointment Rules* set out guidelines for appointing arbitrators in the cases as of *Sections* 13, 23 and 24. Two distinct procedures are indicated in two separate *Parts* of the *Appointment Rules*: *Part* III is dedicated to the procedure for the appointing of the arbitrators (*Rules* 6 and 7), while *Part* IV deals with the number of arbitrators (*Rules* 8–9).

Let us begin with *Part* III. *Rule* 6 describes the means by which the appointment of an arbitrator is to be requested (*Subrule* 1). This request must be presented to the HKIAC using Form 1 of the schedule annexed to the *Appointment Rules*. The use of a single form for the presentation of the application is praiseworthy, since this means that the procedure will certainly be swifter and more secure.

Rule 6 then specifies the means by which the other party is to be informed of the request. It states that a copy of the request is to be served upon the other party at the last known address of that party.

We have said "address" because this is the term used by *Subsection* 3. It does not clarify whether this is to be understood as "residence" or "domicile." It is clear that, in some legal systems at least, an endless series of misunderstandings could take place concerning this term and, therefore, whether or not the request has been properly served upon the party.

A solution to this problem could be sought in an analogous interpretation of the provisions of *Section* 10 of the *Ordinance*. This *Section* refers, in turn, to the provisions of *Article 3 of the UNCITRAL Model Law (Receipt of written communications)*.

Article 3 of the Model Law states that a written communication between the parties should be delivered, where possible, "personally." Failing this, it should be delivered at the "place of business, habitual residence or postal address." "Place of business," that is to say the place where economic interests lie, may be taken as similar to ***domicilio*** [domicile] under Italian law.

The order in which the rule lists these options does not appear to be a purely random one. Possibly, it should be taken as indicating the order in which the attempts at service should be made. This point is not entirely clear, however.

If none of these can be found "after making a reasonable inquiry," Article 3 states that any written communication shall be deemed as received which has been sent to the party's last known place of business, habitual address or postal address, provided it has been sent by ***registered letter*** "or any other means that provides a record of the attempt to deliver it."

Rule 7 deals with the arbitrators' subjective qualifications, or rather, the suitability of a person to be appointed as arbitrator on the basis of the features of each specific dispute. Before analysing the factors that determine this choice, it is interesting to note that *Sub-rule* 2 allows a measure of prior debate. The party that has not requested the appointment of an arbitrator is permitted, in fact, to submit any information it deems relevant to the decision or any motives for which it deems that no arbitrator should be appointed.

12.2.6 Criteria used to choose arbitrators

In making its decision, HKIAC must choose arbitrators having regard to the following factors relating to their suitability:

a the nature of the dispute;
b whether arbitrators who possess the required qualifications would be available to accept the appointment;
c the nationality of the parties;
d the independence and impartiality of the arbitrator;
e any stipulations in the relevant arbitration agreement;
f any suggestions made by the parties themselves.

The factor as of (a) would seem to be the only real criterion for choosing a suitable subject, if suitability is to be understood as the capacity to find a solution to a dispute regarding a specific matter. This means that, in a panel of three arbitrators, it would be strongly advisable to ensure the presence, as well of a professional from the legal field (a judge, a lawyer or a professor), of at least one person with technical expertise covering the matter to be dealt with (an engineer, an architect, a chartered accountant and so forth).

Factor (c), if properly observed, could avoid waste of time in the subsequent stages of the arbitration due to challenges against the arbitrators.

Factor (d), too, could be decisive for the success of the arbitration procedure, but it also raises a question. Can the HKIAC be held liable if one or more of the arbitrators it appoints proves to be partial or corrupt? It would seem that it can, under certain circumstances. Let us see why. It is necessary, first, to find a correct interpretation of Article 43.1 of the *Administered Arbitration Rules*. This "exclusion of liability" states that neither the Secretary General of HKIAC nor other staff members of the Secretariat of HKIAC "shall be liable for any act or omission in connection with an arbitration conducted under these Rules, save where such act was done or omitted to be done dishonestly."

This provision would appear entirely clear. However, it has to be seen in relation to the law applicable to the case, even though the procedure is being handled by the HKIAC. If, for example, the parties had chosen Italian law as the applicable law, this clause would be null and void on the basis of Article 1229 of the Italian Civil Code. So, what happens if the applicable law does not allow clauses that limit liability? Let us examine, according to Italian law, the hypothesis of HKIAC's liability.

12.2.7 Relationship between HKIAC and the parties

Let us consider, first of all, the relationship existing between HKIAC and the parties involved in the arbitration. This relationship could be interpreted as a contract, "a consultancy or assistance contract," even if a rather unusual one, characterised by two counterbalancing services: the payment of the fee by the parties and HKIAC's decision on the request they have submitted.

HKIAC's service amounts to making a decision that is not merely any decision. It has committed itself to identifying the correct number of arbitrators and, much more important than this, to providing arbitrators with those same subjective qualities, including impartiality and independence, that HKIAC itself has declared necessary.

Now, it is clear that, if HKIAC has appointed impartial or corrupt arbitrators, this is in the first place a breach of contract and, furthermore, a valid motive to claim compensation for the damage suffered. Since this is a contractual liability, it would not be necessary for the parties (still supposing that the applicable law were that of Italy) to prove a subjective element. The parties would therefore not have the burden of proving a lack of due diligence or expertise on the part of HKIAC. This latter would be a diabolical evidence trap indeed, even for parties that happened to be well versed in legal technicalities, given the Commission's wide powers of discretion and the fact that it does not need to motivate its decisions. Instead, all that would be needed is proof of the damage suffered and the causal link.

Even if we did not allow the existence of a contract between the parties and HKIAC, liability could nevertheless arise, at least under Italian law, on grounds of *contratto sociale*. This Italian legal concept means that the Commission's high professional standing and its implicit duty to protect those to whom it provides a service by appointing impartial arbitrators would make it liable if it did not act according to its reputation and provide properly the service requested. Here, too, the parties would only have to prove damage in order for HKIAC to be liable for compensation.

However, the above scenario depends on whether the applicable law is deemed applicable to the arbitration itself or also to the process for setting it up. It would also seem that the authority that would have to decide on the question is the Hong Kong Court itself. Opposing the HKIAC's exclusion of liability clause might not be easy, therefore.

Returning to the single factors, (e) underlines the importance of the will of the parties in these procedures. This is very important, given that arbitration is based, in general, on a relationship of trust between the parties and the arbitrators. The parties resolve to entrust certain subjects with the resolution of their disputes, on the condition that these subjects satisfy certain conditions that the parties may have envisaged in their arbitration agreement. The factor at (e) evidently intends to protect this type of agreement.

Last but not least, the factor (f) allows for dialogue between the Commission and the parties. This not only protects the debate between the parties in the future arbitration but also enables them to discuss, in relation to the hypothesis of HKIAC's civil liability (in situations where the law applicable to the case does not allow clauses limiting liability), the extent of shared liability and compensation where the parties' own suggestions, as of (f), have contributed to the appointment of a partial arbitrator. This is in accordance with Italian laws on contributory negligence, as of Article 1227 of the Italian Civil Code.

As we anticipated, this list of factors shows clearly that the assessment made by HKIAC in accordance with Rule 7 is aimed at identifying subjects who are suitable to act as arbitrators. Logically and temporally, this assessment would follow a decision on the number of arbitrators. The order in which the rules appear is, therefore, the correct one.

12.2.8 Decision about the number of arbitrators

Rule 8, like Rule 6, regards a decision-making procedure. But, while Rule 6 concerns the procedure for appointing the arbitrators, Rule 8 concerns the procedure for deciding the number of arbitrators for each dispute.

Subsection 2, as with Rule 6, sets out the procedure for making the application, which must be sent to HKIAC using form 2 of the schedule annexed to the Appointment Rules.

Subsection 3, like Subsection 3 of Rule 6, describes the means by which the request must be served on the other party. The observations made with regard to Rule 6 may also be applied to Rule 8.

Rule 9, appearing in Part IV, concerns the decision on the number of arbitrators. It nevertheless introduces an assessment that, de facto, revolves around the suitability of the subjects to act as arbitrators. This Rule envisages a series of factors that HKIAC has to take into consideration every time it has to make a decision on the number of arbitrators needed for each single dispute. These factors are the following:

a the amount in dispute;
b the complexity of the case;
c the nationality of the parties to the arbitration agreement;
d any relevant customs of the trade, business or profession involved in the dispute;
e whether there are any appropriate arbitrators and
f the urgency of the case.

Let us examine the factors on this list one by one. Factors (a) and (b) contain two important general criteria that should always guide a decision on the number of arbitrators. They enable choice of the structure best suited to the matter under dispute, balancing the need for swiftness and flexibility with the capacity to examine properly the merits of questions that are economically more significant or harder to resolve.

The nationality of the parties, as of (c), is an element that the Arbitration ordinance itself considers fundamental, for the reasons we have seen. It is clear, therefore, that this list of factors could not ignore the question of nationality. So far, so good. But, we are bound to wonder what correlation exists between the number of arbitrators and the nationality of the parties. Does the legislator feel that cross-border questions need to be examined more carefully than internal ones? This might be the answer, but then, why not impose, where an agreement between the parties to the contrary does not exist, a panel of three arbitrators for all international questions? It seems, instead, that the Hong Kong legislator has wished to be prudent and has preferred to entrust to HKIAC's discretion the question of whether a greater number of arbitrators is needed in relation to the international nature of the case.

Point (d) raises an interesting point. The idea of taking into consideration "any relevant customs of the trade, business or profession involved in the dispute" sounds attractive, even if it is not clear what sort of customs are intended.

Point (e) is also somewhat critical. What happens if, in the opinion of HKIAC, there are no "appropriate arbitrators"?

Subrule 2 follows the footsteps of Subrule 2 of Rule 7. It allows the parties in dispute to present, in writing, their considerations on whether one or three arbitrators are to be appointed. Under Subrule 4, HKIAC itself may also ask the parties for further information. It is not clear why Rule 7, concerning the appointment of the arbitrators, does not envisage HKIAC making a similar request.

Under Rule 12, HKIAC may specify additional forms with respect to those in the annexed Schedules. This would provide an excellent starting point for the creation of forms that are differentiated according to the subject dealt with in each single dispute. It would also enable the creation of simplified forms for the more straightforward cases.

Rule 13, lastly, sets out the fees to be applied when HKIAC is asked for a decision. The fee is the same, whether for a decision on the number of arbitrators or for the appointment of these same.

12.3 The arbitration ordinance

Let us now examine the content of *HKIAC's Administered Arbitration Rules.* Section III (Articles 6–12) is entirely dedicated to the figure of the arbitrator and the arbitration panel.

12.3.1 Number of arbitrators

Article 6 concerns the number of arbitrators. The first paragraph states indirectly the principle of the parties' freedom to decide the number of arbitrators, in line with the provisions of the *Arbitration Ordinance.*

We have said "indirectly" because, in reality, the *Administered Rules* confer default powers upon HKIAC, in accordance with the role of *Appointing Authority* entrusted to it by the *Ordinance.* The paragraph states that "If the parties have not agreed upon the number of arbitrators, HKIAC shall decide whether the case be referred to a sole arbitrator or to three arbitrators, taking into account the circumstances of the case."

12.3.2 Procedure

An interesting question is raised by the provisions under paragraph 2 of Article 6. This paragraph refers, in fact, to the so-called "Expedited Procedure" as of Article 41, which appears in *Section* VI ("Other Provisions") of the *Administered Rules.* It would seem advisable to examine the regulations of Article 41 concerning the "Expedited Procedure," in order to understand what is meant and why it is referred to under Article 6. As we can see from the title of the article, this procedure aims to provide the parties with the swiftest arbitration possible.

According to Article 41.1, "Prior to the constitution of the arbitral tribunal, a party may apply to HKIAC in writing for the arbitration to be conducted in accordance with Article 41.2 where:

a the amount in dispute representing the aggregate of any claim and counterclaim (or any set-off defence) does not exceed HKD 25,000,000 (twenty-five million Hong Kong Dollars);
b the parties so agree or
c in cases of exceptional urgency."

It appears, therefore, that if the case falls within the twenty-five million Hong Kong dollars threshold, even a single party can request the Expedited Procedure, whether or not the arbitration agreement foresees it.

In the interests of swiftness, every effort is made to have the dispute heard by a sole arbitrator. Article 41.2 (b) states that "the case shall be referred to a sole arbitrator, unless the arbitration agreement provides for three arbitrators." Even if the arbitration agreement does provide for three arbitrators, paragraph (b) continues, "HKIAC shall invite the parties to agree to refer the case to a sole arbitrator." However, it concludes, "If the parties do not agree, the case shall be referred to three arbitrators." A further incentive for the parties to modify their agreement in favour of a single arbitrator might arise from the additional cost of three arbitrators, based on the table of fees annexed to the HKIAC *Administered Rules.*

Article 41 (2) continues by listing the differences to the arbitration procedure if the Expedited Procedure is adopted. Under letter (c), "HKIAC may shorten the time limits provided for in the Rules, as well as any time limits that it has set" (so, this would therefore include the terms for appointing the arbitrators as of Article 7 paragraphs 1 and 2).

d states that "after the submission of the Answer to the Notice of Arbitration, the parties shall in principle be entitled to submit one Statement of Claim and one Statement of Defence (and Counterclaim) and, where applicable, one Statement of Defence in reply to the Counterclaim."

e implicitly gives the arbitral tribunal very wide powers indeed: "The arbitral tribunal shall decide the dispute on the basis of documentary evidence only, unless it decides that it is appropriate to hold one or more hearings."

f becomes clear and consistent only if we assume that, in general, no hearing is envisaged. It would therefore be necessary, given the limit on evidence, for the parties to draw up the Statements as of (d) as completely as possible, in terms of evidence. Not only this, but also if the rule allows hearings to be called because more evidence is to be heard, it must be supposed that such evidence will, of necessity, be different from the documentary evidence.

The core of the question concerns the limit of this waiver, apparently a double limit, referring in the first place to the type of evidence admitted and in the second place to the admissibility of certain official investigative powers (in the broadest sense). In other words, what types of evidence can be introduced during the hearings envisaged under letter (e)? Must this evidence be expressly requested by the parties, or can the arbitrator(s) request further evidence if it is deemed necessary?

We need, first of all, to clarify certain basic principles of procedural law, which must, of necessity, be applied also to arbitration. Without any shadow of doubt, the adversarial principle – the right of reply – has to be applied to the admission and formation of evidence.

As we have seen, the Hong Kong legislator has, on many occasions, protected the parties' right of reply. It would be paradoxical to suppose that this would not also be applied in the field of evidence.

More doubtful is the application of the principles of the nature of the evidence and the rules of the evidence.

Regarding the principle of the nature of the evidence, this would require it to be established, at first, what "nature" of evidence should be applied to the case in question (for example, evidence from witnesses, from technical experts and so forth).

In general, it would appear that the principle of the nature of the evidence is, at the very least, weakened by the last paragraph of Article 23, which states that the arbitration panel will not only decide on the admissibility and relevance of the evidence produced, but it will also decide whether or not strict evidentiary rules are to be applied. This provision arises from the basic principle of the "discovery stage in free form," which leaves only a residual role for "strict evidentiary rules," which are introduced at the express decision of the tribunal. They are not a general rule, but rather, a waiver of the general rule. The aim of the provision is to produce an arbitration procedure that is streamlined and flexible, because it is informal but without being summary.

Following this interpretation, it could even be argued that, in the face of a free discovery phase and the lack of an express exclusion of official powers on the part of the arbitral tribunal, the legal policy chosen as most suitable could actually amount to the setting aside of the rule of evidence, with an officially conducted discovery phase.

We should not confuse the rule of evidence with the principle of the right to plea. This latter cannot be set aside, since, if this were done, we would end up with a substantially inquisitorial process, conducted moreover by arbitrators not by judges. This would be in conflict with the right to public trial, a principle that no modern legal order worthy of the name can suppress.

The rule of evidence, on the other hand, may be a choice of suitability. Once the parties have delimited the facts that are the object of the proceedings, it would seem admissible to allow greater freedom over the means of ascertaining their truth.

Continuing our analysis of the "Expedited Procedure," (f) states that "the award shall be made within six months from the date when HKIAC transmitted the file to the arbitral tribunal." It allows, however, that "In exceptional circumstances, HKIAC may extend this time limit."

The result of this last proviso is that the term under (f) could be considered only indicative, with yet another example of HKIAC's sweeping powers. HKIAC, as we have seen, may decide to extend the term of six months in exceptional cases, and no definition is offered of what "exceptional" means in this case. HKIAC is therefore attributed powers of discretion that are, in reality, incompatible with a peremptory term. There could indeed be cases where an extension of the term is in the parties' best interests, but the discretion allowed raises to infinity the possible motives for extending the term and uncertainty reigns.

g finally, disposes that "the arbitral tribunal shall state the reasons upon which the award is based in summary form, unless the parties have agreed that no reasons are to be given."

This, then, is the "Expedited Procedure." Let us now return to our analysis of the provisions concerning the appointment of the arbitrators.

The *Administered Rules* differentiate between the rules for appointing a sole arbitrator and those for appointing a tribunal of three. Article 7 deals with the appointment of a sole arbitrator. Paragraph 1 begins by making it clear that these rules only apply where the parties have not agreed otherwise between themselves. The procedure for appointing a sole arbitrator envisages a term of thirty days, within which the parties themselves should appoint the arbitrator.

The term of thirty days runs as follows:

1 under (a), if both parties have agreed that there should be a sole arbitrator, from the date in which Notice of Arbitration has been received by the Respondent;
2 under (b), if the decision to refer the dispute to a single arbitrator has been made by HKIAC, from the date on which HKIAC's decision has been received by the last of the parties.
3 The term of thirty days is peremptory. Article 7.2 states that, if the arbitrator has not been designated within that term, HKIAC will make the appointment.

Article 8 deals with the procedure for appointing a panel of three arbitrators. Once again, the article begins by stating that the following rules apply, "unless the parties have agreed otherwise." As with Article 7, Article 8 differentiates between cases where the parties have agreed that there will be three arbitrators (a), and cases where this decision has been made by HKIAC (b).

12.4 Conclusion

Arbitration, using the rules of HKIAC, is a useful instrument for the settlement of disputes between Western and Chinese subjects. Often, in fact, the resolution of disputes through ordinary judgements (but also through local) arbitration in China is seen by Western counterparts, for historical and cultural reasons, as well as for effective mistrust of local institutions, such as overly complex and difficult feasibility. In such cases, an arbitration made in Hong Kong, but considered closed also by its counterpart (such as Hong Kong is generally seen from China), can be a good negotiated settlement to resolve a dispute between the parties on the point.

The rules governing the arbitration is based on standards for international arbitration in commercial matters suggested by the United Nations, and therefore takes the form of rules (specifically applied to domestic and international arbitration), very similar to common arbitration rules in force in many Western countries – therefore, easy to understand even for a stranger professional trader.

On the territory of Hong Kong, the "Convention on the Recognition and Enforcement of Foreign Arbitral Awards" (the so-called New York Convention) is applicable. This Convention assigns the signatory countries the role of promoting the appropriate recognition of arbitral awards made in the context of States Parties with the same ban, among other things, to implement law envisaging tougher conditions for the recognition of foreign awards than those applicable to domestic arbitration awards. Based on the principles and rules expressed in the New York Convention, an express Treaty was finally signed in 2000 between China and Hong Kong on the mutual recognition of the (respective) arbitral awards (remember in this regard that China, a country of civil law, and Hong Kong, a country of common law of Anglo-Saxon influence, will retain formal different legal and judicial systems until 2047).

From the overall legal framework mentioned above, it clearly emerges that the choice of Hong Kong as the venue for arbitration in case of disputes can be a viable solution that ensures, on the one hand, the Western contractor's interest within a third legal system and, on the other hand, the interest of the Chinese party to maintain a geographical and cultural proximity to the site of a future dispute between the parties.

Bibliography

Bateson David, 1989, *Commercial Arbitration in Hong Kong*, Longman.

Di Michael J. Moserand Teresa Y. W. Cheng, 2004, *Hong Kong Arbitration*, Kluwer Law International.

Helen (Hong) Shi and Michael Edwards, 2015, *CIETAC's 2015 Arbitration Rules Analysed*, China Law & Practice.

Katherine Jo, 2014, *CIETAC Raises Its Game*, China Law & Practice.

Lynch, 1999, *Arbitrato commerciale internazionale a Hong Kong e in Cina: un paese, due sistemi di principi nella pratica*, in Dir. comm. int., fasc. 4, 1999, 801–839.

Neil Kaplan, Jill Spruce, and Michael J. Moser, 1994, *Hong Kong and China Arbitration: Cases and Materials*, Butterworths.

Shaun Wuand Kobre & Kim, 2013, *What the New HKIAC Rules Mean for China-Related Arbitration*, China Law & Practice.

13 The difficulties with law and language of arbitration in India

A challenge for domestic environmental arbitration?

Charu Sharma

Introduction

The language of law rules all issues, disputes and their resolution, including processes and procedures. Juxtaposing environmental disputes within the language of Indian arbitration law for dispute resolution, however, seems to bring forth an initial gut reaction of squaring a circle or creating conflict. It does not sit well within the scope and objective of the statutory enactment of the Indian Arbitration Act 1996, (hereinafter ACA) by its very nature.[1]

That is a strange fallacy, whether by default or design, one can only surmise. Within domestic law, none of the public environmental legislation in India that protects public interest provides for arbitration, conciliation or mediation as a method for public–private environmental conflicts and issues.[2] This chapter posits that the language of arbitration law and its interpretation not only pose a challenge for the resolution of commercial disputes but also completely ignore the possibility of resolution of environmental disputes through arbitration.

Arbitration is being increasingly used to resolve business and commercial disputes within India. Simultaneously, commercial and business disputes are oftentimes mixed with environmental questions and violation of public environmental laws or private rights. As disputes are becoming complicated within the industrial, power, energy, pharmaceutical and environmental sectors, the challenge of arbitration law becomes particularly complex when one considers resolution of environmental disputes within the domestic law where no provisions exist for arbitration. Thus, there exists a multilevel challenge within language, its interpretation and the need for amendments to accommodate for environmental disputes that are increasingly mixed with commercial arbitrations. In contrast, at the international level, arbitration law has been drafted to resolve major environmental disputes that may have stood alone or invariably mixed with commercial arbitration. This is to say that although the environment and commercial arbitration fall within different legal domains and any conflicts are accordingly categorised as questions falling within private and public law, there are examples of successful environmental/commercial arbitration within international law. Such arbitration transcends legal language barriers or those of public and private domain,

1 Arbitration and Conciliation Act 1996, Act No 26 of 1996, amended in 2015 and Arbitration and Conciliation Act 2015, No. 3 of 2016 available at http://lawmin.nic.in/ld/P-ACT/1996/The%20Arbitration%20and%20Conciliation%20Act,%201996.pdf; and No 3 of 2016 available at www.indiacode.nic.in/acts-in-pdf/2016/201603.pdf.

2 Compare from the American Arbitration Association: Areas of Expertise – "Real Estate, Construction and Environmental" rules and guideline that exist in resolution of complex multi-party construction, industry and environmental disputes available at https://www.adr.org/aaa/faces/aoe/cre/environmental;jsessionid=TuQ3M-.

which has been achieved through legal expertise at drafting such laws. Within the Indian scenario, examples can be drawn where law provides for arbitration within private/public dispute resolution. Lamentably, no legislation or rules within domestic environmental law provides for arbitration clauses. This impasse, if it can be so called, needs a close examination, because contemporary environmental issues within India are tetra-headed, and resolving environmental disputes through courts and the National Green Tribunal has limitations.

Arguably, it is logical to examine the difficulties that arbitration law poses in the following areas to identify and determine what situations could probably demand futuristic provisions that are increasingly becoming significant for environmental conflicts. This involves an examination of the difficulty that has been identified with the following: the language of the ACA 1996; scope of tetra-headed environmental and development conflicts within which public and private nature of environmental disputes overlap; an examination of international and cross-border environmental disputes to derive strength for making a case for domestic environmental arbitration, inquiry and synthesis of other sectors that provide for arbitration as an alternative for dispute resolution, through specific statutes and an examination of the scope for having arbitration clauses, where necessary, within environmental regulations in the domestic sphere of India. This chapter is divided into four parts. Part I examines the challenges posed by the language of law to arbitration within the ACA. It examines the provisions that have required clarification of the legal language by the Supreme Court. Part II examines where and how international environmental disputes have been resolved using arbitration and highlights provision of arbitration clauses for environmental dispute resolution within international institutions and other jurisdictions, e.g., the United States and Canada. Part III then examines domestic laws, where provisions have been made for the arbitration of disputes and the language is clear so as to specify situations where arbitration or conciliation, mediation/Alternative Dispute Resolution (ADR) techniques have been used to resolve disputes that are both public and private in nature. Part IV provides a conclusion and reiterates the need to tide over language and drafting difficulties in providing effective dispute resolution strategies within domestic environmental laws and the need to amend arbitration and various environmental laws for this purpose.

Part I: Examining the ACA and its language

The ACA was enacted to consolidate and amend the law relating to domestic arbitration, international commercial arbitration and the enforcement of foreign arbitral awards, and also to define the law relating to conciliation and for matters connected therewith or incidental thereto.

It provides for dispute resolution through arbitration, conciliation and by passing court-adjudicated orders in resolution of conflicts between private and public parties. Many conflicts under the ACA have reached the Supreme Court for interpretation and clarification of the language of the ACA provisions. These arbitration decisions illustrate the challenges posed by the language of law and the impediments to speedy resolution of disputes.[3] Recent Supreme Court and State High Court decisions also provide the dynamics

3 See Sumeet Kachwaha and Dharmendra Rautray, Kachwaha & Partners, India available at https://ipba.org/media/fck/files/Arbitration%20in%20India.pdf (2009); Manav Kapur "Judicial Interference and Arbitral Autonomy: An overview of Indian Arbitration Law", *Contemporary Asia Arbitration Journal* 2: 325 (2009); Mauro Rubino Sammartano, *International Arbitration Law and Practice*, Kluwer Law International, 2nd

and trends in respect of commercial arbitration within India in an increasing number of cases. The questions that have been examined under recent decisions have ranged from applicability and varying interpretation of the ACA; language and words used in the ACA that have proved to be obstacles: words such as *may*, *shall*, *intention to go to arbitration*, *consent for arbitration*, *agreement to go for arbitration*, amongst others, to hold or deny the existence of an arbitration agreement; adherence of the courts to strict interpretation of legal clauses (indicating rigidity and literal interpretation rules followed by the courts) and determination of intention of the parties in a commercial contract that requires evidence in writing. The decisions from the last ten years reflect a higher percentage of arbitration disputes, but increasing judicial pronouncements/intervention.[4]

ACA overview

The overall objective of the ACA has been to provide speedy, cost-effective justice and resolution of disputes, as an alternative to litigation in India, thereby upholding the rule of law. Ideally, if parties to a legal relationship, whether contractual or not, have stated and used the word *arbitration*, such a clause ought to be interpreted widely to have an out-of-court settlement. The trend in the courts in the United Kingdom or the United States reiterates this position, where the words *may proceed to arbitration* have been given a wider interpretation to resolve a dispute or conflict without proceeding to litigation in court.[5] In Ceres Marine Terminals, Inc. v. Int'l Longshoremen's Ass'n, Local,[6] it has been held that any ambiguity created by the word *may* was to be properly construed in favour of arbitration. Moreover, the US federal Arbitration Act mandates a policy in favour of arbitration, and any doubts concerning the scope of arbitrable issues should be resolved in favour of arbitration.[7] In Ziegler v. Knuck,[8] the Florida Court has held that the use of the word *may* in an arbitration clause "is little different than the use of the compulsory language – it creates in either party the right to insist upon arbitration; it creates in neither party the right to resist arbitration insisted upon by the other." In Allis-Chalmers Corp. v. Lueck,[9] the court held that "the use of … *may* is not sufficient to overcome the presumption that parties are not free to avoid the contract's arbitration procedures."[10] Similar to the decision in India, the US courts have clarified the law on the issue of whether there ought to be arbitration or not, and where the arbitration clause makes it unclear whether arbitration is mandated and it cannot be stated that there is a "clear and unmistakable evidence" that the parties agreed to have the arbitration panel decide arbitrability logically, the court decides whether the

Revised Edn, 2001, Chap. 6, pp. 143–145 (international commercial arbitration law and international public arbitration law distinction).

4 Manav Kapur "Judicial Interference and Arbitral Autonomy: An overview of Indian Arbitration Law", *Contemporary Asia Arbitration Journal* 2: 325, 326–327 (2009).

5 See for example, *Hirshenson v. Spaccio,* 800 So. 2d 670, 674 (Fla.App.2001).

6 *1969, AFL-CIO,* 683 F.2d 242, 247–48 (7th Cir. 1982).

7 *Moses H. Cone Hosp. v. Mercury Const. Corp.,* 460 U.S. 1, 24–25, 103 S. Ct. 927, 74 L. Ed. 2d 765 (1983). See also Conax Florida Corporation v Astrium Ltd 499 F Supp. 2d 1287 Fla. However, arbitration is not to be imposed on parties who did not agree to it. *EEOC v. Waffle House, Inc.,* 534 U.S. 279, 289, 122 S. Ct. 754, 151 L. Ed. 2d 755 (2002).

8 419 So. 2d 818, 819 (Fla.App. 1982).

9 471 U.S. 202, 204 n. 1, 105 S. Ct. 1904, 85 L. Ed. 2d 206 (1985).

10 Similarly, in *Deaton Truck Line, Inc. v. Local Union 612,* 314 F.2d 418, 422 (5th Cir. 1962) ("Clearly, … 'may' should be construed to give either aggrieved party the option to require arbitration").

parties agreed to mandatory arbitration.[11] However, the presumption can be said to be in favour of arbitration to give credence to the policy of the US Federal Arbitration Act.[12] In contrast, however, the words and language used in the Indian ACA have created difficulties and confusion for parties. In other cases, courts have not interpreted these words to mandate arbitration, even where words such as ***may adopt arbitration*** have been used. The ACA under Sections 6, 7(4), 7(5) and 44(a) has provision for parties to consent to arbitration in certain commercial disputes in order to have relief or to be able to enforce an award, whether domestic or foreign. However, on examination of the language of the law and the recent decisions, one can discern that the interpretation of the law has been an obstacle to speedy resolution of disputes and parties to the dispute, arbitrators, lawyers and counsel have used this language to the disadvantage of the overall objective by invoking court jurisdiction and dragging the dispute, thus thwarting the very objective for which ACA has been enacted.

Section I of the ACA provides the objective and lays down that:

a the object of arbitration is to obtain the fair resolution of disputes by an impartial tribunal without unnecessary delay or expense;
b the parties should be free to agree how their disputes are resolved, subject only to such safeguards as are necessary in the public interest.

In other words, the parties are free to agree without any economic duress to obtain a consensus ad idem to go for an arbitration where they have a legal relation and may anticipate a dispute. This consensus ad idem and the agreement clause so provided in Sections 3 and 7 emphasise a mutual agreement in writing to each other or the parties involved in the contract.[13] Section 3 emphasises the requirement of written communication between the parties to their business/work/communication addresses.

One of the early cases to be decided after the enactment of the ACA in 1996, referring to the old Arbitration Act of 1940, was K.K. Modi v. K.N. Modi, decided by the Supreme Court in 1998.[14] Here, the Supreme Court determined the nature of the clause in question for the settlement of a dispute between the parties and discussed the attributes necessary for considering an agreement as an arbitration agreement listed by Mustil and Boyd.[15] It held, inter alia, that amongst the attributes that ought to be present, the arbitration agreement must

a contemplate that the decision of the tribunal will be binding on the parties to the agreement,
b state that the jurisdiction of the tribunal to decide the rights of the parties must derive from their consent, or from the order of the Court or a statute, the terms of which make clear that the process is to be an arbitration,

11 Conax Florida Corp v Astrium Ltd 499 F. Supp. 2d 1237.
12 Ibid.
13 Section 7(1) In this Part, "arbitration agreement" means an agreement by the parties to submit to arbitration all or certain disputes that have arisen or that may arise between them, in respect of a defined legal relationship, whether contractual or not.

(2) An arbitration agreement may be the form of an arbitration clause in a contract or inform of a separate agreement.

14 AIR 1998 SC1297.
15 Mustil and Boyd, *Commercial Arbitration*, 2nd Edn, pp. 30–31 as cited in KK Modi v KN Modi AIR 1998 SC 1297 at 1311.

c ... that substantive rights of the parties will be determined by the tribunal,
d ... that the agreement of the parties to refer their disputes to the decision of the tribunal must be intended to be enforceable in law.

In the instant case, differences and disputes arose between one Kedar Nath Modi and his sons constituting Group A, the respondents and the sons of late Gujjar Mal Modi constituting Group B, the appellants on the other hand. On 24 January 1989, a Memorandum of Understanding was arrived at between Group A and Group B. There were numerous clauses in the Memorandum of Understanding, of which Clause 9 of the Memorandum was at dispute. The clause provided that

> Implementation will be done in consultation with the financial institutions. For all disputes, clarifications etc., in respect of implementation of this agreement, the same shall be referred to the Chairman, Industrial Finance Corporation of India (IFCI). IFCI or his nominees whose decisions will be final and binding on both the groups.

The Chairman of the IFCI rendered a decision which was not acceptable to group B. On 18 May 1996, the appellants (Group B) filed an arbitration petition under Section 33 of the Arbitration Act, 1940, in the Delhi High Court challenging the legality and validity of the said decision.

The proceedings raised two main questions:

1 Whether Clause 9 of the Memorandum of Understanding, dated 24 January 1989, constituted an arbitration agreement; and whether the decision of the Chairman, IFCI, constituted an award; and
2 Whether Suit was an abuse of the process of court.

After examining the attributes for an arbitration agreement, the Supreme Court held that this was not an arbitration clause. It did not envisage that any difference or dispute that may arise in execution of the works should be referred to the arbitration of an arbitrator.

The Court stated that while there are no conclusive tests, by and large, one can follow a set of guidelines in deciding whether the agreement is to refer an issue to an expert or whether the parties have agreed to resolve disputes through arbitration. It emphasised that the court would look into the following factors:

1 Existence of disputes as against intention to avoid future disputes;[16]
2 The tribunal or forum so chosen is intended to act judicially, after taking into account relevant evidence before it and the submissions made by the parties before it;
3 The decision is intended to bind the parties and
4 Nomenclature used by the parties may not be conclusive.

16 Crusteji Jamshedji Ardaseer Wadia & Anor v Dr R D Shiralee AIR 1943 Bombay 32; KK Modi v KN Modi AIR 1998 SC 1297 at 1315.

> One must examine the true intent and Purport of the agreement. There are, of course, the statutory requirements of a written agreement, existing or future disputes and an intention to refer them to arbitration (Vide Section 2 Arbitration Act 1940 and Section 7 Arbitration and Conciliation Act, 1996). Undoubtedly, in the course of correspondence exchanged by various members of Groups A and B with the Chairman, IFCI, some of the members have used the word arbitration in connection with Clause 9. That by itself, however, is not conclusive.[17]

The court concluded that:

> the intention of the parties was not to have any judicial determination on the basis of evidence led before the Chairman, IFCI. Nor was the Chairman, IFCI required to base his decision only on the material placed before him by the parties and their submissions. He was free to make his own inquiries. He had to apply his own mind and use his own expertise for the purpose. He was free to take the help of other experts. He was required to decide the question of valuation and the division of assets as an expert and not as an arbitrator. He had been authorised to nominate another in his place. But the contract indicates that he has to nominate an expert. The fact that submissions were made before the Chairman, IFCI, would not turn the decision-making process into an arbitration.[18]

In Jagdish Chander v. Ramesh Chander and Ors,[19] the court held that where the clause provides that, in the event of disputes arising between the parties, the disputes shall be referred to arbitration, it is an arbitration agreement. But, where the clause relating to settlement of disputes contains words that specifically exclude any of the attributes of an arbitration agreement or contains anything that detracts from an arbitration agreement, it will not be an arbitration agreement. Thus, mere use of the word *arbitration* or *arbitrator* in a clause will not make it an arbitration agreement, if it requires or contemplates a further or fresh consent of the parties for reference to arbitration.[20] For example, use of words such as *parties can, if they so desire, refer their disputes to arbitration* or *in the event of any dispute, the parties may also agree to refer the same to arbitration* or *if any disputes arise between the parties, they shall consider settlement by arbitration,* in a clause relating to the settlement of disputes, indicate that the clause is not intended to be an arbitration agreement.[21] Such clauses merely indicate a desire or hope to have the disputes settled by arbitration, or a tentative arrangement to explore arbitration as a mode of settlement, if and when a dispute arises. Such clauses require "the parties to arrive at a further agreement

17 KK Modi v KN Modi AIR 1998 SC 1297.

18 In case of Smt Rukmanibai Gupta v Collector Jabalpur (1980) 4 SCC556, the court held that the fact that disputes were referred to arbitration and the fact that the decision of the person to whom the disputes were referred was made final as illustrative of the nature of agreement thus the court held it to be an arbitration agreement. In contrast, in State of UP v Tipper Chand (1980) 2 SCC 341, a clause in the contract that provided for decision of the Superintendent Engineer shall be final and conclusive and binding on all parties pertaining to questions relating to meaning of specifications, designs, drawings and instructions was interpreted as not being an arbitration clause, as there was no mention in the clause of any dispute; the purpose of the clause was to vest the engineer with supervisions of execution of the work and administrative control from time to time.

19 (2007) 5 SCC 719.

20 State of UP v Tipper Chand (1980) 2 SCC 341.

21 (2007) 5 SCC 719.

to go to arbitration, as and when the disputes arise."[22] Any agreement or clause in an agreement requiring or contemplating a further consent or consensus before a reference to arbitration is not an arbitration agreement, but an agreement to enter into an arbitration agreement in future.

In Karnataka Power Transmission Cables Ltd v M/s Deepak Cables (India) Ltd,[23] the court examined a contractual clause for arbitration and appointment of an arbitrator. It interpreted the clause in light of Section 7 of the ACA and held that

> it is graphically clear that unless an arbitration agreement stipulates that the parties agree to submit all or certain disputes which have arisen or which may arise in respect of defined legal relationship whether contractual or not, there cannot be a reference to an arbitrator.[24]

In order to determine the true meaning, the court looks at intention, expressing the consensual acceptance to refer the disputes to an arbitrator.[25] In the absence of an arbitration clause in an agreement, as defined in Subsection (4) of Section 7, the dispute/disputes arising between the parties cannot be referred to the arbitral tribunal for adjudication of the dispute.

Similarly, in Powertech World Wide Limited v. Delvin International General Trading LLC,[26] the Supreme Court reiterated the law on subsistence of an arbitration agreement, but also, in addition, looked into particular facts and circumstances of the case, and thereby specified an additional factor to establish the existence of an Arbitration agreement. The Dispute resolution clause provided that:

> Any disputes arising out of this Purchase Contract shall be settled amicably between both the parties or through an Arbitrator in India/UAE.

The Court held that there exists consensus ad idem between the disputing parties to amicably settle their disputes or settle through arbitration in India or UAE. Also, notwithstanding the judgement in Jagdish Chander, the correspondence letters between parties signify that the petitioner invocated the arbitration and the respondent did not refute the existence of the said invoked clause, which also referred to the appointment of an arbitrator.[27] Thus, along with the requirements of the factors required to determine the existence of an arbitration agreement, the Court, in this case, also enumerated an additional factor to determine the existence of an arbitration agreement – i.e., the related correspondence/ documents that would point to the intention of parties.[28]

However, the smooth application of arbitration law has been riddled with difficulties, as parties to commercial disputes have taken recourse to the courts

22 (2007) 5 SCC 719.

23 (Civ App 4431 of 2014, Supreme Court of India).

24 ibid, paras9 and 22.

25 Jammu Kashmr State Forest Corporation v Abdul Karim Wali & Ors 1989 2 SCC 701, para 24.

26 2011(4) ARBLR 278 (SC).

27 See also *Bharat Bhushan Bansal v. U.P. Small Industries Corpn. Ltd* (1998) 3 SCC 573; *Bihar State Mineral Development Corpn. v. Encon Builders (I) (P) Ltd.* (2003) 7 SCC 418; *and State of Orissa v. Damodar Das* AIR 1996 SC 942.

28 See also M Dayanand Reddy v AP Industrial Infrastructure Corporation Limited and Ors (1993) 3 SCC 137; Bihar State Mineral Development Corporation & Anor v Encon Builders Ltd (2003) 7 SCC 418. See also John Kendall, *Sutto Russell on Arbitration*, 21st Edn, Sweet & Maxwell, 1996, p 37, para 2–014.

> where parties have either disagreed on the existence of an arbitration clause, or proper consent, or have litigated to thwart the purpose of an arbitration clause to get speedy resolution by arguing, dissecting and over emphasizing the usage of certain words in specific sections of the ACA, especially ss3, 5, 7, 11, 34, 35, 45 etc.[29]

In Avant Garde Clean Room & Engg Solutions Pvt Ltd v. Ind Swift Limited,[30] the dispute resolution clause read as follows:

> Arbitration-Dispute if any arising out of this Agreement shall be subject to the exclusive jurisdiction of the courts in city of Delhi.

The High Court of Delhi held that the above clause merely uses *arbitration* in the heading of the clause, while the reference to courts having jurisdiction if dispute arises does away with any agreement to arbitrate.

In State of Orissa & Ors v Bhagyadhar Dash,[31] the Court, while discussing the non-requirement of a particular form in order to constitute an arbitration agreement and determine the intention of the parties to an arbitration, stated with approval the elements to determine arbitration through the language of a written clause or document. So, one can surmise that *arbitration agreement* is to follow the well-settled principles, whereby the "specific and direct intent of the parties to refer to arbitration proceedings is reflected clearly in writing and is precise from the language and terms of the clause in the agreement."

The abovementioned cases provide an insight into how parties have raised issues related with language and litigated to drag cases into the courts or how courts themselves have provided various decisions that have further complicated recognition of an arbitration clause, largely due to the use of certain language drafted by the legal counsel of parties. This difficulty further compounds arbitration and ADR for environmental disputes, whether international or national.

Part II: Nature of environmental disputes

One notes that in contemporary times, by the very nature of overlap between commercial, developmental and environmental sectors, strategies for dispute resolution are changing. The use of Arbitration for commercial disputes is spilling over into environmental disputes at the international level and transboundary sectors. Pollution, spills, explosions from chemical plants, landfills, land acquisition for protected forests, mineral acquisitions and other types of industrial projects form a major part of disputes. This is in addition to violation of the Environment Protection Act 1986, Water Act 1974, Air Act 1981, Wildlife Act 1972, Forest Act 1927, Handling of Hazardous Substances Rules 1989 and Management of Plastic Waste Rules 2016 under the EPA, amongst others, all of such violations transgress into both private law and public law domain.

People, administrative agencies, investors, governments and legislative authorities face a myriad of issues in resolving these types of disputes, from cutting through the maze of

29 See Arpinder Singh, Ernst & Young, Partner and Head, Fraud and Investigation, Disputes, Report on "Emerging Trends in Arbitration in India", 2013 available at www.ey.com/in/en/services/assurance/fraud-investigation---dispute-services/ey-emerging-trends-in-arbitration-in-india (pdf).

30 210 (2014) DLT 714 Court held that in the present case, the main body of the clause does not even contemplate that the parties may agree to arbitration in future.

31 (2011) 7 SCC416.

multiparty and multi-jurisdiction disagreements to finding an arbitrator with environmental expertise. Thus, environmental arbitration poses a challenge.

As environmental disputes within a state are largely a province of public and regulatory law, interspersed with private law, dispute resolution in most countries, especially developing countries, is governed by court adjudicatory mechanisms, instead of ADR.

Further, in the context of environmental law and natural resources law, disputes that arise might invariably involve other substantive areas of law to include, inter alia, right to development, right to trade, right to health, right to livelihood, being similar to those faced at the international level such as those involving investments, WTO-trade agreements, human rights, use and sharing of energy, technology exchange vis-a-vis access to genetic resources, relationships between any international treaty and domestic customary law or State responsibility. All these questions are usually addressed by the law at the national or international level, and disputes are resolved through courts or specialised tribunals.[32] However, as environmental disputes are mixed up with commercial aspects of energy, technology and human rights subject to settlement of disputes through arbitration, there is a strong argument that the ACA or the environmental statutes in existence should take into account arbitration rules for environmental conflicts and not merely litigation. This is despite the fact that environmental disputes often involve rights in rem rather than rights in personam. It also suggests that what is needed is an adjudicatory or dispute resolution method that comprises a mixture of general and specialised experts.

An impetus for consideration for environmental arbitration into the ACA and or environmental statutes comes within the Indian economy, looking at the rate of commercial arbitration that is on the rise where environmental questions may be seen mixed with construction, energy and pharmaceutical disputes, amongst others.[33] Thus, parties are increasingly turning to arbitration over traditional court litigation for resolution of domestic and cross-border disputes.[34] For instance, The Kishenganga arbitration award, dealing with the interpretation of the Indus Water Treaty between India and Pakistan over distribution, use of the river waters and construction of dams, has been interpreted by the "Court of Arbitration" under the Treaty by taking into account international environmental principles of environmental protection and sustainable development.[35] One also notes such

32 Phillppe Sands, "Litigating Environmental Disputes: Courts, Tribunals and the Progressive Development of International Environmental Law", OECD Global Forum on International Investment OECD Investment Division 27–28 March 2008 available at www.oecd.org/investment/globalforum/40311090.pdf.

33 See a Whitepaper Report by PriceWaterhouse Coopers, India on "Corporate Attitudes and Practices towards Arbitration in India" available at https://www.pwc.in/assets/pdfs/publications/2013/corporate-attributes-and-practices-towards-arbitration-in-india.pdf.

34 Arpinder Singh, Ernst & Young, Partner and Head, Fraud and Investigation, Disputes, Report on "Emerging Trends in Arbitration in India", 2013 available at www.ey.com/in/en/services/assurance/fraud-investigation---dispute-services/ey-emerging-trends-in-arbitration-in-india (pdf). See also India v Pakistan (The Indus Water, Kishenganga arbitration) Partial Award of February 18, 2013), available at www.pca-cpa.org/showfile.asp?fil_id=2101, The Indus Waters Treaty 1960 was drawn between the Government of India, the Government of Pakistan and the International Bank for Reconstruction and Development, Pakistan–India, 19 September 1960, 419 U.N.T.S. 126. It was signed by India, Pakistan and the World Bank on 19 September 1960, and entered into force on 12 January 1961, upon the exchange of instruments of ratification, with retroactive effect from 1 April 1960, see also Shashank Kumar, "The Indus Water, Kishenganga Arbitration (India v Pakistan)", vol 17 issue 13 ASIL at https://www.asil.org/insights/volume/17/issue/13/indus-waters-kishenganga-arbitration-pakistan-v-india.

35 See Shashank Kumar, "The Indus Water, Kishenganga Arbitration (India v Pakistan)", vol 17 issue 13 ASIL at https://www.asil.org/insights/volume/17/issue/13/indus-waters-kishenganga-arbitration-pakistan-v-india.

environmental arbitrations that are taking place under international bilateral investment treaties (BITs) in countries such as the United States, Europe and Canada.[36]

Part III: Statutory arbitration provisions in other sectors

Arbitration clauses are provided for in many other areas where disputes arise or might arise by creating a provision under a specific statute that provides for, inter alia, arbitration. For example, the labour tribunal has a clause for arbitration amongst employee–employer disputes (on a myriad of issues that may arise in a labour/worker relationship).[37] Another contemporary area where arbitration clauses help disputing parties is sport. Disputes between various sport activity rules, codes and players carry an arbitration clause provision and redress in specific sport tribunals, e.g., Indian Court of Arbitration for Sport, 2011,[38] similar to the Court of Arbitration for Sports (CAS) at the international level and the International Council of Arbitration for Sport (ICAS 2016).[39] The purpose of ICAS is to

36 Such cases involve disputes between both states and/or states and private individuals or companies as parties. It would usually involve disputes rights arising under the treaty, factual environmental violations in the context of commercial dealing under the investment treaty. For example, nationalisation of oil resources may violate a contract between an oil company and a state (Texaco Overseas Petroleum Co. and California Asiatic Oil Co. v. Libya, 53 ILR 389 [1977] and Kuwait v. American Indep. Oil Co., 66 ILR 519 [1982]); Argentina brought a claim against Uruguay under a 1975 bilateral treaty, alleging that a new pulp mill will discharge toxins into the Uruguay River; Vattenfall – Swedish-owned energy company – contracted with the city of Hamburg to build a coal-fired power plant. New elections led to a coalition involving the Green Party, resulting in new environmental restrictions over air and water emissions. Vattenfall claims it is no longer economically feasible and filed an arbitration for over US $1 billion.

37 See The Industrial Disputes Act 1947 that provides for, inter alia, resolution of employer-employee disputes through arbitration. Industrial Disputes Act, 1947 was enacted with the object of making provision for investigation and settlement of industrial disputes and for other ancillary purposes. It provides for settlement of "industrial disputes." For this purpose, it provides a three-fold machinery for settlement of "industrial disputes": (1) negotiation-Collective Bargaining, (2) mediation and adjucation-arbitration. See also O P Malhotra, "Arbitration of Labour Disputes: Labour Adjudication", In The Law of Industrial Disputes, LexisNexis, 2015, pp. 27–28, available at http://14.139.60.114:8080/jspui/bitstream/123456789/731/7/Arbitration%20of%20Labour%20Disputes.pdf.

38 In July 2015, an Indian female athlete, Duttee Chand, challenged the decision to disqualify her by the International Athletics Federation from participating in Women's Athletic events due to the presence of higher amount of testosterone in her blood for events under Women's category/sex verification in sports or hyperandrogenism. The CAS issued an interim award suspending the regulations issued by the International Federation (IAAF) that stated that athletes with testosterone levels above 10 nmol/L were not allowed to compete in the female category. The panel ordered the IAAF to file scientific evidence regarding the connection between athletic performance and elevated testosterone levels within two years of the issuance of the interim award. CAS/2014/A/3759 Duttee Chand v Athletics Federation of India and International Association of Athletics Federation available at www.tas-cas.org/fileadmin/user_upload/award_internet.pdf.

The Procedural Rules of CAS that provide for general provisions, appointment of arbitrators, award, appeal amongst other procedural and evidentiary rules that the Court needs to follow to determine resolution of the disputes, available at www.tas-cas.org/en/arbitration/code-procedural-rules.html (Provision A to G (Rules1–70) A General Provisions, B. Ordinary Arbitration Procedure, C. Appeals, D. Consultation, E. Interpretation, F. Costs, G. Miscellaneous Provisions).

39 See The Procedural Rules of CAS that provide for general provisions, appointment of arbitrators, award, appeal amongst other procedural and evidentiary rules that the Court needs to follow to determine resolution of the disputes, available at www.tas-cas.org/en/arbitration/code-procedural-rules.html (Provision A to G (Rules1–70) A General Provisions, B. Ordinary Arbitration Procedure, C. Appeals, D. Consultation, E. Interpretation, F. Costs, G. Miscellaneous Provisions). The Court of Sport Arbitration and the 2016 Code for Sports Arbitration that provides for arbitration and mediation of sports related disputes through creation of

facilitate the resolution of sports-related disputes through arbitration or mediation and to safeguard the independence of CAS and the rights of the parties. It is also responsible for the administration and financing of CAS.[40]

Similarly, statutes, such as the Cooperative Societies Act (Delhi) (2003)[41] and the Multi-State Cooperatives Societies Act (Mumbai) (2002), also provide for disputes between private parties and registered societies. The specific law or statute is couched in words that specifically provide for arbitration between the members of the society or a private member against the society. In the Delhi Cooperative Societies Act 2003, Chapter VII provides for the settlement of disputes through arbitration. Sections 70 and 71 are pertinent sections that provide as follows:

> Disputes may be referred for arbitration in case the disputes are with respect to society members. This could be pertaining to the constitution of the cooperative society, disciplinary issues, action against a paid employee or past employee or member as against the cooperative society.

Section 70(1) states that

---

two statutory bodies, International Council of Arbitration for Sports and the Court of Arbitration for Sport (ICAS and CAS), the statute for which is available at www.tas-cas.org/fileadmin/user_upload/Code_2016_final__en_.pdf (the preamble of the Code provides that the disputes to which a federation, association or other sports-related body is a party are a matter for arbitration pursuant to this Code, only insofar as the statutes or regulations of the bodies or a specific agreement so provide).

40 Decisions rendered by the Court have included anti-dopping decisions against international sports players, e.g., The International Tennis Federation (ITF), a special tribunal passed an arbitration award that disqualified Ms Maria Sharipova from playing international tennis matches for two years in June 2016. Ms Sharapova appealed to the CAS against this decision for which decision is awaited to be announced in October 2016, see the decisions in the Arbitration Procedure between Maria Sharapova vs International Tennis Federation, June 2016 available at www.tas-cas.org/fileadmin/user_upload/Media_Release_sept_2016_-_final.pdf; CAS 2014/A/3639 Amar Muralidharan v. National Anti-Doping Agency, National Dope Testing Laboratory, Ministry of Youth Affairs & Sports available at www.tas-cas.org/fileadmin/user_upload/FINAL_AWARD_3639__internet_.pdf (anti-doping rule violation by a national swimmer); CAS 2016/A/4745 Russian Paralympic Committee v. International Paralympic Committee available at www.tas-cas.org/fileadmin/user_upload/Award_4745_Final.pdf (On 18 July 2016, the report commissioned by the World Anti-Doping Authority (WADA) from Professor Richard McLaren as the Independent Person was released (the "IP Report"). In the IP Report, Professor McLaren and his team reported that they had identified and verified evidence that led them to conclude beyond reasonable doubt that the Russian Government had developed, implemented and controlled a State-run doping program over a period from at least late 2011 until August 2015. (The report also stated that Russian athletes from Paralympic sport benefitted from this program.) The Russian Paralymic Committee, comprising government bodies and sports organisation, appealed against the International Paralymic Committee. Amongst others, the CAS held that there was a breach of the IPC Anti-Doping Policy and the RPC duties and obligations... Furthermore, the IPC had before it reliable information from Professor McLaren in the IP Report, as well as the subsequent information provided by him to the IPC, as set out in the McLaren Affidavit. The CAS has rendered many arbitral decision since 1986 over various international sports issues, including cricket, football, olympic, paralympics and Asian games. See CAS Home: Recent Decisions available at www.tas-cas.org/en/jurisprudence/recent-decisions.html.

41 Passed by the Legislative Assembly of the National Capital Territory of Delhi on 29 July 2003 is an Act to consolidate and amend the laws relating to cooperative societies, to facilitate the voluntary formation and democratic Functioning of Cooperatives as People's Institutions Based on Self Help and Mutual Aid to Enable Them to Promote Their Economic and Social Betterment and to provide for better regulation, management, functional autonomy of such societies and for matters connected therewith or incidental thereto in the National Capital Territory of Delhi.

> notwithstanding anything contained in any law for the time being in force, if any dispute touching the constitution, management or the business of a co-operative society other than a dispute regarding disciplinary action taken by the co-operative society or its committee against a paid employee of the co-operative society arises among members, past members and persons claiming through members, and the co-operative society, its committee or any officer, agent or employee, such disputes shall be referred to the Registrar for decision and no court shall have jurisdiction to entertain any suit or other proceedings in respect of such disputes.

Section 70(2) lays down similar elements as listed by the Supreme Court for identification of arbitration agreement by virtue of statute and provides that if any question arises whether a dispute referred to the Registrar under this section is or is not a dispute touching the constitution, management or the business of a cooperative society, the decision thereon of the Registrar shall be final and shall not be called in question in any court.

Section 70(5) is the savings clause that provides that

> Save as otherwise provided under this Act, the provisions of the Arbitration and Conciliation Act, 1996 (26 of 1996) shall apply to all arbitrations under this Act, as if proceedings for arbitration were referred for settlement or decision under the provisions of the Arbitration and Conciliation Act, 1996.

To make the matter clear, Section 71 empowers the Registrar to decide the dispute himself, or transfer it for disposal to any person who has been invested by the government with powers in that behalf or refer it for disposal to an arbitrator. The Delhi Cooperative Societies Act 2003, for example, also provides specifically for arbitration, whether or not a person affected in the dispute has given any consent or not.

Elsewhere, efforts to create a specialist tribunal have only been partially successful to take up the resolution of an environmental dispute, especially where a multinational company has invested in a state to establish a manufacturing unit. These specialist tribunals have been created from time to time to deal with specific environmental problems and deal with victim compensation within India. A good example of a partial successful instance of constitution of a tribunal comes from the dispute between Hindustan Coca Cola Beverages Pvt Ltd. and the people of Plachimada, in the state of Kerala. The dispute involved violation of environmental and water pollution laws. The Kerala State Assembly introduced a Bill, the Coca Cola Tribunal Victim Compensation Bill 2011,[42] which was established when untreated heavy metals seeped into the groundwater supply where the Coca Cola Company operated its manufacturing plant in Pachimadaa, Kerala. The presence of metals like cadmium, lead and chromium in the

42 The Plachimada Coca-Cola Victims Relief and Compensation Claims Special Tribunal Bill, 2011 available at www.niyamasabha.org/bills/12kla/plachimada%20victims.pdf (The aim of this bill was *to provide for the establishment of a Special Tribunal for the expeditious adjudication of disputes and recovery of compensation for the victims from the Hindustan* Coca-Cola *Beverages Private Limited and matters connected therewith or incidental thereto*).
Preamble—Whereas it is expedient to establish a Special Tribunal for the adjudication of disputes and recovery of compensation for the damages caused by the Hindustan Coca-Cola Beverages Private Limited by entertaining original applications and by transferring cases pending before the various courts and other authorities to the Tribunal and to provide for matters connected therewith or incidental thereto; And Whereas, there has been environmental degradation, soil degradation, water contamination by over extraction of ground water and thereby causing scarcity of drinking water by the Coca-Cola Company at Plachimada.)

sludge affected the general health of people with skin ailments, breathing problems and other diseases, and there was environmental degradation, soil degradation and water contamination by overextraction of ground water, which caused scarcity of drinking water.

The Bill was passed by the Kerala State Legislative Assembly, but did not receive assent from the President.[43] However, the quasi-judicial function of the tribunal for dispute resolution is clearly discernible from the language of the Preamble to the Bill. The preamble provides for establishment of a specialist tribunal for the adjudication of disputes and recovery of compensation for the damages caused by the Hindustan Coca-Cola Beverages Private Limited by entertaining original applications and by transferring cases pending before the various courts and other authorities to the Tribunal and to provide for matters connected therewith or incidental thereto.[44] Such a creation of an ad hoc tribunal leaves a negative impression on the government environmental policy, which treats dispute such as this in a piecemeal manner to provide redress by establishing a temporary tribunal.

The controversies that have surrounded the Bill have necessitated the examination of not only Center-state relations and the feasibility of adjudication of the victims but also governmental priorities when it comes to conflicts between stakeholders, due to development, investment and use of natural resources. Such conflicting situations and unanticipated futuristic environmental problems ought to be provided for, not only through judicial determination but also through ADR techniques, especially arbitration, particularly in respect of civil compensation. To provide for arbitration under the Environmental Protection Act 1986 or the Central and State Pollution Control Laws, the National Green Tribunal Act 2010 may go a long way in overcoming environmental conflicts.

Another example can be seen when the government enacted the Bhopal Gas Victims Accident compensation Act, 1985, when a specialist tribunal was set up after a major catastrophe stuck when isocyanate gas leaked from a multinational company subsidiary that had set up a chemical fertiliser plant with state government's assent. Over 3,000 lives were lost overnight, due to leakage of toxic gas in 1984, and over 100,000 people were affected.[45] The claims of the victims have, till date, not been satisfactorily settled, mostly due to dispute between claimants and the compensation authority for one, and difficulties in interpreting the language and intent of the Act that has not been precise.[46] These specialist tribunals have not been very successful. Yet another example is provided by the establishment of the interstate tribunal, which gave an award on the Cauvery River Water

43 The 2011 Bill was to adjudicate disputes relating to compensation of Rs 216.25 crore to be paid by the company for the damage its cola bottling plant caused in the village. See Soumya Misra, "Center returns Plachimada Bill", *Down to Earth* 17 February 2011 available at www.downtoearth.org.in/news/centre-returns-plachimada-tribunal-bill---34039 (accessed on October 2, 2016), Sujith Koonan, "Constitutionality of the Plachimada Bill: An Assessment", 7/2 *Law, Environment and Development Journal*, p. 151 (2011), available at www.lead-journal.org/content/11151.pdf.

44 As the Bill did not receive Presidential assent scholars and ecologists and NGO workers have severely criticised the non-assent to the Bill and questioned Center-State relations, criticised governmental policies in respect of investments by multinational companies and highlighted the conflict between economic development and environmental protection, see S Faizi, "Cocoa Cola Compensation Bill: Government of India subverts The Constitutional Process" at www.countercurrents.org/faizi260515.htm.

45 See Union Carbide Corporation v Union of India, 1989 SCALE 910 380 available at http://cseindia.org/userfiles/scbhopal.pdf.

46 See Sunita Narian and Chandra Bhushan, "Thirty Years of Bhopal Gas Tragedy: A Continuing Disaster", Down to Earth, December 15, 2014 available at www.downtoearth.org.in/coverage/30-years-of-bhopal-gas-tragedy-a-continuing-disaster-47634.

Distribution between the States of Karnataka and Tamil Naidu.[47] The dispute between sharing of river waters has been drawn for over forty years, and despite many interim and final awards, and also interference by the Supreme Court of India, the matter is still unsettled. It has recently led to heated statewide protest in both states and disruption of civil and daily life due to strikes and unrest.[48]

Within the regulations and notification of the Environmental Impact Assessment 2006 issued under the Environment Protection Act 1986, there could be the introduction of ADR and conciliation, which at the moment is absent. The specific benefit of an alternate dispute resolution lies in the fact that it enhances efficiency, reduces time taken, encourages parties to adopt constructive approaches and most of all gives a sense of ownership to stakeholders that is most significant in environmental disputes and determination of rights and recognition of communities. Arbitration is adopted by the parties agreeing to a neutral third party, while mediation and conciliation are ideally adopted at the beginning of the dispute, although it may still be adopted during a trial; however, the essence of such techniques is that parties can resolve their differences or disputes and save time and money not only for themselves but also for the courts and judiciary.

Environmental arbitration at the international level

International environmental law, treaties and specialist institutions provide for ADR processes, including arbitration and mediation, under environmental conventions and treaties, and environmental and trade disputes or conflicts. Many developed countries have adopted clear rules, e.g., the American Arbitration Association (AAA), or the EU, Canada, for environmental arbitration as proven methods for resolving disputes in certain developmental and environmental conflicts.[49] Resolution of environmental disputes can be extremely complex and is at par with commercial contractual/international/domestic disputes with multiparty, multi-jurisdictional issues.

Though environmental arbitration as a method for dispute resolution has had a long history, especially within international environmental border treaty disputes, within India, it is not as mainstream as commercial arbitration. However, in contemporary times, environmental aspects are increasingly mixed with industrial, construction and trade disputes or very often dealt with mixed aspects of environmental facts under BITs.[50] Although there are challenges

47 The Cauvery Water dispute tribunal was formed under directions of the Supreme Court in June 1990 see at www.wrmin.nic.in/forms/list.aspx?lid+378, Ministry of Water Resources, River Development & Ganga Rejuvenation, Government of India website.

48 See Avarnita Mathur, "Cauvery dispute: statewide Bandh in Karnataka, Heavy security deployed", *India Today*, 9 Sep 2016, available at www.indiatoday.intoday.in/story/cauvery-water-row-karnataka-bandh/1/17602.

49 See AAA: Industrial Construction and Environmental Dispute/Guidelines and Rules for Arbitration Process.

50 See Beharry, Christina L., and Melinda E. Kuritzky. "Going Green: Managing the Environment through International Investment Arbitration." *American University International Law Review* 30(3): 383–429 (2015). (The authors have explored to what extent investor-state arbitration is equipped to deal with environment-related disputes and, after examining investor-related international environmental cases, treaties and BITS agreements in the US, Canadian and international context, concluded that that to ensure greater support from both the users and observers of the system, investor-state arbitration could be more sensitive to environmental policy concerns, through the invocation of various procedural, evidentiary, and conceptual tools, See also Lisa Bingham and David Cameroon Prell, "Arbitration of Environmental Disputes that Cross National Borders", vol II *Conflict Resolution, UNESCO, Encyclopedia of Life Support Systems available at www.eolss.net/ Eloss-sampleAllchapter* (.aspx on file with author); Philippe Sands, "Litigating Environmental

faced by arbitrators in resolution of BITs and environmental aspects of cases that are traditionally more suited to court administration, increasing cases have come up at the international level, involving issues that were earlier the province of the courts. There are now a range of specialist courts and tribunals, as well as "green benches" for environmental cases, and many countries have established specialist courts such as Australia, Bangladesh, India, Ireland, New Zealand, Sweden, Denmark, Canada: Ontario, US: Vermont, Africa: Tanzania.[51] Amongst different stakeholder groups, which are relevant for achieving different elements such as the environmental policy, goals and strategy, it is such courts or tribunals that determine the resolution of conflicts. Generally speaking, the percentage of disputes in energy, biodiversity, water and waste sectors remain the highest. If one examines the Indian Biodiversity Act 2002 (BDA),[52] one finds that the law was enacted after India acceded to the United Nations Convention on Biological Diversity, 1992.[53] The Preamble to the BDA states that it is an Act to provide for conservation of biological diversity, sustainable use of its components and fair and equitable sharing of the benefits arising out of the use of biological resources, knowledge and for matters connected therewith or incidental thereto.[54] However, despite the fact that all sorts of stakeholders are involved under the BDA, the statutory Authority under Section 3(1) may grant an approval to any person, company or organisation who is a citizen of India or a foreign person, company or organisation with conditions to obtain any biological resource occurring in India or knowledge associated thereto for research or for commercial utilisation or for bio-survey and bio-utilisation. Disputes and conflicts are likely to arise while determining rights, customary practices, benefit sharing directly with communities, drafting agreements for funding and research, bioprospecting, bio-utlilisation and research or exchanging old traditional knowledge in respect of use of biodiversity. The BDA does not provide for any arbitration clauses or any ADR technique to be adopted before proceeding with a formal complaint to the National Biodiversity Authority (NBA) that activates a civil court. Other stakeholders, such as traditional and customary communities, local bodies, panchayats or even gram sabhas and village councils,[55] could potentially resolve their disputes through mediation, negotiation or even arbitration, before proceeding to the State Biodiversity Authority, or NBA.[56]

Juxtaposed with development and investment in the biodiversity and natural resources sector, tribal and traditional communities, farmers, fishing communities and indigenous

Disputes: Courts, Tribunals and the Progressive Development of International Environmental Law", OECD Global Forum on International Investment, OECD Investment Division, www.oecd.org/investment/gfi-7; Derek McDonald, "Arbitrating International Environmental Disputes", Baker Botts LLP, Law360, October 2010 (on file with author).

51 National Green Tribunal of India (2010); New Zealand Environmental Court (1991); Kenyan Environmental Court (w.e.f. 2002); Austria, Tanzania (specialist tribunal) these tribunals are established to largely resolve public interest questions and are not bound by the rules of evidence and the proceedings are less formal than the general courts.

52 Available at http://nbaindia.org/uploaded/Biodiversityindia/Legal/31.%20Biological%20Diversity%20%20Act,%202002.pdf.

53 See Sections 36 (directions by the Central Government), 57, 60 and 63 (Rules).

54 Section 52. BDA establishes and creates a National Biodiversity Authority, a statutory body with powers of a civil court Code of Civil Procedure, 1908, for the purposes of discharging its functions.

55 Gram Sabhas are village councils and recognised under the Constitution of India article 243(I) as executive units at the village level.

56 However, despite the fact that the Act mentions Environmental Impact Assessment procedures for various activities that might involve use of such an instrument to assess environmental and development harm, settlement of disputes stays under the rubric of the judicial authority of NBA.

people – those reliant on traditional knowledge – are heavily dependent upon biodiversity for their survival and livelihood, and there are higher chances of dispute and threat to such populations. The BDA only recognises conservation of biodiversity – sustainable use of such resources and equitable sharing in benefits as its wider objectives in consonance with the Convention on Biological Diversity. However, the 2004 Rules and the provisions under the Act do not, inter alia, allow for affected persons to directly approach the courts or call for settlement of disputes through any alternative means, such as ADR or arbitration, where appropriate.[57]

In respect of clean air and water and waste management disputes under respective central and state legislation, stakeholders like the central government, state governments, Ministry of Environment, Forests and Climate Change, Ministries like Urban Development, Rural Development, Planning, Health, Renewable Resources, industrial corporations, development banks, scientific institutes, centres and state pollution control boards may have a role to play when it comes to an environment and development dispute. Currently, all or any such disputes are to be referred to the Green Tribunal, as there is no statutory provision that exists making such procedures mandatory.[58]

Sectors, such as forest conservation protection of forest dwellers, demand such strategies, and a few provisions and processes under statutory law have been adopted when one examines the Stakeholder consultation under the Forest Conservation Act 1980. The proposals for diversion of forest land under the Forest Conservation Act 1980 are received from the concerned State Government after due consultation with respective "Gram Sabhas."[59] Stakeholder Consultation is also provided for under the Scheduled Tribes and other Forest Dwellers recognition of Forest Rights Act, 2006.[60] The Scheduled Tribes and other

57 Powers of a civil court are provided under the Act to the NBA that acts as a judicial authority. BDA and its Rules also do not fully empower these communities to protect their resources and knowledge from being misused or to generate benefits (except charging collection fees). There is no representation of local communities at the State Biodiversity Board or at the NBAF or a critique of the Biodiversity Act and Rules see Ashish Kothari, Kanchi Kohli, Shantha B at Kalpvriksh, "Biodiversity Act 2002 and Biodiversity Rules 2004", available www.kalpvriksh.org (on file with author).

58 The National Green Tribunal Act 2010, Section 14(1) read with schedule 1 lays down that the tribunal shall have jurisdiction over all civil cases where a substantial question of environment is involved and such questions arises over enforcement of any enactment as listed in schedule 1 to the NGTA. This also includes enforcement of any legal right over the environment. Schedule 1 lists seven laws that include the Water (Prevention and Control of Pollution) Act 1974, Water (prevention and Control of Pollution) Cess Act 1977, the Air (prevention and Control of Pollution) Act 1981, The Forest Conservation Act 1980, the Environment Protection Act 1986, Public Liability Insurance Act 1991, The Biodiversity Act 2002: see Sections 14(1), 15(1), 17(1) (a) 17(2), 19(4)(j), 34(l) see Central India AYUSH Drug Manufacturer's Association v State of Maharashtra Write petition No 6360/2015.

59 Lowest administrative units at the village and community level recognised under the Constitution and or institutions of self-government constituted under article 243B, 243Q or any other provision of the Constitution or any Central Act or State Act, Article 243B defines gram sabha as a body consisting of persons registered in the electoral rolls relating to a village comprised within the area of the Panchayat at the village level. With regard to its powers and authority, Article 243 (A) of the Constitution says that the Gram Sabha may exercise such powers and perform such functions of the village level as the Legislature of a State may, by law, provide. It is in the light of this that State legislatures have endowed certain powers to this corporate body relating to the development of the village. Provisions of the Panchayats (Extension to the Scheduled Areas) Act 1996 has not only extended development, planning and audit functions to the gram sabha but also endowed it with the management and control of natural resources and the adjudication of justice in accordance with traditions and customs. See Mahi Pal, "Effectiveness of Gram Sabha", available at http://pib.nic.in/feature/feyr2000/fapr2000/f030420001.html.

60 The law concerns the rights of forest-dwelling communities to land and other resources, denied to them over decades, as a result of the continuance of colonial forest laws in India.

Forest Dwellers Recognition of Forest Rights Act, 2006 has a built-in mechanism for stakeholder consultation. The concerned Gram Sabhas that are equivalent almost to Village Councils provide a resolution passed by at least 50% of their strength, indicating that all the rights have been recognised.[61] The settlement of rights is analogous to a negotiation and conciliation exercise that provides for dispute resolution between individuals and the village council.

Gram Sabhas or Panchayats at appropriate level shall also have powers to manage minor water bodies; power of mandatory consultation in matters of land acquisition; resettlement and rehabilitation and prospecting licenses/mining leases for minor minerals; power to prevent alienation of land and restore alienated land; regulate and restrict sale/consumption of liquor; manage village markets; control money lending to Scheduled Tribes and ownership of minor forest produce.

ADR and arbitration for environmental- and natural resources-related disputes at the Permanent Court of Arbitration

Furthermore, since the establishment of the Permanent Court of Arbitration (PCA), arbitration is being used as a tool for compliance with international environmental law.[62] In this field, the PCA is acting, or has acted, as registry for a few cases, as in:

- Ireland v. United Kingdom (MOX Plant Case), which was instituted in November 2001;[63]
- Malaysia v. Singapore, which was instituted in July 2003 and terminated by an award on agreed terms rendered on 1 September 2005;[64]

61 The village council have to enclose copies of the resolution. Further, the concerned Deputy Commissioner has to provide a certificate in this regard. Section 6(1) of the Act provides that the gram sabha, or village assembly, will initially pass a resolution recommending whose rights to which resources should be recognised (i.e., which lands belong to whom, how much land was under the cultivation of each person as on 13 December 2005, and so forth). This resolution is then screened and approved at the level of the subdivision (or taluka) and subsequently at the district level.

62 The Permanent Court of Arbitration, PCA was established by the 1899 Hague Convention on the Pacific Settlement of International Disputes. It is headquartered at the Peace Palace in The Hague, the Netherlands. The PCA facilitates arbitration, conciliation, fact-finding and other dispute resolution proceedings among various combinations of States, State entities, intergovernmental organisations and private parties, see information on PCA and the cases it has been involved in at: www.pca-cpa.org/. On 18 June 2001, Ireland commenced arbitration to resolve a dispute with the United Kingdom, pursuant to the 1992 Convention for the Protection of the Marine Environment of the North-East Atlantic ("OSPAR Convention"). The dispute concerned the access to the information about the MOX nuclear fuel plant at Sellafield, on the Irish Sea. Ireland requested access to certain information about processing of the plant. The UK refused to provide it, arguing that the information was withheld from public reports on commercial confidentiality grounds. In its final award of 2 July 2003, the OSPAR Arbitral Tribunal ruled that Ireland failed to demonstrate that the information that it desired to obtain was information falling within the meaning or Article 9(2) of the OSPAR Convention, namely being "information on the state of the maritime area" or on "activities and measures adversely affecting or likely to affect it." The final award was given in June 2008.

The International Bureau of the Permanent Court of Arbitration served as registry in these arbitration proceedings. Although PCA, is not an enforcing body, the cases arbitrated by the PCA in the Tribunal set under Annex VII of the United Nations Convention on the Law of the Sea (UNCLOS) could be considered as enforcement.

63 Available at www.pca-cpa.org. See also Philippe Sands.

64 Malaysia/Singapore. An Award on Agreed Terms was issued by the Tribunal on September 1, 2005. Available at www.pca-cpa.org.

- Barbados v. Trinidad and Tobago, which was instituted in February 2004 and decided by a final award rendered on 11 April 2006[65] and
- Guyana v. Suriname, which was instituted in February 2004 and decided by a final award rendered on 17 September 2007.[66]
- Chagos Marine Protected Area Arbitration (Mauritius v. United Kingdom): on 20 December 2010, the Republic of Mauritius instituted arbitral proceedings concerning the establishment by the United Kingdom of a Marine Protected Area around the Chagos Archipelago, final award was given by the tribunal in March 2015.[67]
- The Atlanto-Scandian Herring Arbitration (The Kingdom of Denmark in respect of the Faroe Islands v. The European Union): The Kingdom of Denmark in respect of the Faroe Islands instituted arbitral proceedings against the European Union under Annex VII to the United Nations Convention on the Law of the Sea (the "Convention"). The dispute concerned the interpretation and application of Article 63(1) of the Convention in relation to the shared stock of Atlanto-Scandian herring. The Permanent Court of Arbitration acted as Registry in this arbitration. The Final award was given by the tribunal in September 2014.[68]

Since the 1970s, the PCA has also regularly been included as the forum for arbitration of disputes arising out of multilateral environmental treaties in various cases in which international environmental law and sustainable development principles have been applied.[69] The PCA's Environmental Rules arise out of a special working group, convened by the PCA in 1996 for the purposes of exploring the role of the PCA in the settlement of environmental disputes.[70]

Arbitration and conciliation as methods of dispute resolution have been built within the PCA Optional Rules in respect of Natural Resources.[71] The Rules Relating to Natural Resources and/or the Environment[72] apply to conciliation of disputes relating to natural resources and/or the environment.

The Rules define conciliation as a process, whereby parties request a third person, or a panel of persons, to assist them in their attempt to reach an amicable settlement of their dispute relating to natural resources and/or the environment. The characterisation of the dispute as relating to the environment or natural resources is not necessary for the application of these Rules, where all the parties have agreed to settle a specific dispute under these Rules.

65 Award of 11 April 2006, available at www.pca-cpa.org.

66 Award of 17 September 2007, available at www.pca-cpa.org.

67 See at www.pcacases.com/web/view/11.

68 See at www.pcacases.com/web/view/25.

69 See *e.g.* Convention on International Trade in Endangered Species of Wild Fauna and Flora, Mar. 3, 1973,27 U.S.T. 1087, T.I.A.S. No. 8249, 993 U.N.T.S. 243; *Iron Rhine Arbitration (Belgium v. Netherlands)* PCA Case No. 2003–02; *Indus Waters Kishenganga Arbitration (Pakistan v. India)*, PCA Case No. 2011–01.

70 Philippe Sands *Environmental Disputes and the Permanent Court of Arbitration: Issues for Consideration, Background Paper for the Secretary-General of the PCA*, March 1996; P. Sands and R. Mackenzie, *Settlement of Disputes under International Environmental Agreements: A Potential Role for the Permanent Court of Arbitration, Background Paper for the Bureau of the PCA*, July 1997.

71 The 2001 Permanent Court of Arbitration's Optional Rules for the Arbitration of Disputes Relating to Natural Resources and/or the Environment. Available at: www.pca-cpa.org/ENVIRONMENTAL(3)d0a4.pdf?-fil_id=590. See D. Ratliff "The PCA Optional Rules for Arbitration of Disputes Relating to Natural Resources and/or the Environment" *Leiden Journal of International Law* 14: 887–896 (2001).

72 Article 1, Scope of Application.

The PCA has recently been a part of the 2015 Paris Climate Change Declaration and has been involved in the drafting of environmental-related dispute settlement clauses.[73] In this drafting and negotiation with various international bodies, it has been actively assisted by several United Nations Convention secretariats.[74] The United Nations Economic Commission for Europe, for example, has approved a reference to the PCA Environmental Arbitration Rules in its draft "Legally Binding Instrument on Civil Liability under the 1992 Watercourses and TEIA Conventions."[75]

Furthermore, the PCA participated in several international negotiations at the Conferences of the Parties of Multilateral Environmental Agreements (MEAs), amongst others the United Nations Convention on Biodiversity (UNCBD) and the Intergovernmental Committee for the Biosafety Protocol, as well as the United Nations Framework Convention on Climate Change (UNFCCC).[76] The PCA is also involved in drafting dispute-resolution clauses for placement in Emissions Trading Contracts and references the PCA Secretary-General as appointing authority in proceedings under the UNCITRAL.[77] Rules may be found in the World Bank's Instrument Establishing the "Prototype Carbon Fund."[78]

The International Emissions Trading Association (IETA) recommends the PCA Environmental Arbitration Rules in its guidelines on drafting carbon contracts. The PCA also provides guidance on drafting environmentally related dispute settlement clauses, and participates in international environmental conferences to that effect.[79] The PCA covers a range of issues that form the subject of the main MEAs that include the Law of Seas, biodiversity, Climate Change and carbon contracts. The MEAs that have been dealt with by the PCA include, inter alia, Convention on International Trade in Endangered Species of Wild Fauna and Flora,[80] Convention on the Conservation of Migratory Species of Wild Animals[81] and Protocol to the Antarctic Treaty on Environmental Protection.[82]

Environmental governance is thus increasingly acquiring a global dimension at the international level. There are major MEAs in the areas of Biodiversity, Climate Change, Persistent Organic Pollutants, Hazardous wastes and chemicals, Ozone depleting substances,

73 PCA Press Release, *"PCA Participation in COP21 and Conference on Climate Change Disputes"*, Paris, 8 December 2015 available at https://pca-cpa.org/wp-content/uploads/sites/175/2015/12/PCA-Press-Release-dated-8-December-2015.pdf (address by the Secretary General of the Permanent Court of Arbitration (the "PCA"), Hugo H. Siblesz, at the Plenary Session of the UN Climate Change Conference. The PCA's Secretary-General delivered a speech during the High Level Segment of the talks, alongside Ministers, and senior representatives of UN bodies and other intergovernmental organisations discussing existing and future use of international arbitration and alternative dispute resolution (ADR) mechanisms to resolve climate change related disputes and promote sustainable development objectives.

74 Available at https://pca-cpa.org/en/services/arbitration-services/environmental-dispute-resolution/.

75 Available at https://pca-cpa.org/en/services/arbitration-services/environmental-dispute-resolution/.

76 Rio Declaration on Environment and Development, 14 June 1992, U.N. Doc. A/CONF.151/26 (vol. I), 31 I.L.M. 874 (1992).

77 Available at https://pca-cpa.org/en/services/arbitration-services/environmental-dispute-resolution/.

78 Section 18 (2) states that any dispute between the Trustee and a Participant arising out of or relating to this Instrument or such Participants Participation Agreement shall be settled by arbitration in accordance with the UNCITRAL Arbitration Rules as at present in force. The number of arbitrators shall be three. The appointing authority shall be the Secretary-General of the Permanent Court of Arbitration at The Hague. Available at https://pca-cpa.org/en/services/arbitration-services/environmental-dispute-resolution/.

79 See PCA website at www.pca.org.

80 3 March 1973, 973 U.N.T.S. 14537.

81 23 June 1979, 1651 U.N.T.S. 28395.

82 4 October 1991, 30 I.L.M. 1461.

Wildlife and so forth. With India's evolving economic and geopolitical role, we can look upon these MEAs as an opportunity to adopt global environmental standards and, similar to commercial arbitration, to provide for ADR techniques for environmental matters nationally.

Part IV: Conclusion

Overall, the contemporary dynamics of environmental conflict demands the adoption of all kinds of dispute resolution techniques, including arbitration and existing law, and one needs to make room for the adoption of ADR and statutory recognition for arbitration, conciliation, mediation and similar strategies while one is engaged in meaningful environmental dispute resolution.

Despite the challenges posed by the language of domestic arbitration law in India that is geared to ideally resolve commercial disputes replete with the obstacles of legal language and its interpretation, environmental disputes, when mixed with commercial and private disputes, ought to be resolved through formally recognised and alternative methods at the ground level, at the first instance. Hence, legal rules for the arbitration of environmental disputes, where appropriate, ought to be incorporated not only within the domestic arbitration law with clear language but also within other environmental rules and legislation that exist for environmental dispute resolution within the country. In fact, apart from lessons from international environmental arbitration, in sectors such as sport and cooperative societies, there exist domestic laws that reflect the adoption of arbitration, even where dispute is of a private/public nature. A higher potential for justice, speed and efficiency exists for disputes to be resolved through alternate methods of dispute settlement within sectors that involve investment agreements for use and access to natural resources, energy, minerals, biodiversity, medicines or development and construction sectors domestically.[83]

Businesses are increasingly adopting arbitration over traditional court adjudication. This provides further persuasive dicta to tide over the public nature of environmental disputes and the private nature of business ventures that are commercial in nature. As environmental disputes transcend both the private and the public law domain, it makes sense to argue that domestic arbitration law be made easier to understand and incorporate environmental conflicts where appropriate, so that the language of law, which has so far been difficult, doesn't act as an impediment to effective environmental dispute resolution and environmental justice or pose an outright challenge to the resolution of environmental disputes within both the public and private sphere.

Arguably, if arbitration is not suited for all kinds of environmental disputes, questions of agreement on the assessment of damages to environmental victims of harm, assessment of value of natural resources, loss of livelihood, land acquisition, erosion of customary practices of forest dwelling communities, environmental victims of accidents or megaprojects, people affected due to the development of forest or river valley areas, process of determining rights, interests and land issues while performance of an Environmental Impact Assessment exercise are issues where statutory arbitration could help and be used, instead of court-protracted litigation. The fact that such techniques of ADR have been used in India under the Gram Sabhas adds another stronger support to have arbitration clauses built in environmental laws, such that the legal language supports effective and efficient resolution of disputes.

83 Arpinder Singh Ernst & Young Partner and National Leader in his foreword to a Report published in 2013 by the Fraud and Investigation, Disputes Team at EY, India.

14 Production and discovery of documents in arbitration in India – a comparative analysis

Ashok Kumar Singh

14.1 Introduction

Every dispute between two parties is a contour of facts that requires substantiation. In matters of dispute brought before a third party for adjudication, such substantiation is only possible with the help of evidence. Therefore, all legal systems across the globe in any dispute recognise the need for adducing evidence. This is done in order to accord meaning to the proceedings and provide the parties with an equal and adequate opportunity to present and defend their case.

Evidence can be adduced in the form of witnesses and documents. It is a settled proposition of law that the *witness may lie but a document will not.* The production of contemporary documents has proved to be one of the most reliable forms of evidence that can be presented in relation to any issue of fact. It is easy and less time-taking, as opposed to the other traditional forms of leading evidence (Redfern, 2006).

With arbitration rapidly growing as one of the preferred choices of alternative dispute resolution for the parties in a dispute, there is no reason why an arbitral tribunal should not have access to all relevant documents while deciding on any dispute submitted to it. The arbitrators primarily rely on the contemporaneous documents to arrive at a right decision and pass the award. Such documentary evidence may ascribe an altogether different meaning to any dispute and assist the arbitral tribunal in determining any disputed issue. It is an admitted practice across the globe that no party under custody, control or possession of documents relevant to the dispute be permitted to conceal the documents from the other party or the tribunal.

While the parties have referred their disputes to arbitration, it may happen that either of the parties before or during the arbitration proceedings may request the other party to produce the documents in its possession and control. Exchange of undisputed documents between the parties reduces the burden on the parties to prove them and cuts short the arbitration proceedings.

The party requested may refuse to produce the documents, sought by the other party on the following or other grounds:

- The documents are confidential (Delta Distilleries v United Spirits Ltd. and Anr., 2014).
- The documents are not available.
- The requested party is barred or exempted from producing such documents under a statute (Delta Distilleries v United Spirits Ltd. and Anr., 2014).
- The requested party does not want to produce the documents, apprehending that production of such documents would be fatal and detrimental to their interest in an arbitration proceeding.

The aggrieved party may, under these circumstances, request the arbitral tribunal for a direction to the other party to produce the documents, which are material to the dispute and are in possession of the other party.

In this section, we have dealt with the law of discovery and production of documents in arbitration in India. We have further analysed the arbitration law followed in India in light of international practices. This has been done in order to analyse and also establish a nexus between what has already been adopted and implemented by India in its arbitration legislation and what is still left to be explored apropos discovery and production of documents.

14.2 Legal framework governing arbitration in India

In India, arbitration proceedings are governed under The Arbitration and Conciliation Act, 1996 hereinafter referred to as 'Act of 1996'. Most of the provisions of the Act are in line with the United Nations Commission on International Trade Law Model Law on International Commercial Arbitration, 1985 hereinafter referred to as 'Model Law'. Prior to the enactment of the Act of 1996, arbitration proceedings in India were substantially governed by three enactments, namely The Arbitration Act, 1940 hereinafter referred to as 'Act of 1940', The Arbitration (Protocol and Convention) Act, 1937 and The Foreign Awards (Recognition and Enforcement) Act, 1961.

The Act of 1996 is divided mainly into three parts, namely Part I for Domestic Arbitrations, Part II for Enforcement of certain Foreign Awards and Part III for Conciliation. There are some institutions governing Institutional Arbitrations in India. However, there is no institution governing institutional arbitration, which has offices all over India. The existing institutions governing arbitrations have not been able to create confidence among the business community. As a result, institutional arbitrations are not prevalent, and the majority of domestic arbitrations in India are conducted through Ad-Hoc Arbitrations. In cases where the international commercial arbitration is seated in India, the Act of 1996 (The Arbitration and Conciliation Act 1996, s. 2(2) (4) (5)) governs the proceedings.

14.2.1 Conduct of arbitral proceedings under the act of 1996

While drafting the provisions of the Act of 1996, all efforts have been made to accord equal treatment to all the parties involved in the proceedings, and to enable the arbitral tribunal to arrive at a just decision in minimal possible time.

Section 18 of the Act of 1996, which deals with the equal treatment of parties (The Arbitration and Conciliation Act 1996, s. 18), ensures that each party is treated with equality and given equal opportunity to present the case. Section 19 of the Act of 1996, which deals with the determination of rules of procedure (The Arbitration and Conciliation Act 1996, s. 19), gives wide powers to the arbitral tribunal.

The entire judicial system and the courts in India dealing with civil disputes are governed by the Code of Civil Procedure, 1908, and the Indian Evidence Act, 1872. Section 19(1) of the Act of 1996 is a departure from this fundamental rule. As per Section 19(1), the arbitral tribunals are not bound by the provisions of the above referred Code and Act. In other words, to arrive at a right decision, the arbitral tribunals do not have to follow the technicalities of law like the courts.

The Supreme Court of India, in order to facilitate the arbitration proceedings, has held time and again that although arbitral tribunals are not bound by the Code of Civil

Procedure, 1908, and The Indian Evidence Act, 1872, the Act of 1996 does not expressly prohibit their application and thus, arbitral tribunals may take guidance from their general principles while conducting the arbitration proceedings (ITI Ltd. v Siemens Public Communication Network Ltd, 2002).

The parties are given the freedom to agree on the procedures to be followed by the arbitral tribunal in conducting its proceedings. In case the parties do not arrive at an agreement on the procedures to be followed by the arbitral tribunal, the arbitral tribunal may conduct the proceedings in the manner it considers appropriate, subject to the provisions of Part II of the Act of 1996. Conferment of such powers on the arbitral tribunal includes, amongst others, the power to determine the admissibility, relevance, materiality and weight of any evidence (The Arbitration and Conciliation Act 1996, s. 19(4)).

Once the parties have appointed the arbitral tribunal and agreed upon the procedures to be followed by the Tribunal or the Tribunal has determined the said procedure in case of failure of the parties to arrive at an amicable agreement on procedure, the parties are required to submit their statement of claims and defence with supporting evidence and material documents, to the arbitral tribunal (The Arbitration and Conciliation Act, 1996, s. 23). After consulting both parties, the arbitral tribunal decides whether the proceedings are to be conducted on the basis of documents and other materials adduced by the parties or whether the parties will lead their evidence by examining their witnesses (The Arbitration and Conciliation Act, 1996, s. 24). The parties are required to communicate and exchange with each other the statements, documents and other information supplied to the arbitral tribunal, which would be relied upon by the arbitral tribunal while making its decision (The Arbitration and Conciliation Act, 1996, s. 24(3)). The arbitral tribunal, based on the evidence produced and arguments placed by both parties, passes the award. If the party against whom the award has been passed is not satisfied with such an award, the party may challenge the said award by moving an application before a competent court under Section 34 of the Act of 1996 (The Arbitration and Conciliation Act, 1996, s. 34), within the period prescribed under Section 34(3) of the Act of 1996, in order to get the award set aside on the grounds enlisted under Section 34(2). The provisions of Section 34(2) of the Act of 1996 leave very narrow scope for setting aside the award.

14.3 Applicable law in different jurisdictions in relation to discovery and production of documents before the arbitral tribunal

In this section, the general laws/rules followed in a few jurisdictions are taken into consideration for comparison with the corresponding provisions of the Act.

14.3.1 Singapore

Singapore has two separate Acts to govern Domestic and International Arbitration, namely the Singapore Arbitration Act, 2001 and the International Arbitration Act, 1994.

Section 28(2)(b) of the Singapore Arbitration Act, 2001 and Section 12(1)(b) of The International Arbitration Act, 1994 empower arbitral tribunals to make orders or directions to any party for discovery of documents and interrogatories.

Rule 27(f) of Arbitration Rules of the Singapore International Arbitration Centre, 2016 (SIAC Rules) empowers the tribunal to order any party to produce to the tribunal and to the other parties for inspection and to supply copies of any document in their possession or control that the tribunal considers relevant to the case and material to its outcome.

14.3.2 Malaysia

In Malaysia, the arbitration proceedings are governed under Arbitration Act, 2005. Section 19(1)(b) and Section 21(3)(f) of the said Act empower the arbitral tribunal to order the discovery and production of documents or materials within the possession and power of a party.

As per Article 27(3) of Kuala Lumpur Regional Centre for Arbitration UNCITRAL Rules (as revised in 2010), the arbitral tribunal may require the parties to produce documents, exhibits or other evidences within such a period of time as the arbitral tribunal shall determine.

14.3.3 The United Kingdom

In the United Kingdom, the governing arbitration legislation is Arbitration Act, 1996. Section 34(2)(d) of the said Act confers on the tribunal the power to decide whether any, and if so, which, documents or classes of documents should be disclosed between and produced by the parties and at what stage.

Article 22.1(v) of London Court of International Arbitration (LCIA) Rules 2014 grants the arbitral tribunal power to order any party to produce to the arbitral tribunal and to other parties documents or copies of documents in their possession, custody or power, which the arbitral tribunal decides to be relevant.

14.3.4 Hong Kong

In Hong Kong, a new Arbitration Ordinance (Arbitration Ordinance, 2011) came into effect in 2011, reforming the arbitration law of Hong Kong, based on the Model Law. Section 56(1)(b) of the said Act (Arbitration Ordinance, 2011) entrusts power to the arbitral tribunal to make an order directing the discovery of documents or the delivery of interrogatories.

Rule 6.7 of Hong Kong International Arbitration Centre Domestic Arbitration Rules, 2014 permits the tribunal, at any stage of the proceedings, to order the parties to produce any additional document that the tribunal may specify. Similarly, in Article 22.3 of Hong Kong International Arbitration Centre Administered Arbitration Rules, 2013, the arbitral tribunal is vested with the power to require a party to produce documents, exhibits or other evidence that the arbitral tribunal determines to be relevant to the case and material to its outcome at any time during the arbitration.

From the perusal of the relevant provisions of the applicable laws of the various jurisdictions, it is evident that in all jurisdictions, while making the law or rules, precaution has been taken to empower the arbitral tribunal to issue directions to the parties for discovery and production of the relevant documents.

14.3.5 India

Prior to the enactment of the Act of 1996, arbitration in India was governed by the Act of 1940. Para 6 of the first schedule of the Act 1940 (The Arbitration Act 1940, Para 6) states:

> The parties to the reference and all persons claiming under them shall subject to the provisions of any law for the time being in force, submit to be examined by the arbitrators or umpire on oath or affirmation in relation to the matters in difference and shall, subject as aforesaid, produce before the arbitrators or umpire all

> books, deeds, papers, accounts, writings and documents within their possession or power respectively, which may be required or called for, and do all other things which, during the proceedings on the reference, the arbitrators or umpire may require.

This provision gave specific powers to arbitrators to issue directions to the parties to the reference and all persons claiming under them to produce before the arbitrators or umpire all books, deeds, papers, accounts, writings and documents within their possession or power, respectively, that may be required or called for and do all other things that, during the proceedings on the reference, the arbitrators or umpire may require.

Such a provision is lacking in the present Act of 1996. There is no specific provision in the Act of 1996 that empowers the arbitral tribunal to issue the directions to the parties to the reference and all persons claiming under them to produce the documents in their possession as may be deemed relevant by the arbitral tribunal.

Since the Act of 1996 is enacted taking inspiration from the Model law, Section 27 is introduced in the Act of 1996 (The Arbitration and Conciliation Act, 1996, s. 27) for court assistance in taking evidence. The said section is borrowed from Article 27 of the Model Law (UNICITRAL Model Law on International Commercial Arbitration 1985, Article 27), which provides that the arbitral tribunal or a party with approval of the arbitral tribunal may seek the assistance of a competent court of their state in taking evidence.

Section 27 of the Act of 1996 is an enabling provision, which allows the arbitral tribunal or a party with the approval of the arbitral tribunal to apply to the court for assistance in taking evidence.

Section 27(2) of the Act of 1996 specifies the particulars, which are to be mentioned in an application to be moved before the court. The necessary particulars, which are required to be submitted to the court, include the general nature of the claim and the relief sought, the description of the evidence to be obtained, in particular the name and address of any person to be heard as witness or expert witness, and the description of any document to be produced or property to be inspected.

The court, on receipt of the application, may, within its competence and according to its rules on taking evidence, execute the request by ordering that the evidence be produced directly to the arbitral tribunal.

In case of non-compliance of the directions given by the court, the defaulting party shall be subject to disadvantages, penalties and punishment by order of the court on the recommendation of the arbitral tribunal as the defaulting party would incur for the like offences in the suits tried before the court.

Since there is no provision like Para 6 of the first Schedule of the Act of 1940, in the Act of 1996, the general interpretation has been that in order to secure the discovery and production of documents or evidence in power and possession of the other party, the requesting party should approach only the Court under Section 27 of the Act of 1996. Needless to say, this process may increase the expenses of the proceedings, as well as delay the settlement of the dispute, which is contrary to the spirit of Alternative Dispute Resolution.

Does this mean that an arbitral tribunal, which is not bound by the Code of Civil Procedure, 1908, or The Indian Evidence Act, 1872, is powerless to issue directions for discovery and production of the documents to the parties to the proceedings? The answer to the foregoing question is, 'No'.

Analysis of Section 27(1) of the Act of 1996 shows that an application for court assistance in taking evidence can be moved either by the arbitral tribunal or by a party with the approval of the arbitral tribunal. It presupposes that, in both cases, the arbitral tribunal has applied its mind and directed the party in possession of documents for discovery and production of documents referred to in Section 27(2)(c)(ii) of the Act of 1996. On failure of the party to comply with such directions, the court is approached. The tribunal thus gets the power from the provisions of Section 27(1) of the Act of 1996 for issuing directions for discovery and production of documents.

Further analysis of Section 19 of the Act of 1996 shows that the arbitral tribunal is given wide powers. It is not bound by any technicalities. Like courts, it is not bound by the provisions of the Code of Civil Procedure, 1908, and the Indian Evidence Act, 1872. The arbitral tribunal is empowered to conduct the proceedings in the manner 'it considers appropriate', which implies that the arbitral tribunal is given extensive powers to make its own rules or procedures and issue necessary directions, as and when required to meet the ends of justice, including the rules for discovery and production of documents by the parties in appropriate cases. Thus, the arbitral tribunal derives the power to issue directions for discovery and production of documents under both the above provisions.

The party to whom the directions are issued has two alternatives: either to comply with the directions and to produce the documents or refuse to follow the said directions. In case the directed party refuses to produce the documents required by the arbitral tribunal, the tribunal may take an adverse inference against the party and proceed with the matter.

In case the requesting party is not satisfied with the adverse inference taken by the arbitral tribunal and insists for production of documents by the requested party, the arbitral tribunal may apply on its own or permit the requesting party to apply for court's assistance for compliance of its directions under Section 27 of the Act of 1996.

14.4 Judicial pronouncements by Indian courts on powers of the arbitral tribunal on discovery and production of documents in arbitration in India

In the absence of a specific provision in the Act of 1996 empowering the arbitral tribunal to issue directions for discovery and production of documents, time and again, questions have been raised that such powers are not vested with the arbitral tribunal and are only available with the courts under Section 27 of the Act of 1996.

These issues also came for adjudication before the Supreme Court of India and the various High Courts. The Courts had an opportunity to examine the provisions of the Act of 1996 to resolve the issues apropos of the powers of the arbitral tribunal to issue directions to the parties for discovery and production of the documents. The courts in India, to maintain the highest standards of equity, fair play and justice and to make the arbitration proceedings more effective and meaningful, have held that the arbitral tribunal has the power to issue directions for discovery and production of documents to the parties to the proceedings. The reasoning may differ from one court to another, but the ratio decidendi of the judgements is that the arbitral tribunal has such powers within the framework of the Act of 1996.

The role of the judiciary expands to the interpretation of the laws enacted by the legislature and passed by the parliament. This role of the judiciary to interpret laws includes inter alia the power to explain and clarify any law and the intent of the legislature behind enacting such law in question. It also includes creatively filling the void in the legislation. Judicial treatment not only adds light and luminosity to the law but also polishes it like a diamond.

The Delhi High Court had an opportunity to examine the role of the arbitral tribunal while adjudicating an application moved under Section 27 of the Act of 1996 in Hindustan Petroleum Corporation v. Ashok Garg, 2006 and held:

> Section 27 envisages an application to be made to the court for seeking assistance to take evidence. Such an application can be made either by the arbitral tribunal or a party with the approval of the arbitral tribunal. Thus, in case of an application by a party, the legislature itself envisaged an approval of the arbitral tribunal. This in turn puts an obligation on the arbitral tribunal to apply its mind and not to mechanically direct an application to be filed before the court.

The Delhi High Court, in another landmark judgement, Thyssen Krupp Werkstoffee GMBH v Steel Authority of India, 2010, held:

> Discovery is extremely important but it should be used by a contesting party to either contest its case or demolish the case of the opposite party. In majority of situations early production of relevant documents would not only cut cost and time but would also ensure a fair outcome. Under the Arbitration Act 1940, the arbitrator had the power to direct discovery by virtue of Para 6 of the first schedule which provided that a party shall produce before the arbitrators or umpire all books, deeds, papers, accounts, writings, documents within their possession or power. There is nothing in the Act which suggests any limitation or any curtailment of this power. Though there is no specific provision in the Act, 1996 which specifically confers power on the Arbitrator to direct discovery, the Arbitrator has absolute power and flexibility by virtue of Section 19 of Act, 1996 to conduct the proceedings in the manner it considers appropriate without being bound by the rules of the Indian Evidence Act, 1872 and Code of Civil Procedure, 1908. Section 27 of Act, 1996 in my view, only deals with third party discovery and not with regard to discovery of parties before the arbitral tribunal. This inherent power of discovery, in my view, is found in Section 19(3) of Act, 1996.

The Supreme Court of India in Delta Distilleries Limited v United Spirits limited, 2014 held:

> It cannot be ignored that the tribunal is required to make an award on the merits of the claim placed before it. For that purpose, if any evidence becomes necessary the tribunal ought to have the power to get the evidence.

The Supreme Court further interpreted that the term *any person* in Section 27(2)(c) of the Act is wide enough to cover not merely the witnesses but also the parties to the proceeding.

The preceding view of the Apex Court was further dwelled upon by the Delhi High Court in Silor Associates v Bharat Heavy Electrical Limited, 2014. A Single Judge of Delhi High Court held:

> There is nothing in the Act to contra indicate the existence of jurisdiction/power in the tribunal to require the parties to produce documents, exhibits or other evidence, as the arbitral tribunal may determine. The aforesaid provision has the effect of vesting the tribunal with much greater autonomy in the matter of regulating its procedure for conduct of the arbitration proceedings, than that exercised by a civil court-which is bound by the rigour of the Code of Civil Procedure (CPC) and the Indian Evidence Act. The scheme contained in Section 19 of the Act is not to denude the arbitral tribunal of its power to regulate its procedure for effective and expeditious conduct

of the arbitration proceedings in a transparent and fair manner. On the contrary, the legislative intent appears to be vest the arbitral tribunal with autonomy and flexibility in the matter of conduct of its proceedings so as to expedite the proceedings and cut the procedural wrangles witnessed in courts-which are governed by the CPC and the Evidence Act.

Consequently, it is evident that the discovery, inspection and production of documents by a party, at the request of the opposite party, is a matter of procedure. It is for this reason that the same has been dealt with in Order XI Rules 12 to 15 and 21, and Order 16 of the CPC. Thus, the arbitral tribunal is not powerless to direct production of a document-considered to be relevant evidence by it, by one or the other party to the proceedings. This power is statutorily conferred upon the tribunal under Section 19 of the Act. Exercise of this statutory power by the arbitral tribunal does not tantamount to assumption of 'inherent power' by the arbitral tribunal-which power does not vest in an arbitral tribunal.

Therefore, it is evident that the arbitral tribunal is empowered on its own, without taking resort to Section 27 of the Act, to direct, a party to produce documents, and upon the failure to comply with the tribunals direction to produce documents, the aggrieved party-who is aggrieved by the non production of documents, may either require the arbitral tribunal to draw an adverse inference against the defaulting party, or may chose to require the arbitral tribunal to enforce the direction to produce the relevant document with the assistance of the court by resort to Section 27 of the Act.

It may be that the aggrieved party (who is aggrieved by the non production of the documents by the opposite party) may be satisfied by the arbitral tribunal drawing an adverse inference against the defaulting party, and may not wish to pursue the aspect of production of documents by the opposite/defaulting party by resort to Section 27 of the Act. It is not necessary for the arbitral tribunal in every such case to seek assistance of the court, and it would depend on the facts and circumstances of each case, whether such assistance should be sought. In any event, there would be no cause to seek assistance of the court by resort to Section 27 of the Act, without first issuing a direction to the concerned party to produce the document, and only upon the failure to comply with such a direction, the arbitral tribunal would be justified in seeking the assistance of the court under Section 27 of the Act-if so desired by the aggrieved/non defaulting party.

I find merit in the submission advanced by the petitioner before the arbitral tribunal that if the arbitral tribunal is held not to have jurisdiction to evolve its procedure requiring production of documents (when there is no agreed procedure laid down by the parties themselves), the same would delay the conclusion of the arbitration proceedings as, in every case, the arbitral tribunal would necessarily have to move for the courts assistance under Section 27 of the Act to obtain a direction for production of the relevant documents by one of the parties, even though the party from whom documents are required to be produced may be willing to comply with such a direction if it were to be so directed by the arbitral tribunal. It would also mean that even in a case where a party requiring production of documents were to be satisfied with the drawing of adverse inference against the defaulting party, the resort to Section 27 of the Act would necessarily have to be undertaken-leading to unnecessary waste of time and resources of the parties and delay in the arbitral process.

In an appeal against the aforesaid order of the Ld. Single Judge, the Division Bench of Delhi High Court in Bharat Heavy Electrical Limited v Silor Associates S.A., 2014, while concurring with the view taken by the Ld. Single Judge, held:

> Thus, if an application is filed before a tribunal requiring a party before the tribunal to produce a document in its power and possession, the tribunal would be competent to deal with the same without any reference being made to a court.

14.5 Conclusion

The Supreme Court of India in FCI v Joginderpal Mohinderpal, 1989 held:

> We should make the law of arbitration simple, less technical and more responsible to the actual realities of the situation, but must be responsive to the canons of justice and fair play and make the arbitrator adhere to such process and norms which will create confidence, not only by doing justice between the parties, but by creating a sense that justice appears to have been done.

The successive interpretations of the relevant provisions of the Act of 1996 by the Supreme Court of India and various High Courts imply that the arbitral tribunal has the power to direct the parties for discovery and production of the documents, despite there being no specific provision under the Act of 1996. It is in the direction to achieve the above goal and to create confidence among the international community that Indian laws relating to arbitration are at par with the corresponding international arbitration laws and practice.

It is recommended that Indian legislators should consider making specific provisions under the Act of 1996, empowering the arbitral tribunal to issue directions for discovery and production of the documents to the parties, instead of leaving this issue open for judicial interpretation.

References

Arbitration Act, 2005: Malaysia: The Commissioner of Law Revision, Malaysia.

Arbitration Ordinance, Chapter 609 Gazette Number E.R.2 of 2014, 1/06/2011.

Bharat Heavy Electrical Limited V Silor Associates S.A., 2014 (3) ARBLR 522 (Delhi).

Delta Distilleries V United Spirits Ltd. and Anr. AIR 2014 SC 113.

Arbitration Act, 1996, Part 1 at http://www.legislation.gov.uk/ukpga/1996/23/section/34.

FCI V Joginderpal Mohinderpal, (1989) 2 SCC 347.

Hindustan Petroleum Corporation V. Ashok Garg, AIR 2006 Delhi 365.

Hong Kong International Arbitration Centre Administered Arbitration Rules 2013. (Section IV): Hong Kong: Hong Kong International Arbitration Centre.

Hong Kong International Arbitration Centre Domestic Arbitration Rules 2014 (Section III): Hong Kong: Hong Kong International Arbitration Centre.

ITI Ltd. v Siemens Public Communication Network Ltd. AIR 2002 SC 2308.

Kuala Lumpur Regional Center Arbitration UNCITRAL Rules (As Revised In 2010), (S.3): Kuala Lumpur: Kuala Lumpur Regional Centre For Arbitration.

London Court of International Arbitration Rules, 2014: London: The London Court of International Arbitration.

Redfern, Alan et al., *Law and Practice of International Commercial Arbitration* (S. Asian Edition, 2006, London Sweet & Maxwell, 4th Ed. 2004).
Silor Associates V Bharat Heavy Electrical Limited, 213 (2014) DLT 312.
Singapore Arbitration Act, 2001, (P.VII). Singapore.
Singapore International Arbitration Rules, 2016 (R.27): Singapore: Singapore International Arbitration Centre.
The Arbitration Act, 1940 (Repealed), (First Schedule, Para 6). New Delhi: Universal Law Publishing Co. Pvt. Ltd.
The Arbitration and Conciliation Act, 1996. New Delhi: Universal Law Publishing Co. Pvt Ltd.
Thyssen Krupp Werkstoffee GMBH V. Steel Authority of India, 168 (2010) DLT 250.

List of abbreviations

Act of 1940 – Arbitration Act, 1940.
Act of 1996 – Arbitration and Conciliation Act, 1996.
CPC – Code of Civil Procedure.
ICA – Indian Council of Arbitration.
ICC YAF – International Council of Arbitration Young Arbitrators Forum.
KLRCA – Kuala Lumpur Regional Centre for Arbitration.
LCIA – London Court of International Arbitration.
Model Law – United Nations Commission on International Trade Law Model Law on International Commercial Arbitration, 1985.
NIXI – National Internet Exchange of India.
SIAC Rules – Arbitration Rules of the Singapore International Arbitration Centre, 2016.
UNCITRAL – United Nations Commission on International Trade Law.

Part IV

Towards an Asian arbitration model

15 Legalisation of international arbitration in Asia

Paving the way for cultural homogenisation?

Shahrizal M. Zin

15.1 Introduction

How does one think about the past and about its grip on the present? Some have said that we can either accept the past and its teaching or we can think about it critically. Tradition would therefore exist, but everyone would have the option of either being an adherent to it or of being an external critic, free to move on to other concerns. For centuries of Western thought, tradition has been associated with static forms of social order.[1] A traditional society was one that did not change and that was largely impervious to valid reason for change.[2] Legal culture, in its most general sense, is one way of describing relatively stable patterns of legally oriented social behaviour and attitudes.[3]

The identifying elements of legal culture range from facts about institutions, such as the number and role of lawyers or the ways judges are appointed and controlled, to various forms of behaviour, such as litigation or prison rates, and, at the other extreme, more nebulous aspects of ideas, values, aspirations and mentalities.[4] It is also worth noting that like culture itself, legal culture is about who we are, not just what we do.[5] Clifford Geertz defines culture as the fabric of meaning in terms of which human beings interpret their experience and guide their action.[6] In light of this definition, law is also part of culture, for, to be meaningful to the people it regulates, the law must partake of the resources within the culture. Enquiries into legal culture attempt to understand puzzling features of the role and rule of law within given societies. The concept of legal culture, if deployed well, can help reveal the broader historical and societal context that shapes the interpretation and development of law. Why do East Asian communities prefer conciliation or mediation to resolve dispute instead of litigation? This chapter argues that the increasing legalisation of arbitration rules seems to be accompanied by a homogenisation of legal culture in Asia. This chapter examines to what extent legalisation represents the attempted imposition of a particular legal culture on other societies.

1 H. Patrick Glenn, *Legal Tradition of the World* (Oxford University Press, Oxford, 4th ed, 2010) 23.

2 Ibid.

3 David Nelken, 'Using the Legal Concept of Legal Culture,' (2004) *Australian Legal Journal of Philosophy* 29: 2. Also See Jeremy Webber, 'Culture, Legal Culture, and Legal Reasoning: A Comment on Nelken,' (2004) *Australian Legal Journal of Philosophy* 29: 27.

4 Ibid.

5 Many aspects of law are the result of colonialism, immigration and conquest. Non-European countries frequently have mixed or pluralistic legal systems, which testify to waves of colonial invasions or imitations of other systems.

6 Clifford Geertz, *The Interpretation of Cultures* (Basic Books, New York, 1977) 145.

15.2 Legalisation of arbitration in Asia: another triumph for international law?

Writers have defined the concept of legalisation as 'a particular set of characteristics that institutions may, or may not, possess'.[7] These characteristics have been defined in terms of obligation (whether a state or actor is legally bound by a rule), precision (the extent to which the rule is unambiguously defined) and delegation (the ability of third parties to 'implement, interpret and apply the rules to resolve disputes and possibly to make further rules').[8] Although these elements may exist in a continuum, a high degree of legalisation would assume a stronger stand on all three elements in an international arrangement.[9] Nevertheless, one negative feature of legalisation is that it seeks to provide harmonisation of laws without regard for the social, cultural or environmental concerns of domestic policies.

A review of the literature shows that scholars are divided in identifying legalisation trends. Some have observed a preference towards the legalisation approach, whilst others have seen the drift away from legalisation in favour of informality. For example, in the context of international economic law, Davidson argues that there is a tendency towards a greater reliance on international law, especially with the establishment of the World Trade Organisation (WTO) and its dispute settlement mechanism, which is a hybrid of conciliation and arbitration.[10] Other writers suggest that 'in many issue-areas, the world is witnessing a move to law', although the extent of legalisation in different fields is variable.[11] Not all commentators would agree that there has been a trend towards legalisation in all areas of international cooperation. But, for the most part, the drift away from establishing formal institutions would appear to be compatible with a desire to form fewer binding obligations under international law, if only due to a fact that informal organisations are not created by an international convention between states. In listing the advantages of this move to informality in international cooperation, Lipson suggests that 'informal bargains are more flexible than treaties'. He describes them as 'willow, not oaks'.[12] Ease of amendment, the lack of a detailed ratification process and the ability to sign such agreement in a less public setting are all cited as benefits of informality.[13] Law is seen as impediment. It is not able to reflect political agreement and cannot accommodate political change in a flexible manner.[14] Whether or not these arguments are an accurate reflection of the advantages of informality and the move away from international organisations in the international community, they appear to have much in common with the approach to international law that is often attributed to Asian nations. Kahler states that 'if Europe and North America provide an implicit benchmark for high legalization, the Asia-Pacific region offers an important example of low legalization and possibly an explicit aversion to legalization'.[15]

7 Kenneth W. Abbott, Robert O. Keohane, Andrew Moravcsik, Anne-Marie Slaughter and Duncan Snidal, 'The Concept of Legalization' (2000) *International Organization* 54: 401, 406.

8 Ibid.

9 Ibid, 404.

10 Paul J. Davidson, 'The ASEAN Way and the Role of Law in ASEAN Economic Cooperation' (2004) *Singapore Yearbook of International Law* 8: 165, 166.

11 Judith Goldstein, Miles Kahler, Robert O. Keohane and Ann-Marie Slaughter, 'Introduction: Legalization and World Politics' (2000) *International Organization* 54: 385.

12 Charles Lipson, 'Why Are Some International Agreements Informal?' (1991) *International Organization* 495, 500.

13 Ibid, 500–501.

14 Jan Klabbers, 'Institutional Ambivalence by Design: Soft Organization in International Law' (2001) *Nordic Journal of International Law* 70: 403, 411.

15 Miles Kahler, 'Legalization as Strategy: The Asian-Pacific Case' (2000) *International Organization* 54: 549.

As evidence from this pattern, states in this region are said to prefer consultation between parties and informal decision-making, rather than formal adjudication, as a method of dispute resolution. Multilateral and bilateral treaties between states in Asia rarely incorporate clauses for a formal dispute resolution body involving adjudication, according to international law. For example, the Treaty for Amity and Cooperation in Southeast Asia (TAC) emphasises the need to settle dispute through friendly negotiations or, if need be, by good offices, mediation, inquiry or conciliation, rather than by a court of tribunal. However, recent developments demonstrate a trend to the contrary. There are a number of cases involving Asian nations that have been referred to a formal adjudication of disputes, particularly based on territorial sovereignty claims through the International Court of Justice (ICJ).[16] This may indicate a reluctance to utilise the ICJ, which may be seen as past phenomenon.

Much recent discussion of governance beyond the level of nation-state has drawn attention to 'legalisation' or the tendency to bring more and more aspects of international life into the ambit of law-like processes. The legalisation discussion has looked at the growing importance of rules governing the behaviour of many actors, from states to private entities, in more and more areas of international life. Attention has been given to the rules, processes to interpret and apply the rules and questions of compliance. Legalisation as a concept in the literature on international relations was developed by the authors to explain 'the use and consequences of law in international politics'.[17] According to the authors, legalisation refers to characteristics that institutions may possess. The elements of their concept of legalisation are obligation, precision and delegation.[18] Obligation refers to international actors being legally bound by legal rules and procedures, whether international or domestic. Such legal rules and procedures impose obligations that are distinct from obligations resulting from coercion, comity and morality.[19] Precision means that these rules and procedures define rights and obligations in unambiguous ways.[20] That is, the scope of reasonably interpreting them is narrow. In Franck's parlance, this means that such rules are determinate.[21] Finally, delegation relates to the grant of authority to third parties, such as courts, arbitrators and administrative bodies to interpret and apply rules during dispute settlement and also to make further rules. Dispute resolution mechanisms are highly legalised when parties agree, on the basis of clear and generally applicable rules to be bound by the decisions of these third parties.

15.3 How has globalization influenced legalisation?

Globalisation is fundamentally about mobility across frontiers – of goods and commodities, capital and investment, information and communication, services and people. Although not all scholars agree on the terminology, there is relatively broad consensus that the periods of recent globalisation, including measures to open barriers and facilitate increased contact

16 Tommy Koh, 'The Asian Way to Settle Disputes.' *Straits Times*, 10 June 2015 http://www.straitstimes.com/news/opinion/invitation/story/the-asian-way-settle-disputes20150610#sthash.uenR6VBf.dpuf. The author discusses various cases in Asia where the states submitted sovereignty claims through the international legal process. The cases involved are the Preah Vihear (Cambodia v Thailand), Sipadan and Litigan (Indonesia v Malaysia), Pedra Branca/Pulau Batu Puteh (Malaysia v Singapore) and Myanmar v Bangladesh.

17 Judith Goldstein et al., above n 11, 386.

18 Kenneth W. Abbott et al., above n 7, 403.

19 Ibid, 408.

20 Ibid, 403.

21 Thomas Franck, *The Power of Legitimacy Among Nations* (Oxford University Press, USA, 1990) quoted by Abbott et al., above n 7, 27.

between nation-states, derived from the three waves of democratisation classified by Samuel Huntington in his renowned thesis (*The Third Wave*).[22] The lengthy First Wave took place in the century prior to the 1920s and effectively ended with the Great Depression; the Second Wave took place after the Second World War and ended in the early 1960s and the Third Wave began in the 1970s–1980s. The beginning of the Third Wave, in the context of the Cold War and international tensions caused by the unwinding of colonisation, was slow to take root.[23] In the face of rising commodity prices and oil shocks, however, many countries deregulated their economies, as the world struggled to stave off a global recession. By the time of the disintegration of the Soviet Union in 1991, a new dawn of global political and economic symbiosis had been born. This was intensified by advances in modern technology, which greatly increased the opportunities for international contact through global trade and investment.

Each of these waves of globalisation has been accompanied by changes in the international legal landscape.[24] The First Wave created the League of Nations; the Permanent Court of Arbitration and many treaties of friendship, commerce and navigation. The Second Wave created the United Nations, the ICJ, the General Agreement on Tariff and Trade (GATT) and the Bretton Woods institutions. The Third Wave was triggered, in part, by the collapse of the gold standard in 1971 and the subsequent removal of foreign exchange control by the early 1980s, leading to the increased movement of capital. The modern proliferation of bilateral investment treaties (BITs) accordingly began in earnest in the 1970s and increased exponentially in the 1990s. The most profound legal change wrought by the Third Wave was the metamorphosis of the 1994 GATT in the WTO in the 1993 Uruguay Round of negotiations.[25]

These changes created the need for new forms of international regulation. Classical public international law, which heavily depended on the law of custom and *opinio juris*, was not equipped to provide necessary certainty, predictability and specificity. The rise of nonstate actors – in particular, international governmental organisations (IGOs) and multinational corporations (MNCs) – has created institutional structures that rapidly mould treaty regimes. This is evident in the international institutions and treaties that govern specific issue areas. Globalisation has resulted in some issue areas being relatively lightly regulated and others being much more heavily regulated. In addition, treaty regimes have played the most fundamental role in responding to the challenges of globalisation. This is exemplified in the different issue areas comprising international economic law, which have arisen as a response to gradual integration of national economies into one borderless global economy. This phenomenon is hardly surprising at all, given the fact that the main advantage of treaty regimes is their binding and enforceable character for dispute resolution. This offers a form of certainty and leverage that classic international law could not provide.[26] These treaty

22 S. P. Huntington, *The Third Wave. Democratization in the Late Twentieth Century* (University of Oklahoma Press, Norman, OH, 1991).

23 R. Robertson, 'Globalisation Is Not Made in the West', *Yale Global Online*, 13 April 2005.

24 Daniel Kalderimis, 'Is Transnational Law Eclipsing International Law?' in Pieter H.E. Bekker et al., *Making Transnational Law Work in the Global Economy, Essay in Honours of Detlev Vagts* (Cambridge University Press, 2010) 96.

25 Ibid.

26 Cassese indicated this position that most members of the international community tend to prefer treaties to custom, as the former are more certain and result from the willing participation of contracting parties. He also argued that custom is not the most suitable instrument for achieving change in the international legal system. Therefore, a number of states have turned to treaty-making for the codification or progressive development

regimes have not arisen by accident. They have arisen because of the increase in economic integration and liberalisation of trade and foreign direct investment due to globalisation, which requires clear and enforceable rules. Merchants and international actors wanted precisely what classical international law could not offer, which was a resemblance of domestic dispute resolution characters, producing binding and enforceable decisions. Thus, a new dawn of international legal landscape has taken shape.

Economic globalisation leads to cultural globalisation by discouraging diversity. Globalisation of trade, for example, challenges domestic cultural values. Culture is not immune from the coercion of global forces and a global culture is merging alongside economic globalisation. Although economic globalisation has its limits, globalisation inevitably leads to some degree of cultural homogenisation. States generally pursue a variety of goals in addition to economic development, such as cultural autonomy. A solid rule-based international trade mechanism diminishes the ability of nations to structure their own domestic laws, which often reflect the cultural values of that nation. Imposing a superseding international law, therefore, undermines the social values reflected in domestic laws. Economic globalisation, to some extent, rests on the foundation of cultural imperialism.

15.4 Harmonising laws and their justification in the context of international commercial arbitration

The concept of harmonisation of laws refers to the unification of laws, particularly in conjunction with inter-jurisdictional private transactions. It has been applied in many diverse areas of law within different states, including monetary and fiscal policy, contract law, banking law, securities regulation, labour law, environmental law and, of course, international trade and commercial law.[27] Harmonisation and uniformity have played a particularly important role in efforts to 'internationalise' arbitration law. The two terms are in many ways complementary, although harmonisation generally involves a common understanding of the meaning of certain terms or the substance of certain concepts. By contrast, uniformity is generally a part of a larger process, requiring agreement on rules.[28]

---

of international law. For a general discussion of treaties as sources of international law see Antonio Cassese, *International Law* (Oxford University Press, 2nd ed, 2005).

27 Rene David, 'The International Unification of Private Law,' (1971) *International Encyclopaedia of Comparative Law* 2(1): 7–17.

28 The unification movement originally arose within comparative law and was applied with the objective of eliminating as much of the diversity of laws as reasonably possible in international or inter-jurisdictional transactions. Unification of laws had as its original goal the standardization of legislation by means of uniform model codes or statutes that would be adopted and consistently applied by sovereign states. While the unification movement was originally characterised by an ideal of uniform legislation, however, it has in recent times moved away from uniformity and become associated with the less ambitious and yet more indeterminate notion of harmonisation. The move away from uniformity towards a flexible and indeterminate notion of harmonisation is due to the realisation that true uniformity of laws among sovereign jurisdictions is highly unlikely to materialise. See Martin Boodman, 'The Myth of Harmonization of Laws,' *American Journal of Comparative Law* 39: 699, 704. For a critique of unification and harmonisation in private international law, see Malcolm Evans, 'Uniform law: A Bridge Too Far?' (1995) *Tulane Journal of International and Comparative Law* 3: 145, 146–153 (suggesting three main criticisms of unification efforts: (1) uniformity compromises certainty and effectiveness, (2) inconsistent interpretation of uniform law when applied to national law and (3) inability of national legislation to keep pace with the international unification process).

David Leebron has loosely defined harmonisation of laws as 'making the regulatory requirement or governmental policies of different jurisdictions identical, or at least similar'.[29] Rene David has defined harmonisation as involving 'an understanding about the significance of certain concepts, on certain modes of rules formulation, and on the recognition of authoritative sources'.[30] Still others refer to the process of harmonisation as one under which 'the effects of a type of transaction in one legal system are brought as close as possible to the effects of similar transactions under the laws of other countries'.[31] There is no clear consensus on the definition of harmonisation. Nevertheless, it has various definitions, depending upon the context in which it is used.

Within the international arbitration context, the main justifications for the harmonisation of national arbitration laws and practices generally include the following: (a) providing a jurisdictional interface to enable parties from different systems to interact or communicate; (b) fairness in international transactions and international trade competition; (c) assurance of trade transparency (ensuring that jurisdictions adopt policies that are consistent with trade liberalisation).[32] The most common economic justification given for the need to harmonise international commercial arbitration is the need to provide a jurisdictional interface for parties from different jurisdictions engaged in international commercial transactions, so as to avoid uncertainty and increased transaction costs in international transactions. The aim is to limit the differences between national arbitration laws and therefore reduce the uncertainties associated with the multiplicity of arbitral regimes.[33] The notion of harmonisation is considered desirable because it will reduce the costs of transacting inter-jurisdictional business, which are increased by diversity of legal rules.[34] An equally prevalent argument in support of harmonising laws is fairness in trade competition. In this sense, Alan Redfern and Martin Hunter, in the context of international commercial arbitration, refer to it with the notion of a 'level playing field'.[35]

15.5 Growing harmonisation of national arbitration law

With the continuing expansion of international trade and investment, the number of arbitration cases in general is also on the rise.[36] Domestic arbitration does not exist in isolation but is subject to and influenced by its domestic political, economic and legal climate,

29 David Leebron, 'Seoul Conference on International Trade Law: Integration, Harmonization and Globalization,' (1996) *Colombia Journal of Asian Law* 10(2): 305, 209.

30 David, above n 27.

31 John Goldring, 'Unification and Harmonization of the Rules of Law,' (1978) *Federal Law Review* 9: 284.

32 For a general discussion of harmonisation justification see Jagdish Bhagwati, *The Demands to Reduce Domestic Diversity among Trading Nations,* in Fair Trade and Harmonization: Prerequisite For Free Trade 41 (Jagdish N., Bhagwati & Robert E. Hudec eds., 1996).

33 Katherine Lynch, *The Forces of Economic Globalisation: Challenges to the Regime of International Commercial Arbitration*, (Kluwer Law International, The Hague, London, New York, 2003) 201.

34 Ibid.

35 Alan Redfern and Martin Hunter, *Law and Practice of International Commercial Arbitration* (Oxford University Press, Oxford, 3rd ed, 1999).

36 International arbitration mainly developed in Europe and has been quasi-codified by predominantly European-based or European-influenced international organizations and associations. The best examples of quasi-codification have come from UNCITRAL, ICCA, the ICC and the IBA. While these are all truly international bodies these days, they have European-influenced origins. These supranational sources of arbitration law have no binding effects, but provide guidance on arbitration practice. See Y. Dezalay and B.G. Garth, *Dealing in Virtue: International Commercial Arbitration and the Construction of a Transnational Legal Order*

as well as the practice of state courts and the usages of the national business community. For the different regions across the globe, cultural diversities will continue to play a role in relation to dispute settlement.[37] For the Asian nations, where previously conciliation and mediation were primarily utilised to settle disputes,[38] a study of the Asian Development Bank confirmed that, as markets expand beyond the national frontiers, informal dispute settlement mechanisms become less reliable and formal institutions and procedures with powers of decision and enforcement become more important. By the same token, there is growing harmonisation between national arbitration laws. National legislators will continue to be urged by their own constituencies, particularly their business communities, to adapt their respective legal frameworks to the demands of international business practice for efficient dispute settlement mechanisms. Therefore, this growing momentum of harmonisation will eventually lead international arbitration to become more internationalised. With the growing number of international arbitration cases and the increasing numbers of lawyers and arbitrators involved in international arbitration, it would make them less dependent on their specific national particularities. Instead, they would be more open and flexible to the specific needs of disputes in the international context.

International law has become more relevant in many ways for commercial arbitration. The most obvious relevance in this context is the role of public international law, which directly deals with international commercial arbitration. This is illustrated in the application of treaties as sources of international law, such as the United Nations Commission on International Trade Law (UNCITRAL) Model Law and the New York Convention, which have a bearing with international commercial arbitration.[39] Furthermore, in past and present practice, subjects of public international law have been highlighted in many cases of international commercial arbitration. In most of them, states, as well as their bodies, institutions or enterprises, are involved. In this context, many issues of international law arise.

(University of Chicago Press, Chicago, 1996) who explain that international arbitration was created in Europe by a group of European 'grand old men.'

37 In order to understand how the ASEAN legal framework is developing, it is necessary to appreciate how ASEAN has been operating based on the notion of 'the ASEAN Way'. For more than forty years, ASEAN has functioned without a formal constitution. By choice, it has conducted its affairs in a loose, informal way, with few legally binding arrangements and weak institutions. Indeed, the ASEAN Way, a term derived from the Malay concepts of ***musyawarah*** and ***mufakat,*** emphasizes decision-making by consensus. The approach involves conducting informal behind-the-scene discussions to reach a general consensus, which will form that starting point for a unanimous decision to be made at formal meetings. This can be contrasted with across-the-table negotiations, which result in deals enforceable in a court of law. In short, the ASEAN Way is distinct from the formal legalism present in most Western international legal institutions.

38 See Shin-Yi Peng, 'The WTO Legalistic Approach and East Asia: From Legal Cultural Perspective' (June 2000) *Asian-Pacific Law & Policy Journal* 13. Peng contends that the legal culture of East Asia differs considerably from the West, because the former focuses on the Confucian principle of harmony and kinship, while the latter stresses the use of formal legal rules to govern relationship. Peng then argued that in the age of globalisation, the prosperity of East Asia depends on the region's adherence to the Western legalised framework of the WTO, because Western legal culture has now transcended regional boundaries. Peng concludes that with East Asia's extended stake in the WTO, the region has to reshape its legal culture in conformity with the WTO standards and norms. This suggests that while the starting point of a non-legal basis to international relationship may be a cultural preference in East Asia, East Asian pragmatism usually overcomes such cultural preferences. This may also be true for Southeast Asia.

39 In addition, the role of soft law has been increasingly important. Hand in hand with tendencies to legalisation and proceduralisation, we see the increasing use of soft or non-binding norms. For example, there are various soft laws that apply directly in the context of international commercial arbitration. These include the IBA Evidence Rules, the IBA Conflict of Interest Guidelines and the UNCITRAL Notes on arbitral procedure.

While in most cases a national law will be the applicable law, in quite a number of ways, the principle of public international law will be applicable as part of substantive law in international arbitration. Certain contracts, such as concession contracts or economic development agreements, usually contain a choice of law clause expressly selecting public international law or at least general principles of international law, in accordance with Article 38 of the Statute of the ICJ.[40] Then, there is reference to public international law in the rules of certain institutions, such as Article 42 of the ICSID Convention.[41] Certain obligations of private law contracts are transformed into obligations under public international law either by umbrella clauses in BITs or as being covered by the property protection provisions in BITs or in customary international law. But, even without such express reference, certain parts of public international law may be considered relevant as part of the applicable substantive law, particularly if states are involved as parties.

15.6 Of *Li* and *Fa* – never the twain shall meet

If one wants to understand fully the present role of arbitration, one will have to start by looking at past developments that were the basis for the present situation. In this respect, Confucianism is the greatest traditional source of normativity in East Asia. It is not generally seen as a religion, while other East Asian religions, such as Buddhism, Taoism or Shintoism, have concerns that are largely other than legal.[42] At the same time, Confucian legal tradition differs from Western legal traditions, at least since the thirteenth century, in its reluctance to root normativity in formal structures and sanctions.[43] In other words, the essence of Confucianism seeks to persuade and not oblige. It is a tradition of great and friendly persuasion based on the centrality of a communal interest to create harmonious societal relations. It intends to develop social harmony and moral philosophy, which seeks to induce and persuade rather than command and punish. Confucius is the philosopher of the *Li*, which emphasises on denial of the lasting and effective normativity of formal law and formal sanctions. There is

40 Article 38 of the Statute of the ICJ reads as follows:

1 The Court, whose function is to decide, in accordance with international law, such disputes as are submitted to it, shall apply:

a international conventions, whether general or particular, establishing rules expressly recognised by the contesting states;
b international custom, as evidence of a general practice accepted as law;
c the general principles of law recognised by civilised nations;
d subject to the provisions of Article 59, judicial decisions and the teachings of the most highly qualified publicists of the various nations, as subsidiary means for the determination of rules of law.

2 This provision shall not prejudice the power of the court to decide a case *ex aequo et bono*, if the parties agree thereto.

41 Article 42 of the ICSID Convention reads as follows:

1 The Tribunal shall decide a dispute in accordance with such rules of law as may be agreed by the parties. In the absence of such agreement, the Tribunal shall apply the law of the Contracting State party to the dispute (including its rules on the conflict of laws) and such rules of international law as may be applicable.
2 The Tribunal may not bring in a Finding of non liquet on the ground of silence or obscurity of the law.
3 The provisions of paragraphs (1) and (2) shall not prejudice the power of the Tribunal to decide a dispute ex aequo et bono if the parties so agree.

42 Glenn, previously n 1, 320.
43 Ibid.

therefore little place for detailed Confucian regulation of an entire society. One has to understand its general teaching. The moment one understands, there is no need to concern oneself with the detail of formal law. As a result, there were many legal maxims that lend support to this non-adversarial or persuasion approach. Confucius himself wrote that 'what we need is for there be no lawsuit;' 'win a lawsuit and lose a friend', 'better to be vexed to death than bring a lawsuit', 'litigation ultimately ends in disaster'.[44] Confucians preferred conciliation. In other words, if legal complaint was possible, it had to be deterred by all possible means.

The notion of law in the form of *Li*, based on informal tradition of normativity, reflects persuasiveness that could effectively control all those areas of life that were not given over to the formal world of *Fa*-edicted sanction. The domain of *Li* is thus greater than the domain of law, at least as it is understood in the West. *Li* has been variously defined in its totality as 'moral law',[45] as 'customary, uncodified law, internalised by individuals',[46] as the 'moral and social rules of conduct',[47] as 'propriety',[48] and as the 'courtesy, customs and traditions we come to share ... following the human way'.[49] Confucianism thus lies somewhere between religious norm and positive law, necessarily defending itself in both directions.

There is, however, a long tradition of formal law and formal sanctions, which is known as *Fa*, though it has played a subordinate role to the *Li* or persuasion of the Confucian. Myth has it that *Fa* was invented by a barbarian people, the Miao, who blossomed around 2300 BC, even before Hammurabi.[50] At some point, the word *Fa*, originally 'model, pattern or standard', was taken over to mean an imposed standard, closely associated with criminal conduct and conduct repugnant to established order.[51] Law was perceived not as a means of regulation of private, economic activity, nor as a means of upholding religious values, but rather as an instrument of politics and public order.[52] It is known as rule by law, and much flows from this premise. *Fa* is thus concerned with criminal conduct and administrative regulation. It is primarily directed not to the people but to administrative officials. It was closely associated with militarism (enrich the state, reinforce the army) and, in practice, exhibited as a measure of doctrinal intolerance, including burning of the books of Confucianism.[53]

15.7 The Confucians' worldview on dispute resolution

The Confucian tradition is often noted as an important factor in understanding many East Asian societies, such as South Korea, China and Taiwan. A review in the literature suggests that there are four cultural traits that underpinned the Confucians' worldview on dispute resolution. These are the anti-lawsuit attitude, law as punishment, collectivism and family-centred

44 Confucius, *The Analects* (Columbia University Press, New York, 2007) Book XII, 13, 83.

45 D. Tan, 'Judicial Independence in the People's Republic of China: Myth or Reality?' (1994) *Australian Law Journal* 68: 660, 663.

46 J. Ching, 'Human Rights: A Valid Chinese Concept?' In W. De Bary and Tu Weiming eds., *Confucianism and Human Rights* (Columbia University Press, New York, 1998) 67, 74.

47 Derek Bodde and Clarence Morris, *Law in Imperial China* (Harvard University Press, Cambridge, MA, 1967) 19. Also see C. Hahn, 'Ritual and Constitutionalism: Disputing the Butler's Legitimacy in a Confucian Polity' (2009) *American Journal of Comparative Law* 57: 135, 141.

48 A. Chen, *Introduction to Legal System* (LexisNexis, Hong Kong, 2004) 10.

49 W. De Bary, *Trouble with Confucianism* (Harvard university Press, Cambridge, MA, 1991) 33.

50 Bodde and Morris, previously n 47, 13.

51 Ibid, 11.

52 Ibid.

53 Ibid, 27.

ethics.[54] This worldview on dispute resolution can be attributed to the Confucian legal culture that stressed social harmony and opposition to lawsuits. As discussed above, the notion of *Li* and *Fa* have deeply influenced the Confucian thinking on dispute resolution in relation to attitude towards 'disputes' and approach to 'settling' disputes. The East Asian's unique culture and social values account for the relationship between law and other social factors. These values, to a significant degree, determine how East Asian laws operate either domestically or internationally. In addition, the Confucian worldview on dispute resolution has provided a fertile ground for the development of mediation amongst the East Asian nations.

First, the anti-lawsuit attitude explains that in maintaining interpersonal harmony, Confucianists expressed disfavour towards resolving disputes through a lawsuit. Accordingly, Confucians perceived litigation as a last resort in resolving a dispute. This negative attitude towards lawsuit has taken shape for centuries, resulting in the preference for mediation as a means for dispute resolution. This is due to the advantages of mediation that allow disputants to seek a solution to their conflict in a harmonious way, while maintaining the relationship. Second, law has always been seen as punitive in character. Moreover, law is nothing more than the imposition of fines and penalties for official transgression.[55]

The ancient Confucianist believed than an ideal society would never require extensive legislation or litigation, because the law was for barbarians, not for a civilised society.[56] All types of litigation, including marriage and property distribution issues, were subject to criminal proceedings that include torture and corporal punishment.[57] As a result, being a party to a lawsuit was viewed as involvement in a crime, from both the judges' eyes and in societies' eyes. Therefore, settling a dispute out of court is always a better option to avoid humiliation in court litigation. Third, collectivism emphasised on selfless righteous deeds in favour of others than personal interest.[58] As a result, asserting one's personal rights was generally discouraged by society. This traditional expectation on selfless personal interest of the individual becomes a hindrance for the adoption of modern civil litigation.[59] This is in contrast with the Western legal culture that asserts the rights of the individual in a conflict. Collectivism, which stressed group and communal goals, has been the norm for traditional East Asian society. Fourth, the family plays an essential role and is regarded as the most basic unit in East Asian society.[60] The mutual obligation between the individual and the family serves as a powerful social control agent. The individual's responsibility to the family and the family's responsibilities to the individual are interdependent.[61] The notion that a parent's status was higher than that of a child was embedded in state law throughout Chinese legal history. Filial piety and brotherhood are the fundamental elements of benevolence, the highest moral standard of a gentleman. Over the centuries, these traditional guidelines have shaped people's expectations and behaviour, which profoundly influenced the Chinese way of dealing with family disputes.

54 Peng, previously n 38 and see Yun-Hsien Diana Lin, 'Civil Mediation in Taiwan: Legal Culture and the Process of Legal Modernization' (2011) *University of Pennsylvania East Asia Law Review* 6: 192.

55 William H. McNeill and Jean W. Sedlar, *Classical China* (Oxford University Press, Oxford, 1960) 76.

56 Bodde and Morris, previously n 47, 21–22.

57 Lin, previously n 54, 196.

58 See *Analects of Confucius*, ch IV, verse 23 (containing Confucius's statement that 'a gentlemen understands righteousness while a petty man understands profits'); ch. XVII, verse 23 ('a gentlemen who has courage but not righteousness will cause disorder; a petty man who has courage but not righteousness will cause thievery'.)

59 Lin, previously n 54, 196.

60 Peng, previously n 38, 24.

61 Ibid.

15.8 Integrating mediation into arbitration (Med-Arb): the Chinese experience

Apart from the impact of the Confucian tradition and Communist ideology,[62] the China International Economic and Trade Arbitration Commission's (CIETAC) mediation practice also has its own historical background. Although the modern commercial arbitration process is a product of the market economy, the Chinese arbitration system emerged and developed in the environment of a planned economy. As a consequence, there were few laws in China that could be applied to commercial disputes before the 1980s. In such a legal vacuum, arbitral tribunals could only decide cases in accordance with the principles of fairness and reasonableness, or they could encourage the parties to resolve their disputes by mediation with the assistance of the arbitral tribunal. Deeply influenced by the practice of the Chinese courts, CIETAC empowered its tribunals to mediate arbitration cases since its inception.[63] It is worth noting that cases submitted to CIETAC during its infancy stages were straightforward mediation, given the simplicity of disputes, such as the small value of the claims.

Prior to the enactment of the Arbitration Law, CIETAC attempted to mediate its arbitration cases, even though the first Arbitration Rules of CIETAC did not contain provisions on mediation but merely a provision stating that an arbitration case should be dismissed if the parties reached an amicable settlement agreement.[64] Mediation was first provided for in the CIETAC Rules of 1989, which stated that CIETAC and its arbitral tribunals may mediate the cases accepted by CIETAC, and, if an amicable settlement was reached by the parties through mediation, the arbitral tribunal should render an arbitral award in accordance with the contents of the settlement agreement.[65] The statistics show that from the 1950s to the 1980s, most CIETAC arbitrations were concluded by way of mediation. In the 1980s and 1990s, CIETAC still enjoyed a considerable rate of success with the combination of mediation and arbitration.[66]

62 Apart from the traditional legal culture, the prominence of mediation in contemporary China also appears to be attributable to the Communist ideology of society, social control and social conflict. Like Confucianism, Communism is hostile to litigation and places a great emphasis upon 'criticism-education', 'self-criticism' and 'voluntarism'.

63 In general, the modern mediation system in China can be divided into five categories: (1) people's mediation, or mediation undertaken by people's mediation committees; (2) administrative mediation, or mediation conducted by local people's governments or administrative departments; (3) institutional mediation, or mediation conducted by permanent mediation centres; (4) mediation within litigation proceedings and (5) mediation within arbitral proceedings. In contrast, the Taiwanese legal system has two types of mediation: (1) town mediation and (2) court mediation.

64 Gabrielle Kaufmann-Kohler and Fan Kun, 'Integrating Mediation into Arbitration: Why It Works in China' (2008) *Journal of International Arbitration* 25(4): 479, 485.

65 See Art 37 of the CIETAC Rules 1989. Structured mediation is a relatively new addition to the dispute resolution process in Western jurisdictions and has arisen largely in response to perceived inadequacies in the adversarial system. It is worth noting that the Model Law does not provide for mediation by the tribunal, either before or during the arbitration proceedings. Nevertheless, certain Model Law jurisdictions and rules have introduced the possibility for mediation by the tribunal. Examples can be found in s 33 of the Hong Kong Arbitration Ordinance (Cap 609), in the rules of the Chinese European Arbitration Council (CEAC) and in s 17 of the Singapore International Arbitration Act (Cap 143A).

66 Wang Wenying, 'The Role of Conciliation in Resolving Dispute: A PRC Perspective,' (2005) *Ohio State Journal of Dispute Resolution* 20: 421, 436.

15.9 Advantages and concerns of the Med-Arb practice

15.9.1 Advantages

The Med-Arb practice is intended to allow the parties to profit from the fruits of both dispute settlement processes. It is an integrated process of combining both mediation and arbitration. A neutral third party works with the disputing parties towards a settlement, first using the techniques of mediation. If this is unsuccessful, the mediator changes a hat and becomes an arbitrator.[67] One of the obvious advantages of this practice is that it allows the arbitration phase to proceed if the parties fail during the mediation phase without having to start afresh. This is due to the fact that the same person is involved in both phases and hence is familiar with the issues in the dispute. To find an adequate resolution in the arbitration phase, the Med-Arbitrator will use an understanding of the relationship between the parties during the mediation phase or knowledge of their respective underlying interests.[68] In addition, a settlement agreement entered into in the course of a pending arbitration may form part of a consent award and become enforceable under the New York Convention. These particular advantages are the core strength in Med-Arb practice. Therefore, this explains why Chinese legal culture and the present Chinese domestic legislation appear susceptible towards Med-Arb practice as a means of dispute resolution.

15.9.2 Concerns

The Med-Arb practice has been criticised with the serious concern as to whether both phases are legitimate when handled by the same person.[69] Here, a concern on the impartiality of the mediator-arbitrator arises. If the settlement fails and the arbitration continues, the impartiality of the mediator-turned-arbitrator may come into question, because of the confidential information he or she may have obtained during the mediation phase.[70] Moreover, if the parties anticipate that the mediator may become an arbitrator and decide the case if the mediation fails, they might be less candid during the caucusing, which could weaken the effectiveness of the mediation process.[71] As a result of active engagement during the mediation phase, the mediator-arbitrator may lose impartiality by becoming privy to confidential information that would have never been revealed to a real arbitrator.[72] It is doubtful that the mediator-arbitrator will remain unaffected as an arbitrator after engaging and becoming privy to confidential, perhaps intimate, emotional, personal or other legally irrelevant information.

By the same token, there is a risk of breach of due process safeguards if caucusing is used in the mediation phase. On such occasion, a party may disclose facts that the other side is unaware of and has no opportunity to respond to. This prompts a question as to whether *ex parte* caucuses violate due process. Confidential private caucuses with one party arguably violate due process, since they deny the other party the opportunity to challenge what is presented as evidence to the mediator-arbitrator, who can use it to reach a judgement.

67 James P. Peter, 'Med-Arb in International Arbitration,' (1997) *American Review of International Arbitration* 8: 83, 90–91.

68 Ibid.

69 Carlos De Vera, 'Arbitrating Harmony: 'Med-Arb' and the Confluence of Culture and Rule of Law in the Resolution of International Commercial Disputes in China' (2004) *Columbia Journal of Asian Law* 149, 157.

70 Kohler et al., previously n 64, 491.

71 Ibid.

72 De Vera, previously n 69, 158.

Recently, the arbitration community in Asia was faced with a controversial case in which the key issue is whether the use of Med-Arb is incompatible with a fair procedure in arbitration. In Gao Hai Yan & Another v Keeneye Holdings Ltd & Others (Keeneye),[73] the Hong Kong Court of First Instance (CFI) refused enforcement of an arbitral award made in mainland China on public policy grounds. The court held that the conduct of the arbitrators turned mediators has caused a fair-minded observer to apprehend a real risk of bias. However, the Court of Appeal then overruled the decision and approved enforcement of the award based on the two principal grounds as follows.

15.9.2.1 Waiver by Keeneye *of its right to object*

The first ground for the Court of Appeal's decision was that Keeneye had failed to raise any objection to the 'Arb-Med' procedure during the arbitration itself and had therefore waived its right to do so in the enforcement proceedings. This was the effect of the Xian Arbitration Commission Arbitration Rules, which governed the proceedings and specifically provided for waiver of the right to object in such circumstances. Similar rules on waiver exist in many institutional rules (for example, Article 28.1 of the HKIAC Administered Arbitration Rules, Article 33 of the current ICC Rules, Article 39 of the new ICC Rules which take effect from 1 January 2012, and Article 36.1 of the SIAC Rules). The Court of Appeal also emphasised the principle that it is not open to a party to keep a complaint about impropriety or bias 'up its sleeve' for potential use at a later point. For these reasons, it held that a clear case of waiver had been established and that Keeneye had lost its right to complain about the Arb-Med procedure.

15.9.2.2 No apparent bias

The second ground for the Court of Appeal's decision was that, in any case, the 'Arb-Med' procedure adopted in this case did not disclose apprehended bias, giving rise to an issue of public policy. This part of the Court of Appeal's judgement is likely to give rise to considerable discussion and debate, given the striking factual circumstances of this case. These included the facts that (i) the mediation took place in the form of a private meeting over dinner at the Xian Shangri-la Hotel, (ii) it was not held in the presence of both parties and (iii) the mediators appeared to make a settlement proposal on their own initiative. It was based on these facts, amongst others, that the CFI had held apprehended bias to be established. In considering the factual circumstances of the 'Arb-Med' procedure and concluding that there was no apprehended bias, the Court of Appeal appeared to consider that whether there was an apprehension of apparent bias might depend upon an understanding of how mediation was conducted in mainland China. In this regard, it placed considerable weight upon the fact that the local court in Xian, with supervisory jurisdiction over the arbitration, had refused an application to set aside the award, and cited with approval English authority that such circumstances will be a 'very strong policy consideration' for the court to take into account in deciding whether or not to enforce the award. In other words, the Court of Appeal indicated that, in determining whether or not to deny enforcement of an award, weight may be accorded to any decision of the courts of the seat as to whether or not to set aside the award.

73 *Gao Hai Yan & Another v Keeneye Holdings Ltd & Others (Keeneye)* [2011] HKEC 514 and [2011] HKEC 1626.

Having found that there was no apparent bias, the Court of Appeal noted that the test for determining what is contrary to public policy in Hong Kong is whether the relevant matter is contrary to 'fundamental conceptions of morality and justice' in Hong Kong. Accordingly, the mere fact that the procedure adopted would give rise to an apprehension of bias if adopted in Hong Kong will not necessarily amount to a breach of public policy. If the procedure is acceptable practice in the jurisdiction in which it took place, it will not be in breach of public policy in Hong Kong, unless it was so serious as to be contrary to 'conceptions of morality and justice'. This is a pro-enforcement decision, which emphasises that the Hong Kong courts will not readily refuse to enforce arbitral awards, whether rendered in China or elsewhere. In particular, the public policy ground should be interpreted narrowly.

The Court of Appeal's decision demonstrates that some concerns about the Med-Arb practice affecting the enforceability of an arbitral award were inflated. In the same vein, it reinforces the power of the New York Convention that it is very difficult to resist enforcement of a valid arbitration award once an unsuccessful attempt has been made to set it aside in the place it was originated. Of note, Keeneye has sparked a debate because it places two cardinal principles of international arbitration in conflict.[74] First, that an arbitration award should be widely enforced and public policy objections kept within narrow grounds.[75] Second, that arbitration requires 'due process' or 'fair procedure,' in which it cannot be seriously denied that there was a major failure in that regard in the Keeneye case.[76] Accordingly, this begs a question as to what extent the court tasked with enforcement should give deference to the decision of the court having jurisdiction over the seat of the arbitration.

15.10 Conclusion

In sum, three conclusions seem to follow from this in terms of legalisation. The first is that international arbitration will be more internationalised. This is evident with a steady growing of harmonisation of national arbitration laws and increasing participation of lawyers and arbitrators involved in international arbitration. In this sense, the specific need of disputes in the international context would prompt the application of international arbitration laws. As a result, they become less dependent on the peculiarities of national arbitration practices. There will be an exponential transition from the centrality of national arbitration towards international arbitration practice and procedure. This may lead the diversity of legal cultures to converge into uniform international standards. All policy, however, should recognise that commercial law and dispute between parties from different jurisdictions require an international perspective, based on an underlying commonality of principles and approach.

Second, Asian legal culture is not immune from the coercion of global forces that reverberated across the globe. Change occurs when it is forced by necessity. That said, recognition of necessity happens when a crisis is looming upon a society. In this regard, economic globalisation has been a catalyst for change. Further, the legalisation of international arbitration has paved the way for harmonisation of national arbitration law to conform to international standards and practices. Consequently, Asian legal consciousness, attitudes and values are experiencing cultural homogenisation.

74 Mark Goodrich, 'Arb-Med: Ideal Solution or Dangerous Heresy?' (2012) *International Arbitration Law Review* 15(1).

75 Ibid.

76 Ibid.

Finally, despite the fact that much progress has been made towards the promotion of arbitration in East Asia and Middle East, much still needs to be accomplished. This is particularly obvious in relation to the recognition and enforcement of arbitral awards by local courts. Cases such as Keeneye have demonstrated how the judicial interpretation approach in relation to public policy led to different outcomes. An interpretation adopted by the Hong Kong Court of Appeal in Keeneye is a strong pointer that arbitration awards should be widely enforced and public policy should be capped within narrow parameters. A further oddity shown in the Keeneye case is that there was an apprehension of apparent bias and lack of due process or fair procedure in that regard.

References

Carlos De Vera, 'Arbitrating Harmony: 'Med-Arb' and the Confluence of Culture and Rule of Law in the Resolution of International Commercial Disputes in China' (2004) *Columbia Journal of Asian Law* 149.

David Nelken, 'Using Legal Concept of Legal Culture,' (2004) *Australian Journal of Legal Philosophy* 29: 2.

Gabrielle Kaufmann-Kohler and Fan Kun, 'Integrating Mediation into Arbitration: Why It Works in China' (2008) *Journal of International Arbitration* 25(4): 479.

H. Patrick Glenn, *Legal Tradition of the World* (Oxford University Press, Oxford, 4th ed, 2010).

Jan Klabbers, 'Institutional Ambivalence by Design: Soft Organization in International Law' (2001) *Nordic Journal of International Law* 70: 403.

Jeremy Webber, 'Culture, Legal Culture, and Legal Reasoning: A Comment on Nelken,' (2004) *Australian Journal of Legal Philosophy* 29: 27.

Jingzhaou Tao, *Arbitration Law and Practice in China* (Kluwer Law International, The Hague, London, New York, 2nd ed, 2008).

Judith Goldstein, Miles Kahler, Robert O. Keohane and Ann-Marie Slaughter, 'Introduction: Legalization and World Politics' (2000) *International Organization* 54: 385.

Katherine Lynch, *The Forces of Economic Globalization: Challenges to the Regime of International Commercial Arbitration* (Kluwer Law International, The Hague, London, New York, 2003).

Kenneth W. Abbott, Robert O. Keohane, Andrew Moravcsik, Anne-Marie Slaughter and Duncan Snidal, 'The Concept of Legalization' (2000) *International Organization* 54: 401.

Michael Pryles, *Dispute Resolution in Asia* (Kluwer Law International, The Hague, London, New York, 3rd ed, 2005).

Miles Kahler, 'Legalization as Strategy: The Asian-Pacific Case' (2000) *International Organization* 54: 549.

Paul J. Davidson, 'The ASEAN Way and the Role of Law in ASEAN Economic Cooperation' (2004) *Singapore Yearbook of International Law* 8: 165.

Shin-yi Peng, 'The WTO Legalistic Approach and East Asia: From Legal Cultural Perspective' (June 2000) *Asian-Pacific Law & Policy Journal* 13.

Simon Greenberg, Christopher Kee and J. Romesh Weeramantry, *International Commercial Arbitration: An Asia-Pacific Perspective* (Cambridge University Press, Cambridge, 2011).

Yun-Hsien Diana Lin, 'Civil Mediation in Taiwan: Legal Culture and the Process of Legal Modernization' (2011) *University of Pennsylvania East Asia Law Review* 6: 192.

16 Emerging trends in the dispute settlement mechanism in the Free Trade Agreements of China, South Korea and Japan

Rajesh Sharma[1]

Asian countries jumped on the bandwagon signing Free Trade Agreements (FTAs) at a considerably fast speed, after the collapse of the Ministerial Meeting of the World Trade Organization (WTO) at Cancun in 2003. The Asian economic drivers like China and India were new in this journey. ASEAN countries, on the other hand, were focusing on establishing their ASEAN free trade zone, which was in the early stages of development. At the same time, ASEAN started negotiating with China, Japan and South Korea to form an ASEAN+3 Agreement. India also joined the same club by forming an extended ASEAN+4. Among Asian countries, Singapore, Japan and South Korea started negotiating and signing FTAs with other economically developed countries, like the US and the EU. These countries were considered as like-minded countries, so FTAs with them were a natural course of action. Otherwise, the rest of the Asian countries were moving slowly in signing FTAs. Once China started flexing its economic prowess, the FTAs negotiation and conclusion started taking new turns. This was further fuelled by the commencement of negotiations on East Asian Communities (EAC) envisaging the EU-type communities for the Asian Countries.

The EAC negotiations were conducted on the sidelines of the ASEAN meetings. However, soon, the EAC negotiations faced a stumbling block on the issue of leadership, the definition of Asia, mainly in terms of coverage of Asian countries within the EAC, including whether Australia and New Zealand should be part of the EAC or not, and above all, on security concerns. This inclusion issue went beyond its anticipation when Russia requested to join the EAC as a member, or at least, as an observer. Now, the discussion on the EAC has become a mere event on the side of the ASEAN meetings. Once the EAC negotiation started to cool down, the Asian countries started negotiating separately with developed and developing countries, including those in Africa and Latin America. From Asia, the target countries were China, Japan, South Korea, India, Malaysia, Indonesia and Singapore. Australia and New Zealand also started FTA negotiations with these countries.

Over a period of time, Asian countries started negotiating their FTAs in more sophisticated ways, as compared to their earlier approach of negotiating on the basis of the text prepared by the other parties, mainly by the developed countries. New approaches of Asian countries have shown new innovations in their FTAs provisions. What was considered an unfeasible task has started becoming a reality. New experiments have been made. This chapter focuses on these new experiments and trends emerging from the State-to-State dispute settlement

1 Senior Lecturer, Justice and Legal Studies, RMIT University, Melbourne, Australia; author of book *Dispute Settlement Mechanism in the FTAs of Asia*; Arbitrator at Korean Commercial Arbitration Board; Chief-Editor of *ADR World*.

provisions of the FTAs of Asia. For this purpose, recently signed FTAs of China, South Korea and Japan with Australia will be considered. These three countries are powerful economies of Asia, and their approach in the dispute settlement in their FTAs can be considered as representative of the Asian trend. The FTAs under consideration in this chapter have also raised discussions on the Investor-State dispute settlement mechanism. For example, the Australia-China FTA has proposed to negotiate an appellate mechanism for Investor-State disputes, which is very innovative, and a hot topic in the international arena. However, as the focus of this chapter is on State-to-State dispute settlement, discussion on Investor-State disputes is beyond the scope of this chapter.

FTAs of China, South Korea and Japan with Australia

The Australia-China FTA was signed on 17 June 2015 and became effective on 20 December 2015. The Australia-China FTA is the newest FTA of China, which represents a new trend in the dispute settlement mechanism of China.

Chapter 15 of the Australia-China FTA contains the State-to-State dispute settlement mechanism. In addition to the main provisions, this chapter includes three new items: (1) Code of Conduct (Annex-15-A), (2) Model Rules of Procedure for the Arbitral Tribunal (Annex-15-B) and (3) Indicative Time Table for the Arbitral Tribunal attached with Annex B (Annex 15-B). Code of Conduct, Model Rules and Time Table have now become part of the FTA applicable to the State v State disputes. Among these three, the Code of Conduct for Arbitrators has been used for the first time.

The Korea-Australia FTA was signed on the 8 April 2014 and became effective on 12 December 2014. Like the Australia-China FTA, the Korea-Australia FTA also shows some new trends in dispute settlement. The Korea-Australia FTA also includes a Code of Conduct (Annex 20-A), Model Rules of Procedure (Annex 20-B) and an Indicative Time Table for a Dispute Settlement Panel as part of the Model Rules of Procedure for Dispute Settlement Panel Proceedings (Attachment to Annex 2-B). From the structural point of view, the dispute settlement mechanisms of both the Australia-China FTA and the Korea-Australia FTA look similar, as Australia is the common partner in both the FTAs. Both FTAs were signed in close proximity, so one may see the influence of one on the other.

The other major Asian economy, Japan, has also signed an agreement with Australia, which included the Code of Conduct in its dispute settlement mechanism.[2] In contrast with Korea and China, the Australia-Japan FTA requires not only arbitrators or panelists but also assistants and administrative personnel to comply with the Code of Conduct.[3] The Obligation of Self-Disclosure contained in the Code of Conduct is exclusively applicable on arbitrators.[4]

The Code of conduct imposes a duty on arbitrators to remain independent and impartial[5] and stresses the performance of duties by arbitrators[6] and maintenance of

2 The Australia-Japan FTA was signed on 8 July 2014 and became effective on 15 January 2015.

3 Australia-Japan FTA, Rules of Procedure of Arbitral Tribunals, Para 6.

4 Section IV of the Code of Conduct of the Australia-Japan FTA contains the provisions of Obligation of Self-Disclosure.

5 Australia-China FTA, Code of Conduct, Paras 12–17; Korea-Australia FTA, Code of Conduct Paras 11–16.

6 Korea-Australia FTA, Code of Conduct, Paras 4–10; Australia-China FTA, Code of Conduct, Paras 5–11.

confidentiality.[7] As these obligations are important in maintaining the integrity of the dispute settlement system, these obligations are included in both the Australia-China FTA and the Korea-Australia FTA through the Code of Conduct. The Australia-Japan FTA enforces the Code of Conduct on arbitrators, arbitrators' assistants and administrative personnel, thus, the coverage of the Code of Conduct is wider as compared to the Australia-China FTA and the Australia-Korea FTA.

Cooperation – a new means of dispute resolution

The Australia-China FTA follows the consistent pattern of China for the dispute settlement mechanism in the FTAs of Asia, which encourages "cooperation" as the first means of resolving disputes and obliges the parties to "make every attempt through cooperation to arrive at a mutually satisfactory resolution of any matter that might affect" the operation of the Australia-China FTA including the agreement on "the interpretation and application of this Agreement."[8] The importance of cooperation as the first port of call may be assessed by the fact that the recently concluded Trans-Pacific Partnership (TPP) also emphasises "cooperation."[9]

The Korea-Australia FTA has also emphasised "cooperation" and requires parties to "endeavour to agree" on the interpretation and implementation of the FTA. Similar to the Australia-China FTA, the parties to the Korea-Australia FTA also have to "make every attempt through cooperation" to arrive at a mutually satisfactory resolution of any matter that might affect the operation of the Korea-Australia FTA.[10]

The Australia-Japan FTA does not have any stand-alone provision on cooperation, like the Australia-China FTA or the Korea-Australia FTA. However, the Australia-Japan FTA has "Good Offices, Conciliation and Mediation," and the Australia-China FTA has "Good Offices, Conciliation and Mediation," together with a cooperation provision. The Korea-Australia FTA does not have "Good Offices, Conciliation and Mediation." Though the Australia-Korea FTA shows the trend of including cooperation as a means of resolving disputes, at the same time excluding the means of "Good Offices, Conciliation and Mediation," it is still too early to say whether this will be a future trend. It is also a fact that almost every FTA includes "Good Offices, Conciliation and Mediation"; however, the use of this method for dispute resolution is insignificant. Even at the level of WTO, the method of "Good Offices, Conciliation and Mediation" is seldom used.

Though we see the use of cooperation in the dispute settlement mechanism of FTAs now, it is too early to understand the implication of this provision. For example, is it an obligation that, if breached, may give rise to an action under the FTA? In other words, if parties do not cooperate during consultation or at a post-award phase, e.g., for fixing of a reasonable period of time, would that mean the cooperation provision has been violated by the recalcitrant party and therefore the claimant may initiate another action against the party at fault? What standard should be used to ascertain whether a party has breached the cooperation obligations or not whenever the tribunal does face such a question? Considering the general approach of Asian countries to resolve the dispute amicably, the inclusion of cooperation

7 Australia-China FTA, Code of Conduct, Paras 19–21; Korea-Australia FTA, Code of Conduct, Paras 18–20.
8 Australia-China FTA, Article 15.1.
9 TPP, Article 28.2
10 Korea-Australia FTA, Article 20.1.

as the first port of call for dispute resolution is laudable, but for the rule-based system of dispute resolution, this is far from complete and practical.

Independence and impartiality of arbitrators

Independence and impartiality in any decision-making process is a very important aspect. Therefore, the Code of Conduct in the Australia-China FTA, Korea-Australia-FTA and Australia-Japan FTA has paid special attention to it and provided a general obligation on the arbitrators to be "independent and impartial," to act in a "fair manner" and to avoid "creating an appearance of impropriety or bias".[11] It further adds that an arbitrator must not be influenced by self-interests, outside pressure, political considerations, public clamour, loyalty to a party or fear of criticism.[12] Arbitrators are also required to take action in such a manner that it should not give any indication that people at a special position influence them. In order to counter that impression, arbitrators are required to make every effort to displace such an impression. Moreover, arbitrators are not allowed to use their position on the arbitral tribunal to advance any personal or private interests.[13]

Past dealings of arbitrators are also under the scanner in the Code of Conduct of the Australia-China FTA, Korea-Australia FTA and Australia-Japan FTA. According to this Code, arbitrators should not let "past or existing financial, business, professional, family or social relationships or responsibilities influence the arbitrators' conduct and responsibilities."[14] Following this responsibility, arbitrators should also refrain from "entering into any relationship, or acquiring any financial interest" that may affect arbitrators' "impartiality" or "which may create an appearance of impropriety or bias."[15] In addition to that, arbitrators are also suggested to dispel the appearance that the outcome of the decision may, in some way, give benefit to them.[16]

The Code of Conduct of the Australia-China FTA imposes the responsibility on arbitrators to "avoid impropriety and the appearance of impropriety," to be "independent and impartial," to avoid "direct and indirect conflicts of interests" and to observe a "high standard of conduct so that the integrity and impartiality of the dispute settlement process are preserved."[17] The exact similar responsibility has been imposed on the panelist serving under the Korea-Australia FTA.[18] Similarly, the Australia-Japan FTA also imposes the same obligations on arbitrators.[19] Such responsibilities towards the process of dispute settlement are very important and therefore each arbitrator or panelist must adhere to them.

11 Australia-China FTA, Code of Conduct, Para 12; Korea-Australia FTA, Code of Conduct, Para 11; Australia-Japan FTA; Code of Conduct, Para III (c) and VI (1).

12 Australia-China FTA, Code of Conduct, Para 13; Korea-Australia FTA, Code of Conduct, Para 12; Australia-Japan FTA, Code of Conduct, Para VI (1).

13 Australia-China FTA, Code of Conduct, Para 15; Korea-Australia FTA, Code of Conduct, Para 14; Australia-Japan FTA, Code of Conduct, Para VI (4).

14 Australia-China FTA, Code of Conduct, Para 16; Korea-Australia FTA, Code of Conduct, Para 15; Australia-Japan FTA, Code of Conduct, Para VI (1).

15 Australia-China FTA, Code of Conduct, Para 17; Korea-Australia FTA, Code of Conduct, Para 17; Australia-Japan FTA, Code of Conduct, Para VI (2).

16 Australia-China FTA, Code of Conduct, Para 18; Korea-Australia FTA, Code of Conduct, Para 14; Australia-Japan FTA, Code of Conduct, Para VI (4).

17 Australia-China FTA, Code of Conduct, Para 2.

18 Korea-Australia FTA, Code of Conduct, Para 1.

19 Australia-Japan FTA, Code of Conduct, Para VI (1).

The Code of Conduct of the Australia-China FTA, Korea-Australia FTA and Australia-Japan FTA imposes self-disclosure obligations on arbitrators from the time they are invited to sit on a panel to resolve a dispute.[20] Arbitrators are required to disclose "any interests, relationship or matter that is likely to affect his or her independence or impartiality or that might reasonably create an appearance of impropriety or bias in the proceedings."[21] Moreover, it is an obligation on the candidate for arbitration to make "all reasonable efforts to become aware of any such interests, relationships and matters."[22] Such obligation is a continuous one, which is applicable even during the arbitration process. Therefore, arbitrators are required to make their own "reasonable efforts to become aware of any interest, relationships and matters and disclose them to the FTA Joint Commission."[23] However, it does not say whether arbitrators are required to report to the Joint Commission or Committee promptly or as soon as they come to know about any interest, relationships and matters that may affect their independence and impartiality. As a matter of common practice, the reporting should be prompt and take place as soon as such knowledge is acquired. The Australia-Japan FTA does not have any provision of reporting to the Joint Committee or Commission. In these FTAs, it is to note that the code of conduct is not putting any obligation on parties to find out about any conflict, but the onus is on arbitrators, so that in the future, arbitrators may not argue that such information was already known to the parties either directly and indirectly or was available in the public domain.

The Australia-Japan FTA has also warned that the application of these disclosure requirements should not be made administratively so burdensome that it becomes impracticable for qualified persons to serve as arbitrators. Another point of caution has been suggested in the Australia-Japan FTA that while meeting the disclosure requirements, the personal privacy of arbitrators should be respected.[24] In this respect, the Australia-Japan FTA has set the good trend that requirements of disclosure must not transgress into the personal and private domain of arbitrators.

Maintenance of confidentiality by arbitrators and parties

There is a general obligation of confidentiality in all the three FTAs under discussion here. With regard to the obligation of confidentiality, in the Australia-China FTA, the only exception is that an arbitrator or former arbitrator may only disclose confidential information as required by legal or constitutional requirements.[25] Legal obligations are common as an exception to the confidentiality requirement; however, inclusion of "Constitutional" requirements is new. Neither China nor Australia has ever included code of conduct in their FTAs. Inclusion of Constitutional requirements may be significant for Australia, but the same is not true in China. In the Chinese Constitution, there is no particular provision binding on arbitrators. However, in Australia, Constitution plays a significant role

20 Australia-China FTA, Code of Conduct, Para 3; Korea-Australia FTA, Code of Conduct, Para 2; Australia-Japan FTA, Code of Conduct, Para IV.

21 Australia-China FTA, Code of Conduct, Para 3; Korea-Australia FTA, Code of Conduct, Para 2.

22 Australia-China FTA, Code of Conduct, Para 3; Korea-Australia FTA, Code of Conduct, Para 2.

23 Australia-China FTA, Code of Conduct, Para 4; Korea-Australia FTA, Code of Conduct, Para 3. It is to note that there is a terminological difference here because in the Korea-Australia FTA there is a Joint "Committee" and not the Joint "Commission".

24 Australia-Japan, Code of Conduct, Para IV (3).

25 Australia-China FTA, Code of Conduct, Para 21.

in dispute settlement. Parties more frequently, unlike China, refer to the Constitutional provisions in court cases.

The Korea-Australia FTA does not include "Constitutional" requirements. The panelists or former panelists can only disclose the deliberations of the panel or views of an individual panelist as "required by law."[26] The panelists, as well as the person retained by the panel, are required to maintain the confidentiality of panel proceedings and deliberations.[27] It is a significant departure from the Australian point of view between the two FTAs signed with China and Korea. Since Korea is a civil law country, the use of Constitution in disputes may not be frequent, but there is no explanation for the presence of Constitutional requirements in the Australia-China FTA, considering China is a civil law country, too. It is also unexplainable as to why Australia prefers inclusion of Constitutional requirements in the Australia-China FTA and ignores the same in the Korea-Australia FTA, knowing both China and Korea are civil law countries.

The Australia-Japan FTA provides for absolute confidentiality, because even under legal or Constitutional order, any covered person, such as arbitrators, arbitrators' assistants and administrative personnel, is not allowed to disclose confidential information. Unlike the Australia-China FTA and Korea-Australia FTA, there are no exceptions, e.g., "except as required by legal or constitutional requirements." Moreover, the Australia-Japan FTA does not impose confidentiality obligation on former arbitrators, as they are obliged to maintain confidentiality under the Australia-China FTA and Korea-Australia FTA.

Arbitrators are obliged to keep a nonpublic document confidential or even cannot use it for the purpose other than the arbitration proceeding. It is also imperative that arbitrators do not use such information for their own benefit or for the advantages of others or even to adversely affect the interest of others.[28] In the Australia-Japan FTA, prohibition against the use of confidential information does not include "interest of others" and, in that sense, if any confidential information is used to affect the interests of others, then it is debatable whether it is against the code of conduct.[29] The Korea-Australia FTA is similar to the Australia-China FTA, which prohibits the use of confidential information that may affect the interests of others.[30]

Arbitration proceedings, including hearings and deliberations, as well as documents submitted for the purpose of arbitration, are confidential.[31] Not all documents can be confidential, only those documents that are marked confidential by the party providing that they are treated as confidential by the other party. However, the party submitting confidential information to the tribunal may have to submit a nonconfidential summary of the designated confidential information within 15 days of such a request. This nonconfidential information may be made public.[32] The Australia-China FTA has made it clear that the documents submitted for arbitration may be confidential, and the obligation to keep that information confidential is on the receiving party and not on the party providing

26 Korea-Australia FTA, Code of Conduct, Para 20.

27 Korea-Australia FTA, Rules of Procedure, Para 8.

28 Australia-China FTA, Code of Conduct, Para 19.

29 Australia-Japan FTA, Code of Conduct, Para VII (1).

30 Korea-Australia FTA, Code of Conduct, Para 18.

31 Australia-China FTA, Model Rules, Para 17. As the hearings of the arbitral tribunal is in close session and in deliberation only arbitrators are present so these parts of the arbitration proceeding are also confidential. See Australia-China FTA, Model Rules, Paras 9 &13.

32 Australia-China FTA, Model Rules, Para 17.

that confidential information. Therefore, the party providing that information may make that information, i.e., its own position, public, and that will not be considered breach of confidentiality obligation. It is also to note that only documents submitted in arbitration are confidential, whereas any document prepared for arbitration or related to arbitration is not within the scope of the confidential obligations.

In the Korea-Australia FTA, a party may designate any specific information confidential that it considers strictly necessary to protect privacy or legitimate commercial interest of particular enterprises, public or private, or to address essential confidentiality concerns.[33] Therefore, the scope of confidentiality has been extended to private and legitimate commercial interest in the Korea-Australia FTA.

Conduct of arbitration proceedings

The Australia-China FTA, Korea-Australia FTA and Australia-Japan FTA provide for the duties and performance-related code for arbitrators.[34] The first duty is to conduct arbitration proceedings "with fairness and diligence."[35] No arbitrator is allowed "to deny other arbitrator from taking part in any aspect of the proceeding."[36] This may also include the deliberation process. It should be the responsibility of the Chairman to make sure that all arbitrators are included in the process from the beginning till the end. There is no such provision in the Australia-Japan FTA; however, it may be assumed that all arbitrators will take part in the decision-making process. The Australia-Japan FTA assumes that each arbitrator understands that "prompt settlement of disputes is essential to the effective functioning of the Australia-Japan FTA".[37]

Arbitrators are not allowed "to delegate their duties of making decision on any other person."[38] In the Australia-Japan FTA, the same obligation is included; however, the arbitral tribunal may permit arbitrators' assistants, administration personnel, interpreters and translators to be present during its deliberations.[39] This is because the Code of Conduct allows delegation of "duty to decide" to any person "except as provided in the Rules of Procedures."[40] However, the Rule of Procedures only allows covered persons to be present during deliberation; it may not be assumed that the covered person will make the final decision.

This obligation of non-delegation is quite significant in terms of the rumours that arbitrators ask their assistants to draft the award. The controversial Yukos award has been challenged by Russia, on the basis that the assistant to the tribunal spent more hours and was paid for those hours, which was more than the time spent by the arbitrators, suggesting that perhaps the assistant was asked to draft the award, which was the duty of the arbitral panel.[41]

33 Korea-Australia FTA, Model Rules Para 21.

34 Australia-China FTA, Code of Conduct, Paras 5–11; Korea-Australia FTA, Code of Conduct, Paras 4–10; Australia-Japan, Code of Conduct, Para V (1–5).

35 Australia-China FTA, Code of Conduct, Para 6; Korea-Australia FTA, Code of Conduct, Para 5; Australia-Japan, Code of Conduct, Para V (2).

36 Australia-China FTA, Code of Conduct, Para 7; Korea-Australia FTA, Code of Conduct, Para 6.

37 Australia-Japan FTA, Code of Conduct, Para V (1).

38 Australia-China FTA, Code of Conduct, Para 8; Korea-Australia FTA, Code of Conduct, Para 7.

39 Australia-Japan FTA, Rules of Procedure, Para 18.

40 Australia-Japan FTA, Code of Conduct, Para V (4).

41 Dmytro Galagan, "The Challenge of the Yukos Award-An Award Written by Someone Else-A Violation of Tribunal's Mandate?", Kluwer Arbitration Blog, available at http://kluwerarbitration

In arbitration, if the tribunal requires or a party requests, an expert may be engaged to assist the tribunal to reach a conclusion. The expert can be an individual or a body. The parties will agree on the terms and conditions for engagement of the expert. Any technical information or views of the expert so obtained by the tribunal must be provided to the parties also for comments.[42] This is, of course, to maintain the due process within the arbitration proceeding.

Use of Indicative Time Table

The Australia-China FTA provides for a clear timeline for the operation of a dispute resolution process. In order to strengthen the importance of time limit and timely execution of various activities, an "Indicative Time Table for the Arbitral Tribunal" is also added as an Annex 15-B attached with the "Model Rules of Procedure for the Arbitral Tribunal."[43] An outer limit for the completion of a dispute resolution procedure is set at 270 days "from the date of establishment of the arbitral tribunal until the issuance of the final report."[44] This time limit is a general rule, and parties with agreement may change the number of days. If the general rule is adhered to, then it is possible to resolve disputes faster under the Australia-China FTA, as compared to any other forum.

A similar trend is also noticed in the Korea-Australia FTA, which includes an Indicative Time Table for Dispute Settlement Panel, attached to the Model Rules of Procedure for Dispute Settlement Panel Proceedings.[45] According to this time table, a final report is expected to be issued between 170 and 240 days from the date of establishment of the panel. However, the upper limit of deadline for the issuance of final report is 270 days, which is the same as that of the Australia-China FTA.[46]

The Indicative Time Table in the Australia-Japan FTA is even shorter than that of the Korea-Australia FTA. In the Australia-Japan FTA, a period of 23–26 weeks is given, which is approximately 161–182 days from the date of establishment of the tribunal to release the award to the parties.[47] At the same time, Proceedings of Arbitral Tribunal declares that the maximum days to issue the award to the parties must not be more than 6 months, which is approximately 180 days.[48] Therefore, in terms of number of days, arbitrators have less time under the Australia-Japan FTA as compared to the Australia-China FTA and Korea-Australia FTA. From the parties' point of view, the tribunal can decide a dispute faster in the Australia-Japan FTA. All these dates are, of course, a general guideline and with the agreement of the parties, it can be extended.[49]

A time period for the written submissions and documents is also set under the Australia-China FTA. For example, the complaining party is required to submit its first

---

blog.com/2015/02/27/the-challenge-of-the-yukos-award-an-award-written-by-someone-else-a-violation-of-the-tribunals-mandate/.

42 Australia-China FTA, Model Rules, Para 20; Korea-Australia FTA, Model Rules, Para 26.

43 See Annex 15-B of Australia-China FTA.

44 Australia-China FTA, Model Rules, Para 2.

45 See Annex 20-B of Korea-Australia FTA.

46 Korea-Australia FTA, Model Rules, Para 2 and Annex 20-B.

47 Australia-Japan FTA, Indicative Time Table, Attachment A.

48 Australia-Japan FTA, Para 19.9 (6).

49 Australia-China FTA, Model Rules, Para 2; Korea-Australia FTA, Model Rules, Para 2; Australia-Japan FTA, Article 19.9 (6).

written document within 14 days from the date of appointment of the final arbitrator, and the party complained against is then supposed to submit its reply within 30 days from the date of delivery of the first written submission by the complaining party.[50] The complaining party, in the Korea-Australia FTA, also has 14 days to make its written submission, but the respondent has only 21 days.[51] In the Australia-Japan FTA, both the complaining party and the party complained against have a shorter time, i.e., 10 days and 20 days, respectively.[52]

It may seem unreasonable to give less time to the complaining party as compared to the party complained against. However, this may not be the case, as the complaining party might have prepared and already submitted most of the information regarding the dispute at the time of filing the notice for consultation and for the request for the establishment of the panel to resolve the dispute. Therefore, a lesser time period given to the complaining party is justified.

The arbitral tribunal, in the Australia-China FTA, is obligated to commence hearing 30 days after the submission of the party complained against.[53] The initial report also needs to be issued 30 days after the receipt of the written supplementary submissions by the parties.[54] That means that the tribunal has to work at a fast pace to complete the writing of the report. Parties are also required to react faster, as they are given only 10 days to make written comments on the initial report.[55] Thereafter, the tribunal gets only 20 days to make the final report to the parties.[56]

The process is even faster in the Korea-Australia FTA, as the tribunal fixes the first hearing with parties within 20–45 days, and the initial report is issued 60–90 days thereafter. However, parties get more days (14 days) to give their comments on the initial report, as compared to the Australia-China FTA. The final report is made available to the parties in 31 days.[57] As a general rule, in the Korea-Australia FTA, the panel is bound to give "sufficient time to the parties to prepare their submissions."[58]

The arbitration process is very fast in the Australia-Japan FTA; therefore, all time limits are shorter, as compared to the Australia-China FTA and Korea-Australia FTA. However, in the Australia-Japan FTA, parties get two substantive hearings, whilst in the Australia-China FTA and Korea-Australia FTA, parties get only one hearing.[59] In the Australia-China FTA, however, parties are allowed to provide written supplementary submissions after the first hearing.[60] Though the time limit is very short in the Australia-Japan FTA, the time period to give comments on the draft award is longer, i.e., 15 days, as compared to the Australia-China FTA (10 days) and Korea-Australia FTA (14 days). The final award in the Australia-Japan FTA is issued to the parties in 15 days after the

50 Australia-China FTA, Model Rules, Para 4.

51 Korea-Australia, Model Rules-Indicative Time-Table, Para (a).

52 Australia-Japan FTA, Indicative Time-Table, Para (b).

53 Australia-China FTA, Model Rules-Indicative Time-Table, Para 2.

54 Australia-China FTA, Model Rules-Indicative Time-Table, Para 4.

55 Australia-China FTA, Model Rules-Indicative Time-Table, Para 5.

56 Australia-China FTA, Model Rules-Indicative Time-Table, Para 6. The time limit is 30 days from the date of issuance of the initial report which includes 10 days for the comments to receive from the parties.

57 Korea-Australia FTA, Model Rules-Indicative Time-Table, Annex 20-B.

58 Korea-Australia FTA, Model Rules, Para 3.

59 Australia-Korea FTA, Indicative Time-Table, Annex A, Paras c & e.

60 Australia-China FTA, Model Rules, Indicative Time-Table, Para 3.

submission on their comments, which is faster than the Australia-China FTA (20 days) and Korea-Australia FTA (31 days).

Presence of arbitrators in hearings and deliberations

All arbitrators in the hearings and deliberations under the Australia-China FTA are required to be present, even though assistants, translators and designated note-takers may be present during the hearings who are not allowed to take part in the deliberations.[61] In the Korea-Australia FTA, assistants, interpreters or translators or designated note-takers may be present in the hearings, and with the permission of the parties, they may also be present in deliberations.[62] In the Australia-Japan FTA, the tribunal may permit the presence of arbitrators' assistants, administration personnel, interpreters and translators during deliberations.[63] For this purpose, the tribunal in the Australia-Japan FTA may not be required to consult parties. Therefore, whilst the Australia-China FTA allows assistants, note-takers, interpreters and translators only during hearings but not in deliberations, the Korea-Australia FTA allows them to be present in deliberations (and assumed to be present during hearings, too). However, according to the Australia-Japan FTA, the tribunal on its own may allow those people to be present during deliberations and assume that they are allowed to be present during hearings; this is also similar to the situation in the Korea-Australia FTA.

All the meetings of the tribunal must be presided over by the Chair of the Tribunal. Other arbitrators may delegate authority to the Chair to deal with administrative and procedural decisions.[64] Such delegation of the authority is good for the efficiency of the arbitral tribunal to resolve disputes in a speedy matter. There are several administrative and procedural decisions that are important that can be taken by the Chair alone, without involving other arbitrators.

In the Australia-China FTA, arbitral hearings are not mandatory. They can only be organised if parties agree to an oral hearing.[65] In case the oral hearing is arranged, the tribunal must ensure an equal amount of time for each party.[66] The Chair of the Tribunal fixes the time limit with a view to providing equal time to parties.[67] It is to note that due process is satisfied by giving an equal amount of time, and there is no obligation to provide a "reasonable," "full" or "adequate" opportunity to present the case. At the hearing, first the complaining party is given the opportunity to make its argument, followed by arguments of the party complained against. After the main arguments, the complaining party is given time to make a reply, followed by a counter-reply by the party complained against.[68]

61 Australia-China FTA, Model Rules, Para 9.

62 Korea-Australia FTA, Model Rules, Para 7.

63 Australia-Japan FTA, Rules of Procedure, Para 18.

64 Australia-China FTA, Model Rules, Para 10; Korea-Australia FTA, Model Rules, Para 5; Australia-Japan FTA, Rules of Procedure, Para 16.

65 Australia-China FTA, Model Rules, Para 12.

66 Australia-China FTA, Model Rules, Para 14.

67 Australia-China FTA, Model Rules, Para 14.

68 Australia-China FTA, Model Rules, Para 14.

Language in arbitration

Chinese is the language of China, and English is the language of Australia, but the Australia-China FTA includes English as the working language of the arbitral proceeding. This is not a strange provision, considering China has agreed to use English as the working language in other FTAs that it has signed.

The Australia-Japan FTA provides use of dual language in arbitration. It provides that the proceedings of the arbitral tribunal are to be conducted in both English and Japanese. The same condition is also applicable on oral and written submissions.[69] It is the obligation on a party to provide translation of the written submission in the language of the other party and consequently bear the cost of translation.[70] In other words, if Australia submits a document in English, then it has to get that document translated into Japanese and also bear the cost of the translation. However, the cost of interpretation is borne by the parties in equal share. For the purpose of interpretation, the Australia-Japan FTA provides a general rule that the party in whose capital a meeting is held will be responsible for organising interpretation services for the meeting.[71] One may argue that the use of dual languages may delay the process; at the same time, it may also be argued that a proceeding in a native language of the parties may result in a well-informed decision. China and Korea also have language differences with Australia, but those two countries have not agreed to the dual languages proceeding with Australia.

Venue of hearing

It is believed that parties in a dispute may enjoy the local advantage if the venue of the hearing is set in their country. This presumption is dispelled in the Australia-China FTA. The parties' agreement is respected in the Australia-China FTA, so the first method of deciding the venue of the hearing is through parties' agreement. If, for some reasons, parties cannot agree on the venue of the arbitration hearing, then as default rule, the first hearing will be conducted in the territory of the parties complained against. The second hearing and any further hearings thereafter will be conducted alternatively in the territories of the parties. In other words, the second hearing will be conducted in the territory of the complaining party, and the third hearing will be organised in the territory of the party complained against.[72] A similar approach has been adopted in the Korea-Australia FTA, too.[73] However, the decision on the venue of the meeting has been left to the Chair in the Australia-Japan FTA to decide in consultation with the parties and other arbitrators.[74] There is no default rule on venue in the Australia-Japan FTA, similar to the Australia-China FTA and Australia-Japan FTA.

Considering the size of China and Australia, parties still have to agree on the venue, for example, whether the venue of the hearing should be in the capital or any other place. The Model Rules in the Australia-China FTA do not shed any light on that. Therefore, for all practical purposes, both Australia and China have to agree on a venue. The only innovation

69 Australia-Japan FTA, Rules of Procedure, Para 37.
70 Australia-Japan FTA, Rules of Procedure, Para 38.
71 Australia-Japan FTA, Rules of Procedure, Para 39.
72 Australia-China FTA, Model Rules, Para 22.
73 Korea-Australia FTA, Model Rules, Para 29.
74 Australia-Japan FTA, Rules of Procedure, Para 4.

one can note in this provision is that the venue is not limited to the capital city; rather, it could be organised anywhere within the territory of a party. Depending upon the nature of the dispute, sometimes it would be helpful to organise the hearing at a place that has more evidence of the measures in dispute.

Implications of violations of the Code of Conduct

Violation of the Code of Conduct by an arbitrator is itself a determinable matter; therefore, no arbitrator is allowed to "communicate matters concerning actual or potential violations."[75] If the matter is necessary to ascertain whether an arbitrator has violated or may violate the Code of Conduct, then an arbitrator may communicate such matter, otherwise that arbitrator has to inform both parties. This is perhaps for the purpose of maintaining the integrity of the questionable arbitrator, unless the FTA Joint Committee of the Australia-China FTA or Korea-Australia FTA, as the case may be, finally resolves the matter. China, Korea and Japan have set the trend of making the violation of code of conduct itself a disputable ground.

Arbitrators in a commercial arbitration are familiar with such codes, but the same arbitrators may not be compelled to follow such codes when deciding State v State disputes under FTAs. Now, with the inclusion of the Code of Conduct in the Australia-China FTA, Korea-Australia FTA and Australia-Japan FTA, arbitrators will be bound by the code, and violation of this code may lead to removal of arbitrators.

Conclusion

China, South Korea and Japan have set a new and positive trend in the dispute settlement mechanism of their FTAs. The most important trend is to include the Code of Conduct for arbitrators in the dispute settlement system. This Code of Conduct is a package, which covers independence, impartiality and other necessary measures that are important for maintaining the integrity of the dispute-resolution mechanism. In the commercial arbitration world, such measures are common and have been in use for a long time; however in the FTA dispute-resolution system, such measures were not used until recently. In other words, arbitrators under the FTA dispute settlement system were not under strict scrutiny, as compared to any commercial arbitration. The whole Code of Conduct is binding on arbitrators, which is a very positive development, but the rule relating to self-disclosure is far more important. According to this rule, the obligation is on the arbitrator to disclose any situation of actual or apparent bias and not on the parties. From the parties' perspective, this is a big relief. In this regard, it is also important to note that the personal and private information of arbitrators should not be of public scrutiny. Therefore, Japan has made it clear that the obligations of self-disclosure on arbitrators should not be administratively cumbersome and go beyond its purpose, so that a qualified person may not be able to perform the main duty of resolving disputes. In essence, a fine balance should be maintained for this purpose. Separate Model Rules of Procedures for arbitration are another significant development in the FTAs of China, South Korea and Japan, which provide default rules for arbitration, unless parties agree otherwise. In

75 Australia-China FTA, Code of Conduct, Para 11; Korea-Australia FTA, Code of Conduct, Para 10. Australia-Japan FTA, Code of Conduct, Para V(5)

the FTA dispute settlement system, earlier emphasis was not put on rules of procedure, but rather, it was left open for the tribunal to design or adopt them in consultation with parties. The default rules are now available for the arbitral tribunal to follow, which has been negotiated between the parties. The presence of default rules in the FTAs of China, South Korea and Japan will help develop a consistent application of rules in any arbitration under the respective FTAs. Similarly, an Indicative Time Table sets the clock right from the beginning for the parties, as well as for the Tribunal, to resolve the disputes in a timely manner. From a logistics point of view, the Time Table is easy to refer to now, as compared to the past. In the earlier FTAs, one could only calculate the time period by reading various provisions in the FTAs. From the users' point of view, one may quickly compare as to which FTAs may help resolve the dispute in a timely manner. Arbitrators will also be mindful of the time limit before they accept appointment. Otherwise, in commercial arbitration or in investment arbitration, delay in issuing the award has become very common. Finally, use of cooperation as the means of dispute resolution has become the hallmark of Asian FTAs, particularly those of China and South Korea. From an Asian perspective, cooperation between disputants is always appreciated in resolving their disputes. However, it is not settled yet, the legal implication of this cooperation provision as to whether any violation of this obligation may give rise to any cause of action or not.

It has been argued that proliferation of FTAs may have an impact on the domestic courts in the administration of justice. Similar arguments have been raised about the impact of the World Trade Organisation (WTO) on domestic jurisdiction, which is a valid point. This is because, as a member of the WTO, all members are required to align their domestic rules with the WTO rules. For example, law on intellectual property rights, anti-dumping and so on are a few examples that forced every members of the WTO to amend their local laws in line with the WTO rules. China is one example, which has to amend more than a thousand legislations and rules to bring them in line with the WTO requirements. If there is any violation of WTO rules, then a member of the WTO may initiate dispute against the member who is alleged to violate WTO rules. The general impact of FTA on domestic legislation has not been evident. One may see the change in rules in favour of FTA partners. For example, change in rules of origin, lower threshold for establishing service companies and so forth may have been put in place in light of specific FTAs. To this extent, one may argue that FTAs have some impact on domestic legislations. At the same time, it should be noted that such favourable treatment to a FTA partner is allowed under the WTO, and it is not considered as the violation of Most Favoured Nation (MFN) principle. Disputes under FTAs are not common. In Asia, no bilateral FTA has been invoked yet for a formal dispute settlement. However, a rule-based dispute settlement system in a FTA gives predictability about how a dispute might be resolved as and when that may arise.

With these new trends in action, one may conclude that China, South Korea and Japan are developing a new Asian style of dispute resolution mechanism in their FTAs, whether signed with developed or developing countries.

Index

For Product Safety Concerns and Information please contact our EU representative GPSR@taylorandfrancis.com
Taylor & Francis Verlag GmbH, Kaufingerstraße 24, 80331 München, Germany

www.ingramcontent.com/pod-product-compliance
Ingram Content Group UK Ltd.
Pitfield, Milton Keynes, MK11 3LW, UK
UKHW050754180926
475701UK00007B/1045
* 9 7 8 0 3 6 7 5 9 4 8 2 4 *